D0221060

The Economic Impact of Demographic Change in Thailand, 1980–2015

The Economic Impact of Demographic Change in Thailand, 1980–2015

An Application of the HOMES Household Forecasting Model

Edited by
Burnham O. Campbell, Andrew Mason,
and Ernesto M. Pernia

published in cooperation with the

Asian Development Bank

Distributed by the University of Hawaii Press

Library of Congress Cataloging-in-Publication Data

The Economic impact of demographic change in Thailand, 1980–2015 : an application of the HOMES household forecasting model / edited by Burnham O. Campbell, Andrew Mason, and Ernesto Pernia.
p. cm.
Includes bibliographical references and index.
ISBN 0-86638-135-X : $19.00
1. Thailand—Population—Mathematical models. 2. HOMES (Computer file) 3. Households—Thailand—Mathematical models. 4. Population forecasting—Thailand—Mathematical models. I. Campbell, Burnham O. II. Mason, Andrew, 1947- . III. Pernia, Ernesto M., 1943- .
HB3644.55.A3E28 1993
304.6'09593'01—dc20 93-16845
CIP

Published in 1993 by the East-West Center
1777 East-West Road, Honolulu, Hawaii 96848

Distributed by the University of Hawaii Press
2840 Kolowalu Street, Honolulu, Hawaii 96822

Contents

List of Figures *vii*

List of Tables *xi*

Contributors *xvii*

Acknowledgments *xix*

Preface *xxi*

1. Demographic Change and the Thai Economy: An Overview *1*
   Andrew Mason and Burnham O. Campbell

2. Households and Their Characteristics *53*
   Andrew Mason, Mathana Phananiramai, and Nipon Poapongsakorn

3. Labor Force and Wage Forecasts *83*
   John Bauer, Nipon Poapongsakorn, and Naohiro Ogawa

4. Domestic Resource Mobilization: Analysis of Survey Data *115*
   Andrew Mason, Varai Woramontri, and Robert M. Kleinbaum

5. Consumer Expenditures *143*
   Andrew Mason, Varai Woramontri, and Robert M. Kleinbaum

   Appendix 5.1. Estimation Results from Expenditure Analysis *175*

6. The Education Sector: Enrollment Rates and Expenditures on Schooling *185*
   Mathana Phananiramai and Andrew Mason

   Appendix 6.1. Results from Survey Analysis *217*

   Appendix 6.2. Costs of Education *221*

7. Forecasts of Health Care Costs 229
Naohiro Ogawa, Nipon Poapongsakorn, and Andrew Mason

Appendix 7.1. Detailed Results: Statistical Analysis of Health Care Use, 1981 Socio-Economic Survey of Thailand 263

8. Housing Demand and Required Residential Construction 269
Burnham O. Campbell and Nipon Poapongsakorn

Appendix 8.1. Estimation of Occupied Housing–Household Ratio (A_f) in Thailand 301

Appendix 8.2. Estimated "Normal" Vacancy Ratios (A_{v1}) for Thailand 305

Appendix 8.3. Estimated Withdrawal Rates (A_w) in Thailand 309

Appendix 8.4. Detailed Age-of-Head Projections 313

Appendix 8.5. Estimates of the Price of Housing 317

APPENDIX A
Household Characteristics and Household Projections Using HOMES 321
Andrew Mason

References 343

Index 349

List of Figures

1.1 Principal activity of household members: 1990–2010 9

1.2. Demand and supply of labor: 1977 and 1985 13

1.3. Forecast annual increase in the labor force: 1985–90 to 2010–15 13

1.4. Educational attainment of male workers 25–29 years of age: 1985, 2000, and 2015 17

1.5. Age distribution of the Thai labor force: 1980–2015 19

1.6. Median age of workers: 1980–2015 19

1.7. Age profile of dependency: 1985–2015 23

1.8. Age profile of household saving: 1980 and 2005 25

1.9. Purchasing power of households: 1985–2015 27

1.10. Impact on monthly household expenditure of an additional child age 0–2 28

1.11. Monthly household expenditure: The impact of additional members 29

1.12. Population 5–14 years of age, average annual change: 1960–65 to 2005–10 34

1.13. Inpatient care: Childbearing women, children, and the elderly: 1985, 2000, and 2015 43

1.14. New housing requirements: 1950–55 to 2010–15 46

1.15. Expenditures on residential construction: Varying assumptions on income elasticity of housing expenditures, 1950–55 to 2010–15 47

1.16. New housing required by age of head: 1950–55 to 2010–15 49

1.17. Share of residential construction in GDP: 1955–60 to 2010–15 50

1.18. Share of residential construction in GDI: 1955–60 to 2010–15 51

2.1. Number of households by age and sex of head: 1985 59

2.2. Number of households with single heads by age and sex of head: 1985 *60*

2.3. Number of children of head by age and sex: 1985 *62*

2.4. Number of grandchildren of head by age and sex: 1985 *62*

2.5. Number of parents of head by age and sex: 1985 *63*

2.6. Number of other household members by age and sex: 1985 *63*

2.7. Composition of intact households by age of spouse and head: 1985 *64*

2.8. Age and sex of household members by relationship to the head: 1985 *67*

2.9. Population pyramids for 1985 and 2005 *69*

2.10. Age distribution of household heads: 1985 and 2005 *73*

2.11. Average number of household members by age of household head: 1980, 1990, and 2005 *73*

2.12. Population by relationship to the head by age and sex: 1985 and 2005 *78*

2.13. Average household size by age of head for selected cohorts *81*

4.1. Investment versus saving in 97 countries: 1970–81 *116*

4.2. National saving and investment: 1950–85 *117*

4.3. Age of head and the adjusted saving ratio: 1981 *134*

4.4. Age profile of household saving: 1980 and 2005 *140*

5.1. Per capita household expenditure: Comparison of 1980 and 2005 *167*

7.1. Age-specific patient rates: Japan, 1984 *233*

7.2. Age-specific outpatient and inpatient rates: Thailand, 1981 *234*

7.3. Average cost per outpatient visit: Thailand, 1980 *234*

7.4. Average cost per inpatient visit: Thailand, 1980 *235*

7.5. Average cost per patient per use: Japan, 1984 *235*

7.6. Projected differential growth rate in occurrences of 14 illnesses in the total population: 1980–2015 251

7.7. Projected medical expenditures for the MOPH and households: 1980–2015 259

8.1. Projected household formations and required additions to the housing stock: 1950–55 to 2010–15 277

8.2. New housing required by age of head: 1950–55 to 2010–15 278

8.3. Required additions: Sensitivity to doubling and vacancy rate assumptions, 1950–55 to 2010–15 280

8.4. Housing starts, required additions, and withdrawals: 1950–55 to 2010–15 281

8.5. Effect on housing starts of varying withdrawal rates: 1950–55 to 2010–15 282

8.6. Tenure composition of required additions (*RA*) based on 1970 national and urban rates: 1950–55 to 2010–15 285

8.7. Age composition and the value of required additions: 1950–55 to 2010–15 289

8.8. Income-adjusted and benchmark residential construction forecasts: 1950–55 to 2010–15 292

8.9. Actual and forecast residential construction: 1950–55 to 1980–85 293

8.10. Net residential construction expenditures (income-adjusted new units) by age of head: 1950–55 to 2010–15 294

8.11. Required residential construction: Sensitivity analysis comparing estimates based on differing assumptions about income growth and income elasticity, 1950–55 to 2010–15 295

8.12. Share of residential construction in GDP: 1950–55 to 2010–15 296

8.13. Share of residential construction in GDI: 1950–55 to 2010–15 297

A.1. Headship rates for men and women: 1970 and 1980 323

A.2. Children per adult by age of mother: 1950, 1980, and 2010 328

A.3. Likelihood of being a child of the head by age of child and age of mother: 1980 *330*

A.4. Comparison of surviving mothers with mothers of head by age of mother for households with heads 50–54 years of age in 1980 *337*

A.5. Other household members by age and sex of members: 1970 and 1980 *338*

A.6. Other household members 75–79 years of age by age of household head: 1980 *340*

A.7. Other household members 75–79 years of age by age of household head: 1970 *341*

List of Tables

1.1. Population statistics and projections: 1960–2010 *2*

1.2. Household projections: 1970–2015 *5*

1.3. Age distribution of household members: 1990 *8*

1.4. Activity of household members over the life cycle: 1990 *8*

1.5. A comparison of projected and enumerated populations: 1990 *11*

1.6. Distribution of households by age of head: 1985–2015 *24*

1.7. Projected saving: 1980–2015 *25*

1.8. Forecast monthly expenditures: 1980–2005 *31*

1.9. Comparison of forecast and actual budget shares *32*

1.10. Forecasts of number of patients and recurring costs: 1985–2015 *42*

2.1. Population and the number of households: 1960, 1970, and 1980 *58*

2.2. Type of households: 1985 *59*

2.3. Average number of household members by their relationship to the household head: 1985 *60*

2.4. Age and sex of household members: 1985 *65*

2.5. Assumptions underlying population projection *68*

2.6. Population projections: 1980–2015 *68*

2.7. Projected number of households: 1970–2015 *70*

2.8. Type of households: 1980–2005 *71*

2.9. Average number of members of family households by age of members: 1980–2005 *74*

2.10. Relationship to head of total population: 1980–2005 *76*

2.11. Number of children and grandchildren of the head per household: 1980–2005 *80*

2.12. Number of parents of household head per hundred households: 1980–2015 *80*

3.1. Unemployment rate: 1974–84 85

3.2. Real wage rate: 1977–85 86

3.3. Labor-force participation rates by sex and area: 1971–83 86

3.4. Description of variables used in the labor-force participation model 91

3.5. Reduced form participation probits 92

3.6. Total labor force: 1985–2015 94

3.7. Projected labor-force participation rates: 1985–2005 94

3.8. Projected labor-force participation rates by age and sex: 1985–2005 95

3.9. Educational attainment of the labor force by age and sex: 1985 and 2005 96

3.10. Age composition of the labor force: 1985–2005 98

3.11. Average workers per household, household size, and persons per worker: 1985–2005 98

3.12. Labor force by age of head and household type: 1985 and 2005 99

3.13. Average number of workers per household by age of head and household type: 1985 and 2005 100

3.14. Participation probit for women in Bangkok 103

3.15. Wage equation for working women in Bangkok 103

3.16. Wage equation for Bangkok males 104

3.17. Bangkok male labor-force participation probit with wages included 104

3.18. Employment target in the Sixth Plan (1986–91) 106

3.19. Projections of labor supply and labor demand: 1985–2015 106

3.20. Projected labor force by age groups: 1980–2005 107

3.21. Assumptions about labor market behavior 109

3.22. Wage and employment projections: 1985–2015 110

3.23. Number of workers in older households: 1985 and 2010 114

3.24. Average number of preschoolers per household: 1985–2015 114

4.1. Investment and saving: 1950–54 to 1980–85 *117*

4.2. Description of variables used in analysis of consumption *122*

4.3. Descriptive statistics: 1981 Socio-Economic Survey of Thailand *128*

4.4. Household composition and the consumption ratio: Number of children *131*

4.5. Household composition and the consumption ratio: Number of adults *132*

4.6. Adjusted mean consumption ratio *134*

4.7. Average number of household members: 1980 and 2005 *137*

4.8. Age of members, intact households: 1980 and 2005 *137*

4.9. Calculated saving ratio: 1980 *138*

4.10. Projected saving ratio: 2005 *138*

4.11. Projected savings: 1980–2015 *140*

5.1. Description of variables used in expenditure analysis *150*

5.2. Summary statistics: 1981 Socio-Economic Survey of Thailand *152*

5.3. Effects of income on expenditure: 1981 *154*

5.4. Household size and scale effects: 1981 *154*

5.5. Household composition and food expenditure: 1980 *156*

5.6. Household type and adjusted mean expenditures: 1980 *157*

5.7. Age of the head and adjusted mean expenditures: 1981 *159*

5.8. Average number of household members: 1980 and 2005 *163*

5.9. Age of members, intact households: 1980 and 2005 *164*

5.10. Calculated per capita expenditures by household type: 1980 *165*

5.11. Forecast per capita expenditures by household type: 2005 *165*

5.12. Forecast budget shares: 1980–2005 *167*

5.13. Forecast monthly expenditures: 1980–2005 *168*

5.14. Decomposition of budget share changes: 1980–2005 *171*

5.1.1. Detailed expenditure results using per capita income as independent variable 176

5.1.2. Detailed expenditure results using per capita expenditure as independent variable 180

6.1. Proportions enrolled, adjusted means: 1981 195

6.2. Impact of additional household members on proportions enrolled, adjusted means: 1981 197

6.3. Forecast proportions enrolled: 1990–2015 199

6.4. Forecast enrollments: 1990–2015 199

6.5. Transition rates: 1978–85 201

6.6. Assumed transition rates for projection 202

6.7. Enrollment projections: 1990–2015 204

6.8. Projected enrollment ratios by level: 1990–2015 204

6.9. Enrollment projections based on HOMES and the transition-rate method: 2000 and 2015 206

6.10. Estimated cost per student by type and level of education: 1985 208

6.11. Projected education costs borne by government, with assumption of constant unit costs: 1990–2015 210

6.12. Unit costs of education, with assumption of improving quality: 1985–2015 211

6.13. Projection of education costs borne by the government, with increasing unit costs: 1990–2015 211

6.14. Analysis of education expenditures by household: Statistical results 213

6.15. Percentage share of education in household budget and total expenditure on education, by age of head: 1990 and 2005 214

6.1.1. Definition of variables in logistic model 218

6.1.2. Variable means in a logistic model 219

6.1.3. Logistic estimates of school enrollment 220

6.2.1. Regression equation of unit costs 226

7.1. Age- and sex-specific outpatient rates: 1981 232

7.2. Age- and sex-specific inpatient rates: 1981 232

7.3. Projected number of outpatient cases treated under the MOPH health care system and projected total outpatient costs covered by MOPH: 1980–2015 237

7.4. Projected number of inpatient cases treated under the MOPH health care system and projected total inpatient costs covered by MOPH: 1980–2015 239

7.5. Projected recurrent, investment, and total costs for the MOPH: 1980–2015 240

7.6. Projected MOPH costs relative to GDP and GDI: Basic forecast and Japanese profile, 1980–2015 240

7.7. Percentage distribution of outpatients by type of household and age of household head: 1980 and 2015 242

7.8. Percentage distribution of inpatients by type of household and age of household head: 1980 and 2015 243

7.9. Projected demand for doctors, nurses, and beds under two different assumptions: 1980–2015 246

7.10. Estimates of demand for nurses and doctors as a percentage of the total labor force: 1980–2015 246

7.11. Age- and cause-specific distribution of patients treated at MOPH health facilities in 1981 249

7.12. Ranking of 10 leading communicable diseases by morbidity rate for various age groups: 1984 250

7.13. Projected number of patients treated under the MOPH health care system and projected expenditure for MOPH, 1980–2015: An application of Bangkok profiles 253

7.14. Comparison of sex-specific number of inpatients among selected age groups between changing inpatient rate case and constant inpatient rate case: 1980–2015 257

7.1.1. List of variables 264

7.1.2. Regression results 266

8.1. The housing market: 1950–2015 275

8.2. Required housing stock by age group: 1950–2015 277

8.3. Tenure rates by age of head, total and urban: 1970 284

8.4. Benchmark and income-adjusted estimates of real residential construction adjusted for income elasticity of housing demand and growth in per capita income: 1950–55 to 2010–15 290

8.5. Indices of labor force requirements in the residential construction sector: Various estimates 298

8.1.1. A_f's in selected countries 304

8.2.1. Vacancy ratios: Singapore and the Philippines 307

8.4.1. Change in households by age of head in Thailand: 1950–55 to 2010–15 315

8.4.2. Value of required additions by age of head in Thailand: 1950–55 to 2010–15 316

8.5.1. Average rents and housing prices by age of head 320

A.1. Headship rates for non-intact households: 1980 324

A.2. Proportion of women at selected ages who are the spouse of a head in selected age groupings: 1980 324

A.3. Surviving offspring per woman: 1980 326

A.4. Proportion of population who were the child of a head: 1970 and 1980 328

A.5. Ratio of observed to expected daughters per household: 1980 331

A.6. The proportion of grandchildren: 1970 and 1980 332

A.7. Ratio of observed grandchildren to "expected grandchildren" 333

A.8. Proportion of population who were parents of head: 1970 and 1980 335

A.9. Surviving parents per 100 surviving offspring: 1980 336

A.10. Proportions of other household members: 1970 and 1980 339

Contributors

Editors

Burnham O. Campbell was Chief Economist, Asian Development Bank, Manila, while this manuscript was in preparation; he is now a consultant for the Program on Population, East-West Center, Honolulu, Hawaii, and Professor Emeritus of Economics, University of Hawaii at Manoa.

Andrew Mason is Director, Program on Population, East-West Center, Honolulu, and Professor of Economics, University of Hawaii at Manoa.

Ernesto M. Pernia is Economist, Asian Development Bank, Manila.

Authors

John Bauer is Research Associate, Program on Population, East-West Center, Honolulu.

Robert M. Kleinbaum is Senior Research Scientist, General Motors Research Laboratories, Warren, Michigan.

Naohiro Ogawa is Professor of Economics, Nihon University, Tokyo, and Deputy Director of Nihon University Population Research Institute.

Mathana Phananiramai is Associate Professor of Economics, Thammasat University, Bangkok.

Nipon Poapongsakorn is Associate Professor of Economics, Thammasat University, Bangkok.

Varai Woramontri is Acting Director, Economic Statistics Division, National Statistical Office of Thailand, Bangkok.

Acknowledgments

This study was prepared for the Kingdom of Thailand under an Asian Development Bank technical assistance project, Demographic and Economic Forecasting Pilot Study. It was carried out in collaboration with the East-West Center and the National Economic and Social Development Board (NESDB). Without the support of key institutions and the help of many individuals, the project could not have been successful.

Project team members benefited considerably from the leadership provided by Kosit Panpiemras, who was deputy director-general of NESDB during the period we were conducting the study. Jawalaksana Rachapaetayakom served as project coordinator on behalf of NESDB and her support and assistance were vital to the success of the project.

An effort of this kind requires access to an extensive amount of census and survey data and we are grateful to the National Statistical Office for its support and the cooperation and assistance of Secretary-General Niyom Purakam, Wiwit Siripak, and Varai Woramontri.

We would also like to acknowledge the technical and logistical assistance of Laura Shrestha, Noreen Tanouye, Yoke Yun Bauer, and Norma Uejo.

We are indebted to many people who helped bring this book to completion. The Graphics and Production Services Unit of the East-West Center brought the book to a camera-ready state. We are especially indebted to Russell Fujita for the book's design, to Lois Bender for typesetting, and to Brooks Bays for preparation of the 63 figures contained in the book. We are also grateful to Corinne Holland, editorial assistant at the East-West Center's Program on Population, for proofreading the manuscript. We also thank Jan Heavenridge, production manager at the University of Hawaii Press, for her assistance with the project. Finally, without the hard work and perseverance of our editor, Anne Stewart, this project would never have been completed. We thank her for her contribution.

Acknowledgments

Preface

This report summarizes demographic trends, household projections, and substantive findings from six studies undertaken as part of a project, Demographic and Economic Forecasting Pilot Study for Thailand, organized and funded by the Asian Development Bank. The purpose of the project was to provide a household projections package, HOMES, to the National Economic and Social Development Board and the National Statistical Office of Thailand, to train staff to use the package, and to explore the ways in which detailed household projections can be used to improve economic forecasting and planning.

HOMES, Household Model for Economic and Social Studies, is a computer model developed at the East-West Center and used to project the number and demographic characteristics of households and to assess the implications for various sectors of the economy. By applying the model to standard population projections, the user is provided projections of the number of households; the age and sex of the household head; average household size; the number, age, and sex of household members; and other basic demographic information about households. This demographic information is used, in turn, to forecast related social and economic trends and to examine the links between population growth and economic development.

Because this kind of detailed household demographic information has not been available previously, there is little or no experience about how it can be incorporated into social and economic development planning. The six sector studies were undertaken to explore ways in which this information could be effectively used. The sectors studied were: education, health, housing, consumer expenditure, household saving, and labor force, employment, and wages.

The household and the family are often forgotten institutions when it comes to economic research, policy, and development planning. But examples abound of the central role played by these institutions in economic and social activity. Change in the supply of labor provides one example. In many countries, Thailand included, changes in labor force participation are dominated by the employment decisions of women, which are, in turn, closely connected to childrearing responsibilities and the presence of other wage earners in the household. Thus, accurate forecasts of labor supply can not be prepared if the changing family circumstances of women are ignored.

A second example is human resource development. The speed with which educational opportunities can be expanded depends on the value placed on schooling by the target population. Economic models of school attendance have stressed the importance of economic returns from higher wages and the opportunity costs of foregone employment. As important as these factors are, they neglect the importance of the family. Analysis of survey data from Thailand shows that the educational attainment of parents is the most important determinant of whether a child continues in school or not.

A third example is economic security. In industrialized and developing countries alike, but particularly in developing countries where extended or multigenerational households prevail and government sponsored social security programs are limited, the household is the basic provider of economic security. Individuals are protected from bouts of unemployment because in Thailand, for example, households average close to three workers. Thus, labor earnings of the household are much less sensitive to unemployment than labor earnings of an individual. Old age security is also effectively handled by multiearner, extended households. In Thailand, family households with a head over age 65 typically have two or more wage earners, reducing the need to rely on saving and government support.

Few would deny that the household is an important institution, but many might argue that it's role need not be *explicitly* modeled except in a limited number of cases, e.g., the demand for housing. This view would have some merit if the household were a stable and unchanging institution, but such is not the case. All Asian developing countries are experiencing major demographic change that is having a profound impact on the the Asian household. The average size of households in Thailand is dropping rapidly, the average age of the head is increasing, the number of dependent children is declining, and so on. Moreover, in some developing countries, there is evidence that the extended family may be declining in importance, whereas nuclear households are becoming increasingly important.

This report and the detailed studies it summarizes examine demographic trends in Thailand, forecast changes in the number and demographic characteristics of households, and assess the implications for the national economy and for demographically sensitive sectors—education, health, and housing. A number of general conclusions stand out.

First, the number of households will continue to grow quite rapidly for many years to come, increasing from 12 million in 1990 to exceed 22 million by 2015. The demographic character of the Thai household, its size and age composition, will change a great deal as a consequence of declining fertility and improved mortality. However, currently available evidence does not indicate that the rules governing household formation are undergoing significant change, i.e., there is no apparent movement toward the Western model of the nuclear household.

Second, the Thai labor force will continue to grow at a relatively brisk pace and roughly in line with the expected growth in demand for the next 15 years. After that, growth in labor demand is forecast to exceed labor supply, with excess demand reaching 11.7 percent of the labor force in 2000 and 54.9 percent in 2015. Real wages are expected to increase several times between 1990 and 2015, even taking account of the substitution of capital for labor and the real wage elasticity of the labor supply. The increasing scarcity of labor will lead to rapid changes in Thailand's comparative advantage and in the relative profitability of different lines of economic activity. Clearly, being forewarned of these possibilities is very valuable to both private and public planners.

A third component of the study deals with household saving, the most important component of national saving in Thailand. Although the household saving ratio, at the aggregate level, had not responded to favorable demographic trends, analysis at the micro level shows that reduced child dependency has a salutory effect on saving. Continued decline in the number of children per household is forecast to increase household saving to about 14 percent of national income over the next two decades. This increase probably represents the minimum effect of coming demographic change because households in modern sectors of the economy are more sensitive to demographic trends than those in traditional sectors.

Household expenditure patterns will change in response both to changing demographic characteristics and improved standards of living. Relative to the growth forecast in total consumption demand, miscellaneous expenditures and expenditures on transportation and communication, recreation and reading, medical care, housing and apparel, in that order, will grow more rapidly than total demand. Expenditures on personal care, education, and particularly food will grow less rapidly. Changes in the structure of demand are likely to affect relative real wages within the consumption sector and suggest areas where more financially rewarding careers and more profitable investment opportunities lie.

Education is one of the demographically sensitive sectors that will be affected in important ways by changes in Thailand's population and household characteristics. As the population ages the educational resources required in total will increase less rapidly than income barring unanticipated improvements in the quality of schooling. The relative shares of different schooling levels, primary, secondary, and tertiary, will change considerably over the coming decades. There will be opportunity for improving quality and expanding the coverage of education, especially at the secondary level. The challenge for teacher training and other educational programs will be to respond to the changing relative demands for different levels of education and to the demands for adult education associated with the anticipated changes in the structure of the economy and labor shortages. In the longer run, the demographic trends at work may make it possible to reduce education's share of public resources.

As Thailand's population ages, health sector costs will undoubtedly rise.

During the next few decades, however, the greater health care needs of a growing elderly population will be largely offset by the relatively declining health needs of childbearing women and the very young. Thus, broad measures of health care, e.g., number of inpatients, number of outpatients, and recurring expenditure, are expected to grow at about the same pace as the population, in the case of patients, or the economy, in the case of expenditure. However, substantial changes in the demographic characteristics of patients will occur and will require a substantial reallocation of medical resources. This could have an important impact on capital expenditure in the medical sector, but requires more extensive study than could be undertaken here.

Based on quite conservative assumptions, the housing stock necessary to maintain current housing standards will be increased by 82 percent between 1990 and 2015 by demographic changes, with the peak in the flow of new units required coming around the turn of the century. The growth in demand for dwellings meeting the tastes of the mid-life 35–59 age group will be particularly large. On the other side, demand by the 15–34 age group has already peaked and will, in incremental terms, become negative in the next century. If adjustment is made for the effects of withdrawals and of increased income on residential construction expenditures, then the share of residential construction in GDP will increase from now until 2010–15. If, for any reason, this relative growth is not satisfied, given the relatively price inelastic demand for shelter, the result could be a speculative boom in the value of existing housing. Residential construction will also take an increasing share of gross domestic investment until just after the turn of the century, suggesting the possibility of some difficult decisions involving the allocation of Thailand's scarce capital resources. Moreover, these conclusions do not take account of the infrastructure and other effects (including environmental effects) of the forecast increases in housing demand.

In sum, as the brief list of key results presented underlines, taking account of the relation between changes in the number and characteristics of households and in income growth provides information about the future that is extremely useful for both private and public decision makers. Because of the relative reliability with which the number of households and their characteristics can be forecast several decades ahead, the HOMES methodology, as illustrated by the chapters to come, proves to be a useful tool for looking at what the future holds in store for all economic variables sensitive to demographic change.

1

Demographic Change and the Thai Economy: An Overview

by Andrew Mason and Burnham O. Campbell

HOUSEHOLDS AND DEMOGRAPHIC CHANGE

Thailand is in the midst of its demographic transition—rapid changes in mortality and fertility are generating important changes in the size, rate of growth, and age structure of its population. Historical data on fertility and mortality are somewhat sketchy and subject to error, but the available evidence indicates that in 1960 mortality conditions were relatively good for a country with Thailand's material standard of living. Life expectancy at birth for men was around 56 and for women around 62. At the same time rates of childbearing were quite high—women were averaging over six births each. Thus, births far outpaced deaths in any year and rapid population growth was the inevitable result. Between 1960 and 1970, the population grew by 10 million, increasing from 26.3 million to reach 36.4 million, an annual rate of growth of 3.2 percent (Table 1.1).

During the last 30 years, life expectancy has risen modestly but steadily. Fertility, however, has declined rapidly. By 1980 women were, on average, bearing fewer than four children and are bearing closer to two children today. The rate of population growth has responded to declining childbearing, reaching 2.5 percent during the 1970s but slowing to 1.9 percent during the 1980s. Despite the slowdown in growth, the population increased by another 10 million during each of the last two decades to reach 56 million in 1990[1] (Table 1.1).

1. According to the recently released advance report of the 1990 Population and Housing Census, Thailand's enumerated population was 54.5 million in 1990 (NSO 1992).

Table 1.1. Population statistics and projections: 1960–2010

	1960	1970	1980	1990	2000	2010
Population (millions)	26.3	36.4	46.7	56.2	64.4	70.9
Growth rate (%)	—	3.2	2.5	1.9	1.4	1.0
Total fertility rate	6.6	5.6	3.6	2.6	2.0	1.7
Life expectancy						
Male	56.0	58.0	60.0	62.6	66.0	68.5
Female	62.0	64.0	66.0	68.1	70.2	72.2
Age distribution (%)						
Under 15	43.2	45.1	40.0	33.4	27.4	23.0
15 to 59	52.2	50.0	54.6	60.6	65.0	67.7
60 and older	4.6	4.9	5.4	6.1	7.5	9.3

Source: See Chapter 2.

The official projections on which this research is based anticipate a continuation of recent trends in fertility and mortality. Life expectancy is projected to reach 66 for men and 70 for women by the year 2000 and to improve further thereafter (Table 1.1). The total fertility rate is projected to continue its decline reaching 1.7 births per woman by 2010. The continued rapid decline in fertility will provide a further brake on population growth, but driven by the momentum that characterizes any young population, Thailand will experience considerable growth over the next several decades. By the turn of the century the population is expected to reach nearly 65 million and to exceed 70 million by the year 2010.

The age structure of Thailand's population is also in transition, from a very young structure to one that is relatively old (Table 1.1). In 1970 nearly one-half of all Thais (45 percent) were under 15, one-half were between the ages of 15 and 59, and the remainder (5 percent) were elderly. But as is true of any country experiencing improvements in mortality and rapid decline in fertility, Thailand's population is aging quickly. By 1990 one out of three Thais was under age 15 and by the year 2000 barely more than one out of four will be under 15. The number who are of working age (15 to 59) is increasing quite rapidly: from 60 percent in 1990 to 65 percent in 2000. Although a distinct minority of Thais are elderly, the number over age 60 is growing, in percentage terms, faster than any other group. By the year 2000, 7.5 percent will be age 60 or older and by 2010 nearly one in 10 will be elderly.

Household Characteristics

Based on projections detailed in Chapter 2, some of the salient features of Thai households in 1990 were:

- Number of households: 12.0 million
- Average size: 4.6 members per household
- Number of children: 1.6 per household
- Family households: 96 percent
- Household head and spouse present: 78 percent
- Female household heads: 15 percent
- Household heads over 60 years of age: 16 percent

These and other characteristics of Thai households are a product of the demographic trends described in the preceding section and the rules or behavioral decisions that govern the establishment and membership of Thai households.[2] Family households are the rule in Thailand. Ninety-nine percent of all Thais living in a household live with a relative, and only 1 percent live by themselves or with unrelated individuals.[3] As is true in other East and Southeast Asian countries, one offspring usually continues to live with his or her parents after marriage while any brothers and sisters establish separate households.[4] There may be some delay, however, between marriage and the establishment of a separate household. Of men 25–29, only about one-half head their own households and of those 30–34, only about three-fourths do so. But eventually, nearly all men (over 90 percent) become the head of a household (see Chapter 2).

A surprising feature of Thai households is the negligible numbers of parents per household. Does this mean that the parents of young adults are no longer residing with their children? In short, the answer is no. A number of factors account for the small number of parents per household. First, many parents have died. Second, those who are alive may have several surviving offspring and live with only one at any point in time. Third, many elderly living with their children are designated as heads and, thus, would not be recorded as a parent of the head. Finally, some elderly parents may be living on their own or only with their spouse; but in 1980 only 6 percent of all women and 3 percent of all men over age 65 were living alone.

One of the principal concerns of this study has been the extent to which the traditional Thai family system is undergoing change. Are households

---

2. A group of individuals, related or not, who reside together and make common provision for food and other essentials for living are considered a household. Military personnel living in barracks and other institutionalized persons are not considered to be living in households.

3. Although the numbers are still very small, recent census results indicate a significant increase in the number of one-person households. About 4.9 percent of all households are reported as one-person households (NSO 1992) as compared with a projected figure of 3.0 percent based on the 1980 census results. Only 1.1 percent of all Thais are reported to be living in one-person households compared with a projected figure of 0.6 percent.

4. It is common in Thailand, however, for offspring to live nearby or even in compounds with their parents after establishing a separate household.

becoming increasingly nuclearized? Are young adults or the elderly more likely to live by themselves than previously? Do young adults establish households at an earlier or later age than they used to? Although it is commonly believed that the extended family is undermined by economic development and modernization, we found no evidence of significant change in Thailand between 1970 and 1980.

Several indicators confirm that the nuclear household is not replacing the extended household in Thailand. Age-specific headship rates compiled from the 1970 and 1980 censuses show modest declines in the probability that young male adults and modest increases in the probability that young female adults will head their own households. And there has been no substantial or consistent change in the likelihood that men or women will live by themselves or with unrelated individuals. At all relevant ages the probability of being a grandchild of the head increased between 1970 and 1980. Likewise, the probability of being a parent of a head increased between 1970 and 1980. All in all, the extended family appears to be alive and well in Thailand.[5]

Detailed information from the 1990 census has yet to be released but limited data available are consistent with the view that substantial changes in the rules governing living arrangements did not occur during the 1980s. Our projection based on 1980 rates of the number of households in 1990—12.0 million—is quite similar to the enumerated number of 12.2 million. Even this small difference can be partly accounted for by differences in the projected and enumerated adult populations. The ratio of the number of households to the population 20–59 years of age, the age group where headship rates are highest, is 0.351 for the projection and 0.352 for the enumeration.

Although the rules governing the formation and composition of households do not appear to be changing, the demographic characteristics of households will be affected in important ways by the underlying demographic changes noted above. Detailed projections of the number and demographic characteristics of households point to the following major trends:

- <u>The number of households will grow quite rapidly over the next two decades.</u>

  The number of households is projected to increase from 12.0 million in 1990 to 20.1 million in 2010 (Table 1.2). This amounts to an average annual rate of growth over the period of 2.6 percent as compared with a

5. It would be a mistake to interpret these indicators as showing a resurgence of the extended family norm. Much of the change may reflect increased survival of relatives. For example, the probability of being a grandchild of the head will increase just because more elderly are surviving.

Table 1.2. Household projections: 1970–2015

Year	Number of households (thousands)	Household population (thousands)	Average household size	Annual increase (thousands)
1970	6,200	36,370	5.82	—
1980	8,689	46,016	5.30	249
1985	10,215	50,902	4.98	305
1990	12,002	55,498	4.62	357
1995	13,977	59,638	4.27	395
2000	16,030	63,502	3.96	411
2005	18,091	67,006	3.70	412
2010	20,074	69,960	3.49	396
2015	21,870	72,307	3.31	359

population growth rate of 1.2 percent over the same period. The greatest increases, in absolute terms, will occur at the turn of the century when the number of households will be increasing by 400,000 per year (Table 1.2).

- Households are becoming smaller.
  In 1970 households averaged nearly six members apiece, but by 2010 households should average only 3.5 members. The decline in household size will occur across the board. Intact households (where both husband and wife are present), households with single heads, households with young heads, and those with old heads will all be considerably smaller within two decades.

- Household "aging" is an emerging phenomenon.
  Households with a head under 35 years of age will grow most slowly so that by 2010 only 20 percent of all households will have a head so young. Those with heads 35 to 49 years of age will grow most in absolute terms, increasing from 4.3 to 7.9 million between now and 2010. During the same time span, the percentage of elderly households will increase from 5.6 percent to 11.0 percent.

- The family household is not on the decline.
  Family households continue to be the dominant form of living arrangement. The percentage of nonfamily households has increased modestly during the last decade, but fewer than 5 percent of all households are one-person households or households that consist of unrelated persons. Nearly four of five households are headed by a husband and wife and no significant changes in these numbers are projected.

- Lineal households are on the upsurge.
  Fewer household members have a nonlineal relationship to the head. Between 1970 and 1980, the percentage of household members who were brothers, sisters, aunts, uncles, etc., dropped substantially. At the same time, the number of members who were parents, children, or grandchildren of the head increased. The decline in other household members should continue over the next two decades. There is no evidence of a decline in the importance of lineal extended households.

- Households are becoming "adult-ified."
  Over the next two decades, the number of children per household will decline by one-half. In 1990 intact households averaged 1.7 members under age 15 but are projected to average only 0.9 children by 2010. In contrast, the average number of adult members will decline only marginally during the same period. The overall dependency ratio will decline from 78 dependents per 100 prime-age adults in 1980 to 47 dependents per 100 prime-age adults in 2010.

- Elderly parents will not prove burdensome.
  Over the next 20 years, the number of parents per household will increase only marginally and the number age 65 and older hardly at all. By 2010 there should be no more than 10 parents per 100 households, but as aging sets in with more force during the twenty-first century the prevalence of elderly parents in the household should increase markedly.

Household Aging and the Household Life Cycle

The age of the household head is essentially an indicator of the life-cycle stage of a household. There are many different ways that one can characterize the life-cycle stages—by the principal activities of household members, by the important demographic processes that dominate demographic change, or simply by the age and sex of the members of the household. Households with a head under 35 years of age are distinctive demographically because childbearing and rearing of young children is a central part of their lives. Most households with a head 35–49 years of age have moved on to a new stage of the life cycle in that childbearing is essentially complete but the rearing of children remains a central activity. In the next stages of the life cycle, childrearing plays a less important role. In general, the dependency burden for households with a head 50–64 is at a low point, because few children remain and most adults are employed. But for households with an elderly head, adult members are less likely to be economically active so that the dependency burden for older households is generally high.

Although the above characterization of the life-cycle stages of the household is adequate, it is far from precise. The characterization would most readily fit nuclear households, but extended or three-generation households are quite common in Thailand. Thus, households with an elderly head may include economically active adult members who are the offspring of the household head. Or, households with a head over age 50 may include preschoolers who are the grandchildren of the head.

Table 1.3 shows how the demographics of the household vary with the life cycle or the age of the head in Thailand as of 1990. Several features stand out:

- The average number of members varies considerably over the life cycle, rising to a peak size of 5.5 members for households with a head 35–49 years of age, i.e., those who have just completed their childbearing.
- Irrespective of the age of the head, Thai households are not small. Households with an elderly head do not, on average, fit the Western stereotype of an elderly couple or person living alone.
- Households with a head under 35 years of age have more than twice as many preschool children, an average of 0.8, as households with a head 50 or older. Households with a head over age 35, however, average 0.4 to 0.5 preschoolers per household irrespective of the head's age. Even elderly households are actively engaged in raising young children.
- Providing for school-age children is a responsibility shared by households with heads of all ages, but those with heads 35–49 have substantially more children 6–14 years of age than either younger or older households.
- The number of prime working-age adults varies significantly across the household life cycle, rising from 1.7 per household with a head under age 35, peaking at 2.4 per household with a head 50–64 years of age, and dropping off substantially to 1.4 for elderly households.
- The elderly are concentrated in households with an elderly head—1.3 elderly per household as compared with no more than 0.2 elderly per household for households with younger heads.

A slightly different perspective on the life cycle is provided by the data in Table 1.4, which applies labor-force participation data and school-enrollment data to distinguish household members by their principal activity: preschoolers, students, workers, and nonworking adults. A summary of these data is provided by the dependency ratio, the number of all those not working divided by all those working. Young households and elderly households are most disadvantaged with 0.9 and 1.1 dependents, respectively, supported by each worker, but they are distinctive in the sense that elderly households are supporting the elderly whereas young households concentrate more heavily on rearing the young. Each worker in households

Table 1.3. Age distribution of household members: 1990

	Age of head				
	Under 35	35–49	50–64	Over 64	Combined
Average members	3.86	5.48	4.87	4.23	4.62
0–5	0.79	0.52	0.39	0.40	0.59
6–14	0.73	1.42	0.61	0.59	0.92
15–24	0.61	1.33	1.29	0.55	0.98
25–64	1.67	2.12	2.42	1.38	1.95
65 and older	0.06	0.09	0.16	1.31	0.18

Table 1.4. Activity of household members over the life cycle: 1990

	Age of head				
	Under 35	35–49	50–64	Over 64	Combined
Average number of members					
Preschoolers	0.79	0.52	0.39	0.40	0.59
Students	0.75	1.52	0.71	0.62	0.99
Workers	1.99	3.00	3.14	2.03	2.56
Nonworking adults	0.33	0.44	0.63	1.18	0.49
Dependency ratio	0.94	0.83	0.55	1.08	0.81

with a head 35–49 years of age supports only 0.83 dependents and each in households with a head 50–64 supports only 0.55 dependents.

How will the demography of the household life cycle change as Thailand proceeds through its demographic transition? Figure 1.1 shows the "division of labor" for all households combined by reporting the average number of preschoolers, students, workers, and nonworking adults. Between 1990 and 2010, the average household size declines from 4.6 members to 3.5 members per household. In percentage terms, the decline is principally among nonworking members; the number of preschoolers and students declines by more than 40 percent and nonworking adults by 25 percent over the two decades. During the same period, the number of working adults should decline by only 11 percent. As a result, the dependency ratio declines from 0.82 dependents per worker to 0.53 dependents per worker over the 20-year period.

A somewhat different pattern emerges over the remainder of the projection. Average household size declines at a considerably slower pace than during the preceding two decades, but there is a significant increase in the

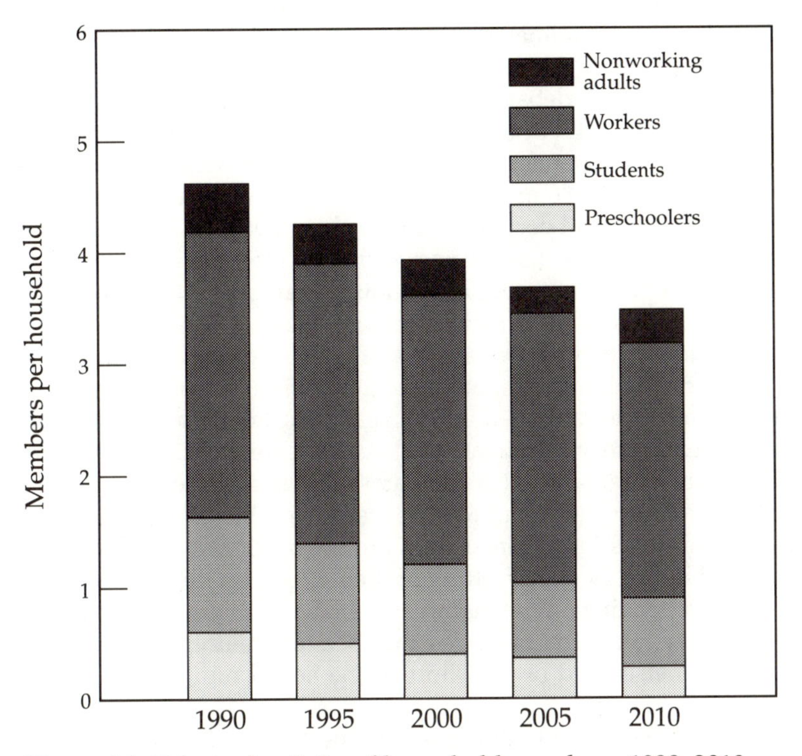

Figure 1.1. Principal activity of household members: 1990–2010

number of nonworking adults. This is the beginning of a trend that reflects the underlying aging of the Thai population; projections further into the future would yield an additional increase in the number of nonworking adults, particularly those who are elderly.

Our picture of future demographic change in Thailand relies on numerous assumptions about trends in mortality, fertility, migration, and living arrangements detailed in Chapter 2. At the completion of this research project, little additional information was available by which to judge the accuracy of the projections. In the past few months, however, limited information from the 1990 census has become available that, along with several demographic surveys, provides some evidence about the extent to which Thailand is following the path described above.

In general, Thailand appears to be proceeding through its demographic transition somewhat faster than anticipated. In particular, fertility has declined more rapidly than projected. The projections presented in this volume are based on a total fertility rate (TFR) of 3.46 for the 1980–85 period and 2.84 for 1985–90. Survey data for the first half of the 1980s are generally consistent with the assumptions. Based on the Current Population

Surveys, the TFR is estimated at 3.68 in 1981 and 3.47 in 1984. Estimates for the second half of the decade point to a substantial decline, the speed of which is subject to debate. The Thai Demographic and Health Survey yields an estimated TFR of only 2.1 for 1987, but the third and fourth Surveys of Population Change yield higher, and more widely accepted, estimates of 2.7 for 1985–86 and 2.4 for 1989. Accepting the latter figures as accurate, the more rapid decline in fertility should be translated into roughly 10 percent fewer births than projected during the second half of the decade and a 0–4 population 10 percent lower than presented in our projection (Thai Population Information Center 1992).

Recent estimates of life expectancy at birth also indicate a more rapid transition in mortality than anticipated. For the 1985–86 period, life expectancy at birth for males is estimated at 63.8 years and for females at 68.9 years. By 1989 life expectancy is estimated to have increased to 65.6 years for males and 70.9 years for females. This compares with an assumed life expectancy at birth of 61.75 for males and 67.50 for females. The lower than projected mortality translates into a larger than projected population. The errors in fertility and mortality are offsetting in their effects on the populations under age 10. Depending on the discrepancy between the actual and projected child mortality rates, the projected numbers of children of ages 0–4 and 5–9 could either exceed or fall short of the actual numbers in those age categories.

Recently released population data from the 1990 census are substantially different from our projections. Table 1.5 compares the projected and enumerated populations for 1990. The greatest discrepancies are between the young and the very old. The enumerated population 0–4 is 25 percent below and the population 5–9 years of age is 12 percent below the projected values. The enumerated population 70 and older is 30 percent larger than the projected population. Although the differences for other age groups are smaller, in percentage terms, they are still substantial. For the 45–64 age groups, the enumerated population exceeds the projected population by 11 to 15 percent.

If the census results are reliable, the deviations from the projected population data will have a substantial impact on the projection of household membership. The number of children per household, particularly the number under age 5, would be substantially below the values projected. There would also be significantly more elderly households and elderly members per household, in percentage terms, than projected.

There are, however, substantial inconsistencies between the 1980 and 1990 censuses and estimated vital rates for the decade that require a thorough assessment before any firm conclusions are possible. The low numbers of children enumerated in the 1990 census imply that either fertility declined much more rapidly than seems likely or that children were underenumer-

Table 1.5. A comparison of projected and enumerated populations: 1990

Age	1990 populations Projected (thousands)	1990 populations Enumerated (thousands)	Ratio	1980 population (thousands)	Intercensal survival rate
0–4	5,939	4,466.6	0.752	6,344	0.923
5–9	6,146	5,387.8	0.877	6,237	0.908
10–14	6,240	5,855.9	0.938	6,112	0.949
15–19	6,172	5,660.8	0.917	5,288	0.970
20–24	6,027	5,799.0	0.962	4,574	1.019
25–29	5,190	5,130.4	0.989	3,750	1.023
30–34	4,475	4,662.2	1.042	2,884	1.056
35–39	3,655	3,834.6	1.049	2,364	1.074
40–44	2,792	3,044.8	1.091	2,180	1.042
45–49	2,262	2,538.2	1.122	1,825	1.044
50–54	2,045	2,271.9	1.111	1,501	0.985
55–59	1,660	1,905.2	1.148	1,132	0.864
60–64	1,300	1,478.5	1.137	878	0.758
65–69	906	978.0	1.079	682	0.625
70–74	619	665.6	1.075	483	—
75–79	327	426.2	1.303	243	—
80+	327	426.6	1.305	242	—

Source: NSO (1992); Chapter 2.

ated in the 1990 census or overestimated in the population data for 1980—the base year for our population projections. For adults 20–24 to 45–49 years of age in 1980, the intercensal survival ratios exceed 1.0. The ratio for the population 65–69 years of age of 0.625 is consistent with a substantially higher expectation of life than prevails in Thailand, suggesting that the elderly population was either understated in the 1980 population data or overstated in the 1990 data.

The importance of demographic change and changes in the character of the Thai household for the Thai economy and for key aspects of Thailand's social and economic development is considerable. The following sections of this chapter summarize the major lessons learned from and questions raised by the analysis detailed in subsequent chapters. First, the results covering the aggregative effects on labor supply, employment, and wages, and on the savings ratio are discussed. Then the effect of changes in demographic and household characteristics on household spending patterns and on the three sectors most affected by such changes—education, health care, and housing—are examined.

LABOR SUPPLY, EMPLOYMENT, AND WAGES

Thailand's recent labor market experience has been mixed. On the one hand, economic growth has been sufficient to absorb a rapidly growing labor force. Between 1971 and 1985 employment grew at an annual rate of 3.0 percent as nearly 8 million additional workers were employed, bringing the total labor force to 26.5 million in 1985. Despite the rapid increase in the numbers seeking jobs, open unemployment was kept largely in check. Labor force surveys conducted two or more times a year since 1974 report an unemployment rate as high as 4 percent on only one occasion, during the July-September round of 1982.

On the other hand, real wages have risen very slowly or not at all in recent years as the agricultural sector continues to absorb most of the labor force growth. Between 1977 and 1985 the real monthly wage of Thai workers is estimated to have been essentially constant. These outcomes have helped in making possible the rapid industrial and trade growth achieved by Thailand in the 1980s.

This is illustrated by Figure 1.2. Between 1977 and 1985, the demand for workers increased rapidly as real gross domestic product (GDP) grew by 6.2 percent per annum. Without any increase in the labor supply, the real wage would have increased substantially.[6] However, the population of prime working age (15–59) grew at slightly more than 3 percent per annum, inducing an increase in the supply of labor that essentially matched the increased demand. As a result, the growing labor force has been absorbed but real wages have been stagnant.

Projected trends in employment and wages are governed by the same forces. Growth in the numbers of working age and changes in labor force participation rates will determine shifts in the supply of labor. The effect on wages and employment will depend on the extent to which the Thai economy can continue to generate demand for additional workers.

Figure 1.3 summarizes forecasts based on extensive analysis of the supply of labor and alternative assumptions about the ability of the Thai economy to generate employment opportunities (see Chapter 3). The approach used is much broader than is customary, with both educational attainment by age and sex and household composition included, as well as the usual population variables.

For the 1985–90 period, the labor force is projected to increase from 26.5 to 30.5 million, which amounts to an annual rate of growth of 2.8 percent. Available data indicate that actual growth has been somewhat more rapid—the labor force reached 30.2 million in 1989 (NSO 1991a).

6. Of course, had wages increased rapidly, Thailand's competitive position in labor-intensive goods would have been undermined, retarding the overall rate of economic growth.

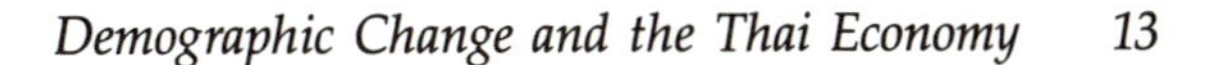

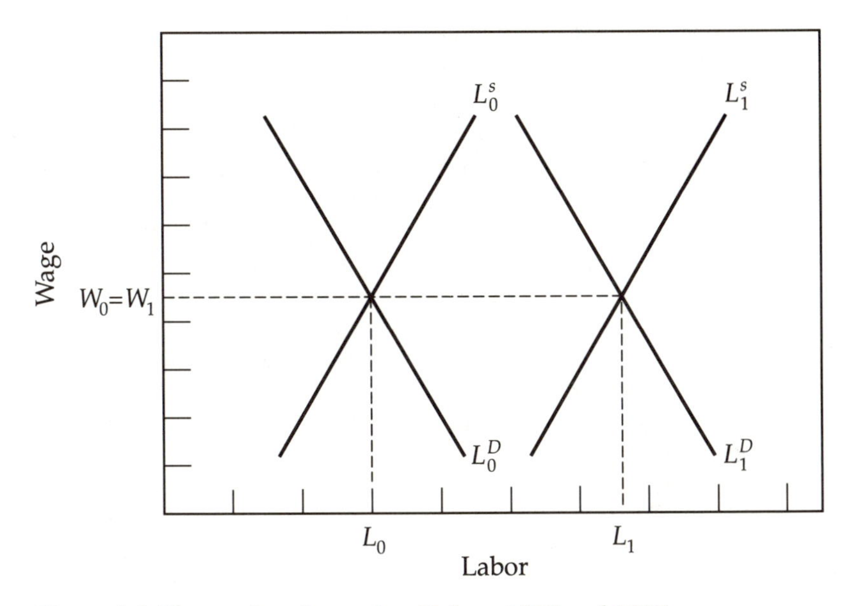

Figure 1.2. Demand and supply of labor: 1977 and 1985

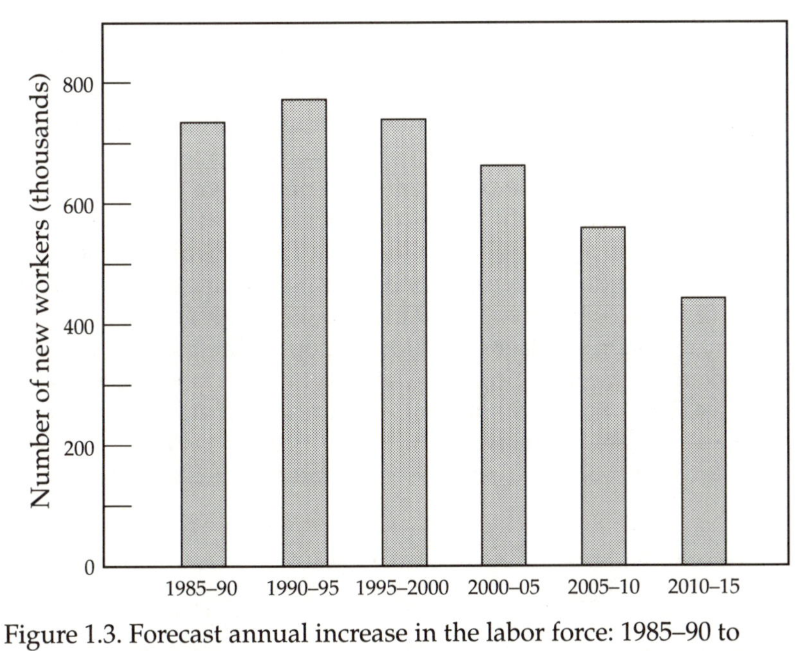

Figure 1.3. Forecast annual increase in the labor force: 1985–90 to 2010–2015

From 1990 to 2015 the labor force is projected to increase from 30.5 to 46.4 million or by 50 percent. However, according to our forecasts, Thailand faces two distinct phases during the next few decades. During the first phase, lasting to the year 2000, the supply of labor will continue to grow at a rapid pace. The number seeking employment will increase annually by over 700,000, peaking at 770,000 annually during 1990–95. Overall, the rate of growth of the labor supply will average 2.2 percent during the remainder of this century—somewhat slower than during the last two decades but still a substantial rate of growth.

Will the Thai economy be able to absorb the additional workers? Expectations for the second half of the 1980s were that the growth in additional jobs would just match the increased supply of workers. The 1986–91 five-year economic plan projected an increase in the number of jobs by 780,000 annually. If these numbers held, supply and demand would be roughly in balance with only slight upward pressure on wages. Following the five-year plan, the growth in labor demand is based on GDP growth of 6 percent or approximately the same growth as attained in the first half of the 1980s. In fact, economic growth has exceeded expectations—GDP grew at an annual rate of 9.4 percent in real terms between 1985 and 1989 (ADB 1991).

If the economy slows to a more moderate rate of growth in the 4 to 6 percentage point range, we expect employment to grow at between 2.3 percent and 2.7 percent annually between 1990 and the year 2000, so that total employment should stand somewhere between 36.9 and 38.3 million workers by 2000. Wages should rise only modestly during this period. If GDP had increased at 4 percent per annum during the 1985–95 period, we would have expected wages, in real terms, to continue to be essentially stagnant. If GDP had increased at 6 percent per annum, we would have expected wages to grow at less than 1 percent per annum.[7]

Depending on the speed with which the Thai economy expands, the Thai labor market should enter a second phase sometime shortly after the turn of the century, or if current economic growth continues, somewhat sooner. Significant labor shortages should develop as the increase in the supply of workers begins dropping quite rapidly. Because labor-force participation rates will be at or near 90 percent, it is unlikely that higher wages will induce a significant expansion of the labor force.[8] The annual increase in supply is forecast at 665, 560, and 444 thousand for the first three quinquennia

7. Recent experience in Thailand is broadly consistent with this view. Despite the rapid growth in GDP, nominal wages earned by private urban employees between 1987 and 1989 just kept pace with the rate of inflation in Bangkok (NSO 1991a; IMF 1992).

8. The participation rate is measured as the labor force divided by the population 15–64 years of age.

(2000–15) of the next century. But if low wages and economic growth in the 4–6 percentage point range continue unabated, as many as one to two million additional workers could find employment annually.

The impact on wages will depend very much on the success with which firms deal with labor shortages. At one extreme, if labor is easily substituted by other factors and GDP grows at 4 percent per annum, wages are forecast to grow at 2.9 percent. If, on the other hand, GDP grows at 6 percent per annum and firms find it difficult to reduce their reliance on labor inputs, wages are forecast to grow at 12.7 percent. Irrespective of the speed with which wages increase, employment is expected to grow at a much slower pace between 2000 and 2015. The number of workers should grow at between 1.3 and 1.5 percent per annum and total employment should reach about 46 million workers, more or less, in 2015.

In sum, the forecasts of labor demand and supply show that there will be a continuing but diminishing excess supply of labor in Thailand through the 1990s, assuming GDP growth of 6 percent. After that demand for workers should begin to outstrip supply so that excess demand will amount to 3.9 percent of the labor supply in 1995, 11.7 percent in 2000, 22.4 percent in 2005, 36.6 percent in 2010, and 54.9 percent in 2015. Even with better capital and a more experienced, better educated, and, hence, more productive work force, it does not seem possible that there can be anything but large increases in the national real wage in response to excess demands of the magnitude forecast.

And, in fact, after taking account of both male and female elasticities of supply and the elasticity of demand for labor in the long run, allowing substitution of capital for labor,[9] with 6 percent growth in GDP there will be very large future increases in both real wages and employment. If firms find it difficult to adopt less labor-intensive techniques, male and female real wages will be eight and two-thirds times the 1990 level in 2015. Even if the demand for labor hits the highest elasticity level deemed likely[10] they will be slightly over three times the 1990 level and the unemployment rate will be no more than 1.2 percent of the labor force. These large changes will not begin until the last five years of this century but will accelerate rapidly thereafter.

With increasingly scarce labor in Thailand, there will be some significant shifts in entrepreneurial opportunities and in comparative advantage. Rapid

9. The substitution considered is within sectors. Because labor shortages will raise the relative prices of labor-intensive goods, there will also be substitution away from labor-intensive products. This substitution is ignored, but will, especially through exports, ameliorate the wage pressure to a limited extent.

10. With the elasticity of demand varying only from 0.1 to 0.3 between the high and low forecasts, there are obviously quite large differences resulting from relatively small changes in the elasticity of demand for labor. More intensive study is clearly called for here.

growth in real wages may undermine Thailand's current comparative advantage in labor-intensive exports and impinge on profits and other returns to nonlabor factors, undermining overall growth. Flexibility in responding to the implied shifts in relative profitability between products and sectors, with more capital-intensive sectors gaining in relative terms, will be important if both private and public sector planners in Thailand are to effectively meet the challenges involved.

Although the role of the government in guiding future economic growth in Thailand is necessarily limited, the government can serve an important role by making clear to all decision makers what lies ahead and, *in extremis,* placing roadblocks in the way of projects that will shortly become untenable if the provision of information and the working of the market do not accomplish the task. Because the Thai government via its controls over investment promotion is already involved in guessing where resources ought to go, the emerging labor force developments should be an important consideration in the promotion process.

On the brighter side, the increase in real wages can only be considered positive from the viewpoint of "worker welfare," ultimately the basic rationale for setting sustained economic growth as a national goal. Moreover, higher wages will increase the size of the domestic market and make possible increased economies of scale. As a preliminary step in the process of becoming internationally competitive in the production of consumer goods, a growing domestic market can play an important role and one complementary to the adjustment in factor proportions required by real wage increases.

Labor Quality

The character of the Thai labor force is changing in two important respects—the work force is more educated, on average, and more experienced with each passing year.

The most important features of the educational transition are illustrated by Figure 1.4, which shows educational attainment of male workers in their late 20s. This is a pivotal age group from a manpower planning perspective because these are the workers who are filling many of the new jobs becoming available. Two aspects of educational trends stand out. First, the percentage with only a primary school education is quite substantial in 1985 and forecast to remain so throughout the period under study. Even by 2015, slightly less than half have completed only primary school. Second, of those who have gone beyond the primary school level, there is a remarkable emphasis on tertiary education. By the year 2000, for example, 22 percent are forecast to have completed tertiary education as compared with only 18 percent forecast to have completed only secondary education.

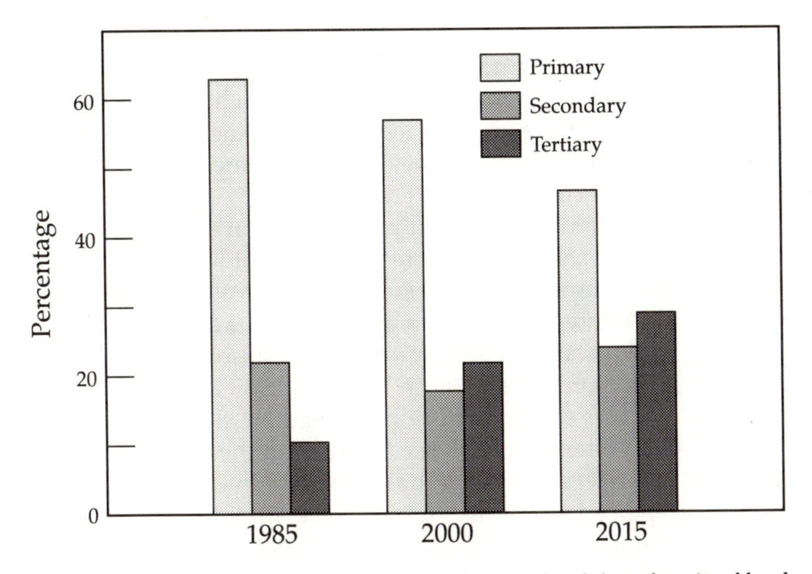

Note: The percentages shown are for persons who completed that educational level but did not complete the next level. Therefore, 62 percent of male workers in 1985 completed only primary school, but 94 percent completed primary school plus some further schooling.

Figure 1.4. Educational attainment of male workers 25–29 years of age: 1985, 2000, and 2015

Although for purposes of illustration, we have highlighted only a small segment of the labor force, the educational trends observed permeate the entire work force. Educational attainment among women in the labor force is very similar to attainment for men. Older workers, of course, have lower attainment than younger workers so that the percentages with elementary schooling only are even higher. And for all but the oldest age groups, the emphasis on tertiary education among those advancing beyond elementary school emerges during the forecast period.

The unusual trends in educational attainment raise important questions. Continued economic growth and the potential labor shortages discussed above mandate a structural shift in the Thai economy away from agriculture and other labor-intensive industries and toward an industrially based economy, which will require a more highly educated labor force. Will educational attainment be sufficient if nearly half of entering workers have not completed secondary school? And if the demand for more educated workers does grow rapidly, how much education is required? Will there be sufficient jobs for the large numbers of college graduates? And if not, will their skills be underutilized or, even worse, not utilized at all?

The forecast trends in educational attainment are by no means inevitable. They are based on assumptions about educational policy that are detailed in Chapter 6 and, as such, are subject to change. However, the aging of the Thai labor force and the accompanying increase in the average experience of the Thai worker is an inevitable consequence of past and continuing demographic conditions in Thailand.

Figures 1.5 and 1.6 provide different perspectives on the aging of the Thai labor force. Figure 1.5 shows the absolute numbers of workers in five broad age categories. The number of workers is growing in all age categories, but the number 11–24 is forecast to begin a gradual decline after 1990. The 25–34 and 35–44 age groups are registering the largest absolute increases, forecast to exceed 1 million workers each between 1985 and 1990. Although the number of workers 45 or older is increasing more slowly than the number under 45, that pattern reverses itself starting in the year 2000 when the growth of workers over 45 will exceed the increase in the number of workers under 45. In percentage terms, the clearest contrast is revealed by comparing workers under 35 with workers 35 or older. In 1985, 60 percent of all workers were under 35 years of age. In 2000 the value is forecast to stand at 50 percent and by 2015 only 40 percent of all workers will be under 35 years of age.

Figure 1.6 presents an alternative and simple summary of the aging of the Thai labor force. The median age in 1980 was just under 32, i.e., half of the Thai labor force was under 32 years of age! Although little change occurred between 1980 and 1985, the median is forecast to exceed 34 by the year 2000 and 39 by 2015.

What are the important implications of the aging of the Thai labor force? First, an increase in the average age and, hence, the experience of the average worker should lead to higher labor productivity. Change over the next 15 years, when the percentage in the 11–24 age category is declining rapidly and the percentage in the 35–44 age category is rising rapidly, should be particularly conducive to higher average labor productivity. Second, at some point innovativeness and labor mobility may be adversely affected by labor force aging. Young workers tend to be more likely to change jobs because they have invested less in developing job-specific skills. Moreover, young workers are more likely to have up-to-date information to the extent that job skills are imparted through formal schooling rather than on-the-job training. In other words, an aging labor force means increased productivity and decreased flexibility. Relatively speaking, fewer and fewer workers will come equipped with the latest technology and with a "have skills will travel" mentality. Not much can be done about the latter beyond providing some way of reducing the risks of moving to new opportunities by reducing information costs, for example. However, older workers can be kept up

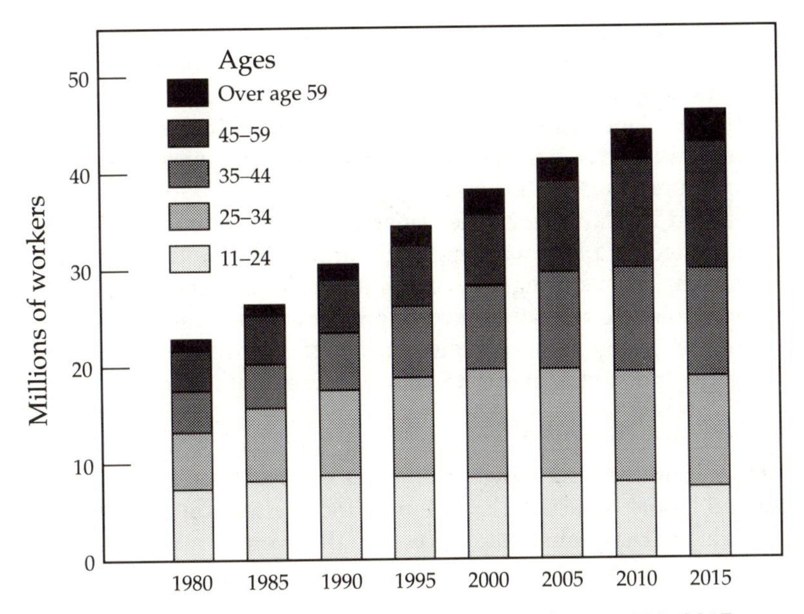

Figure 1.5. Age distribution of the Thai labor force: 1980–2015

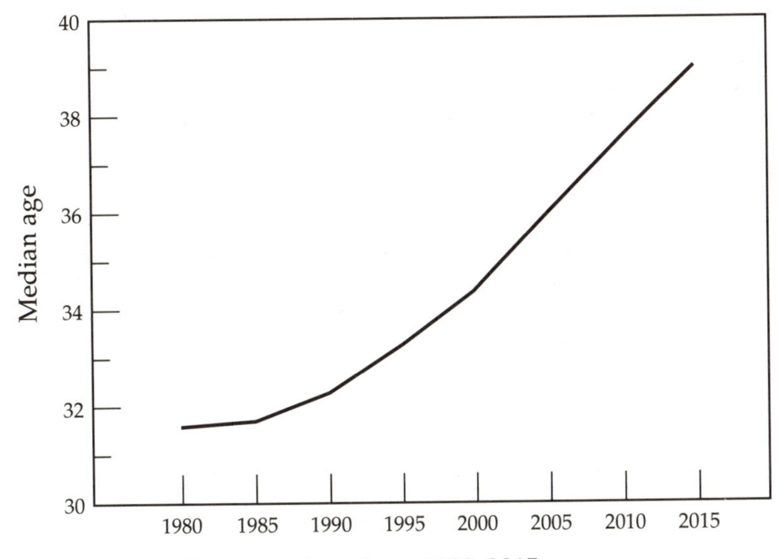

Figure 1.6. Median age of workers: 1980–2015

to date via on-the-job training and adult education. In this context, the open universities[11] in Thailand could play an especially important role.

Finally, the proportion of the labor force over age 35, especially those 35–49 years of age, will increase greatly through the end of the century while the proportion under 25 will fall off. The impact these changes is likely to have on the structure of wages has many important implications.[12] The changes taking place in Thailand mean the wages of young workers should rise relative to the wages of older workers and that the lifetime earnings of members of the smaller incoming labor cohorts should improve beyond the level attributable solely to overall economic growth. As a result, there could be changes in the intergenerational distribution of wealth, the provision of old age security, and saving patterns, among other possibilities.

Labor and the Household

The material summarized above emphasizes national trends in employment, wages, and labor characteristics. We now focus attention on the impact of such trends on Thai households. For one, the average number of workers per household is expected to decline quite steadily over the next several decades. In 1985 the typical household had two or three workers—the average was 2.6 workers per household. Over the next decade, the average will decline only by one-tenth of a worker, but by 2005 the average will decline to 2.3 workers and by 2015 to 2.1 workers per household. The decline, however, will not be uniform across all types of households. In particular, households with elderly heads will experience the greatest declines. Thus, as the relative number of households with members over 65 increases, there will be a relative decline in the number of workers on whom they can depend. This will not happen until well into the twenty-first century. By then later retirement and increased productivity for those employed may take the edge off this problem. For elderly households, the average number of workers will drop from 2.0 workers in 1985 to 1.6 workers in 2005 and then to 1.3 workers in 2015.

Households headed by female workers will also experience a significant decline in the average number of workers per household. For female-headed family households, the average will drop from 2.4 in 1985 to 1.9 in 2005 and to 1.6 in 2015. One result may be a large increase in the number of working women. In the Thai context this may not raise the same child care

11. The first open university in Thailand, Ramkhamhang University, was established in 1971. The objective is to create equal opportunity for higher education, and all persons who have completed upper secondary school are accepted. Open universities rely heavily on mass media and self study.

12. Research on the United States, Japan, South Korea, and Taiwan, among other countries, shows that relative wages are inversely related to the relative size of labor cohorts.

problems it does elsewhere because there are often elderly members present in the household. The possibility exists, of course, that as cohorts beginning to move through the life cycle become the elderly, their greater financial independence will lead them to maintain separate households. But that is 40 to 50 years ahead.

Even for elderly and female-headed households, the decline in the average number of workers should not, on average, result in economic hardship because the average household size and, hence, the number of members relying on labor earnings will decline more rapidly than the average number of workers. Among households with an elderly head, the number of dependents per worker will decline from 1.2 in 1985 to 0.9 in 2005. And among female-headed family households, the dependency ratio will decline from 0.9 dependents per worker in 1985 to 0.7 in 2005. With real wages increasing and each household supporting fewer nonworkers, there should be a rapidly increasing domestic market for both Thai consumer goods and imported consumer goods.

In some cases, however, averages can conceal as well as enlighten. As households come to depend on fewer workers, they will be increasingly vulnerable to unemployment. Households with two or three workers have more protection against unemployment, but households with only one worker lose all labor earnings when hit by unemployment. Although in some cases previously nonworking adults may enter the labor force, there will be relatively few nonworking adults in households with elderly or single heads so that options will be more limited.

HOUSEHOLD SAVING

There are two important reasons why patterns of household saving should be carefully scrutinized. First, household saving is a major determinant of the rate of capital accumulation, which, in turn, is a major determinant of economic growth. Second, by saving, households accumulate financial reserves that protect them against unforeseen contingencies and provide a basis of support if and when household members retire.

In Thailand household saving has generally averaged between 10 and 15 percent of national income since the 1950s and has been an important component of national saving and investment. Between 1980 and 1985, net national saving was 14.5 percent of national income—during the same period household saving averaged 12.7 percent of national income. Thailand compares favorably with other countries in its ability to generate saving in the household sector. For 25 countries reporting figures on household saving to the United Nations (U.N. 1990), household saving averaged only 5.8 percent of GDP (see Chapter 4).

Despite the positive aspects of saving in Thailand, there were some negatives during the 1980s. Starting from 1974, national saving declined steadily until 1985 when the net national saving ratio reached its lowest point in 15 years. Not surprisingly, the reliance on foreign sources to finance domestic investment increased during this period and overall investment may have been adversely affected.

The major portion of the decline in national saving can be traced to a decline in government and business saving rather than household saving, but household saving was, on average, 2 percentage points less during the first half of the 1980s than it was during the 1970s. In some respects this is a surprising development. Many Asian countries have maintained relatively high and even rising saving ratios during the same period. Although experts disagree about the exact reasons behind the higher saving ratios, demographic factors have been increasingly favorable. Fertility decline has led to a reduced financial burden from childrearing. And changes in the age structure have resulted in a relative increase in the number of households at their peak earning years.

Beginning in 1986 the saving rate began to experience a substantial rebound. By 1988 the net saving ratio had increased by 8 percentage points over the 1985 low. About three-fourths of the rise can be traced to government saving and one-fourth to corporate saving. The rate of household saving, however, has been very stable and remains below the levels that prevailed during the early part of the 1980s (U.N. 1990).

The demographic processes that Thailand is experiencing should, in principle, have a beneficial impact on household saving over the next 25 years. Figure 1.7 shows the "dependency" ratio for four different age-of-head categories. The dependency ratio is a simple way of summarizing the burden of members who do not contribute to household earning. Typically, the ratio is calculated by dividing the population under age 15 or over 65 by the population of working age. But the ratio reported in the figure is the number of nonworking members divided by the number of working members per household. The shape of the dependency profile in 1985 was typical of a moderate to high fertility population. It was highest among households with young heads because they had many children to support but fewer members old enough to work. The ratio declines as both the number of children declines and as the number of working adults increases. In 1985, for example, households with a head under age 35 averaged 2.0 workers whereas households with a head 35–49 averaged 3.1 workers and those with a head 50–64 averaged 3.2 workers. The dependency profile turned up again for older households as household members entered their retirement years and withdrew from the labor force.

Between 1985 and 2015, the dependency burden will decline substantially irrespective of the age of the household head. Between 1985 and 2005 the dependency ratio is anticipated to drop by 30 percent for households with a head under age 35 or 35–49 years of age, by over 40 percent for house-

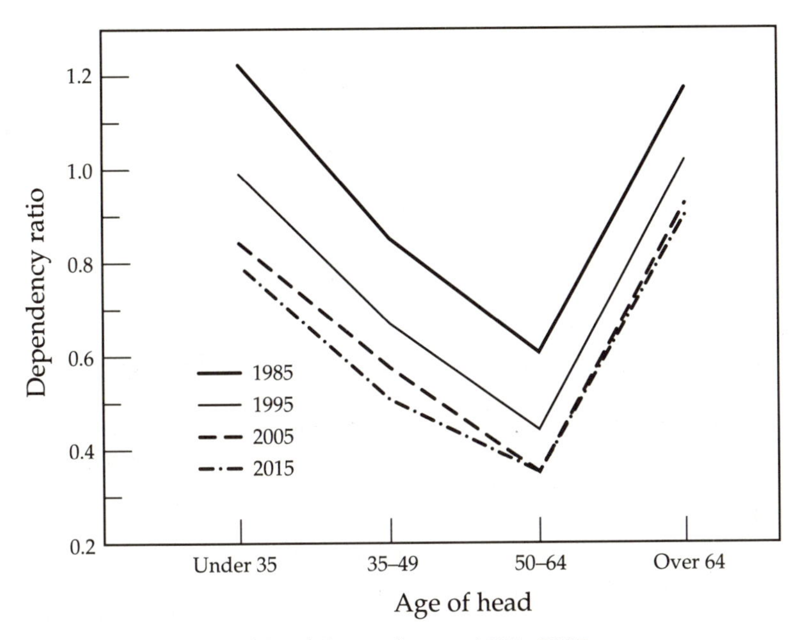

Figure 1.7. Age profile of dependency: 1985–2015

holds with a head 50–64, and by over 20 percent for households with an elderly head. Thus, to the extent that dependency discourages saving, households at all stages of the life cycle should enjoy higher rates of saving in the future than they do today.

Saving should also be affected by shifts in the composition of households. Thai households were concentrated at high dependency stages of the life cycle in 1985 (Table 1.6). Over 30 percent of all household heads were under age 35 and fewer than one-quarter belonged to the low dependency 50–64 age category. By 2015, however, only 20 percent of all households will belong to the high dependency under-35 group and just over 30 percent will belong to the 50–64 group. Over the next 30 years then, households will be increasingly concentrated at stages of the life cycle that, from a demographic perspective, are more conducive to saving.

Analysis of Thai survey data provides fairly clear support for the view that shifts in dependency affect saving. Although children under age 3 have no discernible effect on consumption or saving ratios, an additional child 3–12 years of age is estimated to decrease the saving ratio by about 1 percentage point and an additional child 13–19 by about one-half a percentage point. An additional prime-age adult, however, is estimated to increase the saving ratio by about 1 percentage point. The effect of elderly on household saving is complex and somewhat surprising. Households headed by

Table 1.6. Distribution of households by age of head: 1985–2015

Year	Age of head			
	Under 35	35–49	50–64	Over 64
1985	31.4	35.5	23.7	9.4
1995	29.6	37.7	23.1	9.9
2005	24.8	39.7	25.1	10.4
2015	20.3	37.7	30.1	11.9

an elderly person save less than younger households. But the presence of an additional elderly member leads to higher saving. The impact of demographic change on household saving is shown in Figure 1.8, which compares 1980 and 2005. At every age saving is expected to be greater, but particularly at stages of the life cycle where childrearing is an important activity.

What will be the overall impact on aggregate saving and the overall impact on the economic security of Thai households? A steady increase in the household saving ratio is anticipated during the next two decades (Table 1.7). Demographic and growth factors will raise household saving rates to near the record 1970 values by 2005. Thereafter, household saving is projected to remain relatively constant at about 14 percent of disposable income. The gradual increase in the saving ratio together with rising income combine to push up the absolute amount of domestic resources supplied by households for investment purposes by substantial amounts. Monthly aggregate household saving is calculated to rise from 5.9 billion baht in 1980 to 32.6 billion baht by 2005 and to 55.5 million baht by 2015. Thus, household saving is forecast to increase tenfold over the 35-year projection period, representing a rate of growth of 6.4 percent per annum.

Further analysis of the more "modern" segments of Thai society, e.g., households with educated heads or those employed in the urban sector, shows that more favorable demographic conditions may have an even larger impact than indicated above. Thus, the Thai saving ratio could increase by as much as an additional percentage point, reaching 15 percent at the turn of the century.

How will financial security of households be affected by the changes anticipated? It is very hard to reach any firm conclusions. As indicated above, the average household saving ratio for Thailand is relatively high as compared with other developing countries. It is also relatively high among young households so that most accumulate financial reserves early on to protect themselves against unanticipated economic emergencies. Are sufficient resources being accumulated for retirement? Analysis of the forecast saving behavior of households established in the 1980s indicates that by the

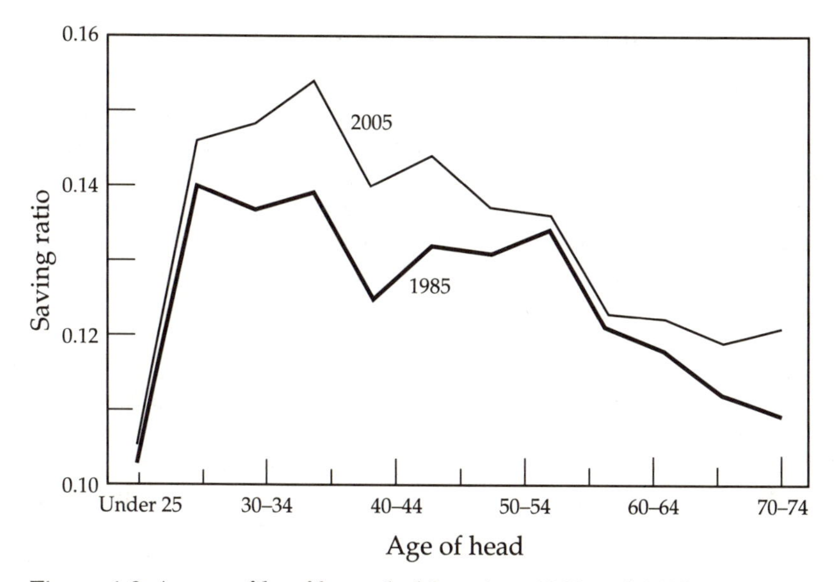

Figure 1.8. Age profile of household saving: 1980 and 2005

Table 1.7. Projected saving: 1980–2015 (millions of baht)

Year	Saving ratio	Aggregate monthly saving
1980	0.130	5,853
1985	0.132	8,571
1990	0.135	12,393
1995	0.137	17,531
2000	0.139	24,199
2005	0.140	32,628
2010	0.140	42,967
2015	0.140	55,498

time household heads reach retirement age, the average household would accumulate wealth equal to four to five times average annual earnings beyond any inherited wealth. Currently, older households clearly do not rely on accumulated financial wealth to support their consumption. In fact, the average household with an elderly head contained two workers in 1985 according to our calculations. It would appear, then, that the combination of labor earnings and accumulated saving provides a reasonable base of economic security for the *average* Thai household.

HOUSEHOLD EXPENDITURE PATTERNS

A recurring theme in this study is that a wide range of activities in Thailand will be influenced by changes in the demographic character of the Thai household. Spending patterns are influenced by the number, ages, sex, and activities of household members. Because Thailand is in the middle of such significant changes in its demographic character, spending patterns will change in the years to come. However, economic growth is more likely to be a dominant force than changes in Thailand's demographics.

The Aging of the Thai Market

The aging of the population is one of the key demographic phenomena that Thailand faces over the next few decades. Like other countries with a recent experience of rapid population growth, Thailand currently has a relatively young age structure, and numbers are translated into purchasing power. Our estimates for 1985 show that 37 percent of all household spending emanated from households headed by an individual under 35 years of age. This figure is surprising for two reasons. First, Thais do not establish households at a young age. In 1980 barely half of adult males 25–29 years of age and not quite three-quarters of those 30–34 had established their own households. Second, adults in their 20s and early 30s are far from their peak earning years. These two factors, however, were offset by overwhelming numerical strength—40 percent of all households in 1985 were headed by someone under 35 years of age.

Figure 1.9 shows the purchasing power of households divided into four age-of-head categories, those 35–49, 50–64, and 65 and older, in addition to "young" households. In 1985 households with a head 35–49 years of age accounted for 37 percent of the market, identical to the market share of young households. Households with a head over age 50 accounted for only one-quarter of expenditure with four out of five dollars spent by households with a head 50–64 and the remaining dollar by households with a head over 65.

The next three decades will be dominated by a shift in spending power from young to middle-aged households. Between 1985 and 2015, the share of purchasing power of young households will decline by 9 percentage points from 37 percent to 28 percent. Households with a head 35–49 years of age will experience a 5 percentage point gain. Those with a head 50–64 will increase their share by 3 percentage points, and those with a head 65 or older by just under 1 percentage point. Thus, in the foreseeable future essentially four of every 10 dollars will be spent by households with a head 35–49. Out of every 10 dollars, between $2.00 and $2.40 will be spent by households with a head 50–64 and from $0.50 to $0.60 will be spent by elderly households.

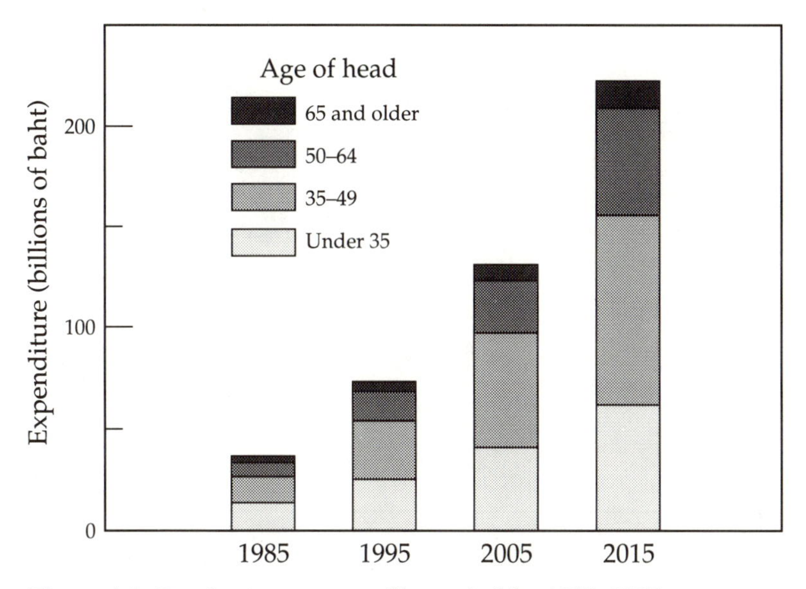

Figure 1.9. Purchasing power of households: 1985–2015

Two aspects of this shift are of further interest. The first aspect is that expenditure patterns will be affected because the demographic and economic character of households vary systematically with the life-cycle stage of the household. Thus, the structure or composition of final aggregate demand will shift toward the goods and services most favored by households with the greatest spending power. A second consideration is that shifts in expenditure shares may represent or coincide with changes in the relative standard of living or economic well-being of one group of households vis-à-vis another.

Expenditure Patterns and Demographic Composition

Changes in the demographic composition of households will affect expenditure patterns in diverse ways that can be difficult to anticipate. Consider, for example, the estimated impact on monthly expenditure of an additional child age 2 or younger as pictured in Figure 1.10. Although providing the material needs for a young child undoubtedly involves substantial cost, the total impact on household expenditure is quite small—average monthly expenditure increases by less than 10 baht per month.[13] This is possible not because a child can be supported on 5 baht per month, but because expenditures on the child are substituted for expenditures on other members,

13. One U.S. dollar equals approximately 25 baht.

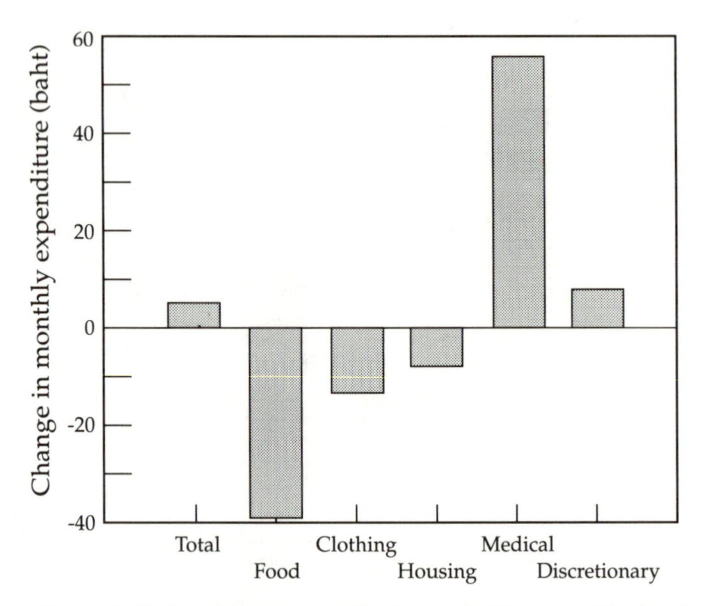

Figure 1.10. Impact on monthly household expenditure of an additional child age 0–2

i.e., others in the household do with less. Changes in the types of goods and services consumed by the household are influenced by the particular needs of the additional members, but may depend as much on what other members can do without. For example, monthly food expenditure is reduced by almost 40 baht per month with the addition of a child age 2 or younger because other family members are spending less on their own food. Expenditure on clothing, housing, and discretionary items[14] are not much affected by the addition of a young member. Expenditure on medical care, however, increases by almost 60 baht per month as a result of the addition of the new member. It would be incorrect, however, to surmise that the additional medical care is devoted solely to the additional child. The change undoubtedly reflects increased maternal health care, as well.

Figure 1.11 shows similar estimates of the budgetary impact of an additional household member of ages 3-12, 13–19, 20–59, or 60 and older. An additional child or teenager induces higher monthly expenditure whereas an additional prime-age adult or elderly member induces lower monthly expenditure.[15] Households with an additional child or teen shift expendi-

14. This is a catch-all category that includes spending on tobacco and alcohol, transportation and communication, education, reading and recreation, personal care, and miscellaneous items.

15. These estimates are based solely on the consumption side and do not include expenditure out of increased earnings associated with additional members.

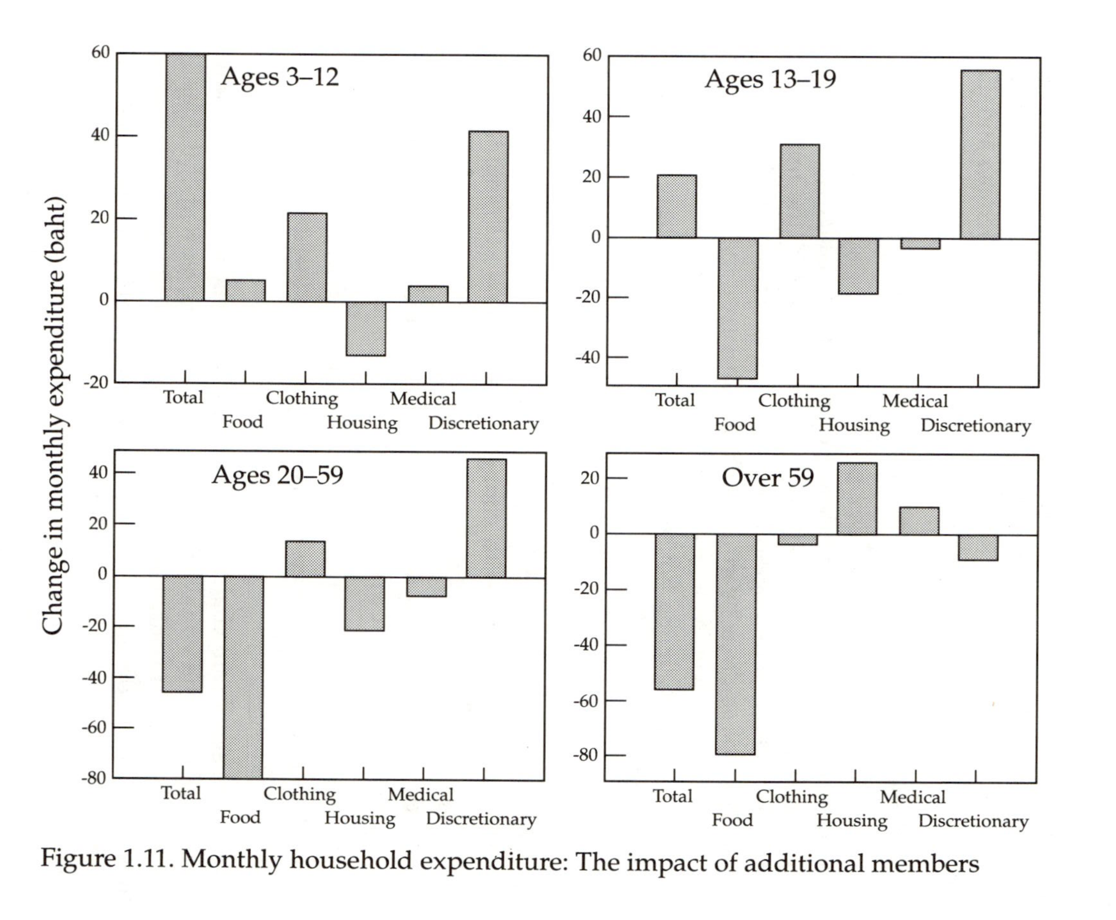

Figure 1.11. Monthly household expenditure: The impact of additional members

ture toward discretionary items and out of housing and, for teens, food. The impact on the composition of the budget of an additional adult is quite similar to the impact of an additional teen. Monthly expenditures on food decline by 80 baht per month and on housing by 20 baht per month while expenditure on discretionary items increase by almost 50 baht per month and on clothing by about 15 baht per month. The addition of a prime-age adult and an elderly member have quite similar impacts on food expenditure, but housing expenditure is higher given an elderly member and discretionary expenditure is lower.[16]

The Impact on Aggregate Expenditure Patterns

HOMES (Household Model for Economic and Social Studies) proves to be a useful tool for forecasting trends in aggregate spending patterns. All necessary demographic data are available because changes in the number of households and their demographic composition are projected. Household membership has a direct bearing, as shown above, on the composition of the household budget. Moreover, household expenditures are indirectly affected because changing household characteristics will have an impact on household income.

In general, aggregate spending patterns will be shaped by the following forces:

- Changes in the age distribution of the population will shift spending power from households with young heads to those with middle-aged heads.
- The demographic character of households will change, affecting the propensity to consume and the composition of the household budget.
- Economic growth and improved standards of living will induce budgetary shifts away from basic essentials, e.g., food, and toward luxury goods and services.

The most significant change forecast is the dramatic decline in the importance of food and nonalcoholic beverages—from over half of the family's budget in 1980 to only one-third of the budget in 2005. The resources thus freed up are devoted to a number of areas. During the same period expenditure on housing is forecast to increase its share of the budget from 19.4 percent to 22.3 percent; apparel increases from 6.6 percent to 7.5 percent; medical care increases from 3.5 percent to 4.3 percent; and discretionary expenditure increases from 19.4 percent to 32.0 percent.

---

16. These results do not distinguish the sex of the additional member. In Thailand, gender has very little effect on spending patterns except for spending on alcohol and tobacco products. See Chapter 5 for more information.

Table 1.8. Forecast monthly expenditures: 1980–2005 (millions of baht)

Expenditure category	1980	1985	1990	1995	2000	2005
Food	13,311	17,717	23,198	29,652	36,979	45,021
Alcohol and tobacco	1,027	1,479	2,102	2,918	3,950	5,222
Apparel	1,721	2,618	3,855	5,476	7,521	10,041
Housing	5,049	7,411	10,774	15,369	21,470	29,387
Medical care	917	1,368	2,006	2,886	4,077	5,624
Personal care	550	779	1,086	1,479	1,965	2,555
Transportation and communication	1,316	2,205	3,592	5,652	8,599	12,723
Recreation and reading	460	760	1,223	1,906	2,882	4,246
Education	260	375	512	661	801	916
Miscellaneous	1,468	2,540	4,284	6,997	11,035	16,848
Total expenditures	26,079	37,252	52,632	72,996	99,279	132,583

Forecasts of total monthly private expenditures are presented in Table 1.8. From a value of about 26 billion baht per month in 1980, expenditures on all goods and services combined are forecast to reach nearly 133 billion baht per month in 2005, which represents a rate of growth of 6.5 percent per annum. The forecast aggregates represent a gradual decline in the rate of growth of private expenditures from 7.1 percent during the 1980–85 quinquennium to reach 5.9 percent during the 2000–05 quinquennium. Although in percentage terms, expenditures on food and nonalcoholic beverages grow more slowly than expenditures on any other category, the absolute increase is greatest. Monthly expenditures on food rise from 13 billion baht per month in 1980 to 45 billion baht per month in 2005. The greatest increases in percentage terms are anticipated for discretionary items. Transportation and communication, recreation and reading, and miscellaneous items are each forecast to rise tenfold between 1980 and 2005.

The forecasts presented above may for several reasons deviate substantially from the shifts in spending Thailand actually experiences. Economic growth may be slower or more rapid than assumed. New products may emerge that were not even included in the 1981 Socio-Economic Survey on which the analysis is based. The possible impact of price changes is neglected altogether.

A comparison of budget shares forecast for 1985 and 1990 with those reported in the 1988 Socio-Economic Survey (NSO 1991b) shows that, in general, the shifts in spending are occurring more rapidly than anticipated (Table 1.9). The share devoted to food had dropped to 40 percent by 1988. Expenditure on housing and transportation and communication increased

Table 1.9. Comparison of forecast and actual budget shares

Expenditure category	1988 Socio-Economic Survey: Expenditure per household	1988 Socio-Economic Survey: Share	Projected shares: 1985	Projected shares: 1990
Food	18,228	0.399	0.476	0.442
Alcohol and tobacco	1,896	0.042	0.039	0.040
Apparel	3,072	0.067	0.070	0.073
Housing	12,144	0.266	0.200	0.205
Medical care	1,716	0.038	0.037	0.038
Personal care	1,296	0.028	0.021	0.021
Transportation and communication	4,848	0.106	0.059	0.068
Recreation and reading	1,104	0.024	0.021	0.023
Education	672	0.015	0.010	0.010
Miscellaneous	672	0.015	0.068	0.081

Source: Chapter 5; NSO (1992).

much more rapidly than expected. Economic growth during the 1980–88 interval was not very different than assumed, but price changes may have played an important role. The price of residential property has increased substantially in recent years, which (depending on the elasticity of demand) could account for the higher share of the budget devoted to housing.

Economic growth and demographic factors both explain part of the variation in household expenditures, but, of the two, economic growth is by far the most important source of change. Only in housing do demographic factors account for as much as half the growth forecast. In education, on the other hand, demographic factors account for the small decline in relative share. In the alcohol and tobacco sectors, income growth increases and the changes in age composition decrease the forecast consumption.

The forecast decline in household size turns out to have a negative impact on food, housing, and alcohol and tobacco expenditures and a large positive impact on apparel, transportation and communication, and recreation and reading. Looking at these results suggests that further investigation of the future effect of modernization, development, and tastes on the expenditures of present and future cohorts as they move through the life cycle would be useful. An even more interesting result is the growth in demand by sector relative to the total growth in demand and relative to the growth in the labor supply. If the growth in expenditures in each category is compared with the growth in total demand as a base only, personal care, food, and education expenditures grow less rapidly than total demand, with education bringing up the rear. Alcohol and tobacco grow at the same rate. On the other side, miscellaneous expenditures exceed the growth in total demand by the largest amount, followed by transportation and communication, recreation and reading, medical care, housing, and apparel, in that order.

These trends, at least in the sectors covered,[17] suggest what is likely to happen to relative real wages in different career or industry specializations and to relative profits in different sectors. They may also help in foretelling where a strong union movement is likely to develop, and, in broad terms, the timing of coming changes in Thailand's comparative advantage. However, to draw any final conclusions requires information on growth in production of nonconsumer goods and services.

THE EDUCATION SECTOR

Thailand's educational sector has expanded rapidly in the last two decades driven by two factors: a commitment to increasing the schooling available to those of school age and rapid growth in the number of school-age children. In 1978, for example, the compulsory level of education was extended from four to six years of schooling. The enrollment ratio for the secondary level increased from 11 percent in 1960 to 30 percent in 1980. An extensive vocational education program has been developed, and university education has been extended to large numbers of Thai citizens through the development of open universities.

These advances took place in spite of a rapid increase in the number of school-age children. The average annual increase in the population 5–14 years of age averaged between 250,000 and 350,000 per year from 1960 to 1975 (Figure 1.12). Thus, the Thai educational system faced a double challenge—improving the quality and level of education achieved by the average Thai child and rapidly expanding the school system to accommodate population growth. To meet this challenge, between 1964 and 1985, the number of students enrolled in primary and secondary public schools doubled from 4.1 million to 8.5 million, the number of teachers increased fourfold from 114,000 to 451,000, and public expenditure increased sixfold from 4.7 billion baht to 28.6 billion baht in 1985 prices.

Starting in 1980 the underlying demographics of schooling have changed quite dramatically. The population belonging to the age groups from which primary and secondary school students are drawn is essentially not growing at all. And beginning in 1995, the primary and secondary school-age population is expected to decline by as much as 100,000 potential students per year.

---

17. Capital goods and services and the impact of foreign demand have not been analyzed.

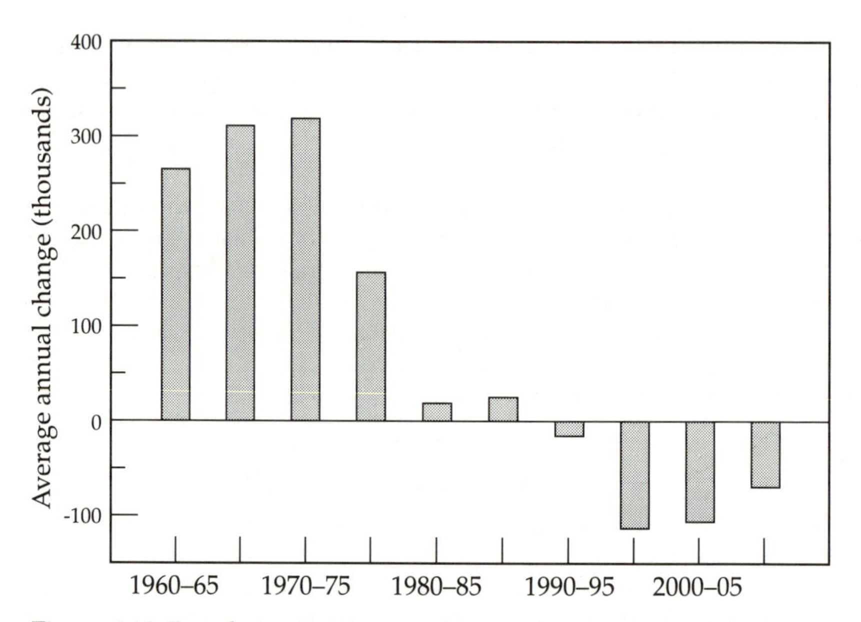

Figure 1.12. Population 5–14 years of age, average annual change: 1960–65 to 2005–10

Enrollment trends will also be affected by changes in enrollment ratios. The greatest percentage increase in enrollment ratios is forecast for those 18–24 years of age. Enrollment among these young adults is forecast to increase from 12 to 21 percent from 1990 to 2015, with most of the increase occurring before 2000. Those 15–17 years of age will also experience a large increase in school enrollment, rising rather steadily from 33 percent to reach 47 percent by 2015. Finally, enrollment among those 12–14 years of age is expected to increase from 67 to 78 percent, spread evenly over the 1990–2015 period (see Chapter 6, Table 6.3). Only those 5–11 years of age are forecast to experience no increase in school enrollment rates as schooling is essentially universal among them in any case.

How will such fundamental population change and anticipated increases in enrollment rates affect school enrollment? Primary school enrollment will almost certainly be relatively constant until 1995 and, at that time, begin a steady and fairly significant decline. Secondary school enrollment is projected to increase substantially over the next decade, rising from 2.6 million in 1990 to over 3.3 million in 2005. But, starting shortly after the turn of the century the growth in secondary school enrollments will level off and experience no additional gain. Enrollment at the closed universities[18]

18. Closed universities (in contrast to open universities) are traditional universities where acceptance is based on academic merit.

should nearly double between 1990 and 2015, reaching 1.2 million students in that year. All told, total school enrollment will increase from 10.5 million in 1990 to 11.4 million in 2000, but will decline to 10.7 million by 2015 (Table 6.4).

Forecasts of increased school enrollment rates are based on analysis of the determinents of school attendance. The most important determinant of school enrollment is the educational attainment of the head. Household income is an important determinant of enrollment in the secondary and tertiary levels. Children of farm families, who have a higher opportunity cost, are less likely to attend school, whereas children from entrepreneurial households are very likely to attend.

Trends in public expenditure on education will depend on the quality of education provided. Assuming no increase in unit costs provides a lower end benchmark. In this case, public costs will increase from 37 million baht in 1985 to 41 million baht in 1990, a rise of 2.2 percent per annum, and to 45 million baht in 1995, a rise of only 1.8 percent per annum, (see Chapter 6). Such rates of increase are far less than the expected growth in real GNP and suggest that education will become much less of a burden, providing an opportunity to improve the quality of education to meet the challenges of the twenty-first century without increases in taxes.

Even with considerable improvements in quality coming from better qualified teachers and lower student–teacher ratios, the growth in real educational expenditure will reach only 4.2 percent between 1985 and 1990 and only 3.4 percent during the 1990–95 period. At least in education, Thailand can perhaps "have its cake and eat it, too."

Policy Implications

During the past 25 years, the challenge facing the education sector has been to improve the availability and quality of schooling in the face of rapid growth in the school-age population. The next 25 years clearly presents a different challenge. Because the school-age population has stabilized, a broader range of policy options is feasible. In general terms, the possibilities include: (1) slowing the growth of public expenditure on education; (2) increasing enrollments by inducing students to extend their years in school; and (3) improving the quality of education by, for example, reducing class size, lowering the student–teacher ratio, or by upgrading the average quality of the teacher corps.

The most concrete and important area in which these options arise is in the area of employment of teachers. Between 1964 and 1985 employment of teachers grew very rapidly, the number of primary and secondary school teachers increased from 114,000 to 451,000—an annual rate of growth of 6.5 percent. To sustain such a rapid rate of growth required the development of a substantial teacher-training program. In 1977, for example, there were over 40,000 graduates of teacher-training programs—enough to increase the number of teachers by 15 percent in a single year (Chapter 6).

But the current student–teacher ratio of 18 to 1 can be maintained over the next 25 years with virtually no increase in employment. Employment would peak in 1990 at 548,000 teachers and begin to decline rather slowly thereafter. By 2015 total employment would be about 10 percent below the 1990 peak. The greatest decline would be in primary school teachers. Between now and 1995 employment would be constant at about 400,000 but by 2015 employment would drop to about 340,000 primary school teachers. Employment of secondary school teachers would increase by about 3,000 teachers per year between now and the year 2000, the year of peak employment. Thereafter the number of secondary school teachers required would decline by about 1,000 per year.

In response to slackening demand for teachers, teachers' colleges have terminated evening programs that award teachers' certificates or diplomas and have increasingly emphasized baccalaureate education. By 1985, 66 percent of those enrolled in teacher-training programs were pursuing a bachelor's degree as compared with 26 percent in 1980. At the same time, total enrollment has declined precipitously to the current level of fewer than 60,000 students. Lower enrollment and a longer training period will reduce the number of newly graduated teachers seeking employment. Is further retrenchment necessary?

From 1977 to 1980, the number of teachers grew annually at between 30,000 and 40,000 per year. In addition, about 10,000 teachers withdrew annually because of retirement, death, or resignation. Because annual graduates from teacher-training programs averaged about 40,000 during this period, the supply and demand for teachers was apparently in fairly close balance during this period. From 1981 to 1985 the number of new graduates dropped to about 32,000 to 33,000 teachers each year while employment grew on average by less than 10,000 per year. Full employment of new graduates could be achieved only through replacement demand of about 20,000 teachers per year. In other words, all graduates could be employed if about 5 percent of the teacher corps turned over each year and all new hires were recent graduates.

For the period 1973 to 1980, the years through which data are available, the withdrawal rate generally varied from 2 to 4 percent. Thus, particularly as total employment grows more slowly, further retrenchment seemed inevitable.

There are several unfortunate aspects of a serious retrenchment in teacher-training programs. First, the capacity of Thailand to train teachers would be damaged, reducing the country's capacity to respond to future expansion of the educational system. Second, current efforts to upgrade the educational achievement of teachers would be undermined. Although most of those currently being trained are pursuing a bachelor's degree, they would have a negligible impact on overall teacher quality were few recent graduates employed.

What are the alternatives to the retrenchment in employment? Three possibilities stand out. First would be to improve the quality of teaching by reducing the student–teacher ratio. The second would be to increase enrollments at the secondary school level. And the third would be to adopt a sabbatical system that would release teachers periodically to upgrade their skills through teacher-training programs.

For the sake of illustration we consider the implications of allowing employment of teachers to increase by 1 percent per annum[19] so that employment would increase by about 6,000 teachers per year increasing to closer to 7,000 teachers per year at the end of the simulation.

We consider three alternatives for absorbing the additional teachers.

- Reducing the student–teacher ratio
  A reduction of the student–teacher ratio from 18, the 1985 level, to 15 in 2005, and 12.6 in 2015 would absorb all additional teachers. This does not appear to be a cost-effective approach to absorbing additional growth in employment. The current student–teacher ratio of 18 is already low by international standards, and compares favorably with ratios even in industrialized countries. In the United States, for example, during the early 1980s the elementary student–teacher ratio was around 20 and the secondary ratio around 17. The United States, of course, has also had to deal with problems of shrinking enrollments.
- Increase secondary enrollment
  The growth in employment up to the year 2000 could be absorbed by increasing secondary enrollment to 4.1 million. This exceeds our basic projection of secondary enrollment by nearly one million and would represent a significant, but plausible, expansion of school enrollment. To absorb growth in the number of teachers after the year 2000 by expanding enrollment probably would be only partially successful. To absorb the full 1 percent annual growth would require 2 million additional students in 2005, 2.8 million additional in 2010, and 3.9 million additional in 2015. Enrollment at these levels could be achieved only with unrealistically high enrollment ratios.
- Teacher training
  If enrollments are maintained at the basic projection levels, student–teacher ratios are held constant, and employment is allowed to increase, the resulting "surplus" of teachers could be absorbed by instituting a sabbatical system by which teachers would take a specified amount of time

19. Between 1980 and 1985 employment grew at an annual rate of 3.9 percent.

off from teaching so as to upgrade their skills, possibly to the levels of education being achieved by current graduates of teaching colleges. By 1995 approximately one teacher in 20 could be on sabbatical without adversely affecting staffing. By the year 2000, one teacher in 10 could be on sabbatical. Thereafter, a sabbatical system, by itself, could not feasibly absorb the additional teachers employed under the 1 percent growth in employment scenario.

The clear message in the education sector is that resource requirements associated with total growth will begin to shrink in the coming years. The remainder of this century seems to offer an excellent opportunity to improve the quality of education and to extend educational attainment, particularly at the secondary level. Thereafter, expansion of the educational system should be relatively limited. Population redistribution, not explicitly considered in this study, will become an important concern. Some localities will begin to face a decline in enrollments, requiring a retrenchment in the educational system, while other localities will experience increasing enrollments, requiring employment of additional teachers locally and construction of appropriate facilities.

THE HEALTH SECTOR

Analysis of health is difficult in almost any country because of the complex mix of public and private providers. The analysis undertaken here relies on a variety of resources so as to provide an overall perspective of likely changes in the health sector. Extensive analysis was carried out using data from the Ministry of Public Health which accounts for about 60 percent of total public cost (see Chapter 7). Public and private sector use of health care facilities was assessed by analyzing micro data collected on 21,000 households in the 1981 Health and Welfare Survey conducted by the National Statistical Office of Thailand. And household expenditure on health care was analyzed using micro data collected on 9,000 households as part of the 1981 Socio-Economic Survey (NSO 1985).

The study has several objectives. The primary objective is to forecast, at the national level, trends in the number of patients and health care expenditures. This has been accomplished by estimating rates of health care use and their dependence on age, sex, household characteristics, and socioeconomic characteristics of the population. The rates of use have then been applied to projections of Thailand's population, number of households, and the demographic characteristics of households to obtain aggregate estimates of the numbers of inpatients and outpatients. Health care costs have been obtained by applying unit costs for inpatients and outpatients to the forecast numbers of patients. The unit costs are also affected by demographic change because the treatment mix and cost varies with the age and sex of the patient. Trends in the private sector were assessed by estimating the impact of social, economic, and demographic characteristics of the households on health care expenditure. Determinants of expenditure were forecast and used to forecast total private health care expenditure.

In addition to the primary purpose of the study, two secondary objectives are pursued in less detail. The first is to describe likely changes in the patient mix that will bear on health sector planning. The second is to assess the impact at the household level of changing health needs.

Major Findings

The principal findings of our health sector study are summarized below.

- The number of patients will grow at about 1 to 1.5 percent per annum.
- Public costs will grow at about 5 percent per annum.
- Private expenditure will grow at about 7 percent per annum.
- Demand for maternal and child care will decline steadily.
- Health care needs of the elderly will grow rapidly.
- The family will continue as a viable support mechanism.

Looked at in overall terms, these findings paint a fairly optimistic picture despite the increasing number of elderly, a by-product of Thailand's demographic transition. In an aging society, it is inevitable that an increased share of resources will be devoted to health care. Such a phenomenon is very apparent in more demographically advanced Japan, for example. But Thailand is in more of a transition period. Although the health care needs of the elderly are increasing, they are balanced by the relative decline in the needs of two other groups of major health care users: young children and childbearing women. As a consequence, the overall demands of the health sector should not be excessive over the next 20 to 25 years.

Although the overall requirements of Thailand's health sector will not increase very rapidly in the near future, the kinds of medical care that will be required should change quite dramatically. It is clear from this study that a detailed assessment of changing health needs and the implication for health care planning should be a high priority.

A recurring issue in health is the question of who should bear financial responsibility for health care: the state or the individual. The choice, in reality, is between the state and the family. The health sector analysis and analysis of other sectors indicate that the family is a viable institution capable of playing a major role in the financing of health care. Most elderly live with their children; households headed by the elderly are not particularly economically disadvantaged, on average; and, households headed by the elderly do not have excessively high per capita rates of treatment. Of course, increased reliance on the family to finance health care costs will require the development of health insurance to protect them against catastrophic medical expenses.

Detailed Discussion

Aggregate trends in three aspects of the health sector have been forecast: (1) the number of patients, (2) recurring expenditure, and (3) capital expenditure.

The number of patients seeking health care will grow in step with Thailand's increasing population, but the amount of health services required will also depend on which segments of the population grow most rapidly. In general, health needs are closely related to age. Thus, three demographic groups that rely more extensively on the health sector can be readily identified: the very young, the old, and childbearing women. In Thailand, the pattern of use is evident in proportions seeking inpatient care. Among males, the three heaviest users are children under age 7, adults 50–59 years of age, and those 60 and older. Among Thai females, the heaviest users are those of childbearing age (20–39), those over 50, and those under 7, in that order. A similar pattern is evident in expenditure data—the presence of an additional child under 3 or an additional member 60 or older results in higher health care expenditure by Thai households. The impact of a child under 3 is particularly noteworthy. An additional child of either sex raises health care expenditure by more than 1 percent of the household's total disposable income. This is a remarkable impact since Thai households on average spend only 3 percent of their disposable income on health care.

The traditional pattern of health care use is less apparent for outpatient care. Male outpatient care follows a U-shaped age profile, but school-age children are also major users of outpatient care. The female pattern is much more complex with use high among children of school age and younger, women of childbearing age, and older women.

Because the age pattern of health care use is complex, the impact of demographic change is complex as well. The first group of heavy health care users, young children, is essentially stationary and beginning to decline in Thailand. Alternative forecasts of inpatient care indicate that the number of patients under age 7 has peaked and will decline very gradually over the foreseeable future.

The second group of heavy users, the elderly, are rapidly growing in numbers. Those 65 and older are forecast to increase from 1.9 million in 1985 to 3.7 million in 2005 and will exceed 5 million in 2015. Over each 10-year forecast period, the average annual growth rate of the elderly population varies from 3.1 percent to as much as 3.7 percent. It should come as no surprise, then, that the total demand for health care by the elderly will rise in step. Detailed forecasts presented in Chapter 7 show a steady increase in inpatient care, for example, averaging 3.4 percent per annum for elderly women and 3.7 percent per annum for elderly men.

Analysis of the final group of heavy health care users, childbearing women, is more complex because two distinct demographic factors affect use. The number of childbearing women in Thailand is currently growing at a fast pace. For example, the number in the 20–29 year age group grew 2.6 percent per annum between 1985 and 1990. But the number of women in their 20s will peak around 1995 and change little over the next 15 years. At the same time, women of childbearing age are having fewer children than in the past so that the typical woman will require less maternal health care than previously. When these multiple factors are taken into account, inpatient care for women 20–49 years of age is forecast to increase by about 1 percent per annum between now and the year 2000, to remain essentially constant between 2000 and 2010, and to begin declining thereafter.

When these demographic impacts are combined with changes in the numbers in other groups seeking health care, the total forecast demand for inpatient and outpatient care, presented in Table 1.10, is obtained. Both the number of outpatients and the number of inpatients grow at a steady but declining rate over the entire simulation period. Inpatient care consistently grows more rapidly than outpatient care and somewhat more rapidly than the population, in general. Outpatient care grows somewhat more slowly than the population in every period.

Figures on recurring costs presented in Chapter 7 reflect a combination of forces including increased number of patients, differences in health care needs and costs associated with age, and expected improvements in the quality and price of health care. Overall health care costs are expected to increase at a fairly steady pace—annual growth for outpatient care is forecast to average 5.4 percent and for inpatient care 5.1 percent. All in all, then, recurring costs will grow at a magnitude similar to the growth in GNP expected in Thailand. Recurring expenditure for health care should be a relatively constant proportion of GNP and the government budget.

Assessing likely changes in investment on health care expenditure is a fruitful area for more extensive analysis. Estimates could be improved by assessing the adaptation of new health technology, the impact of shifts in the type of health care required, and changes in the geographic distribution of the population and, hence, the demand for health care services.

From the discussion of key demographic groups above it is clear that Thailand will experience substantial shifts in the demographic character of patients and, as a consequence, changes in the mix of health care to be provided. Figure 1.13 clarifies this further by showing the relative shares of child care, "maternal" care (care of women of childbearing age), and care for the elderly. In 1985 inpatient cases for the elderly and child care took up about one-quarter of the pie each, whereas women of childbearing age constituted nearly one-half of all patients. But the relative numbers of patients who are children and childbearing women steadily erodes and, by 2015, half of the pie is devoted to care for the elderly, only one-third to care for women of childbearing age, and one-sixth to care for children.

Table 1.10. Forecasts of number of patients and recurring costs: 1985–2015

	Inpatient care		Outpatient care	
Year	Patients (millions)	Cost (millions of baht)	Patients (millions)	Cost (millions of baht)
1985	2.570	2,033	30.360	2,680
1990	2.856	2,755	32.564	3,525
1995	3.112	3,662	34.500	4,588
2000	3.357	4,816	36.249	5,933
2005	3.595	6,285	37.861	7,616
2010	3.801	8,098	39.277	9,745
2015	3.997	10,328	40.368	12,452

Source: Chapter 7, Tables 7.3 and 7.4

The implications of such a shift are far reaching in that they affect the mode by which medical care is provided (less reliance on schools), the pattern of treatment (decline in OB-GYN and infectious and respiratory diseases and an increase in degenerative diseases, e.g., cancer and heart disease), the facilities and equipment required to provide medical care, and possibly the means by which health care is financed.

The implications for health care financing requires additional discussion. There are two aspects of health care financing that may be affected by demographic change. First, the need for user charges and other mechanisms to promote allocative efficiency may increase with the aging of the health market. A recurring problem in the provision of public health care is underutilization of primary health care services and overuse of urban hospitals and specialized services. Schools provide an institutional setting by which children can be screened for their health care needs in a cost-effective manner. But as the overall importance of child care declines, mechanisms for screening, e.g., user charges, may become more important. Furthermore, as experience in the West has shown, the potential costs of providing health care to the elderly are enormous so that unlimited access to health care is not a fiscally viable alternative.

A second aspect of health care financing may be more important. Equity is a principal concern in discussions of increased privatization of health care insofar as paying for health care places an undue financial burden on those who fall ill. As increasing numbers of health care users become elderly, equity concerns may increase to the extent that the elderly are more likely to become ill and are more likely to have low labor earnings or none at all. The burden can be ameliorated in two ways: health insurance or family support. Evidence presented throughout this study suggests that the net-

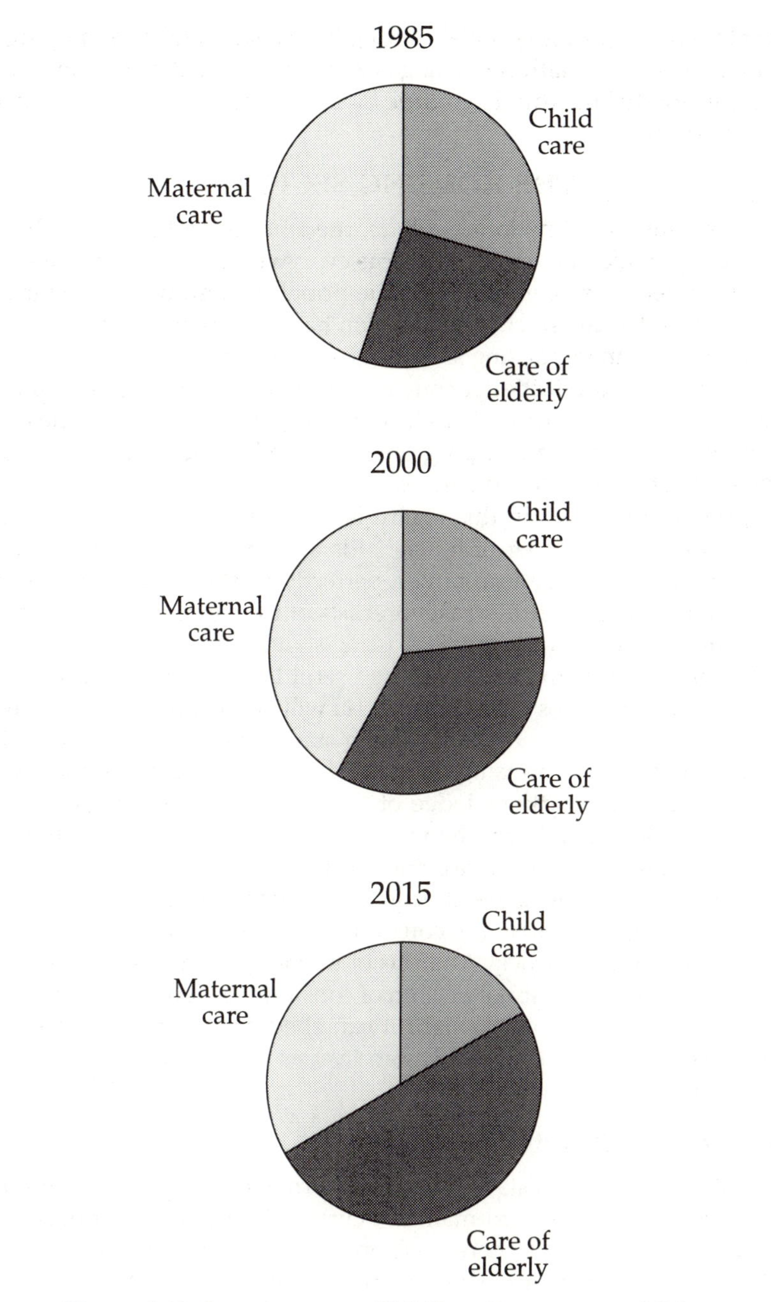

Figure 1.13. Inpatient care: Childbearing women, children, and the elderly: 1985, 2000, and 2015

work of family support is relatively strong in Thailand and shows no signs of crumbling. Thus, health care charges would not fall solely on the shoulders of the elderly but would be borne by a larger and financially stronger extended family.

THE HOUSING SECTOR

From the standpoint of national welfare, the amount and quality of housing services provided are major concerns everywhere. However well existing housing needs are being met, as the population grows or changes in composition and as the stock of housing on hand wears out or is destroyed, maintaining per capita housing standards requires the construction of new dwelling units. And additional construction may be needed in response to the market demand for increased housing quality as real incomes rise or in response to government programs designed to meet some currently unmet social standard for housing services.

Our primary emphasis in this regard is to determine the effect of forecast changes in the number of households and in per capita incomes on the demand for housing, assuming a perfectly elastic supply of housing (see Chapter 8). The resulting base forecasts of the number of newly built dwelling units required to maintain existing standards and to replace withdrawals from the housing stock will be useful to both private and public decision makers. Perhaps even more useful will be the forecasts of the real expenditures needed to maintain existing standards and to adjust for increases in the quality of housing demanded as incomes grow. Armed with such forecasts and with knowledge of the applicable supply conditions, various possible scenarios can be worked out, helping to reduce the uncertainties facing the private sector and, where relevant, aiding the government in its sectorial and general economic policymaking.

The second emphasis is on the consumption of the housing services derived from the housing stock. Analysis of housing consumption is important because such a substantial portion of consumer expenditure is devoted to housing and because of the light it can shed on the income elasticity of housing demand and on how demand varies with the characteristics of households.

Future Housing Requirements

The HOMES-based forecasts of household formations imply that the stock of dwelling units required to maintain current housing stock/household standards in Thailand will increase from 9.7 to 20.5 million between 1985 and 2015, or by 111 percent. The assumptions underlying these forecasts are quite conservative (see Chapter 8).

The peak in the number of newly built units required to meet this growth in demand will not come until the turn of the century when 1.91 million additional units or 33 percent more than were required in 1980–85 will be needed. By 2010–15 the additional units required will have fallen back to 13 percent above the 1985–90 level.

Assuming withdrawals from the housing stock run at the conservative rate of 2 percent per annum, then housing starts will continue to increase, though by smaller and smaller amounts, through 2010–15, exceeding 3 million in that five-year period or 55 percent more than in 1980–85. Thus, in absolute terms, measured by the number of new dwelling units started, housing sector needs in Thailand will continue to expand through most of the period covered (Figure 1.14). Of course, the stock of infrastructure needed to service residential dwellings and of capital needed to produce the furniture and household appliances complementary to residential dwellings will also have to expand just to maintain current service levels.

In the absence of further movement into urban areas, the growth in Thai housing demand will be concentrated in owner occupancy and located largely in rural areas. In fact, after 1990–95, the number of new rental and other nonowner-occupied dwellings required by demographic changes will decline. However, given the much larger relative demand for rental and other nonowner occupancy forms of tenure in urban areas compared with the national averages, a large increase in the share of the urban population could halt or even reverse this decline. Specifically, if urban growth did in fact adjust national tenure rates to something near the current urban ratios by 2015, there would be a boom in rental (or condominium-type) housing rather than a decline.

Future Residential Construction

Analysis of the consumer expenditure data discussed above indicates that housing expenditure by households has a per capita income elasticity of 1.08. Based on this indirect evidence, the income elasticity of the quality of housing demanded is assumed to be 1.0 in estimating the impact of income growth on residential construction. However, the number of dwelling units demanded per household is assumed to be independent of the level of income, i.e., that household formations and the multiple occupancy of dwelling units by households do not respond to income changes and that households demand only one dwelling unit, whatever their income. Thus, if Thai per capita income increases 10 percent, we assume that Thais will not buy more housing units but will upgrade the quality of new housing demanded by 10 percent.

The impact of income growth on housing demand, even with the "conservative" assumption that the income elasticity of 1.0 applies only to newly constructed units, is very large. In fact, under these circumstances residential construction will be almost six times the level required by demographic changes alone by 2010–15. And if the entire housing stock is upgraded with

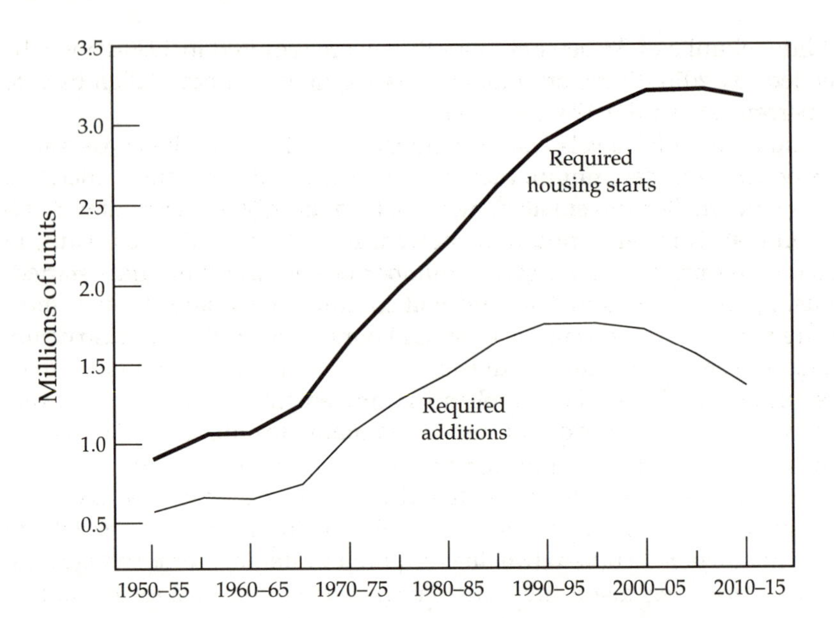

Note: "Required additions" are the number of new dwelling units required to meet the changes in demand coming from the changes in households only, adjusted for the occupancy of some units by more than one household. "Required housing starts" includes a further adjustment for "normal" vacancies and expected withdrawals from the housing stock.

Figure 1.14. New housing requirements: 1950–55 to 2010–15

income changes, residential construction will be 11 times this level by 2010–15 (Figure 1.15).

The projected boom in residential construction should already be underway and should proceed apace through 2010–15 (the forecasts based only on newly built units do show the pace of the increase slowing in the next century and so a long-swing in the growth rate of residential construction). The growth in demand is likely to lead to price increases as well as to new construction because the supply of new units is not perfectly elastic, in that costs in the building industry increase as output grows and government interventions (such as zoning restrictions) impose costs. Given the large increments forecast, the possibility of a speculative boom in housing is clear.

Expansive as these forecasts are, they ignore the apparent backlog from the last two decades. If the income elasticity of demand for housing and the experienced growth in income are considered then the evidence suggests that a considerable quality backlog has built up. Whether due to supply side constraints, including financial constraints, limiting the adjustment

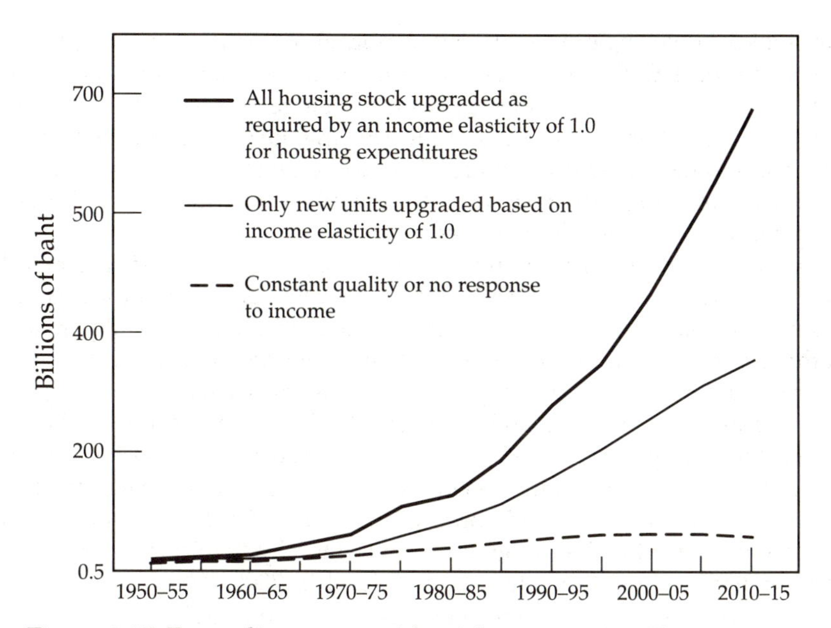

Figure 1.15. Expenditures on residential construction: Varying assumptions on income elasticity of housing expenditures, 1950–55 to 2010–15

or to direct government interventions, actual residential construction has been far less than expected. One implication, confirmed by experience, is that the prices of existing dwelling units should increase more rapidly than the average price level in this period.

Another set of factors likely to affect the characteristics and so average price (quality here) of housing demanded are the changes forecast in the nature of Thai households, especially the decline in average size and the decrease in the number of children per household. Both changes might be expected to raise the relative demand for rental or condominium-style housing and so to reduce, relatively, the average construction cost of new dwellings. Some of the saving on land and dwelling unit size may, however, be put back into a higher quality of housing per square meter. And, in fact, consumer expenditure data suggest that at the same income smaller households spend a larger share of their income on housing than do larger households. Thus, the net effect on per household housing expenditures of these demographic developments may be small.

The Age Composition of Demand

There are systematic differences in the quality, size, location, and tenure of housing demanded in different age groups. Because of these differences, the "typical" dwelling units occupied by households in different age groups are not perfect substitutes. Thus, the variation in net demand by age group can be very important. Relative prices can change to offset excess supply or demand in different segments of the housing market but they are sticky (at least downward) and there are likely to be large differences between the short- and long-run response. Meanwhile, construction will be encouraged in the excess demand segments.

Most impressive in this context is the coming growth in housing demand by the middle-aged (35–59) heads. By 2015 dwellings required for this age group in Thailand will be 253 percent of the 1985 level. Generally, heads in this age group have less postponable housing demand, tend to spend more on furnishings and other housing appurtenances, require better quality or at least larger housing, and are more often homeowners than are heads in the other age groups; therefore, the significance of this growth is apparent. Enroute to this much increased required housing stock, beginning in the 1985–90 quinquennia and continuing through 2000–05, expenditures for new units for the 35–59 age group will literally "explode," reaching a peak of almost three times the 1980–85 level in 2000–2005 (Figure 1.16).

The much slower growth and then decline in 2010–2015 in the required housing stock for the 15–34 age group is also interesting (Figure 1.16). Heads in this age group can postpone demand if necessary and tend to have specialized housing needs, especially in urban areas. The ultimate decline in housing required for this age group could result in a mismatch between the characteristics of the housing produced and the characteristics of housing demanded. In fact, even accounting for growth in per capita income, required residential construction expenditures for this age group have already peaked, though they will remain relatively high through 1990–95. Only a major—but not impossible—increase in the rate of household formations could change this result. Thus, to the extent that housing is specialized to the needs of different age groups, our analysis suggests some difficult times ahead for the builders and owners of properties designed for younger households in Thailand.

Finally, though the growth in housing requirements and expenditures on new units for household heads age 60 or older in Thailand will remain considerably smaller than for the other two age groups, their approximate doubling during 2005–15 (to 329.8 percent of the 1985 level) will offer both an opportunity in a specialized housing category to the Thai building industry and provide a considerable challenge.

Share of Residential Construction in GDP, GDI, and the Labor Supply

To understand the potential impact of the changes described, it is necessary to relate the changes forecast in residential construction to what is fore-

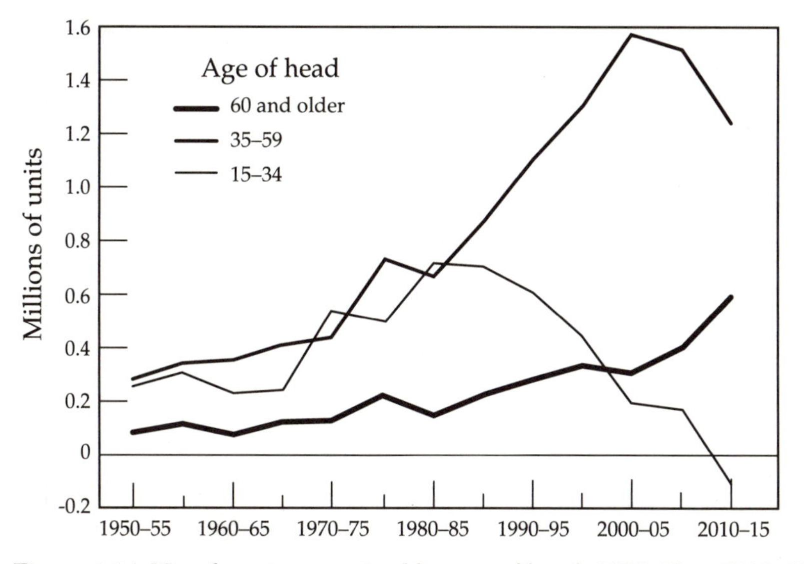

Figure 1.16. New housing required by age of head: 1950–55 to 2010–15

cast to happen in the rest of the Thai economy. The forecasts of residential construction, based on quality changes in the entire housing stock, account for an increasing share of national output (GDP) quinquennium by quinquennium over the next 25 years. The more conservative forecasts based on quality changes in newly built housing only, show the share increasing to a peak in 1990-95 and remaining relatively constant thereafter (Figure 1.17).

The forecast share of residential construction in gross domestic investment (GDI) tells a similar story, with an important exception. Even upgrading the entire stock will not keep Thai residential construction growing as a share of GDI throughout the period covered. If income-adjusted residential construction follows the assumptions underlying either forecast, the share of residential construction in GDI in Thailand would have grown most rapidly during 1985-90, with the peak share coming in during 1990-95. However, while falling off, for both forecasts residential construction's slice of GDI will remain above the 1980-85 level at least through 2000-05 (Figure 1.18).

Between 1980-85 and 2010-15, the share of residential construction in the labor force, based on upgrading the entire stock, would be six times greater than the labor requirement if the stock were not upgraded. Over the same period the labor supply is projected to increase by only two times. Thus, there will be an excess demand for labor in the construction sector and the likelihood is that real wages in residential construction will increase. But

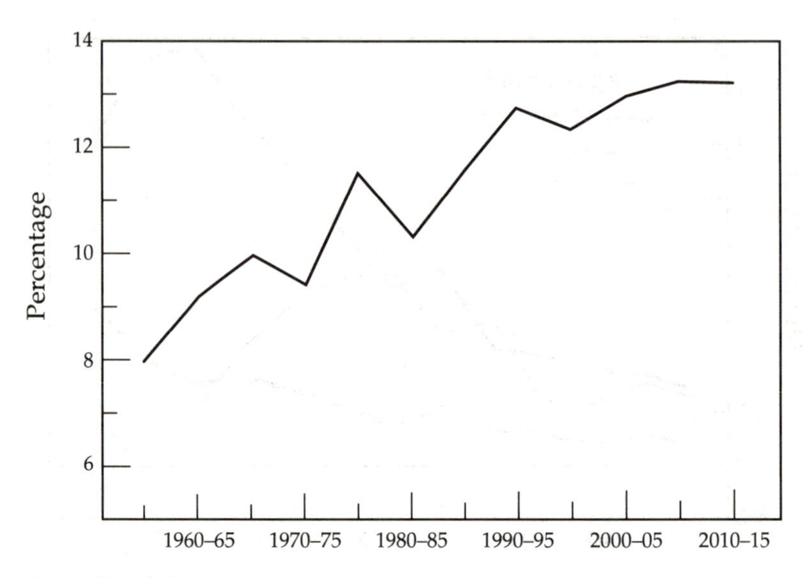

Source: Chapter 8.

Figure 1.17. Share of residential construction in GDP: 1955–60 to 2010–15

real wages in residential construction are not apt to increase as much as the relative growth in the sector might suggest because of the probable existence of a ready supply of construction labor from the agricultural sector. When the economy begins to adjust in the twenty-first century to the national excess demand for labor by substituting more capital-intensive for labor-intensive production in other sectors, the short-run employment effects of this substitution may be softened by the expected growth in labor-intensive residential construction (Chapter 8).

Summary

In sum, our analysis suggests that increasing amounts of real resources will be absorbed by the Thai residential construction sector from now through the first 15 years of the twenty-first century and that, *ceterus paribus,* this will raise the relative share of residential construction in GNP and the share of the future supply of labor absorbed by residential construction. And, although the share of residential construction in GDI will peak in 1990–95, it will remain above past levels at least through 2005–10. Given the many other demands of growth on Thailand's savings and foreign resources, the fact that for most of the next three decades residential construction will use up a larger share of Thailand's domestic saving and foreign borrowing than it has in the recent past has obvious growth implications and suggests that

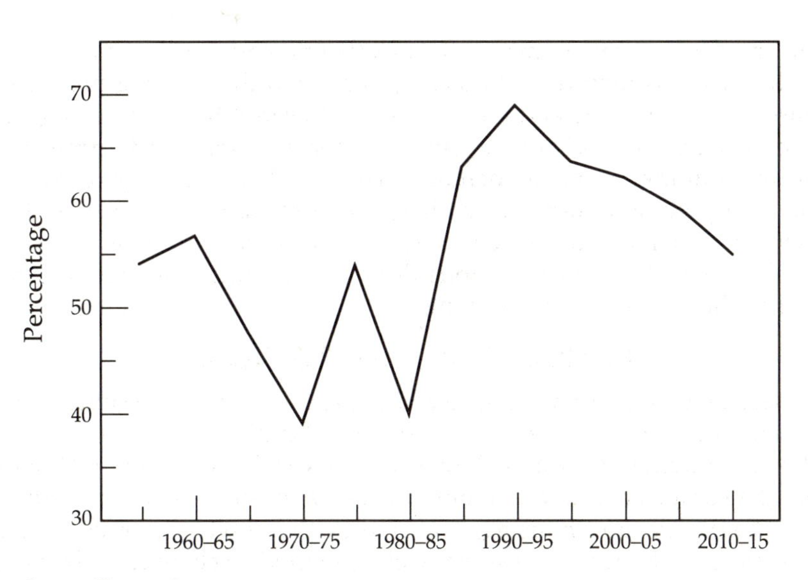

Source: Chapter 8.

Figure 1.18. Share of residential construction in GDI: 1955–60 to 2010–15

some very difficult choices lie ahead—especially when the conservative nature of the forecast is considered.

Our forecasts are based on the assumption that supply is perfectly elastic in the residential construction industry, so that excess demand or supply changes the quantity of new dwelling units produced and not their prices. However, the extent to which the excess demand involved in the forecast residential construction boom will actually be removed through increased prices or through increased production is not predictable. Although the relatively elastic (if seasonal) supply of labor and the relative abundance of land in Thailand suggest the market response will involve increases in output relatively more than in price. In other words, although price adjustments may reduce the number and quantity of new dwelling units produced, the forecast of a major boom in real residential construction stands.

In addition to the real resources used in constructing and improving the dwelling units required by the growth in the required housing stock and in the quality of the housing stock, Thailand's economy and social welfare will be impacted in several other, perhaps equally or more important ways, by the residential construction developments forecast. These include the greater land area absorbed (over twice as much as currently) for housing purposes, the increased infrastructure necessary to service the additional land and new housing required, the greater ongoing expenses to maintain this larger infrastructure and housing stock, and the growing market for household furnishings and appliances. And even if housing units go up rather than out, they will require no less expensive capital and current support expenditure. From the perennial issue of the transportation system and of air pollution on down the line, the possibility that this growth in Thailand's housing requirements will be concentrated in urban areas, especially Bangkok, raises numerous difficult questions that should be addressed through advance planning.

CONCLUDING OBSERVATIONS

The sector studies, summarized here and described fully in accompanying detailed reports, demonstrate the importance of demographic factors as contributors to trends in various dimensions of social and economic activity. Both the composition and amount of goods and services, such as education, health care, and housing, provided by the public sector alone or in partnership with the private sector, will be affected by changes in the number and demographic character of Thai households. Likewise, important dimensions of the Thai macroeconomy, including employment and wages, aggregate rates of saving, and the level and composition of household consumption, will change with the aging of the population, the rapid decline in average household size, and other demographic features of Thailand.

The importance of demographic factors to social and economic development planning have been appreciated for some time. Many countries, Thailand included, regularly prepare population projections as input to their five-year development plans and to other long-range planning documents. The incorporation of demographic factors into the planning process has been limited, however, by the absence of more complete information about households and their characteristics. Labor-force participation, school enrollment, saving behavior, the demand for health services, and the demand for housing are all influenced by the household and its characteristics. Reliable forecasts in each of these sectors is possible only when the importance of the household is recognized and incorporated into the forecasting process. Likewise, the impact of social and economic policy can only be reliably determined when potential responses by households are carefully evaluated.

The major contributions of this project have been to show how more detailed household characteristics can be projected and brought into the planning process. As with any new methodology, however, the full potential of household demographic data can be realized only through extensive interaction between members of the research and planning community. It is hoped that this project will contribute to that process both in and outside of Thailand.

2

Households and Their Characteristics

by Andrew Mason, Mathana Phananiramai, and Nipon Poapongsakorn

The underlying thesis of this study is that Thailand, along with virtually every other country, is experiencing fundamental changes in its demographic character that will influence various aspects of its society and economy. By understanding these demographic processes and their implications, those engaged in economic and social planning can more effectively anticipate future needs and problems. This chapter seeks to lay the groundwork for understanding the effects of demographic change, described in the following chapters, by providing a detailed description of Thailand's demographic situation, both currently and in the future, and a brief description of HOMES, the model used to project the number and demographic characteristics of Thai households.

The preparation and publication of population projections is a firmly established operation in many countries, and population projections have proven useful for a variety of purposes: to evaluate and to establish population policies; as input to the economic planning process; and as basic information for the business community. The preparation and use of household projections is much less firmly established, yet for many purposes household projections are critical. An increasing body of research points to the importance of the household as a determinant of social and economic behavior. Women who are rearing young children behave differently than women who are not. Children raised in homes with both parents present differ from those raised by a single parent. What the household buys and what the household owns varies with the number of members, their age, and their sex. The standard of living of most people depends as much on the earnings of other members of the household as it does on personal income. And the household provides some security from the physical and economic risks of everyday life.

To address these issues requires detailed information about households. Most projection work has attempted little beyond the projection of the number of households and the age of the head. The work reported here, however, is an application of a new computer package called HOMES (Mason 1987) that provides considerable detail about both the number and demographic characteristics of households including:

- Number of each household type
- Age and sex of the household head
- Average household size
- Number of males and females
- Age of household members
- Number of children and grandchildren
- Number of parents

HOMES employs a unique methodology to project the entire membership of the household, including the head, the spouse, children, grandchildren, parents, and other household members, in a manner consistent with underlying mortality and fertility trends. If, for example, childbearing becomes more concentrated among women in their 20s, HOMES accounts for this trend in projecting the number of children in households in subsequent years. Or, if mortality among the elderly declines, HOMES accounts for the impact on the number of households headed by the elderly, the number of elderly living alone, and the number living in households headed by their offspring.

HOMES has been developed to deal with household composition in the developing country context. Its emphasis is on analyzing the impact of demographic change on both the composition and the number of households, and it is particularly well-suited for application to countries where extended or multigenerational families are prevalent. HOMES has been applied to a number of Asian countries, including the Republic of Korea, China, Japan, Indonesia, Malaysia, Nepal, the Philippines, and Sri Lanka, as well as to Thailand.

PRINCIPAL FINDINGS

The number of households in Thailand is projected to grow quite rapidly over the next few decades, increasing from 10.2 million in 1985 to 18.1 million in 2005. This amounts to an average annual rate of growth over the period of 2.9 percent as compared with a population growth rate of 1.4 percent over the same period. The greatest increases, in absolute terms, will occur at the turn of the century when the number of households will be increasing by 400,000 per year.

Young households will grow most slowly. By 2005 only one-quarter of all households will have a head under 35 years of age. Those with heads 35 to 49 years of age will grow most rapidly, increasing their share from 36 percent in 1985 to 40 percent by 2005.

Average household size will continue to decline precipitously. In 1970 households averaged nearly six members apiece, but by 2005 households should average only 3.7 members. The decline in household size will occur across the board. Intact households, households with single heads, households with young heads, and those with old heads will all be considerably smaller by 2005.

The family household does not appear to be on the decline in Thailand. In both 1970 and 1980 family households were dominant, as fewer than 5 percent of all households were one-person or primary-individual households, those consisting of unrelated individuals. Nearly four of five households were headed by a husband and wife and no significant changes in these numbers are projected. Furthermore, there is no evidence of a decline in the importance of the lineal extended household.

Between 1985 and 2005, the number of children living in households will decline by one-half. In 1985 the average intact household had two members under age 15, by 2005 they are projected to average only one child. In contrast, the average number of adult members will decline only marginally during the same period. The overall dependency ratio will decline from 78 dependents per 100 prime-age adults in 1985 to 44 dependents per 100 prime-age adults in 2005.

Over the next 20 years, the number of parents of the head per household will increase only marginally and the number of persons age 65 and older will hardly increase at all. By 2005 there should be no more than 10 parents per 100 households, but as aging sets in with more force during the twenty-first century the prevalence of elderly parents of the head in the household should increase markedly.

AN OVERVIEW OF HOMES

The procedures by which HOMES incorporates demographic change into projections of the number and demographic characteristics of households is quite complex and is, therefore, described at a very general level in the remainder of this section. The model has been implemented using special tabulations from the 1980 population census and population projections prepared by the National Economic and Social Development Board (NESDB) of Thailand. The tabulations on which the analysis is based were compiled in cooperation with the National Statistical Office of Thailand using the 1 percent population sample for 1980. In addition, a 2.5 percent sample from the 1970 census was analyzed to assess the stability of rules governing living arrangements in Thailand. A more detailed discussion of the demographic characteristics of Thai households and a description of how this information is used to project households is given in Appendix A. A complete technical description of HOMES is available in Mason (1987).

HOMES projects the numbers and types of households using an elaboration of the headship rate method (U.N. 1973a). The basic approach relies on headship rates calculated in the base year (1980) as the proportion of men and women in each five-year age group who are the head of a household. The numbers of households are projected by multiplying the projected number of men and women in each five-year age group by the base-year headship rates.[1]

Households headed by males and females are projected separately and four different types of households are further distinguished:

- intact households—those headed by a husband and wife
- single-headed households—those in which no spouse of the head is present
- primary-individual households—those that consist of unrelated individuals
- one-person households

There are two important reasons to distinguish between household types. The first is that these households differ quite substantially in their demographic makeup. One-person households are obviously quite different from family households. As another example, households headed by a single male generally have fewer children than those headed by a single female. The second reason we distinguish these households is that their members behave in very different ways and face varying social and economic circumstances. Persons living alone are more likely to be attending school, for example. Households headed by single women are less likely to benefit from the earnings of a prime-age employed adult male, but female members of such households are more likely to participate in the labor force.

Using the modified headship rate method, the number of households, the type of household, and the age and sex of the head are all identified. The remaining members of the population are allocated among households using a kinship approach that focuses on five relationship-to-head categories: the spouse of the head, children of the head, grandchildren of the head, parents of the head, and a residual category, other household members.

---

1. A number of sophisticated models have been developed in recent years for projecting households and families. The interested reader is referred to Keilman et al. (1988) and Bongaarts et al. (1987).

With each relationship-to-head category, a similar approach is followed. First, candidates for membership in a particular household group are identified. Take children of the head living in households with a spouse of the head 50–54 years of age in 1990 as an example. The candidates for child of head will be males and females, varying in age from 0–4 to 35–39, who were born to women belonging to the 50–54 cohort over the preceding 35 years and who survived to 1990. Second, the numbers of surviving offspring who are actually children of the head, i.e., living in the households in question, are determined by multiplying the candidates for membership by probabilities derived from the 1980 census. Nearly all children under age 15 will be living with their parents, but a much lower percentage of those in their 20s and 30s will still be living with their parents. Similar procedures are followed for each relationship-to-head category until all members of the household population are allocated to their respective households.

The end result of the projection is a cross-tabulation at five-year intervals of the household population by age, sex, relationship to head, age of head, sex of head, and household type. Thus, the basic projection provides a detailed demographic profile of households—the age and sex of the head, the type of the household, the average household size, and the age and sex distribution of the household membership. For each household group, we can determine the number of infants, the number of school-age children (broken down to specific school level age categories, e.g., 6–12, 13–17, and 18–24), the number of prime-age adults, the number of elderly, or any other demographic group of particular interest for analysis of an economic or social sector of the economy.

CURRENT SITUATION

Characteristics of Households

In 1985 Thailand's population passed 50 million and the number of households reached the 10 million mark. This represents a very substantial increase from 1980 (Table 2.1). In that year, we estimate that there were approximately 8.7 million households; therefore, an additional 1.5 million households were added in only five years. The rapid increase in the number of households is the product of two forces. Thailand's population has been growing rapidly since 1960. Averaging an annual growth rate of nearly 2 percent, the population in 1985 was virtually double that of 1960. The number of households has grown even more rapidly as average household size has declined. Households in 1970 averaged nearly six members each, but by 1985, they averaged only five.

The overwhelming majority of households in Thailand are family households, i.e., households in which at least one of the members is related by blood or marriage to the household head. Only about 4 percent of all house-

Table 2.1. Population and the number of households: 1960, 1970, and 1980

Year	Population (thousands)	Households (thousands)	Average household size
1960	26,258	4,600	5.68
1970	36,370	6,200	5.82
1980	46,718	8,700	5.32
1985[a]	50,902	10,215	4.99

Source: Data are from NESDB (1985b).

a. Values for 1985 include only the private household population adjusted for under-enumeration. Values for 1960, 1970, and 1980 are unadjusted values taken from census reports.

holds are one-person households or households consisting of unrelated individuals. Almost four out of every five households are intact, i.e., the head's spouse is present, whereas almost one in five is headed by a man or woman who is unmarried or separated from his or her spouse. Of these single heads, nearly three out of four are women.

These households vary in many ways that will be discussed below, but one important difference is the difference in household size (Table 2.2). Intact households tend to be the largest, with an average size exceeding five members. Single-headed households are smaller, on average, by about one person, and primary-individual households have about 3.5 persons per household.

Many of Thailand's households are headed by relatively young adults. The heaviest concentration of household heads is among men in their 30s (Figure 2.1). The age characteristic of the head is very sensitive, however, to the type of household in question. For example, the age distribution of men who are single heads is bimodal with peaks in the late 20s and late 50s (Figure 2.2). Younger men tend to head nonfamily households. Women in their 50s, 60s, and even 70s frequently head nonfamily and single-headed family households (Figure 2.2).

Who are the members of households in Thailand? There are several ways to answer the question—we can describe their relationship to the head, their age, and their sex. Table 2.3 provides an answer from a relationship-to-head perspective.

In family households, a plurality of members are children of the head. About one-half of the members of intact and single-female-headed households and just under 40 percent of the members of households headed by single males are the child of the head. This is a remarkably high percentage given that households with heads well past the childbearing and child-rearing stages of their lives are included in Table 2.3. Furthermore, an

Table 2.2. Type of households: 1985

Type of household	Number (thousands)	%	Average size
Intact	7,985	78.2	5.3
Single-headed			
Male heads	475	4.7	4.5
Female heads	1,311	12.8	4.6
Primary-individual			
Male heads	50	0.5	3.5
Female heads	31	0.3	3.2
Single-person			
Males	181	1.8	1.0
Females	182	1.8	1.0
Total	10,215	100.0	5.0

Source: Estimated using HOMES and data from NESDB (1985b).

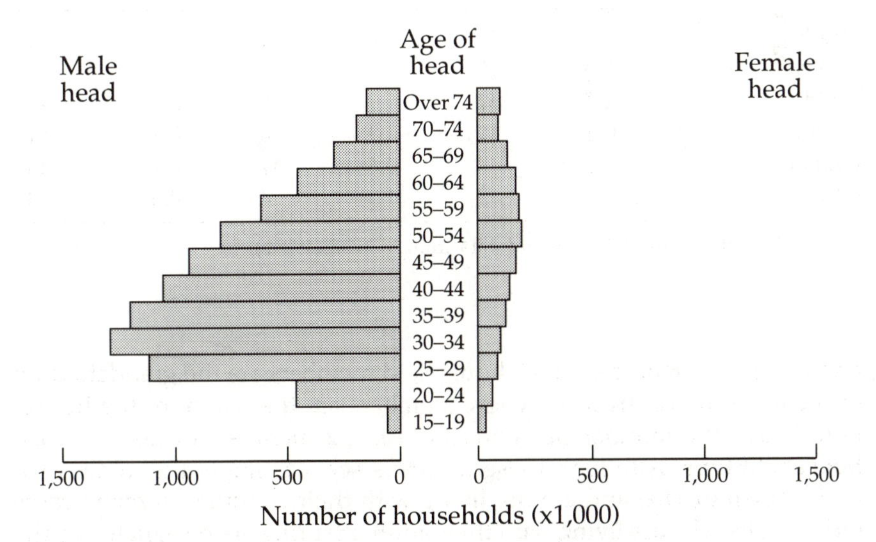

Figure 2.1. Number of households by age and sex of head: 1985

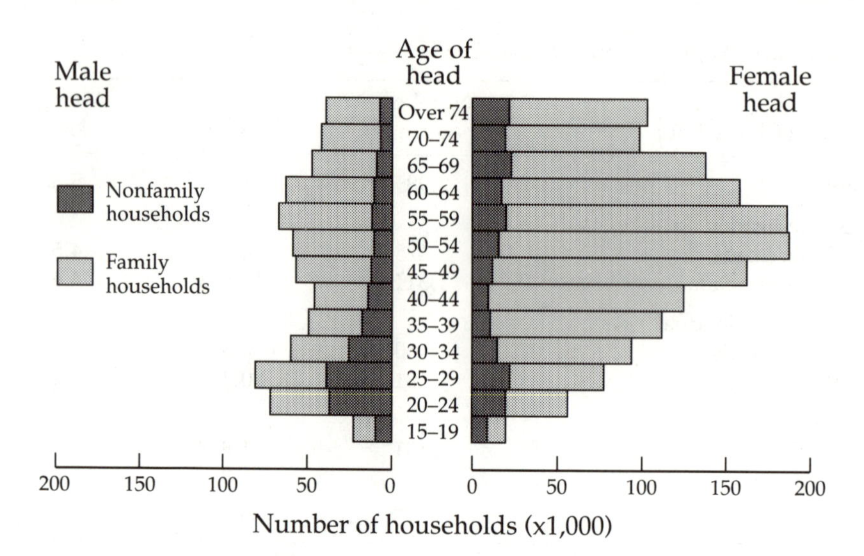

Figure 2.2. Number of households with single heads by age and sex of head: 1985

Table 2.3. Average number of household members by their relationship to the household head: 1985

Relationship	Intact		Single male head		Single female head	
	Number	%	Number	%	Number	%
Head	1.0	19	1.0	22	1.0	22
Spouse	1.0	19	—	—	—	—
Child	2.7	52	1.7	38	2.2	48
Parent	0.1	2	0.2	4	0.1	1
Grandchild	0.2	4	0.6	12	0.7	16
Other	0.2	5	1.1	24	0.6	13

Source: Estimated using HOMES and data from NESDB (1985b).

additional 4 to 16 percent of all household members are the grandchildren of the head. By contrast, very few members are the parent of the household head—the number per household is 0.2 members or less for each household type. Although these numbers seem to imply that older men and women in Thailand are not living with their children, in many cases older adults who are living with their adult offspring are designated as the household head.

The number of household members with the designation child of the head does not indicate how many children (persons 15 years of age and younger) are in the household because the term child, as used here, denotes a biological relationship. Many children of the head are adults and may shoulder a substantial burden in providing support for other members of the household. Figures 2.3–2.6 provide some basic demographic details, namely age and sex, for household members who are children, parents, and grandchildren of the head, as well as those categorized as "other household members."

The great majority of children of the head are, in fact, under age 20, but about 2.5 million males and 2 million females in their 20s are the child of the head. Even at older ages, being the child of the head is far from rare; close to a million persons in their early 30s are the child of the head. Being the grandchild of the head is much more closely associated with age, as nearly all grandchildren are under age 20.

Parents of the head—particularly women—are concentrated at the older ages. "Other household members" are concentrated among young adults and children. About equal numbers of boys and girls under age 20 are other household members, but men outnumber women among those between the ages of 20 and 34.

A somewhat different perspective emerges from examination of Figure 2.7, which shows how the composition of intact households varies with the age of the spouse of the head. By definition, intact households have a male head and a wife at every age whereas single-headed households have one head and no spouse. The number of children of the head increases during the childbearing years and then declines as many children leave the home. Some remain behind, however, and the number of grandchildren increases among older heads. The other categories are generally less significant—parents tend to be concentrated among younger households whereas other household members are more evenly distributed across all households irrespective of the age of the head.

The age composition of households varies substantially among different types of households (Table 2.4). A number of features stand out. Age composition varies significantly with the life cycle of the household. Households with heads under 35 years of age tend to have many young members, whereas households with heads over age 65 tend to have many older members. The life-cycle pattern is usefully summarized by the dependency ratio, which has a distinctive U-shaped age profile for intact and female-headed households. The ratio of the number of dependents per prime-age adult is nearly 1 to 1 for households with a head under age 35, many of whom are shouldering childrearing responsibilities. The dependency ratio declines markedly for intact households with middle-aged heads, but rises again to 1.59 for intact households headed by elderly men and to 1.05 for family

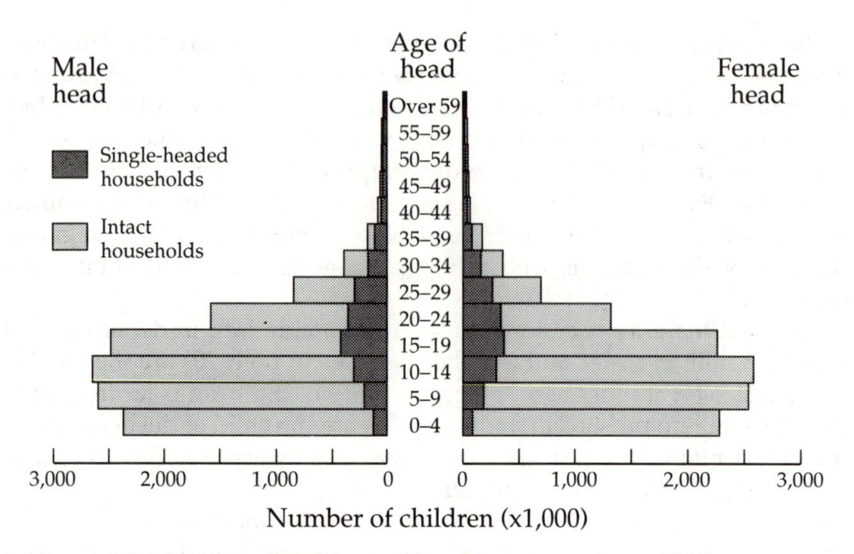

Figure 2.3. Number of children of head by age and sex: 1985

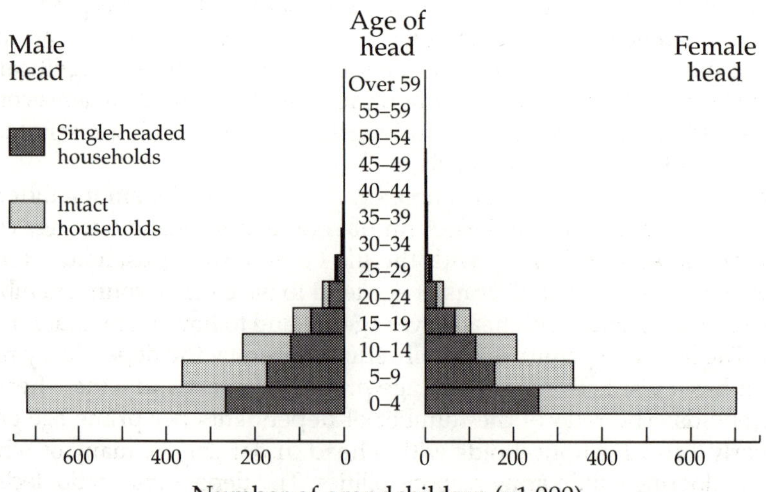

Figure 2.4. Number of grandchildren of head by age and sex: 1985

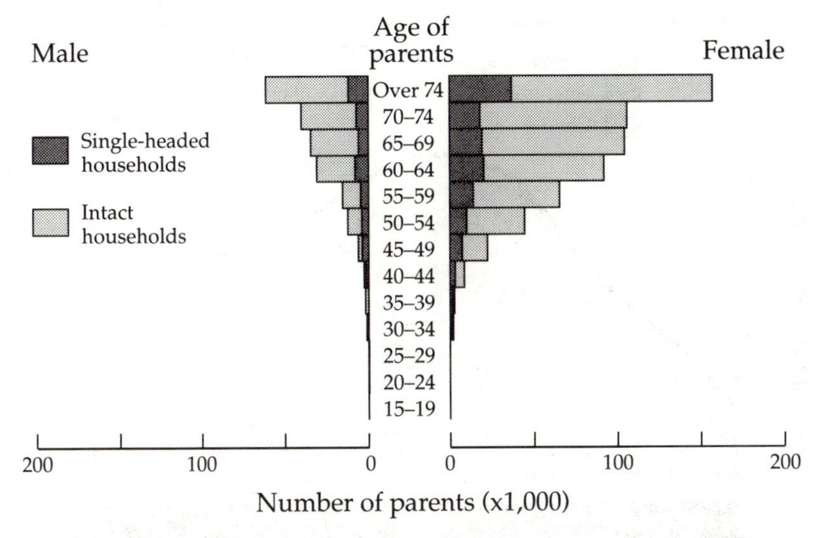

Figure 2.5. Number of parents of head by age and sex: 1985

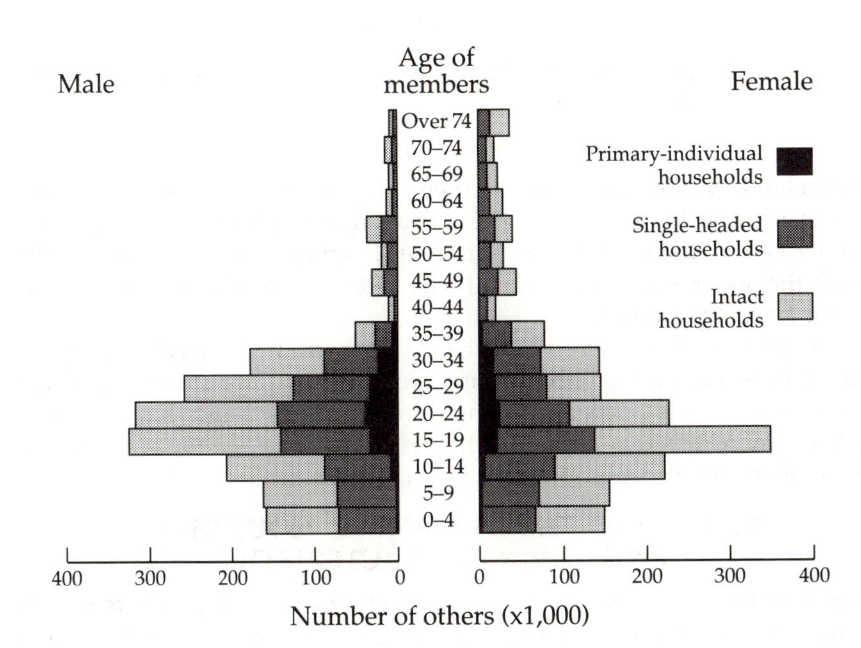

Figure 2.6. Number of other household members by age and sex: 1985

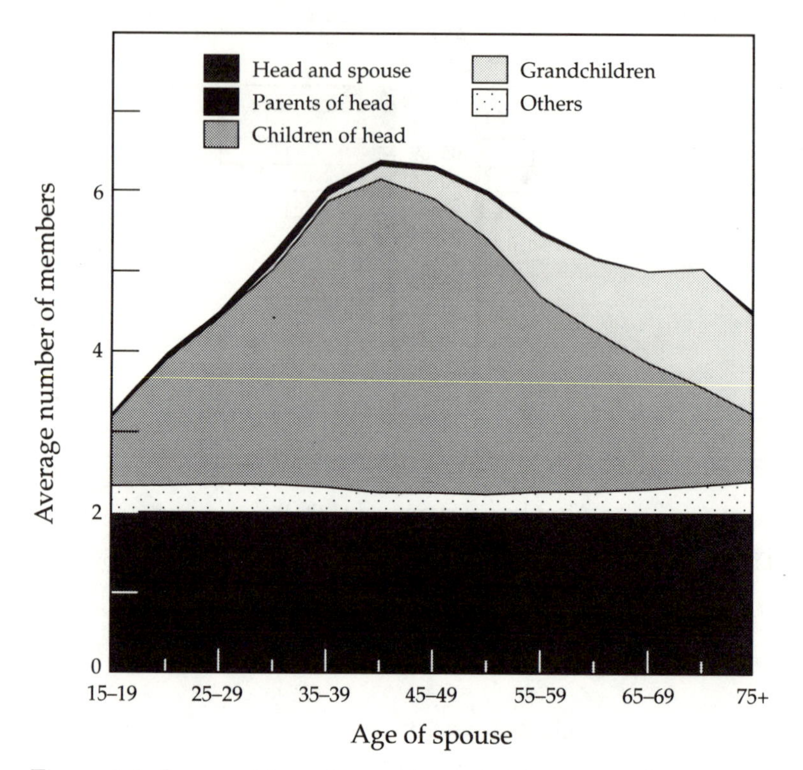

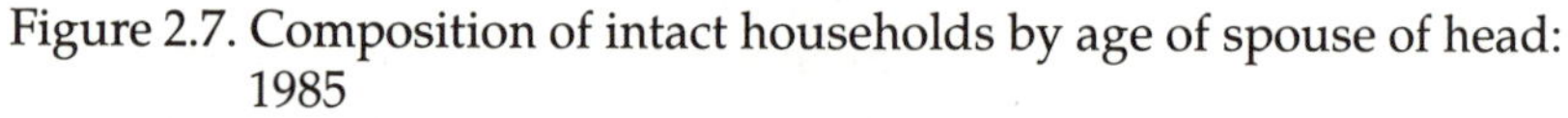
Figure 2.7. Composition of intact households by age of spouse of head: 1985

households headed by elderly women. In general, the dependency ratio is considerably lower for households headed by single males. Among men under age 35, the ratio is a scant 0.36 and, although it rises substantially with the age of the head, it is still well below the level that characterizes other household types.

The sex ratio is also closely associated with household type. Intact households have a fairly even sex ratio irrespective of the age of the household head. Single-male-headed households, on the other hand, have about 50 percent more men than women, whereas single-female-headed households have about 50 percent more women than men.

PROJECTING THE NUMBER OF HOUSEHOLDS AND THEIR CHARACTERISTICS

The number and characteristics of households are the products of two forces: (1) economically, socially, and culturally determined rules that govern the way family and nonfamily members gather into households, and (2)

Table 2.4. Age and sex of household members: 1985

Age of member	Age of marker[a]				
	15–34	35–49	50–64	65+	Total
Intact households					
0–14	2.14	2.31	1.24	1.11	2.02
15–34	1.94	1.76	2.22	1.28	1.90
35–49	0.29	1.73	0.17	0.43	0.78
50–64	0.06	0.26	1.76	0.17	0.41
65+	0.06	0.09	0.23	1.87	0.15
D ratio	0.96	0.64	0.35	1.59	0.70
Sex ratio	100	104	102	98	102
Single head, male					
0–14	0.95	1.33	1.33	1.39	1.25
15–34	2.51	2.01	2.01	1.75	2.08
35–49	0.30	0.65	0.39	0.57	0.46
50–64	0.27	0.36	0.66	0.40	0.44
65+	0.16	0.18	0.27	0.68	0.31
D ratio	0.36	0.50	0.52	0.76	0.52
Sex ratio	165	157	154	144	155
Single head, female					
0–14	1.64	1.75	1.30	1.35	1.49
15–34	1.87	1.89	2.16	1.45	1.90
35–49	0.04	1.06	0.20	0.67	0.52
50–64	0.09	0.04	1.04	0.14	0.44
65+	0.08	0.11	0.04	1.03	0.27
D ratio	0.86	0.62	0.39	1.05	0.62
Sex ratio	55	66	66	62	62

Source: Estimated using HOMES and data from NESDB (1985b).

D ratio—dependency ratio.

Note: Dependency ratio is population 0 to 14 and 65 and older divided by the population 15 to 64. Sex ratio is male population divided by female population times 100.

a. The marker is the head of household, except in intact households where the marker is the spouse of the head.

demographic processes that determine the number of people who are candidates for household membership.

The impact of demographic processes on household composition is in many ways obvious. The number of households will vary with the number of prime-age adults; the prevalence of households headed by widows and widowers will depend on mortality among spouses; and the number of children per household will depend on levels of childbearing and child survival. The impact of other demographic factors are somewhat more elusive. Changes in the timing of childbearing will influence in which households children live, and survival among siblings will affect the probability that any particular sibling will reside with an elderly parent.

One way of illustrating the important link between the characteristics of households and the underlying population is via the specialized age pyramid shown in Figure 2.8. Each bar represents Thailand's estimated 1985 population for a five-year age group—females are charted to the right and males to the left. Each bar is further subdivided by relationship to the household head. Those under age 15 are almost exclusively children or grandchildren of the head; prime-age male adults are almost always heads whereas prime-age female adults are either heads or spouses; and the elderly may be heads, spouses, or parents of a head.

Thailand's current population is very young, hence the bottom-heavy nature of the age pyramid for 1985. Because this is so, Thailand's population is one in which young households are prevalent, a high percentage of household members are children, and a low percentage of members are parents of the head. But, as Thailand's population ages quite rapidly over the next few decades, an entirely different household profile will emerge: household heads will, on average, be older, more members will be elderly parents, and fewer will be young children. The details of these changes are described in the sections that follow.

PROJECTIONS

Population

The number and demographic characteristics of households is projected by applying the projection package HOMES (Mason 1987) to the most recently prepared population projections for Thailand (NESDB 1985b). The results reported here are based on population projections using the medium fertility assumption that the total fertility rate (TFR) will decline from 3.46 for 1980–85 to replacement level during 1995–2000 and continue declining to reach 1.67 in 2010–2015. Gradual improvements in mortality are anticipated so that life expectancy at birth will reach 69.0 for men and 72.75 for women in 2010–2015 as compared with 60.25 and 66.25, respectively, for the 1980–85 period (Table 2.5). Immigration has a negligible impact on Thailand's national population and no account of its impact has been included in the projections employed.

From a total population estimated at 51.7 million in 1985, Thailand's population is expected to reach 67.9 million within two decades, the period on which this study will focus (Table 2.6). The population growth rate during the 1980–85 period was 2 percent per year but will decline to just over 1 percent per year for the 2000–05 period. Household projections are based

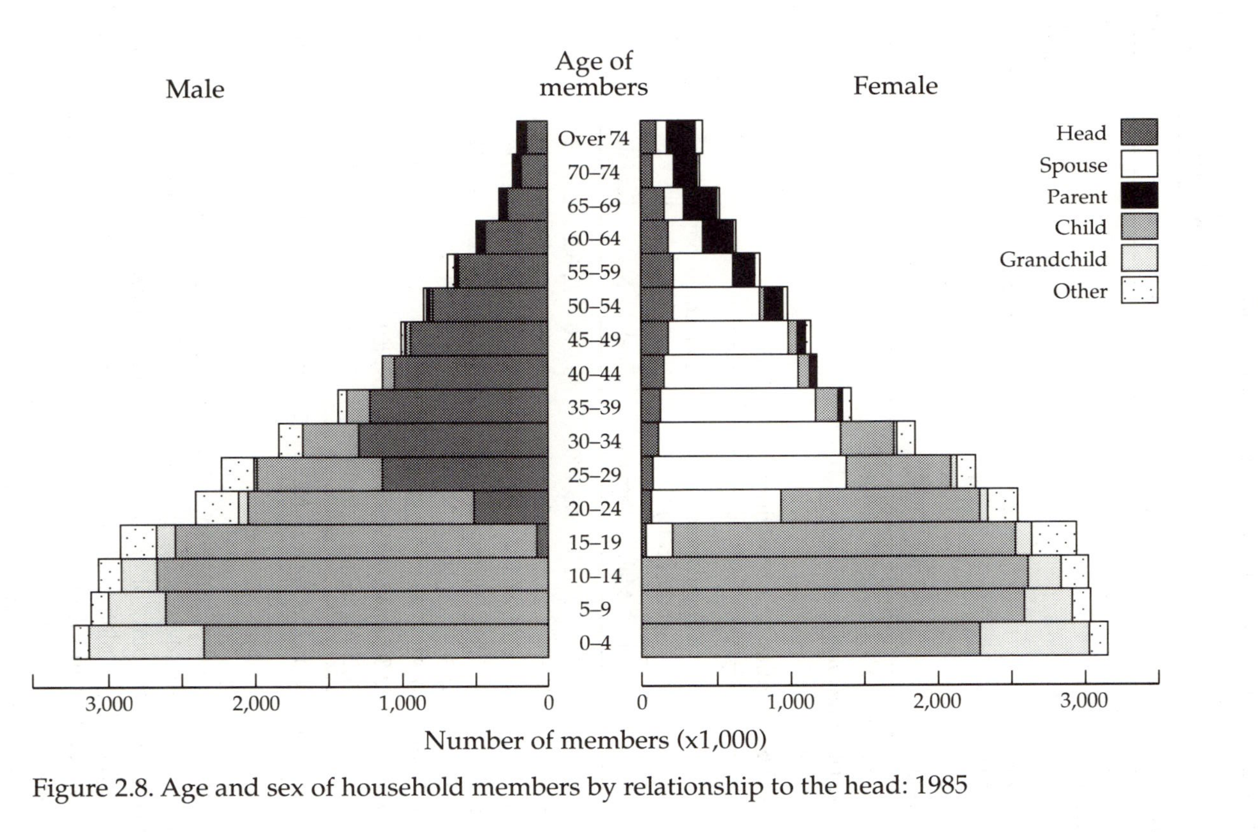

Figure 2.8. Age and sex of household members by relationship to the head: 1985

Table 2.5. Assumptions underlying population projection

Period	TFR	Life expectancy at birth	
		Males	Females
1980–1985	3.46	60.25	66.25
1985–1990	2.84	61.75	67.50
1990–1995	2.35	63.50	68.75
1995–2000	2.11	65.25	69.75
2000–2005	1.94	66.75	70.75
2005–2010	1.78	68.00	71.75
2010–2015	1.67	69.00	72.75

Source: NESDB (1985b).
TFR—total fertility rate.

Table 2.6. Population projections: 1980–2015

Year	Population (thousands)			Household population (thousands)			Annual growth rate (%)
	Total	Male	Female	Total	Male	Female	
1980	46,718	23,428	23,290	46,016	22,835	23,182	—
1985	51,683	25,888	25,795	50,902	25,223	25,679	2.0
1990	56,186	28,117	28,143	55,499	27,476	28,023	1.7
1995	60,506	30,265	30,241	59,638	29,517	30,121	1.5
2000	64,389	32,206	32,183	63,502	31,438	32,064	1.2
2005	67,910	33,975	33,935	67,006	33,188	33,818	1.1
2010	70,865	35,462	35,403	69,960	34,669	35,291	0.9
2015	73,208	36,632	36,576	72,307	35,839	36,468	0.7

Sources: Population figures are from NESDB (1985b); household population was calculated using HOMES.

on the household population, which excludes members of the armed services and individuals living in institutions. The household population includes about 98 percent of the total male population and over 99 percent of the female population. (These values are projected using HOMES, based on constant proportions of each age-sex group being institutionalized or in the military service.)

A particularly salient feature of the population is its age structure. Both decreased mortality and, in particular, declining fertility will join forces to accelerate the aging of Thailand's population. The important changes in the population's age distribution are evident in Figure 2.9.

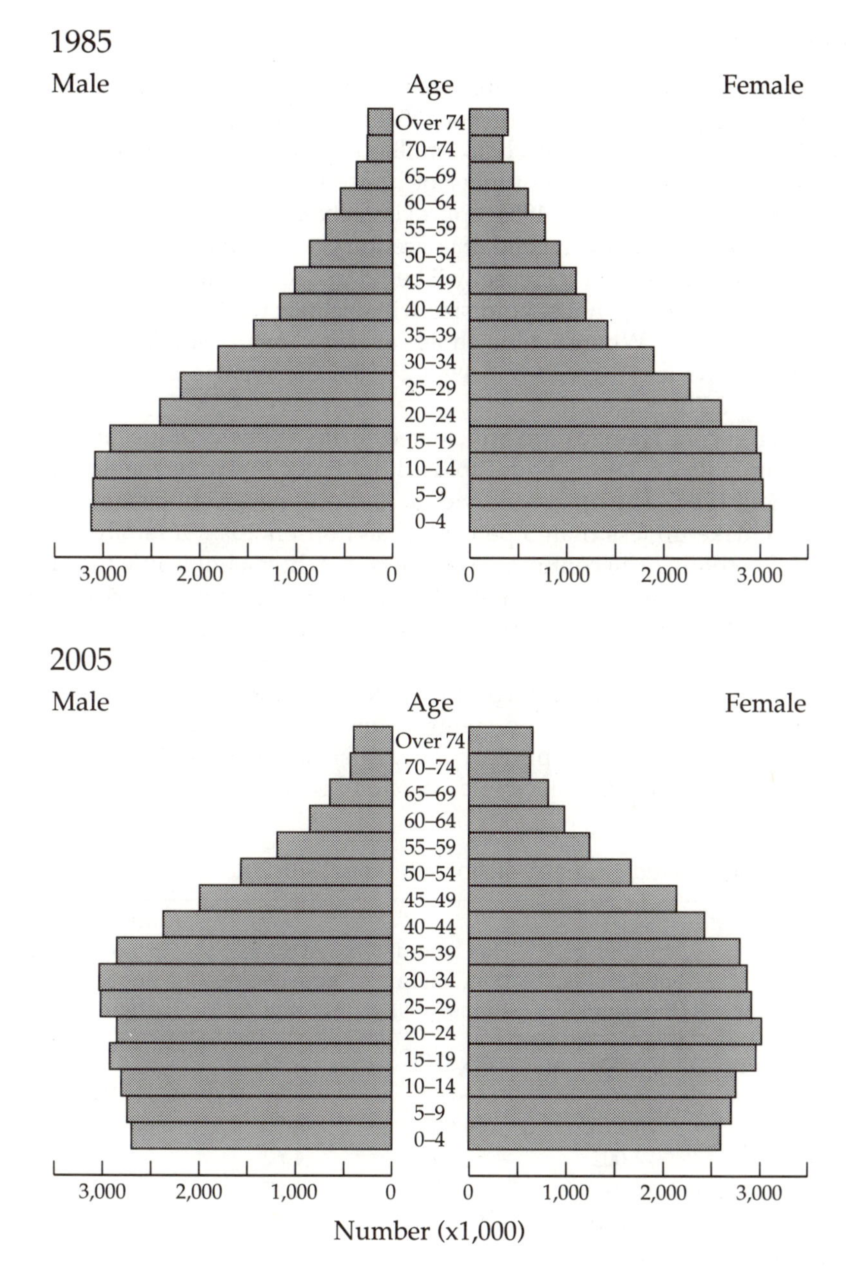

Figure 2.9. Population pyramids for 1985 and 2005

Households

The number of households is projected to grow at a more rapid pace than is Thailand's population. There were 10.2 million households in 1985, but this figure is expected to reach 18.1 million by 2005, which represents an average growth rate in the number of households of 2.9 percent per annum. Between 1980 and 1985 approximately 250,000 households were added each year, and by the end of the century net annual additions should exceed 400,000. This net increase will begin to decline early in the twenty-first century. Average household size will decline steadily throughout the period (Table 2.7). Whereas households averaged nearly six members each in 1970 and five members each in 1985, by 2005 the average size is projected to be only 3.7 members.

No significant changes are anticipated in the types of households. As shown in Table 2.8, family households should continue to be the dominant household type, as primary-individual and one-person households continue to make up less than 5 percent of all households. Of family households, four of five will continue to be intact, i.e., households in which both the head and spouse are present. One in five will be headed by a single adult, most often a female, and little change is anticipated here. It should be clearly understood, however, that the projections do not anticipate substantial social or cultural change. Increasing income, modernization, and delayed age at marriage could combine forces to increase the number of young living alone or in primary-individual households. Similar forces might increase the prevalence of divorce and reduce the number of intact

Table 2.7. Projected number of households: 1970–2015

Year	Number of households (thousands)	Household population (thousands)	Average household size	Annual increase in number of households (thousands)
1970	6,200	36,370	5.82	—
1980	8,689	46,016	5.30	249
1985	10,215	50,902	4.98	305
1990	12,002	55,498	4.62	357
1995	13,977	59,638	4.27	395
2000	16,030	63,502	3.96	411
2005	18,091	67,006	3.70	412
2010	20,074	69,960	3.49	396
2015	21,870	72,307	3.31	359

Source: Estimated using HOMES and data from NESDB (1985b).

Table 2.8. Type of households: 1980–2005

Type of household	1980 Number	1980 %	1985 Number	1985 %	1990 Number	1990 %
Family households						
Intact	6,778,775	78.0	7,985,033	78.2	9,394,088	78.3
Single-headed						
Male heads	406,500	4.7	475,158	4.7	555,652	4.6
Female heads	1,124,421	12.9	1,310,765	12.8	1,535,090	12.8
Total	8,309,696	95.6	9,770,956	95.7	11,484,830	95.7
Nonfamily households						
Primary-individual						
Male heads	42,567	.5	50,300	.5	58,318	.5
Female heads	26,086	.3	30,516	.3	35,273	.3
One-person						
Males	154,063	1.8	180,848	1.8	211,479	1.8
Females	156,728	1.8	182,077	1.8	211,740	1.8
Total	379,444	4.4	443,741	4.3	516,810	4.3
Grand total	8,689,140	100.0	10,214,697	100.0	12,001,640	100.0

Type of household	1995 Number	1995 %	2000 Number	2000 %	2005 Number	2005 %
Family households						
Intact	10,938,232	78.3	12,508,036	78.0	14,027,948	77.5
Single-headed						
Male heads	646,303	4.6	748,324	4.7	863,248	4.8
Female heads	1,798,573	12.9	2,101,304	13.1	2,444,290	13.5
Total	13,383,108	95.7	15,357,664	95.8	17,335,486	95.8
Nonfamily households						
Primary-individual						
Male heads	65,338	.5	70,614	.4	75,251	.4
Female heads	39,851	.3	43,462	.3	47,163	.3
One-person						
Males	242,956	1.7	274,343	1.7	306,180	1.7
Females	245,952	1.8	284,208	1.8	326,688	1.8
Total	594,097	4.3	672,627	4.2	755,282	4.2
Grand total	13,977,205	100.0	16,030,291	100.0	18,090,768	100.0

Source: Estimated using HOMES and data from NESDB (1985b).

households. And although these forces may become important, they are not apparent in the changes in household structure that occurred between 1970 and 1980 (Appendix A).

Although the type of household will be quite stable, the average age of the household head will have shifted significantly by the year 2005 (Figure 2.10). The number of households with a head under age 35 doubles between 1985 and 2005, while the number with a head 35–49 increases threefold. At the same time, the number with a head 50 or older increases by somewhere between two and three times.

Changes in the age distribution of household members will be very significant by 2005 (Table 2.9). The average number of members under 15 years of age will decline by one-half or more; the number of members 15–64 years of age will decline more modestly, with the greatest declines occurring among households with single heads; and the number of elderly will remain relatively constant, but at low numbers through 2005. Whereas over 40 percent of the members of households were under 15 years of age in 1980, by 2005 only 26 percent will be so young. At the same time, the percentage of members over age 65 will increase from 3.3 to 5.3. The overall dependency ratio will decline substantially: from 78 dependents per 100 prime-age adults to only 44 dependents per 100 prime-age adults.

The demographic character of households will change quite dramatically by 2005. Average household size will decline across the board. From 1980 to 1990 average household size is estimated to decline by between 0.5 and 1.0 member, depending on the age of the head, and by another 1.0 to 1.5 members between 1990 and 2005 (Figure 2.11).

Average household size will also decline quite significantly for both intact households and those with single heads. Between 1980 and 2005, average household size will decline by 1.6 members for intact households and households headed by single men, and by 1.7 members for households headed by single women. This represents a decline in average size ranging from 29 percent for intact households to 35 percent for households headed by single women.

Another dimension of the change in the demographic character of the household is the change in relationship to head, which in many respects mirrors changes in age composition (Table 2.10). Between 1980 and 2005, relatively fewer members of the typical household will be children or grandchildren of the head, or other household members, and relatively more will be the head, the spouse, or their parents. By 2005 roughly one-half of all members will be the head or spouse, substantially up from 1980 when just one-third of the members were the head or spouse. During the same period, the percentage who are children or grandchildren of the head will decline from nearly 60 percent to only 45 percent. The close connection

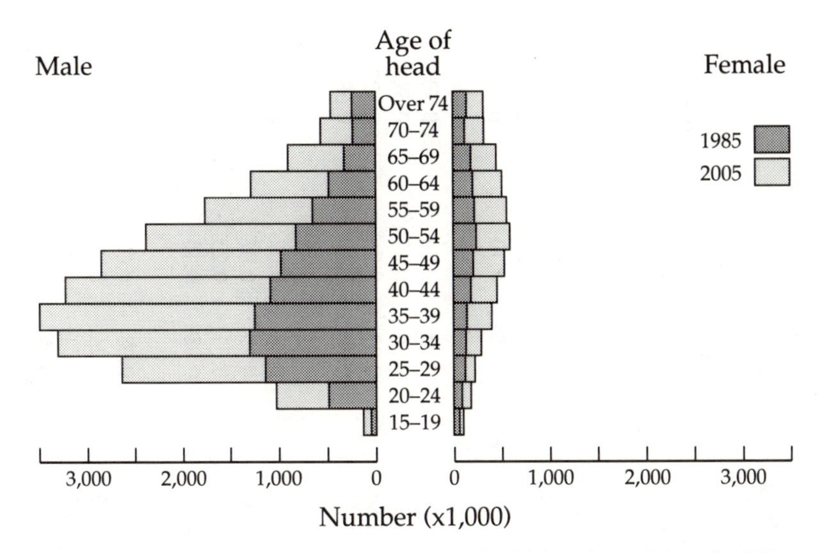

Figure 2.10. Age distribution of household heads: 1985 and 2005

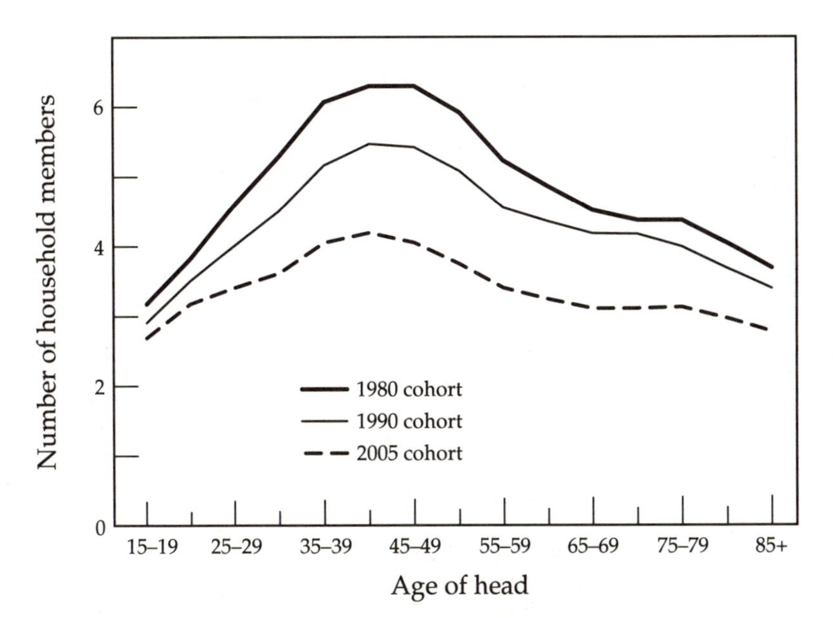

Figure 2.11. Average number of household members by age of household head: 1980, 1990, and 2005

Table 2.9. Average number of members of family households by age of members: 1980–2005

Type of type	Combined	Age of members						Dependency ratio
		0 to 14		15 to 64		65 and older		
		Male	Female	Male	Female	Male	Female	
1980								
Intact	5.61	1.19	1.16	1.56	1.54	0.08	0.08	0.81
Single-headed, male	4.77	0.74	0.71	1.89	1.11	0.24	0.08	0.59
Single-headed, female	4.88	0.89	0.84	1.02	1.84	0.02	0.27	0.71
Combined	5.46	1.12	1.09	1.51	1.56	0.08	0.10	0.78
1985								
Intact	5.28	1.02	1.00	1.56	1.54	0.08	0.08	0.70
Single-headed, male	4.54	0.63	0.61	1.89	1.10	0.24	0.07	0.52
Single-headed, female	4.62	0.76	0.72	1.02	1.84	0.02	0.26	0.62
Combined	5.14	0.96	0.94	1.51	1.55	0.08	0.10	0.68
1990								
Intact	4.88	0.86	0.85	1.52	1.50	0.08	0.07	0.62
Single-headed, male	4.23	0.54	0.52	1.84	1.03	0.23	0.07	0.47
Single-headed, female	4.26	0.64	0.61	0.97	1.78	0.01	0.25	0.55
Combined	4.77	0.81	0.80	1.47	1.51	0.08	0.10	0.60
1995								
Intact	4.51	0.72	0.71	1.47	1.45	0.08	0.08	0.54
Single-headed, male	3.89	0.45	0.44	1.76	0.93	0.24	0.07	0.45
Single-headed, female	3.87	0.52	0.51	0.90	1.67	0.01	0.26	0.51
Combined	4.39	0.68	0.67	1.41	1.45	0.08	0.10	0.53

2000								
Intact	4.20	0.61	0.60	1.43	1.40	0.08	0.08	0.48
Single-headed, male	3.57	0.38	0.36	1.67	0.83	0.25	0.08	0.43
Single-headed, female	3.51	0.43	0.41	0.82	1.56	0.02	0.27	0.47
Combined	4.06	0.57	0.56	1.36	1.39	0.08	0.10	0.48
2005								
Intact	3.96	0.53	0.51	1.39	1.36	0.09	0.08	0.44
Single-headed, male	3.29	0.32	0.30	1.60	0.73	0.26	0.08	0.41
Single headed, female	3.17	0.35	0.34	0.74	1.44	0.02	0.28	0.45
Combined	3.80	0.49	0.47	1.31	1.33	0.09	0.11	0.44

Source: Estimated using HOMES and data from NESDB (1985b).

Note: The dependency ratio is the ratio of the population of ages 0–14 or 65+ to those of ages 15–64. Combined includes primary-individual households.

Table 2.10. Relationship to head of total population: 1980–2005 (%)

	1980			1985			1990		
Relationship to head	Male	Female	Both	Male	Female	Both	Male	Female	Both
Head	16.0	2.8	18.9	17.1	3.0	20.1	18.4	3.2	21.6
Spouse	—	14.7	14.7	—	15.7	15.7	—	16.9	16.9
Child	26.8	25.5	52.3	25.8	24.6	50.4	24.7	23.5	48.2
Grandchild	2.9	2.8	5.7	2.9	2.7	5.6	2.7	2.5	5.2
Parent	0.4	1.1	1.5	0.4	1.2	1.6	0.4	1.3	1.7
Others	3.5	3.4	6.9	3.4	3.3	6.7	3.3	3.0	6.3
Total	49.6	50.4	100.0	49.6	50.4	100.0	49.5	50.5	100.0

	1995			2000			2005		
Relationship to head	Male	Female	Both	Male	Female	Both	Male	Female	Both
Head	19.9	3.5	23.5	21.4	3.8	25.2	22.8	4.2	27.8
Spouse	—	18.3	18.3	—	19.7	19.7	—	20.9	20.9
Child	23.5	22.2	45.6	22.2	20.8	43.1	21.0	19.5	40.5
Grandchild	2.3	2.3	4.8	2.3	2.2	4.5	2.2	2.0	4.2
Parent	0.5	1.4	1.9	0.5	1.6	2.2	0.7	1.9	2.5
Others	3.1	2.7	5.9	3.0	2.4	5.4	2.9	2.0	4.9
Total	49.5	50.5	100.0	49.5	50.5	100.0	49.5	50.5	100.0

Source: Estimated using HOMES and data from NESDB (1985b).

between relationship to head and the age composition of the population is illustrated in Figure 2.12, which shows the age breakdown of the populations of 1985 and 2005 and their relationship to the household head.

Between 1985 and 2005, the greatest percentage decline will be among those under age 15, and both the number of preschoolers and the number of school-age children will decline by 56 percent (Table 2.11). The number of young adults who are children or grandchildren of the household head will, however, decline much more gradually. The average number per household will decline by only 27 percent over the 25-year period under consideration.

In general, the increase in the number of parents of the head per household, small as it is, will be among younger parents—those who are 64 years of age or younger, whereas the number of older parents per household, i.e., those 65 and older, may actually decline somewhat before increasing toward the end of this century (Table 2.12). The number of parents per household will begin to increase with greater regularity and magnitude in the early part of the twenty-first century.

The Household Life Cycle

The information presented above emphasizes the demographic characteristics of households at any point in time, but many decisions of the household depend on a horizon that encompasses expectations about the household's future composition as well as its past experience. One important example would be decisions by the household to buy a residence or other consumer durables. Households that are in the family-building stage of their life cycle would base their decisions, in part, on expectations about eventual household size and the future needs of members, whereas the current residences of households with older heads may reflect past as much as current household membership.

Limited information about the household life cycle can be obtained from the household projections data by following cohorts (of household heads) over the 45 years (1970 to 2015) for which data are available. Figure 2.13 shows average household size for the four cohorts labeled by the year the household heads were 25–29 years of age. This age range is selected as the year in which households are formed because it is the age range at which headship rates reach 50 percent. Households "established" in 1980 averaged about 4.6 members and at their peak (reached at ages 35–39) will average 5.2 members—a surprisingly small increase of 0.6 additional members. Thereafter, household size will decline steadily with average household size reaching 2.8 members when the cohort is 60–64 years of age in 2015.

To the extent that partial cohort "experience" can be used to judge, other household cohorts have had and will have similar life-cycle patterns of average household size, with average size rising during the childbearing years,

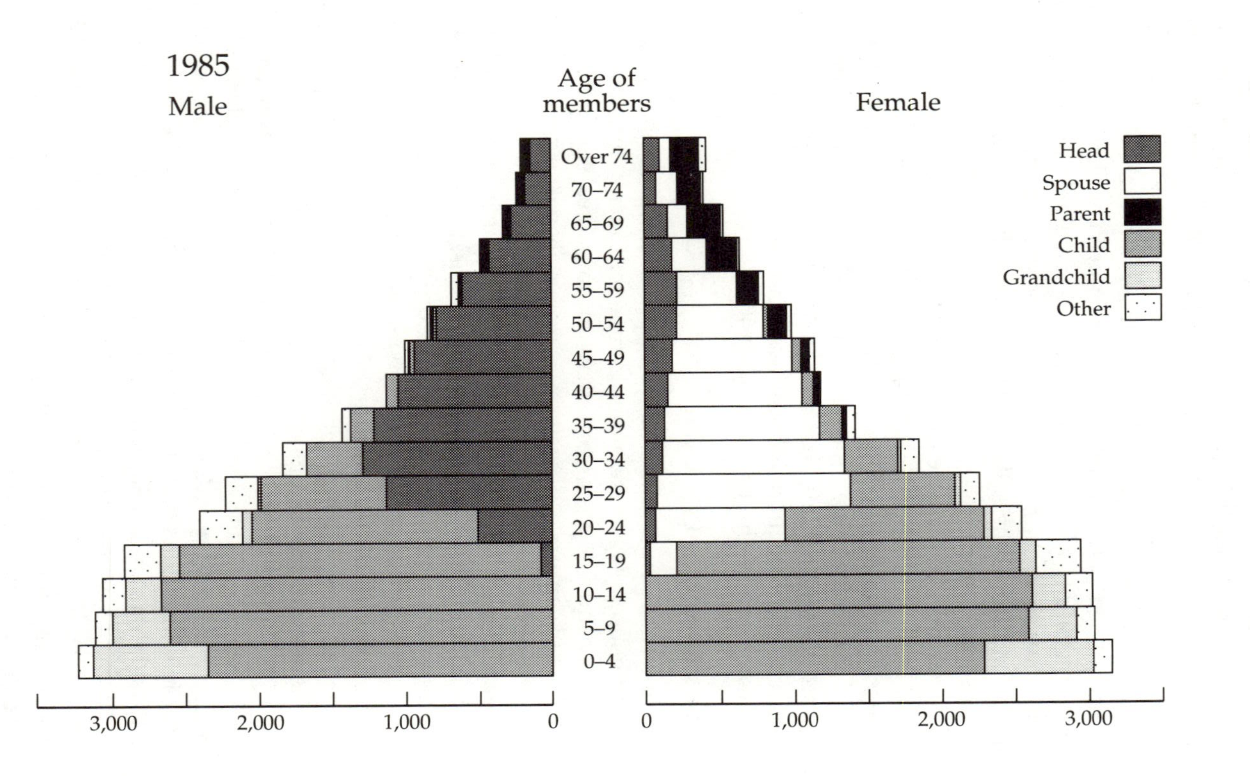
1985
Male
Age of members
Female
Over 74
70–74
65–69
60–64
55–59
50–54
45–49
40–44
35–39
30–34
25–29
20–24
15–19
10–14
5–9
0–4
Head
Spouse
Parent
Child
Grandchild
Other
3,000
2,000
1,000
0
0
1,000
2,000
3,000

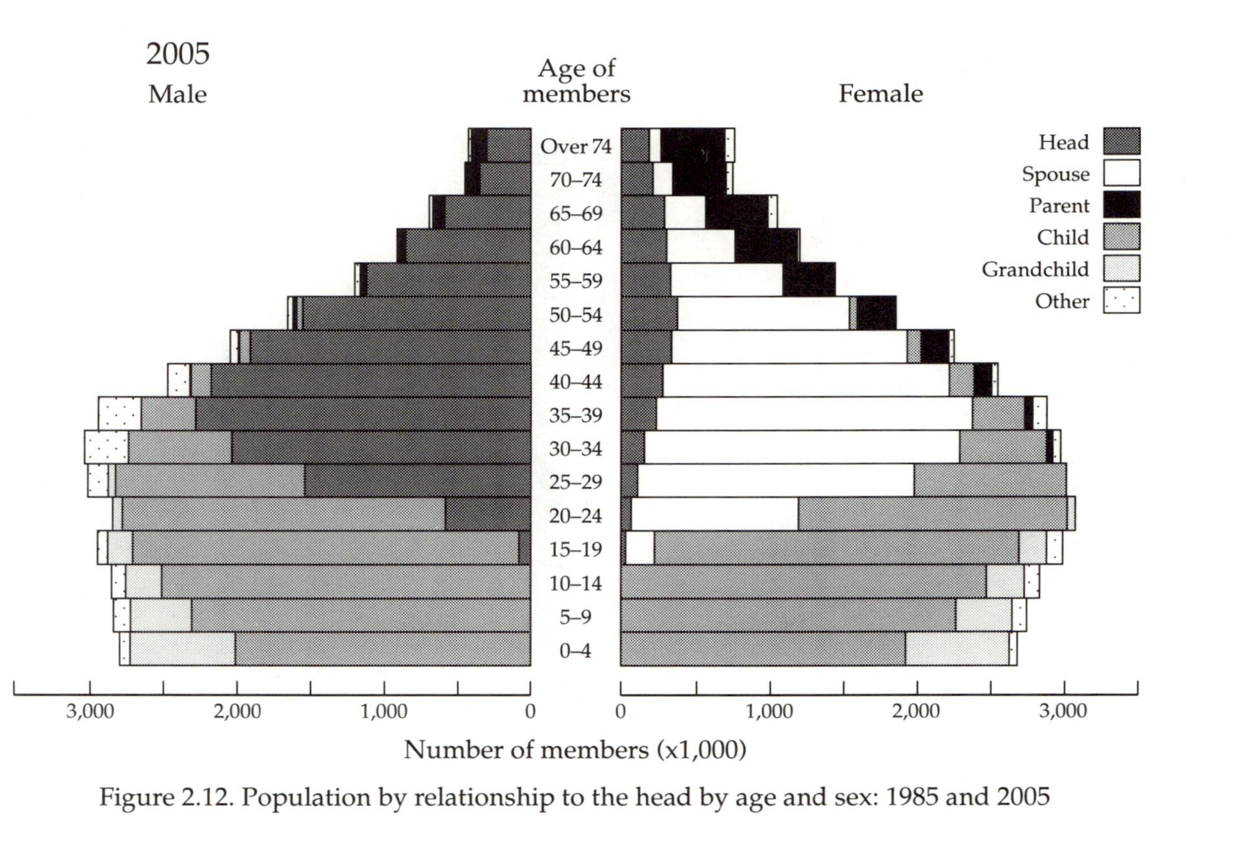

Figure 2.12. Population by relationship to the head by age and sex: 1985 and 2005

Table 2.11. Number of children and grandchildren of the head per household: 1980–2005

Year	Age of members			Total
	0–4	5–14	15 and older	
1980	0.72	1.38	1.11	3.21
1985	0.62	1.18	1.11	2.92
1990	0.52	1.01	1.05	2.58
1995	0.41	0.87	0.97	2.25
2000	0.35	0.72	0.89	1.97
2005	0.30	0.61	0.81	1.73

Source: Estimated using HOMES and data from NESDB (1985b).

Table 2.12. Number of parents of household head per hundred households: 1980–2015

Year	Age of parent				Total
	Under 55	55–64	65–74	75 and older	
1980	0.9	2.0	3.1	2.3	8.2
1985	1.0	2.1	2.9	2.2	8.2
1990	1.0	2.2	2.9	2.2	8.3
1995	1.0	2.3	3.0	2.1	8.4
2000	1.2	2.3	3.2	2.2	8.9
2005	1.6	2.4	3.3	2.4	9.7
2010	1.8	2.8	3.4	2.5	10.5
2015	1.5	3.4	3.5	2.7	11.2

Source: Estimated using HOMES and data from NESDB (1985b).

peaking when the cohorts are in their 30s or perhaps 40s, and declining thereafter. Although the age patterns are similar the levels are not, as average household size at each age of head for successive cohorts has dropped over time. Perhaps the most surprising feature shown in Figure 2.13 is the relatively constant differences in average household size across successive cohorts. Demographic transition in Thailand is not leading only to smaller family size at a narrow "childrearing" interval. Rather it is leading to smaller family size at all stages of the life cycle.

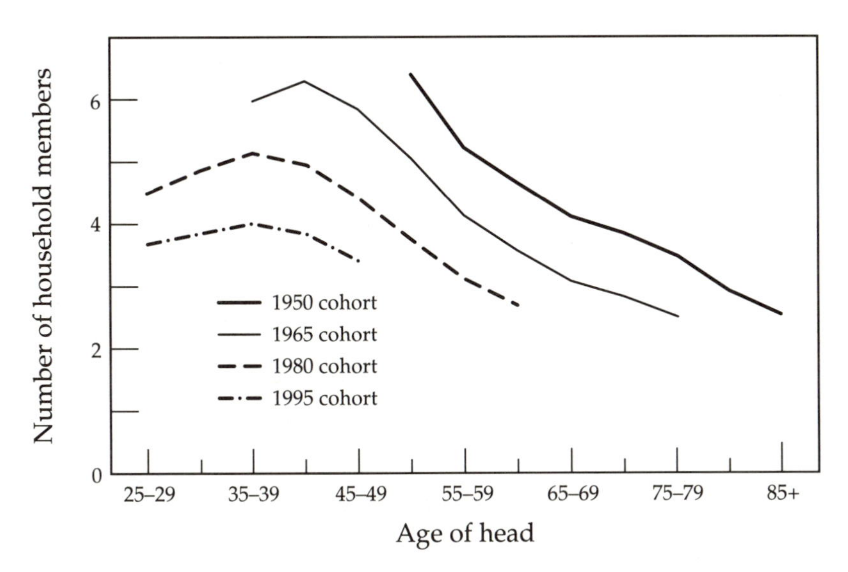

Note: Year indicates year in which cohort was 25–29 years old.

Figure 2.13. Average household size by age of head for selected cohorts

CONCLUSION

In some respects, Thailand has already experienced enormous change in the demographic factors that will influence its economy and society for many years to come. Mortality conditions have improved sufficiently that life expectancy at birth is near levels observed in higher-income countries. Average levels of childbearing are near the two-child level that demarcates countries converging on zero population growth. But many features of Thailand's population are continuing to undergo rapid and significant change. The age distribution of the population is being transformed from a bottom-heavy one, dominated by children and young adults, to a mature distribution with greater representation from those who are middle-aged and elderly.

Household characteristics will mirror the fundamental changes in Thailand's population. The number of households will continue to grow rapidly as do the number of people who establish households. The number of children per household and overall household size will decline as a consequence of reduced rates of childbearing. Households headed by older men and women will become more abundant relative to those headed by younger adults.

These and other changes in the demographic character of the Thai household will have a pervasive effect on how the household organizes itself, the activities of household members, and other features of the household that will drive social and economic change for many years to come.

3

Labor Force and Wage Forecasts

by John Bauer, Nipon Poapongsakorn, and Naohiro Ogawa

Thailand, like other developing countries, has been experiencing a rapid decline in its population growth rate over the last two decades. The rate of population growth declined from 3 percent per year in the 1960s to 1.5 percent during 1985–90. Further declines are expected as a result of economic development, urbanization, increasing educational attainment, and the family planning program. The National Economic and Social Development Board (NESDB) of Thailand forecasts that the population growth rate will drop to 1.3 percent in 1991 and then to 1.1 percent in 2005.

What will happen to the supply of labor and to future wage trends as a result of demographic change? For example, what will happen to the wage rate if labor supply exceeds labor demand? The objectives of this chapter are to:

- Estimate future labor-force participation rates for men and women
- Forecast the future labor supply to the year 2005, using these labor-force participation rate estimates along with demographic projections from HOMES and education projections
- Project the number and characteristics of workers by household type
- Construct a simple model of wage determination to assess the effects of labor market adjustments on wage and unemployment rates in the next few decades

The major source of data used in this study is the Labor Force Survey conducted in August 1984 by the National Statistical Office (NSO) of Thailand (NSO 1984).

THE LABOR MARKET IN THAILAND: AN OVERVIEW

The rapid decline in population growth rates since the mid-1970s has not yet slowed the growth of the Thai labor force. Its annual growth rate was approximately 3.5 percent in the 1971–83 period (NSO 1971–83: Round 2) compared with 2 percent in the 1960s (NSO 1960, 1970).

Most of the increase in the labor force was absorbed by the agricultural sector. In the 1973–83 period 44 percent of employment growth was in the agricultural sector, while the service and the manufacturing sectors accounted for 18.2 percent and 12.7 percent of the growth respectively (Poapongsakorn 1984:35). Despite the rapid growth of output in the manufacturing sector (8.2 percent during 1971–83), its employment share is only 9 percent of total employment. The service sector, which includes the commercial and communication sectors, accounted for 21 percent of total employment in 1984. Its employment growth rate has also been impressive—5.6 percent per year during 1971–83.

The extraordinarily high proportion of the labor force in agricultural employment (68 percent in 1984) relative to the proportion of GDP contributed by the agricultural sector (19.5 percent) reflects the importance of this sector as the major absorber of labor supply. In past decades, increases in agricultural employment (which averaged about 3 percent per year) were made possible by the expansion of cultivated land which grew at about the same rate as that of agricultural GDP (Evenson and Setboonsrang 1985). Since this expansion will not be possible in the future, more nonagricultural employment opportunities will have to be created.

The labor market has performed very well in Thailand. Despite the rapid increase in labor supply (3.49 percent in the 1977–83 period), employment has also grown at an almost equal pace, 3.36 percent per year. The employment elasticity for 1971–83, which averaged 0.584, is impressively high (Poapongsakorn 1986:35). This means that if GDP grows by 5 percent per year, employment will increase by 2.92 percent. As a consequence, open unemployment[1] has generally been well below 2 percent (Table 3.1).

The real wage rate, however, has not been increasing (Table 3.2). Stagnation in the real wage rate can be partly explained by rapid growth in the labor supply and government policies that were biased against the agricultural sector. These policies include the export tax and export quotas on agricultural products, which have reduced farm-gate prices, and the tax exemption on imported machines and equipment for firms promoted by the Board of Investment (World Bank 1983).

Increases in labor-force participation rates, in addition to rapid growth in population, contribute to high labor-force growth rates. Although labor-

---

1. We use the standard definition of not working but looking for work during the survey week.

Table 3.1. Unemployment rate: 1974–84

Year	Survey round	Both sexes	Male	Female
1974	1	0.81	0.96	0.58
	2	0.42	0.58	0.22
1975	1	0.42	0.49	0.31
	2	0.40	0.52	0.27
1976	1	0.93	1.02	0.79
	2	0.83	0.85	0.81
1977	1[a]	1.70	1.71	1.68
	2[a]	1.26	1.21	1.32
1978	1[a]	1.52	1.40	1.71
	2[a]	1.04	1.07	1.00
1979	1[a]	1.37	1.26	1.52
	2[a]	1.12	1.16	1.08
1980	April[a]	3.22	3.50	2.88
	2[a]	1.17	1.15	1.18
1981	1	2.00[a]	2.17	1.78
	2[a]	1.07	1.12	1.02
1982	1[a]	2.31	2.40	2.20
	2[a]	4.12	2.96	5.39
1983	1[a]	1.22	1.30	1.10
	2[b]	2.38	2.16	2.62
1984	1[b]	1.28	1.44	1.26
	2[b]	0.96	1.10	0.80

Source: NSO (1974–84).

Note: Round 3 in 1984 (August) is equivalent to round 2 (July-September) in the preceding years.

a. Includes unpaid family workers who work less than 20 hours and want to work more.

b. Excludes those not looking but available for work.

force participation rates[2] fluctuate from year to year, the general trend has been for them to increase (Table 3.3). The aggregate participation rate in municipal areas averaged 52.4 during 1971–75, 56.6 during 1976–80, and 60.7 during 1980–83. The nonmunicipal rates averaged 71.7, 73.7, and 75.6 over the same periods. The male participation rates increased only marginally over these periods. Female rates grew quickly from levels that were already

2. These rates represent the percentage of the total population age 11 and older who are in the labor force.

Table 3.2. Real wage rate: 1977–85 (baht per month)

Year	Monthly wage
1977	1,154
1978	1,034
1979	1,116
1980	1,123
1981	1,085
1982	1,208
1983	1,232
1984	1,212
1985	1,157

Source: NSO (1977–85).

Table 3.3. Labor-force participation rates by sex and area: 1971–83

	Municipal			Nonmunicipal areas		
Year	Male	Female	Total	Male	Female	Total
1971	64.26	38.99	51.37	81.51	71.07	76.27
1972	66.28	43.54	54.68	79.15	63.71	71.36
1973	64.88	42.04	53.31	78.65	62.92	70.68
1974	64.19	40.26	52.07	76.35	61.30	68.70
1975	63.01	38.67	50.69	77.47	65.45	71.36
1976	62.89	40.30	51.46	77.42	63.45	70.32
1977	65.66	46.49	56.12	78.98	67.79	73.37
1978	67.90	49.20	58.47	80.30	72.60	76.52
1979	67.70	48.60	58.06	77.40	68.00	72.69
1980	68.10	50.20	59.00	79.00	72.40	75.70
1981	68.50	51.90	60.10	79.30	72.40	75.90
1982	68.10	55.50	61.70	80.40	74.00	77.20
1983	67.17	50.49	58.71	78.01	69.46	73.74

Source: NSO (1971–83).

high in 1971. In municipal areas, female participation grew from 40.7 in 1971–75, to 47.0 in 1976–80, and 52.6 in 1980–83. The rates for nonmunicipal females were 64.9 in 1971–75, 68.8 in 1976–80, and 72.0 in 1980–83.

Another interesting aspect of the Thai labor market is that there are large differences between participation rates in the wet season (July–August) and the dry season (January–March). In the wet season, when labor demand is at a peak in the agricultural sector, farm households are so busy that they have to utilize all family members—young and old, male and female—to finish their work on time. After the harvest season most secondary workers pull out of the labor force, resulting in a decline in the participation rate in rural areas. The inter-season differences in the labor-force participation rates in the nonmunicipal areas are 20–26 percent for females and 12–19 percent for males.

In our analysis, we are concerned with the functioning of the labor market. There is substantial controversy about the extent of labor market failure in Thailand (World Bank 1983; Bertrand and Squire 1980; Pongpaichit and Baker 1984; Poapongsakorn 1984; and Sussangkarn et al. 1986). Bertrand and Squire and the World Bank rural employment mission to Thailand argue convincingly that the Thai rural labor markets function very efficiently and are well integrated due to migration. Seasonal unemployment is not really a problem because most marginal workers voluntarily withdraw from the labor market. Also, economists believe that if workers wanted to remain in the labor force, then wages would fall to absorb them. Bertrand and Squire (1980) go further and argue that urban market dualism is not relevant in the case of Thailand because there is a linkage between the two sectors. They also note that some of the jobs in the informal sector pay higher wages than those in the formal sector.

Pongpaichit and Baker (1984) and Sussangkarn et al. (1986) argue that there are imperfections in the Thai labor market. They present evidence that the major cause of seasonal unemployment is imperfect information. Almost 35 percent of seasonally inactive persons did not move to find temporary jobs because they did not know how to find a job. Most of those who moved (65 percent) were assured of a job before they did so. They find that information is a prime determinant of seasonal migration. If some people move from a village, then others are likely to follow. Sussangkarn et al. (1986) conclude, therefore, that seasonal migration tends to be concentrated in certain villages. They also argue that there is evidence of labor market segmentation in urban areas. Workers are more likely to be in the formal sector if they are better educated, male, and not a new entrant to the area. There are also large wage differentials between the formal and informal sectors.

There are reasons to believe, however, that the overall labor market tends to function quite efficiently and that wages are subject to demand and supply forces. First, there are very few government regulations in the labor market. Although there is minimum wage legislation, the compliance rate has been less than 30 percent. Small- and medium-scale enterprises, which employ most of the workers, can easily avoid the law. Second, although there may be barriers to entering the formal sector, the employment share of this sector is only 21.5 percent of total urban employment according to the Sussangkarn et al. (1986) estimate.[3] So it is still a relatively small market amid the informal and self-employed markets. Third, there is evidence that during the 1984–85 period, when most agricultural product prices were at a record low, rural money wage rates did decline slightly (Table 3.2). As a result the real wage rate declined (Poapongsakorn 1986:43). Finally, the tabulated results from the additional questions in Round 2 of the 1984 Labor Force Survey (NSO 1984) show that those facing drastic declines in the demand for labor during the dry season are quite active in seeking work. About 18 percent of the seasonally inactive persons moved to work elsewhere sometime during the dry season and another 18 percent looked for jobs outside their village but did not move.

Therefore, it is reasonable to assume that in the long run excess supply of and excess demand for labor will be eliminated via the wage mechanism.

ESTIMATION OF LABOR-SUPPLY MODELS AND PROJECTION METHODOLOGY

To project the Thai labor force to the year 2015, we use a rather unique methodology that permits us to make projections that are consistent with projected demographic, educational, and household composition trends. Most other labor-supply models let projected population size and age composition drive the labor-force projections.[4] We go beyond this by incorporating both projected educational enrollment rates and educational attainment into our labor-supply model. Also, the effects of future trends in household composition, projected by the HOMES package, are permitted to affect future levels of labor-force participation. The number of household members of various ages and in each household type are included as determinants of participation. For example, the number of young children in the household is allowed to reduce female participation. The absence of the husband in female-headed households is permitted to encourage female participation.

3. About 53 percent of formal sector employment comes from the public sector.

4. Previous studies (e.g., Nitungkorn 1981; Paitoonpong 1976; Maurer et al. 1973; NESDB 1987; Meesook 1976; Poapongsakorn 1979) suffer from at least three problems. First, their study of the female labor supply ignores the problem of selectivity bias. If one is concerned with the effects of wages on the female labor supply, selectivity is an issue. Inferences based on the behavior of working women may not apply to the general female population. Second, most studies do not estimate the male participation equation. The male labor-supply projections are based on constant male labor-force participation rates. This assumption may be satisfactory for prime-age males but may not be correct for youth and the elderly. Our study estimates a male labor-force participation equation and uses the estimated function to forecast male labor supply. Finally, although most studies include demographic variables in the labor-supply equations, these projections are based upon arbitrary assumptions about future trends in the demographic variables. This study uses the HOMES methodology (see Chapter 2) to forecast the future values of demographic independent variables.

Our methodology permits us to project more than just the size and age-sex composition of the labor force. We can also project the educational attainment of the labor force by age and sex. This information is valuable for gauging the future human capital characteristics of the workforce. We can also project the labor force by household compositional characteristics. For example, we can project the number of workers (male and female by age) by various parameters of household composition, such as household type, age of head, household size, and age composition of household members.

Projections of the characteristics of future households provide information that allows us to make forecasts regarding the economic conditions of these households and family welfare. For example, the number of workers in households, along with their age and educational attainment, could generate forecasts of future levels of household income and its distribution. Knowing the number and ages of working and nonworking household members allows for detailed and precise estimates of future trends in dependency. We can also project the number of working mothers, the number and ages of their children, and the presence of other adults in the households with working mothers. This could be used, for instance, to forecast child-care needs. Because the model also projects the incidence of female-headed households, planning for their special needs could be augmented.

Our projection methodology involves several steps. First, we seperate future populations into students and nonstudents using projected enrollment rates. The enrollment rates are taken from an educational model developed by Phananiramai and Mason (see Chapter 6). The projected enrollment rates[5] are presented in Chapter 6, Table 6.8. The second step is projection of the labor-force participation rates of the nonstudent population. We estimate a model of participation whose determinants are age, sex, educational attainment, and various dimensions of household composition. Using these estimates, along with projected trends in educational attainment taken from our education model and future trends in household composition taken from HOMES, we can project future participation rates. In the final step, the nonstudent population is multiplied by the appropriate age-sex-household composition specific participation rates to yeild the projected labor force. We now examine the labor-force participation model in detail.

The conceptual model is presented in terms of market and reservation wages. An individual participates if the offered market wage is greater than the reservation wage. The market wage for each individual is assumed to be a function of experience or age and education. The reservation wage,

5. The ratios are the projected number of students divided by the projected population.

which is not observed, is modeled as a function of education and household composition.

The relationship between labor-force participation and selected variables is estimated with a probit model. In one version of this model, participation is regressed upon wages, education, and household composition. In another version, wages are dropped from the probit regression. Age and education, which determine wages, are substituted for wages in this reduced form model. Estimates using this model are much easier to perform because wages are not observed for nonparticipants. We will concentrate on this reduced form model.

The data supporting this analysis is taken from Round 2 of the 1984 Labor Force Survey (NSO 1984). This round was taken from July though September, the agricultural peak season. The analysis and projections, therefore, will be for peak activity rates.

A liberal definition of labor-force participation is adopted. A labor-force participant is any individual 11 years of age or older who is employed or unemployed during the survey week. The employed include those who worked for payment, unpaid family workers, persons temporarily absent from their jobs because of illness or vacation, or persons waiting to be recalled to a job within 30 days. The unemployed include those who applied for work or who did not apply because of illness, but planned to. We did not include so-called discouraged workers, those who did not look for work because they did not believe work was available.

The variables used in the participation probits for nonstudent men and women are listed in Table 3.4. The determinants of participation that we have selected can be projected using the HOMES model and available population projections. The participation of the nonstudent population is assumed to be a function of education, municipal versus nonmunicipal residence, age, and household composition.

The effect of education is modeled by a set of dummy variables for no schooling and primary, secondary, and university education. A municipal dummy is included to control for the effect of urban residence. The effect of age is modeled with a cubic spline. This flexible form permits the equation to capture the nonlinearities in the age profile of participation. The household composition variables include the number of household members in various age catagories, a dummy variable for female-headed households, and a dummy variable for one-person households.

The results for the male and female participation probits appear in Table 3.5. Consider the male results first. Higher educational attainment has a strong positive effect on male participation. Male participation is lower in municipal areas. The effects of household composition are minor for men, with the exception of the number of members age 60 and above. An increase in this number is associated with lower participation. Living in a female-headed household is also associated with lower participation.

Table 3.4. Description of variables used in the labor-force participation model

Variable	Definition	Mean		Standard deviation	
		Males	Females	Males	Females
LFP	Labor-force participation	0.897	0.725	0.303	0.447
*ED*1	No schooling	0.070	0.153	0.256	0.360
*ED*2	Primary education	0.707	0.711	0.455	0.453
*ED*3	Secondary education	0.156	0.089	0.363	0.285
*ED*4	University education	0.066	0.047	0.248	0.212
MUNI	Municipal resident	0.344	0.362	0.475	0.481
AGE	Age in years	37.1	36.9	16.0	17.0
*AGE*2	Age squared	1,635	1,650	1,392	1,511
*AGE*3	Age cubed	82,460	85,968	0.105*E*+06	0.118*E*+06
*AGE*325	Age spline term[a]	13,924	15,857	31,685	36,764
*AGE*359	Age spline term[a]	285.0	422.2	2,133	2,676
*T*02	Number of household members ages 0–2	0.260	0.252	0.505	0.505
*T*36	Number of household members ages 3–6	0.381	0.362	0.647	0.644
*T*712	Number of household members ages 7–12	0.624	0.607	0.860	0.862
*T*1319	Number of household members ages 13–19	0.841	0.832	1.05	1.15
*T*2059	Number of household members ages 20–59	2.50	2.44	1.23	1.46
T60U	Number of household members age 60 and above	0.345	0.391	0.636	0.650
FHEAD	Female-headed household	0.113	0.268	0.316	0.443
OP	One-person household	0.024	0.034	0.152	0.182
*DW*1**T*02	*T*02 Interaction with age[c]	b	0.514E-01	b	0.257
*DW*2**T*36	*T*36 Interaction with age[c]	b	0.779E-01	b	0.331

Note: N = 3,822 for males, 4,571 for females.

a. $AGE325 = (AGE-25)^3 * D_0$

$AGE359 = (AGE-59)^3 * D_1$

Where: $D_0 = 1$ if $AGE > 25$
$= 0$ if otherwise
$D_1 = 1$ if $AGE > 59$
$= 0$ if otherwise

b. Variable used only for women.

c. $DW1 = 1$ if age is 20–24
$= 0$ otherwise
$DW2 = 1$ if age is 25–29
$= 0$ otherwise

Table 3.5. Reduced form participation probits

Variable	Males		Females	
	Coefficient	*T*-ratio	Coefficient	*T*-ratio
Constant	-4.751	-2.27	-7.252	-4.51
*ED*2	0.374	3.38	0.932*E*-01	1.30
*ED*3	0.292	2.11	-0.349*E*-01	-0.35
*ED*4	0.851	3.72	1.024	6.32
MUNI	-0.294	-3.95	-0.484	-10.27
AGE	0.626	2.18	1.082	4.98
*AGE*2	-0.210*E*-01	-1.68	-0.458*E*-01	-4.90
*AGE*3	0.251*E*-03	1.44	0.632*E*-03	4.85
*AGE*325	-0.247*E*-03	-1.34	-0.680*E*-03	-4.97
*AGE*359	0.558*E*-04	1.27	0.162*E*-03	5.23
*T*02	0.218*E*-01	0.30	-0.235	-5.10
*T*36	0.539*E*-01	0.93	-0.215*E*-01	-0.57
*T*712	0.118*E*-01	0.27	0.877*E*-02	0.33
*T*1319	0.363*E*-01	1.00	0.692*E*-01	3.05
*T*2059	-0.428*E*-01	-1.63	-0.248*E*-02	-0.14
*T*60*U*	-0.206	-3.64	0.136	3.43
FHEAD	-0.247	-2.52	0.657*E*-01	1.27
OP	-0.318	-1.50	0.486*E*-01	0.383
*DW*1**T*02	a	a	-0.286	-3.14
*DW*2**T*36	a	a	-0.179	-2.50

Note: For males: Log – Likelihood = –1,263.9
N = 3,822
For females: Log – Likelihood = –2,690.4
N = 4,571

a. Variables used only for women.

Since male participation is generally stable, the results for women are of more interest. The strongest effect of education is that associated with the higher participation of university women. Municipal residence, once again, is associated with lower participation. The effects of household composition are stronger than those for men. The presence of children less than 6 years of age inhibits female participation, while the presence of older children and adults over 60 years of age encourages it. Women in female-headed households participate more.

LABOR-FORCE PROJECTIONS

The HOMES labor-force projections provide the following output for each five-year period within the projection period.

- Labor-force participation rates by age and sex
- Total labor force by age and sex
- Educational attainment of the labor force by age and sex
- The number of male and female workers by age of the worker, age of the household head, and household type
- The average number of workers per household by household type and age of head
- The total, male, and female labor force by age of head and household type

The program also provides summary tables for the whole projection period. The summary tables include the total labor force, labor-force participation rates, number of workers per household, and the average household size for various years. We present some of the output in this section.

In projecting the number of workers by household type, we concentrate on intact, single female-headed, single male-headed, one-person male, and one-person female households.[6] These household types include most people in the population. Primary-individual households (i.e., households comprised of unrelated individuals) are excluded in our projections. People in these households, which do not readily lend themselves to our methodology, constitute only a small proportion of the Thai population. However, because of their exclusion, we scale up our projected labor force figures. The scaling factors, which vary by sex and age group, are determined so as to make the model's estimated 1984 labor force consistent with the observed labor force as given by Round 2 of the 1984 Labor Force Survey (NSO 1984).[7]

The total labor force in Thailand is projected to increase from 26.53 million in 1985 to 41.38 million by 2005 (Table 3.6). This implies average annual labor-force growth rates of 2.8 percent from 1985 to 1990, 2.4 percent from 1990 to 1995, 2.0 percent from 1995 to 2005, and 1.7 percent from 2000 to 2005.[8]

The aggregate labor-force participation rates increase in the projections from 0.74 in 1985 to 0.77 in 2005 (Table 3.7). Since the male and female rates increase by approximately the same number of percentage points, the proportion of the labor force that is female remains constant at approxi-

6. The husband and wife are both present in intact households. In single female-headed and single male-headed households the spouse is absent.

7. Actually, there are a number of reasons besides our modeling constraints for scaling. Data constraints, problems with sample weights, the possibility of some students working, and other factors necessitate scaling. The model was developed to project change; scaling merely starts the model at the correct initial conditions.

8. NESDB (1987) projected the labor force to grow at an annual rate of 2.83 percent during the Sixth Plan. Sussangkarn et al. (1986) projected an average annual labor force growth rate of 2.72 percent from 1986 to 1991.

Table 3.6. Total labor force: 1985–2015

Year	Number of persons (in millions)	Average annual growth rate[a] (%)
1985	26.53	—
1990	30.50	2.8
1995	34.37	2.4
2000	38.06	2.0
2005	41.38	1.7
2010	44.18	1.3
2015	46.41	1.0

a. Growth rate for previous five years.

Table 3.7. Projected labor-force participation rates: 1985–2005

Year	Male	Female	Total
1985	0.79	0.71	0.74
1995	0.81	0.72	0.76
2005	0.82	0.73	0.77

mately 48 percent. The age-sex specific participation rates over the projection period change only slightly, which is reasonable given that male and female rates were already very high in 1985 (Table 3.8). The rates for men and women 11–24 years of age decline marginally as a result of increasing school enrollment. The participation rates of prime-age women increase slightly. The rates for men and women age 60 and above decline slightly after 1995. One reason the age-specific rates do not change dramatically is because we have projected peak season participation rates. Since these rates are quite high, there is not a large surplus labor pool from which higher wages can draw more than the projected increases.

Education affects productivity and wages. It is therefore of great interest. Our model, because it takes into account the effects of education on labor-force participation, can be used to project the educational attainment of the labor force by age and sex.

The projected educational attainment of the labor force for 1985 and 2005 is shown in Table 3.9. Two interesting facts become apparent in examining the 1985 figures. First, the educational attainments of male and female workers are fairly similar. Of males 25–59 years of age, 12.1 percent have no schooling; 68.9 percent have a primary-level education; 15.2 percent, secon-

Table 3.8. Projected labor-force participation rates by age and sex: 1985–2005

	Males			Females		
Age	1985	1995	2005	1985	1995	2005
11–24	0.58	0.57	0.56	0.57	0.56	0.55
25–34	0.99	0.99	0.99	0.87	0.89	0.89
35–44	0.98	0.98	0.98	0.90	0.91	0.91
45–59	0.96	0.96	0.96	0.85	0.86	0.87
60+	0.58	0.58	0.57	0.33	0.36	0.35

dary; and 4.3 percent, tertiary. The corresponding figures for females are: no schooling, 12.5 percent; primary, 74.7 percent; secondary, 8.6 percent; and tertiary, 4.1 percent. The relatively high proportion of female workers with a tertiary education is partly due to the high labor-force participation of university women. Second, educational attainments are substantially higher for younger as opposed to older workers of both sexes.

These advances in educational attainment are projected to continue. The proportion of male workers 25–59 years of age with a secondary education rises from 15.2 percent in 1985 to 18.4 percent in 2005. The proportion of males with a tertiary education grows from 4.3 percent to 16.8 percent. There are similarly large gains for women.

The aging of the Thai labor force over the projection period will mean a steady increase in the percentage of more experienced workers (Table 3.10). The percentage of the population under age 24 declines from 31.1 percent in 1985 to 20.4 percent in 2005. The proportion 25–34 years of age increases slightly until 1995, then declines. The percentage of workers over 34 increases from approximately 41 percent to 52 percent.

Household income is determined, in large part, by the number of wage earners per household. Our model projects the average number of workers per household. This average is projected to decline from 2.62 in 1985 to 2.30 by 2005 (Table 3.11). The decline in the average number of workers per household, however, probably does not imply a decline in the economic well-being of Thai households. This decline is due to reductions in average household size. In fact, household size declines more quickly than does the average number of workers. As a result, the average number of persons per worker in these households declines from 1.91 in 1985 to 1.62 by 2005. Workers will have fewer people to support.

Tables 3.12 and 3.13 present some of the detail in the HOMES labor projections. The total number of workers in 1985 and 2005 by age of head/spouse[9]

9. The age of the spouse of the head is used for intact households.

Table 3.9. Educational attainment of the labor force by age and sex: 1985 and 2005

	Educational level							
	No schooling		Primary		Secondary		Tertiary	
Age	1985	2005	1985	2005	1985	2005	1985	2005
Male								
11–14	0.0374	0.0000	0.9090	0.8812	0.0536	0.1188	0.0000	0.0000
15–19	0.0190	0.0000	0.6611	0.4973	0.3102	0.4800	0.0096	0.0227
20–24	0.0368	0.0000	0.5842	0.4728	0.2199	0.2799	0.1591	0.2473
25–29	0.0551	0.0000	0.6241	0.5133	0.2169	0.2144	0.1039	0.2723
30–34	0.0679	0.0352	0.7075	0.5711	0.1843	0.1761	0.0403	0.2177
35–39	0.1203	0.0357	0.7247	0.6181	0.1315	0.1830	0.0234	0.1632
40–44	0.1201	0.0356	0.7250	0.6180	0.1315	0.1829	0.0234	0.1635
45–49	0.1191	0.0353	0.7258	0.6178	0.1315	0.1826	0.0236	0.1644
50–54	0.2662	0.0827	0.6518	0.7201	0.0706	0.1642	0.0113	0.0330
55–59	0.2581	0.0796	0.6592	0.7227	0.0709	0.1635	0.0118	0.0342
60–64	0.2433	0.0741	0.6726	0.7270	0.0712	0.1620	0.0129	0.0369
65–69	0.5600	0.1665	0.4002	0.7402	0.0350	0.0748	0.0048	0.0185
70–74	0.5292	0.1495	0.4284	0.7546	0.0365	0.0743	0.0059	0.0217
75+	0.4897	0.1301	0.4644	0.7700	0.0382	0.0732	0.0077	0.0267

Female								
11–14	0.0416	0.0000	0.9042	0.8837	0.0543	0.1163	0.0000	0.0000
15–19	0.0263	0.0000	0.6553	0.5007	0.3084	0.4751	0.0100	0.0242
20–24	0.0377	0.0000	0.6299	0.4656	0.1830	0.2688	0.1495	0.2657
25–29	0.0467	0.0000	0.6963	0.4994	0.1454	0.2019	0.1116	0.2987
30–34	0.0634	0.0329	0.7857	0.5587	0.1099	0.1664	0.0410	0.2419
35–39	0.1202	0.0354	0.7950	0.6454	0.0661	0.1489	0.0187	0.1704
40–44	0.1201	0.0353	0.7950	0.6446	0.0661	0.1484	0.0187	0.1717
45–49	0.1197	0.0351	0.7953	0.6424	0.0657	0.1471	0.0192	0.1754
50–54	0.3033	0.0817	0.6643	0.7952	0.0296	0.0911	0.0058	0.0320
55–59	0.2973	0.0806	0.6671	0.7949	0.0292	0.0895	0.0064	0.0350
60–64	0.2934	0.0791	0.6706	0.7938	0.0286	0.0873	0.0074	0.0398
65–69	0.7487	0.1982	0.2399	0.7568	0.0094	0.0294	0.0020	0.0156
70–74	0.7409	0.1909	0.2470	0.7588	0.0092	0.0279	0.0029	0.0223
75+	0.7305	0.1813	0.2558	0.7573	0.0089	0.0260	0.0048	0.0353

Table 3.10. Age composition of the labor force: 1985–2005 (%)

Age	1985	1995	2005
11–24	31.1	25.4	20.4
25–34	28.2	29.7	27.2
35–44	18.2	21.7	24.5
45–59	17.8	17.8	22.1
60+	4.7	5.4	6.0

Table 3.11. Average workers per household, household size, and persons per worker: 1985–2005

Year	Workers per household	Household size	Household members per worker[a]
1985	2.62	5.00	1.91
1990	2.56	4.64	1.81
1995	2.48	4.28	1.73
2000	2.39	3.97	1.66
2005	2.30	3.72	1.62

a. Average household size divided by average number of workers per household.

and household type appear in Table 3.12. The average number of workers by age of the head/spouse and household type are given in Table 3.13.

It is interesting to compare the average number of workers in intact versus single male-headed and single female-headed households. In 1985 the average number of workers per intact household was 2.73 versus 2.71 per single male-headed household and 2.43 per single female-headed household. On average, therefore, the absence of a female spouse does not significantly reduce household labor supply. The absence of a male spouse reduces it by only three-tenths of a worker on average. The reason for this is that single male-headed and female-headed households are concentrated in households with older heads, where the adult children of the head are the important source of labor. These households, therefore, may not have especially low levels of economic well-being. However, the differences in average numbers of workers per intact versus single male-headed and single female-headed households vary considerably by age of head. In households with prime-age heads, the single male-headed and female-headed households average almost one less worker than the intact households. For example, single male-headed and female-headed households, with heads

Table 3.12. Labor force by age of head and household type: 1985 and 2005 (thousands)

Age of head/ spouse[a]	Household type: Intact	Single male-headed	Single female-headed	One-person male	One-person female	Total
1985						
<25	1,963.45	102.63	68.04	28.53	14.70	2,177.36
25–29	2,639.37	124.32	91.26	36.91	11.69	2,892.54
30–34	2,810.31	93.53	135.71	20.42	11.71	3,071.69
35–39	2,967.88	79.52	210.15	14.58	8.93	3,281.06
40–44	3,172.64	79.69	287.11	12.22	7.76	3,559.43
45–49	3,039.79	113.27	430.94	11.85	10.02	3,605.88
50–54	2,367.95	140.64	507.75	10.18	12.50	3,039.01
55–59	1,499.63	156.63	453.85	9.59	13.07	2,132.76
60–64	769.60	141.30	388.89	8.70	10.76	1,319.24
65–69	342.43	96.89	263.24	4.47	8.47	715.50
70–74	149.79	86.09	168.51	1.59	3.57	409.56
75+	73.47	73.52	177.33	0.69	1.30	326.31
Total	21,796.31	1,288.05	3,182.78	148.72	114.48	26,530.34
2005						
<25	2,422.01	88.18	59.80	31.83	16.31	2,618.14
25–29	3,795.72	123.11	98.51	35.31	15.76	4,068.41
30–34	4,627.55	113.90	177.45	33.75	18.92	4,971.57
35–39	5,479.72	138.23	365.87	30.25	18.42	6,032.49
40–44	5,653.52	152.55	502.27	26.58	16.73	6,351.65
45–49	4,950.31	193.97	685.97	24.22	19.88	5,874.35
50–54	3,504.44	197.39	717.66	20.10	23.96	4,463.55
55–59	2,068.51	203.69	579.18	17.28	23.02	2,891.68
60–64	1,117.60	189.55	526.49	16.22	20.27	1,870.12
65–69	537.83	140.78	403.48	9.27	18.14	1,109.50
70–74	233.97	121.90	260.84	3.16	7.61	627.48
75+	115.28	122.61	262.81	1.45	2.54	504.69
Total	34,506.46	1,785.85	4,640.34	249.42	201.58	41,383.64

Note: Columns may not sum to totals because of rounding.

a. The age of the spouse of the head is used for intact households.

Table 3.13. Average number of workers per household by age of head and household type: 1985 and 2005

Age of head/spouse[a]	Household type: Intact	Single male-headed	Single female-headed	One-person male	One-person female	Total
1985						
<25	1.84	2.36	1.49	0.82	0.79	1.80
25–29	2.03	3.06	1.65	0.94	0.92	2.01
30–34	2.24	2.67	1.72	0.99	0.92	2.19
35–39	2.81	2.69	2.08	0.96	0.92	2.71
40–44	3.40	2.54	2.49	0.95	0.91	3.23
45–49	3.72	2.66	2.80	0.97	0.95	3.48
50–54	3.79	2.97	2.91	0.92	0.88	3.48
55–59	3.49	2.89	2.67	0.81	0.76	3.13
60–64	3.05	2.82	2.72	0.72	0.65	2.78
65–69	2.45	2.64	2.30	0.47	0.39	2.22
70–74	2.07	2.60	2.17	0.26	0.19	1.97
75+	1.80	2.37	2.21	0.10	0.06	1.81
Total	2.73	2.71	2.43	0.82	0.63	2.62
2005						
<25	1.81	1.77	1.12	0.80	0.76	1.74
25–29	2.01	2.23	1.33	0.94	0.93	1.97
30–34	2.16	1.97	1.41	0.99	0.93	2.09
35–39	2.54	2.26	1.77	0.96	0.93	2.44
40–44	2.89	2.24	2.04	0.95	0.92	2.74
45–49	3.07	2.23	2.27	0.97	0.96	2.87
50–54	2.95	2.12	2.17	0.92	0.89	2.69
55–59	2.69	2.10	1.96	0.82	0.78	2.39
60–64	2.37	2.05	1.99	0.73	0.66	2.12
65–69	1.90	1.88	1.69	0.48	0.41	1.68
70–74	1.61	1.90	1.64	0.27	0.20	1.50
75+	1.48	1.94	1.78	0.10	0.07	1.48
Total	2.46	2.07	1.90	0.81	0.62	2.30

a. The age of the spouse of the head is used for intact households.

of ages 40 to 55 average about 0.9 workers less than intact households. These non-intact households, therefore, are at a disadvantage and may deserve special attention from policymakers.

These differences in the labor supply of the various household types increase over time because of declining fertility and changes in age composition. Single male-headed households supply on average 0.39 less workers than intact households by 2005 and single female-headed households supply 0.56 less workers.

LABOR MARKET ADJUSTMENT

In this section, we will make a comparison between the reduced form projections of labor supply, which do not explicitly model the effects of wage trends, and the projections of employment by the NESDB. First, we estimate the wage elasticity of the male and female labor supply. We then discuss the labor demand projections. Finally, three possible types of labor market adjustment will be analyzed. Different assumptions regarding the wage elasticity of demand for labor will be employed.

The Effect of Wages on Participation

This section presents our estimates for the wage elasticities of the male and female labor supply. We correct for the potential selectivity bias that arises in estimating the effects of wages on female labor-force participation. Since many women do not work, we do not observe wages for them and must impute their potential earnings. This imputation is carried out by estimating earnings equations on the subsample of working women. This procedure is subject to selectivity bias, however, because some of the variables that are in the earnings equation also affect the probability that a woman will work, and are already included in the sample used to estimate the earnings equation.

We apply Heckman's (1980) two-step correction procedure for sample selectivity bias. The first step is to estimate a reduced form labor-force participation probit. The results from this estimation are used to generate his Lamda variable which is then added to the wage equation, correcting for the potential bias.

Once again, we use data from Round 2 of the 1984 Labor Force Survey (NSO 1984). In this analysis, we limit our estimates to Bangkok, because rural earnings data are problematic. In fact, there are a number of data problems even when we restrict our analysis to Bangkok. The first concerns earnings.

Earnings are available only for employees, which account for approximately 67 percent of the male labor force in Bangkok and 61 percent of the female labor force. We have to assume that the effects of human capital variables on earnings are similar for employees, self-employed workers, and unpaid family workers. An additional problem is that for many employees hourly wage rates are not available. We are forced to approximate wages by dividing reported earnings by reported hours. This opens the results to well-known potential biases (Schultz 1980).

Perhaps a more serious problem is the absence of unearned income in the survey. Unearned or property income plays an important theoretical role in labor-supply models. Unfortunately, it is often excluded from labor-force surveys. A common practice in studies of female participation is to include the earnings of households as a proxy for the unearned income of wives. We use a similar approach, including the earnings of other household members *(OEARN)* in the female participation equation.[10] A final data problem is that actual labor market experience is not included in the survey. We use a common proxy, age minus years of schooling minus six. While this proxy may be a good one for males, it is unlikely to be so for women (Blinder 1976). With these problems in mind, we turn to the results.

Once again, we have assumed that wages are a function of education and experience. The reservation wage is assumed to be a function of education and household composition. In this case, the dimensions of household composition we have included are the number of household members of ages 0 to 6 (*T06*), 7 to 12 (*T712*), and 13 and above (*T13+*). A dummy variable for female-headed households *(FHEAD)* was also included.

The results of the reduced form participation probit for Bangkok women appear in Table 3.14. Again, the strongest effect of education is that for university women. The presence of children of ages 0 to 6 and 7 to 12 inhibits participation while the presence of more adults encourages it. Women in female-headed households participate more. Higher levels of household income *(OEARN)* reduce participation.

The wage equation estimates, corrected for sample selection bias, appear in Table 3.15. The results seem plausible. Wages increase with education and experience. Using the coefficients for experience in the participation and wage equations, we can calculate the estimated elasticity of participation with respect to wages (see Heckman 1980). We obtain an elasticity of 0.97. This is the elasticity evaluated at the mean participation rate and experience level in the sample and the mean level of wages for workers.[11] This figure is reasonable given estimates for other countries (see Mincer 1985). The estimate suggests that women in Bangkok respond strongly to wage opportunities.

---

10. *OEARN* for any woman is equal to the sum of wage earnings, business profits, and farm profits of other household members.

11. The OLS estimate for this elasticity was 1.27. Poapongsakorn (1979), using the 1977 Labor Force Survey (NSO 1977), estimated the wage elasticity of married Thai women in the labor force to be 1.34.

Table 3.14. Participation probit for women in Bangkok

Variable	Coefficient	*T*-ratio	Elasticity at means
Constant	-0.65	-6.94	-0.54
*ED*2	-0.21*E*-01	-0.28	-0.98*E*-02
*ED*3	-0.87*E*-01	-1.05	-0.19*E*-01
*ED*4	1.03	9.94	0.61*E*-01
*T*06	-0.15	-7.27	-0.64*E*-01
*T*712	-0.16	-7.91	-0.76*E*-01
*T*13+	0.26	3.01	0.95*E*-01
FHEAD	0.16	4.54	0.46*E*-01
X	0.99*E*-01	28.32	1.65
X^2	-0.19*E*-01	-28.03	-1.18
OEARN	-0.35*E*-05	-1.40	-0.17*E*-01

Where *X* = *AGE* - Years of schooling - 6
OEARN = Monthly household income - Earnings of women
N = 6,819
Log - Likelihood = -3,941.7

Table 3.15. Wage equation for working women in Bangkok

Variable	Coefficient	*T*-ratio
Constant	-13.64	-4.90
*ED*2	4.40	3.06
*ED*3	17.52	11.68
*ED*4	34.07	18.14
X	1.20	9.55
X^2	-0.17*E*-01	-6.84
Lambda	5.29	2.66

Dependent variable = Hourly wage in baht.
N = 1,917
R-square = 0.49

We also estimated a participation elasticity for Bangkok men. This was done by first estimating a wage equation for working men. This equation was then used to impute wages for all men, working and nonworking. Since most men work, we did not attempt to correct for selectivity bias. The imputed wage was then used as a regressor in the participation probit. Theoretically, we would want to estimate male participation as a function of wages and property income, but because property income is not observed in our sample we have included education and age as proxy variables.

Table 3.16. Wage equation for Bangkok males

Variable	Coefficient	T-ratio
Constant	3.094	1.9
*ED*3	1.840	0.8
*ED*4	9.895	3.8
X	0.674	5.1
X^2	-0.007	-3.1
*ED*3*X	0.629	3.0
*ED*3*X^2	-0.001	-0.3
*ED*4*X	2.418	7.4
*ED*4*X^2	-0.026	-3.0

Dependent variable = Hourly wage in baht.
N = 2,394
R-square = 0.40

Table 3.17. Bangkok male labor-force participation probit with wages included

Variable	Coefficient	T-ratio
IWAGE	0.056	17.9
*ED*2	0.945	10.5
*ED*3	0.406	4.1
*ED*4	0.360	2.5
AGE	0.176*E*-02	0.9
Constant	-1.086	-9.9

N = 5,745
Log - Likelihood = -3,631.3
Note: IWAGE = Imputed wage from coefficients in Table 3.16.

The results of this exercise appear in Tables 3.16 and 3.17. Wages, again, appreciate with experience. Secondary and university education increase the starting wages of new workers and the rate at which wages increase with experience. The imputed wage has a significant positive effect on male participation. The estimated elasticity of male participation with respect to wages is 0.44.[12]

The labor supply of men and especially of women appears to be quite responsive to wage changes. The high female participation rates are con-

12. Poapongsakorn (1979) estimated the male wage elasticity to be 0.19 to 0.21.

sistent with the estimated high elasticity of participation. This leads us to believe that future wage increases will draw many more women into the labor force.

Employment Projections

In the Sixth National Economic and Social Development Five-Year Plan (1986–91), the employment target is set to increase by 3.9 million persons over the five-year period (Table 3.18). Total employment will be 30.95 million persons in 1991 with an annual growth rate of 2.7 percent.[13] Manufacturing employment is projected to grow at the highest rate—6.4 percent per year—whereas the agricultural sector will have the slowest employment growth rate—1.4 percent.

We made our own employment projections for the 1992–2015 period using the same method that the employment projection working group at NESDB used in their projections. The employment elasticity for the 1971–83 period is estimated at 0.584. As it is difficult to forecast the growth of GDP in the long run, and because the average annual growth rate of real GDP in the last few years has ranged from 4 to 6 percent, it is not unreasonable to assume that after 1991 the annual growth rate of employment will range from 2.34 to 3.50 percent.[14] Table 3.19 contains these employment projections as well as labor-supply projections for the 1990–2015 period.

The following observations can be drawn from Table 3.19. First, assuming a 4 percent rate of GDP growth, there will be excess labor supply until the beginning of the twenty-first century. Excess supply of labor will be gradually eliminated as a consequence of drastic fertility decline. The number of new labor-force entrants eventually declines. Note that the proportion of workers age 35 and over to workers 11–34 years of age will increase rapidly during the projection period (Table 3.20). Not only does the relative size of the labor force 11–34 years of age fall, but its absolute size will also fall. As a result, labor shortages (excess demand) begin to appear after 2000 and grow through 2015. If we assume a 6 percent GDP annual growth rate, then excess demand in the labor market begins around 1995. The excess demand increases continuously through 2015 (Table 3.19).

The labor demand projections have assumed a constant employment elasticity and thus have implicitly assumed that labor productivity will not change. The effect of future gains in labor productivity are not as obvious

13. It should be noted that TDRI projected employment to increase at 2.60 percent per year during the same period (TDRI 1985: table 31, p. 214).

14. Employment growth (2.34 percent) is the product of the GDP growth rate (4 percent) and employment elasticity (0.584). The higher employment growth rate (3.5 percent) is the product of the 6 percent GDP growth rate and the employment elasticity (0.584). Note that these simple employment forecasts ignore the possibility of substitution of labor for capital as excess supply or demand for labor changes the relative price of labor.

Table 3.18. Employment target in the Sixth Plan (1986–91) (thousands)

Sector	1986	1991	Increase	Annual growth rate (%)
Total employment	27,050	30,950	3,900	2.7
Agriculture	18,535	19,835	1,300	1.4
Nonagriculture	8,515	11,115	2,600	5.5
Mining	121	155	34	5.1
Manufacturing	2,194	2,994	800	6.4
Construction	544	686	142	4.8
Public utilities	125	168	43	6.1
Trade and banking	2,276	2,958	682	5.4
Transportation	550	599	42	1.7
Service	2,705	3,555	850	5.6

Source: NESDB (1987).

Table 3.19. Projections of labor supply and labor demand: 1985–2015 (thousands)

		Labor demand 4% GDP growth		Labor demand 6% GDP growth	
Year	Labor supply	Number	Excess supply (+)	Number	Excess supply (+)
1985	26,841[a]	25,853[b]	988	25,853	988
1990	30,503	29,965	538	29,965	538
1995	34,367	33,684	683	35,695	-1,328
2000	38,058	37,865	193	42,522	-4,464
2005	41,384	42,565	-1,181	50,654	-9,270
2010	44,185	47,848	-3,663	60,342	-16,157
2015	46,407	53,787	-7,380	71,882	-25,475

a. Actual labor force in 1985 was 26,847.3 thousand persons.

b. Actual employment obtained from NSO (1985: Round 3).

as one might expect. On one hand, increases in productivity would partially offset the large excess labor demands projected, if we fix GDP growth at the assumed levels. However, productivity increases would result in higher GDP growth rates. The higher GDP growth, in turn, raises the demand for labor. Nonagricultural labor productivity growth is usually associated with higher employment growth.

Table 3.20. Projected labor force by age group: 1985–2005

Year	Labor force by age group (millions)			Ratio of the labor force age 35+ to the labor force age 11–34
	Age 11–24	Age 25–34	Age 35 and older	
1985	8.25	7.48	10.80	0.69
1995	8.73	10.21	15.43	0.81
2005	8.44	11.26	21.68	1.10

In any case, we can expect a number of responses to future labor shortages. In the next section, we forecast rising real wage levels as a result of excess labor demand. Rising wages should induce labor-saving technological innovation, better work-force organization and management, and higher investment in human capital.

Labor Market Adjustment Mechanism

Excess supply or demand for labor cannot last indefinately. Eventually, the labor market should clear. The market may clear, however, at some positive level of frictional unemployment. Past trends in the unemployment rate (Table 3.1) suggest a frictional rate of unemployment of 2 percent.

The increases in labor supply and labor demand presented in Table 3.19 define shifts in the aggregate labor supply and demand curves. We assume the resulting excess demands and supplies are removed, leaving a 2 percent unemployment rate, through wage and employment adjustments. These adjustments, given assumptions regarding the elasticities of labor demand and supply, yield rough forecasts of wage and employment trends in Thailand to the year 2015. One limitation of our forecasts is that they do not fully account for the effect of future investments in human capital and the future aging of the labor force. We do not, therefore, take into full account potential changes in labor productivity. Actual future real wage increses may be somewhat higher than we project.

Assessing the impact of market adjustment requires some knowledge of labor market behavior. Our labor-supply estimates show that the wage elasticity of supply of male workers is 0.4 while that of female workers is approximately 1.0 (Tables 3.14–3.16). Of course, these high supply elasticities cannot persist indefinitely. Even modest wage increases would eventually result in labor-force participation rates greater than 100 percent. What we assume, therefore, is that these supply elasticities persist until a critical aggregate labor-force participation rate for the working age population is reached. In the absence of any strong theoretical or empirical basis on which to choose this critical rate, we somewhat arbitrarily set it at 90 percent. In the forecasts, when an aggregate labor-force participation rate for the working population of 90 percent is achieved, we assume that labor supply then becomes perfectly inelastic. In the 4 percent GDP growth projections, this occurs around 2010. In the 6 percent GDP growth projections, labor supply becomes inelastic around the year 2000.

Another necessary piece of information is the wage elasticity of labor demand. Unfortunately, there are only two previous studies of demand for labor of which we are aware (Chaipravat 1979; Evenson and Setboonsrang 1985). In his macroeconomic model for Thailand, Olarn Chaipravat (1979) found that the elasticity of demand for labor in the nonagricultural sector is –1.23. In another study, Evenson and Setboonsrang (1985) found that the elasticity of labor demand in the agricultural sector is –0.063.

We estimated the wage elasticity of labor demand from the production function. The logarithm of labor share was regressed on the logarithm of relative wage rate (the index of the real wage rate and time trend). This estimated production function gave a wage elasticity of labor demand of –0.175. Contrary to the results obtained in Chaipravat (1979), which did not explain the data source for wage rates, we conclude that labor demand in Thailand is quite inelastic. This conclusion is consistent with findings in the United States.[15] The results from the above studies suggest that in the long run it is reasonable to assume that the wage elasticity of labor demand is between 0.1 and 0.3. The assumptions used to assess the impact of labor market adjustments on the wage rate are summarized in Table 3.21.

Excess supply is assumed to be reduced by lower wage rates and excess demand is eliminated by higher wage rates. Although the supply response of female workers is different from that of male workers, we will assume that the wage rate of males relative to that of females remains constant at the 1984 ratio. Furthermore, we do not have separate estimates of demand for female and male workers, so, although the labor demand for female workers probably differs from that for male workers, we will assume that the two demand functions have the same wage elasticity.[16]

Wage and Unemployment Adjustment

The following procedure is used to estimate the changes in the market wage rate. The forecasts of labor supply obtained in the previous section are

15. Hammermesh (1976) concludes that a consensus value of the fixed output response of employment to real wages in the long run is a bare –0.15. Clark and Freeman (1980), however, argue that the small price effect appears due to the imposition of the constraint that real capital prices have as large a positive effect on demand as the negative effect of real wages. Releasing this constraint results in a higher wage elasticity of –0.285 in the short run and –0.496 in the long run.

16. Because of this assumption, it is not possible to estimate the unemployment rate by sex after the adjustment takes place.

Table 3.21. Assumptions about labor market behavior

Behavior	Wage elasticity
Male labor supply[a]	0.4
Female labor supply[a]	1.0
Labor demand	
Assumption (1)	-0.1
Assumption (2)	-0.3
Male–female wage ratio	Constant

a. The labor supply elasticities become 0 after the year 2010 in the 4 percent GDP growth projections and after the year 2000 in the 6 percent GDP growth projections. See text for explanation.

compared with the labor demand forecast by the NESDB in the Sixth Plan. If the forecast labor supply exceeds labor demand, the real wage rate is assumed to decline.

The proportionate change in the wage rate ($w\sim$) is calculated as follows:

$$w\sim \; = (MS + FS - LD)/(n_d \times LD - n_{ms} \times MS - n_{fs} \times FS)$$

where $w\sim$ = percentage change in wage rate
MS = male labor supply
FS = female labor supply
LD = labor demand
n_d = wage elasticity of labor demand
n_{ms} = wage elasticity of male labor supply
n_{fs} = wage elasticity of female labor supply

The resulting wage and employment projections are presented in Table 3.22. Real wages in Thailand did not grow substantially during the 1971–85 period and wages remain stagnant for several years in our projections. Consider first the 4 percent GDP growth/0.1 elasticity of labor demand projection. Wages in this projection do not grow substantially until 2005. After 2005, excess labor demand becomes acute, resulting in wage growth of 11 percent per year. With a 0.3 elasticity of labor demand, wages grow at around 4 percent per year after 2005. Employment growth in both projections averages around 2.3 percent a year from 1990 to 2000 and 1.7 percent a year from 2000 to 2010.

Next consider the 6 percent GDP growth projections. In these projections, excess labor demand begins to increase wage rates much earlier; rapid wage growth begins around 1995. With an elasticity of labor demand of 0.3, wages would grow between 5 and 6 percent per year after 1995. A labor demand elasticity of 0.1 would result in much more rapid wage increases. Employ-

Table 3.22. Wage and employment projections: 1985–2015

	1985 (Actual)	1990	1995	2000	2005	2010	2015
A. 4% GDP growth, elasticity of labor demand = 0.1							
Annual % change in wage	—	0.05	−0.05	0.38	0.84	11.57	11.02
Male wage	19.87	19.92	19.87	20.24	21.09	33.29	51.64
Female wage	13.97	14.00	13.97	14.23	14.82	23.41	36.30
Equilibrium employment (thousands)	25,853	29,357	33,010	37,037	41,457	44,081	46,428
B. 4% GDP growth, elasticity of labor demand = 0.3							
Annual % change in wage	—	0.04	−0.04	0.30	0.66	3.71	4.41
Male wage	19.87	19.91	19.87	20.16	20.83	24.71	30.16
Female wage	13.97	14.00	13.97	14.18	14.65	17.37	21.20
Equilibrium employment	25,853	29,346	33,009	36,940	41,103	43,713	45,847
C. 6% GDP growth, elasticity of labor demand = 0.1							
Annual % change in wage	—	0.05	1.41	17.06	14.23	12.51	11.38
Male wage	19.87	19.92	21.33	39.54	67.68	110.05	172.70
Female wage	13.97	14.00	15.00	27.80	47.58	77.37	121.42
Equilibrium employment	25,853	29,357	34,722	38,278	41,433	44,140	46,318
D. 6% GDP growth, elasticity of labor demand = 0.3							
Annual % change in wage	—	0.04	1.12	5.39	6.04	6.32	6.34
Male wage	19.87	19.91	21.03	26.70	34.76	45.75	60.27
Female wage	13.97	14.00	14.78	18.77	24.44	32.17	42.37
Equilibrium employment	25,853	29,346	34,367	37,875	41,026	43,718	45,835

ment growth in these projections average from 2.6 to 2.7 percent per year from 1990 to 2000 and around 1.5 percent per year from 2000 to 2010.

In summary, given our demographically driven labor supply projections and our simple demand projections, we would expect very slow growth in real wages for the rest of this century. Wages are projected to grow rapidly after 2005, assuming a 4 percent GDP growth rate. Wages begin to increase rapidly after 1995 in the more optimistic projection which assumes a 6 percent GDP growth rate. Employment growth in our projections ranges from 2.3 to 2.7 percent per year during the 1990–2000 period and from 1.4 to 1.7 percent per year during the 2000–2010 period.

SUMMARY AND ISSUES

The labor-force projections presented in this chapter are consistent with projected trends in demographics, household composition, and education. Our methodology, which incorporates household and educational forecasts into our labor force projection model, permits us to project many dimensions of labor supply. For example, we have projected the Thai labor force by age and sex; labor-force participation rates by age and sex; educational attainment of the labor force by age and sex; number of male and female workers by age of the worker, age of the household head, and the household type; and the average number of workers per household by household type and age of head.

There are several major implications resulting from our analysis and projections. First, consider our labor-force participation analysis. Our estimates indicate that education, fertility, and wages have substantial effects on labor-force participation. Secondary and tertiary education encourages male participation and tertiary education also encourages female labor-force participation. This effect of education on the supply of effort is an added social benefit of education. Future increases in educational attainment will not only improve the quality of the labor force but will also increase its size. Future declines in fertility will also facilitate female labor-force participation. Finally, we estimated a high wage elasticity of labor supply for Thailand. This high elasticity, as our wage forecasts indicate, will tend to dampen wage growth until the year 2000.

Consider next the projected characteristics of the labor force. The educational attainment of the Thai labor force is projected to increase. For example, the proportion of male workers 25–59 years of age with a secondary education increases from 15.2 percent in 1985 to 18.4 percent by 2005. The percentage with a tertiary education grows from 4.3 to 16.8 percent. There are similarly large gains for the female work force. Consider the attainment of new entrants to the work force, say workers of ages 25–29. Approximately 10 percent of male and female workers in this age group had a tertiary education in 1985. By 2005 this group increases to 28 percent.

There are two obvious implications of these projected attainment trends. First, these trends will directly affect the skill composition of the labor force and will be a factor promoting growth in per capita income. Our wage equation estimates indicate substantial returns to education. Therefore, one would expect future attainment gains to promote wage and productivity growth. (We argue below, however, that excess supply of labor will tend to inhibit general wage gains for the rest of this century.) Second, the large projected increases in the number of college-educated workers suggests a need for promoting the generation of appropriate employment. Unemployment among highly educated youth is already a problem in Thailand. This problem may worsen according to these projections.

Our projections also indicate substantial aging of the labor force. The ratio of workers over age 35 to those under age 35 increases from 0.69 in 1985 to 1.10 by 2005. On the positive side, the older work force will be more experienced. Our wage equation estimates indicate that earnings do increase with experience. This suggests that productivity does grow with age. However, aging also creates problems. Relative labor shortages at entry-level positions will arise. Lower and lower proportions of the labor force will be young, mobile graduates bringing the latest techniques to the work place. This should increase the need for on-the-job training and adult education in the future.

Next consider the implications of our labor supply, labor demand, and wage projections. Labor supply is projected to grow at an average annual rate of 2.4 percent between 1985 and 2000. Labor force growth is much less rapid after 2000, averaging only 1.3 percent per year from the turn of the century to 2015. Our rough labor demand forecasts imply that excess labor supply will persist until around 2005, if we assume a 4 percent rate of GDP growth. After this date, excess labor demand becomes increasingly acute. If we assume a more optimistic GDP growth rate of 6 percent, the excess labor supply disappears by 1995.

Applying reasonable labor demand and supply elasticities to these excess labor supply and demand projections generates a range of wage forecasts. The growth in wages should be quite low until the turn of the century, given the projected levels of excess labor supply. Thereafter, wages should grow at a rapid rate.

In broad terms, the results suggest that wage growth will not squeeze profits in Thailand through the end of this century. This should be conducive to growth along the lines of labor-intensive manufacturing. However, the government and industry should start planning for the labor shortages that will arise 10 to 15 years from now. Having this forecast gives the government time to make certain it does not promote projects that will not be viable when real wages begin to increase rapidly and to prepare the way (through educational emphasis, infrastructure, and information) for the changes in Thai comparative advantage that will take place.

Moreover, our projections provide some indication of future levels of economic well-being and possible problems for Thai households. There are reasons to feel optimistic about future standards of living. Although the average number of workers per household is projected to decline, the number of household members drops more quickly. As a result, the dependency burden within households declines. In 1985 every 10 workers had to support themselves plus nine nonworkers. By 2005 every 10 workers will have to support only six nonworkers. Also, even though the number of workers per household declines slightly from 2.6 in 1985 to 2.3 in 2005, each worker will be earning more. Wage levels are projected to rise rapidly after the turn of the century. In addition to these general wage increases induced by labor shortages, workers should command higher earnings because of their greater educational attainments and levels of experience.

The projections do, however, suggest some potential problems for which planning should begin. Although the overall dependency burden does decline because of fewer children, the burden of caring for the elderly will grow. The percentage of household members over age 65 increases from 3.4 percent in 1985 to 6.5 percent by 2015. Also, consider the situation of households with heads over age 60. Because of declines in the number of children, the number of workers supporting these households will drop by 30 percent between 1985 and 2010 (Table 3.23). Private pension plans and public social security schemes will become more important in the future. The decline in the average number of workers in female-headed households is also large (33 percent) relative to the decline for all households (15 percent). This suggests that female-headed households may need greater assistance in the future.

Finally, the projections do provide some insights concerning the demand for child care. The number of young working women will increase rapidly during the next decade. The number of working women 25–34 years of age, for example, is projected to increase at an annual rate of 2.6 percent from 1985 to 2000.

There are reasons to believe, however, that the demand for child-care services will not grow dramatically. First, female labor-force participation rates are already quite high in Thailand. Second, the growth in the number of young working women declines dramatically after the turn of the century. Third, with the projected decline in fertility, the average number of preschoolers per household declines (Table 3.24). Fourth, there will be a growing proportion of elderly people within households. Our analysis suggests that the presence of older adults (60 years and older) within the household facilitates female labor-force participation. This is presumably due in part to child care provided by the elderly. In households with heads under the age of 50, where working women are likely to be found, the average

Table 3.23. Number of workers in older households: 1985–2010

Age of head/spouse	Average number of workers	
	1985	2010
60–64	2.78	1.94
65–69	2.22	1.53
70–74	1.97	1.34
75+	1.81	1.27

Table 3.24. Average number of preschoolers per household: 1985–2015

Year	Age of head/spouse	
	<35	35–49
1985	1.14	0.48
1995	0.80	0.32
2005	0.67	0.23
2015	0.59	0.16

number of members over age 60 is projected to rise from 0.11 in 1985 to 0.16 by 2000.

The household is often forgotten in economic research and development planning. This study has explicitly taken into account change in household composition in projecting labor market trends. The analysis has provided many examples of the central role played by this institution in economic activity.

4
Domestic Resource Mobilization: Analysis of Survey Data

by Andrew Mason, Varai Woramontri, and Robert M. Kleinbaum

Investment in new plants and equipment, the development of improved infrastructure, and many other key components of developing country efforts to achieve higher standards of living require large amounts of investable funds. These funds can come from a variety of sources. Households, businesses, and the government share responsibility for mobilizing domestic resources, and multinational corporations, foreign financial institutions, and multilateral and bilateral lending and development institutions inject foreign resources.

Foreign funds have played an important role in providing investment resources for some countries, but domestic saving is by far the most important source of investable funds. Among the nonindustrialized countries, gross national saving averaged 79 percent of gross domestic investment between 1970 and 1981, according to data from the World Bank (1984). Of the 97 countries with populations exceeding one million, only two, Sierra Leone and Yemen, relied on foreign sources for more than half of their investable funds.

There is a close association between the level of domestic saving and the level of investment in most countries (Figure 4.1). The simple correlation between the saving and investment rate is 0.74 and each percentage point increase in saving is estimated to increase the investment ratio by six-tenths of a percentage point. And if very high saving ratio countries (those with ratios above 30 percent) are excluded from the analysis, the estimated increase in the investment ratio is three-quarters of a percentage point for each percentage point increase in the saving ratio.

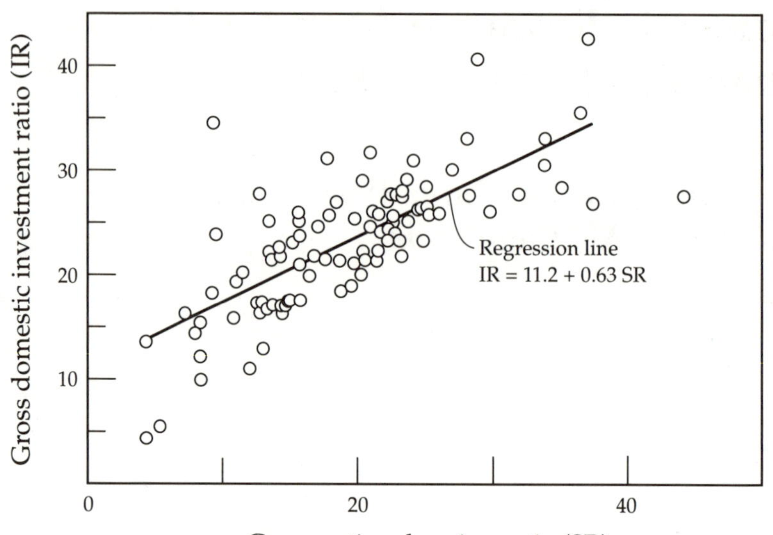

Source: World Bank (1984).

Figure 4.1. Investment versus saving in 97 countries: 1970–81

More sophisticated analyses by Feldstein (1983) and Feldstein and Horioka (1980) support the conclusion of an Asian Development Bank study on domestic resource mobilization in Asia (Abbott 1984:1):

> Asian developing countries . . . will have to raise their national saving rates if they want to keep their investment rates at about the level they have averaged in recent years. But apart from this immediate consideration, higher national saving rates are needed to provide the basis for self-sustained growth and development.

That this generalization is applicable to Thailand is clearly demonstrated by comparing investment to national saving (Table 4.1; Figure 4.2). Foreign saving has only been as high as one-quarter of net investment a few times since 1950, the earliest year for which data are available. More typically, domestic saving has been sufficient to replace depreciated capital and to provide for two-thirds or more of all new investment. The close connection between national saving and investment is particularly apparent in Figure 4.2. Year-to-year changes in investment clearly have a close association to changes in domestic saving rates.[1]

1. A number of economists argue that investment is determined by rates of return and that foreign saving will make up any shortfall in domestic saving.

Table 4.1. Investment and saving: 1950–54 to 1980–85

Period	Investment ratio	National saving ratio	
		Household	Total
1950–54	0.149	0.122	0.144
1955–59	0.160	0.086	0.134
1960–64	0.209	0.120	0.174
1965–69	0.217	0.117	0.184
1970–74	0.222	0.147	0.202
1975–79	0.256	0.148	0.196
1980–85	0.213	0.127	0.145

Source: NESDB (1985a); Burkner (1981).
Note: All values are net of depreciation.

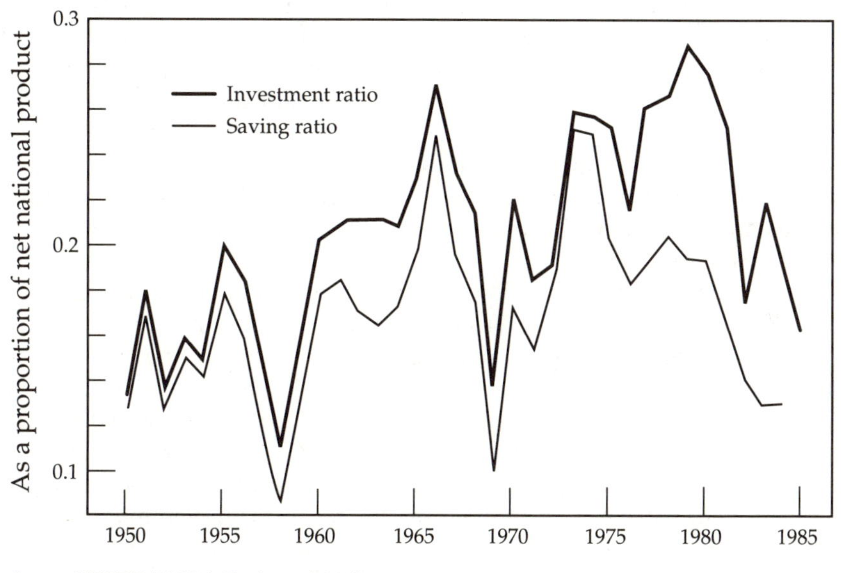

Source: NESDB (1985a); Burkner (1981).

Figure 4.2. National saving and investment: 1950–85

Although government and business share responsibility for mobilizing domestic resources with the household sector, this study is confined to an analysis of saving by households. In most Asian developing countries, household saving is the most important component of domestic saving. Thailand is no exception to this generalization—over the last 35 years household saving has averaged between 65 and 90 percent of national saving (NESDB 1985a; Burkner 1981).

A continuation of the decline in the national saving ratio from its peak in the 1970s could represent a major setback to Thailand's development effort and would be a surprising departure from the upward trend in saving observed over the preceding two decades. A major issue is whether the recent decline in saving is a temporary or a long-run phenomenon. Both government saving and business saving grew much more slowly during the 1975–85 period than did household saving. Business saving grew at an annual rate of 6.5 percent and government saving at an annual rate of –31.4 percent, compared with 10.9 percent for household saving. If government or business saving makes a significant rebound or deteriorates further in the next few years, short-run movements in household saving related to demographic change may not be apparent.

Long-run trends in household saving will continue to be the most important determinant of national saving as long as household saving makes up such a large share of the total. A variety of explanations have been offered to explain the recent decline in household saving, including low rates of real interest, an increase in expenditure on consumer durables, and the emergence of "chit fund" schemes which absorb substantial unreported income and saving. In any case, these adverse factors apparently offset the potential positive effects of Thailand's rapid fertility decline. Unlike several other Asian countries, Japan and Korea being notable examples, high saving has not accompanied lower rates of childbearing in Thailand (Fry and Mason 1982; Fry 1984).

The evidence presented below, analysis of household saving behavior, and forecasts of aggregate household saving to the year 2015, indicate that further changes in Thailand's demographic situation will be sufficient to raise household saving rates to near the record levels achieved during the 1970s. A conservative forecast procedure yields saving rates of 14.0 percent by 2005 as compared with 14.8 percent during 1975–79 and 14.7 percent during 1970–74. Saving among more educated households and those employed in the more modern sectors of the economy tends to be even more responsive to demographic change. If all households were as responsive to a decline in the number of children as are households with college-educated heads, household saving would reach 15 percent by 2005.

SURVEY ANALYSIS

Determinants of Household Saving

Studies of domestic resource mobilization typically focus on government policy and institutional constraints that impede or encourage financial saving. The purpose of the analysis undertaken here is quite different. Our purpose is to identify factors that affect the propensity to save by households, given the existing institutional and legal environment. The results of the analysis can be used in three ways. First, forecasts of household saving will be presented that reflect expected changes in household characteristics. These forecasts can be used to identify possible shortfalls in saving that must be made up by mobilizing saving from alternative sources or by motivating households to increase their rate of saving. Second, forecasts will identify the kinds of households that are contributing the greatest amount to household saving and those that are contributing the least to household saving. This information is useful in identifying groups at which domestic resource mobilization policies should be aimed. Third, the analysis may be useful for identifying households that may not be accumulating sufficient financial resources to provide for their members' old age.

Four sets of variables are used to describe household characteristics that impinge on the propensity to save. First, the age of the household head measures systematic variation in household saving associated with the household life cycle. In many countries, the accumulation of pensions is an important motivation for household saving. During years when the household head and other adult members are working, households accumulate wealth to provide for the old age security of members in later years. If the pension motive is important, saving should be higher for "working" households, particularly when members are at their peak earning years, whereas saving should be lower for "retired" households.[2]

Second, household saving will vary with the demographic composition of the household. The simplest way to visualize this effect is to imagine that each member of a household contributes to household income and, at the same time, consumes some part of household income. Some members, depending on their consumption "needs" and their earning capability, will contribute more to income than to consumption. Their presence will lead to higher household saving. Other members will contribute less to income than to consumption and their presence will lead to lower household saving. One would expect that additional children or elderly household members would depress saving, whereas additional prime-age adults would encourage saving. Depending on attitudes toward women and sex differentials in wages, one might expect females to have a different impact on saving than males.

Of course, the actual effect of demographic composition on household saving is considerably more complex. The behavior of one household member is affected by the presence of another. For example, employment and

---

2. The existence and importance of the pension motive and life-cycle saving are the subject of considerable disagreement within the economics profession. See Ando (1985), Kotlikoff and Summers (1981), King and Dicks-Mireaux (1982), Modigliani (1988), and Kotlikoff (1988) for recent research.

earning by women will be affected by the presence of a young child. Also, the addition of a new member to the household may lead all other members to reduce their consumption or increase their work effort. To the extent that parents reduce their childbearing because they want to spend more on each child, expenditures on children might increase or decrease with lower family size. Analysis of the impact of demographic composition provides an estimate of the "net" effect of an additional member on household saving.

A number of empirical studies of household saving in the developing and industrialized countries have examined the impact of the number of children. For the most part, these studies, including studies of saving behavior in Thailand (Wattanavitukul 1980; Tengumnuay 1981), have been inconclusive or failed to identify statistically significant effects (see Mason 1988 for a recent review). But two recent studies based on the analysis of consumer expenditure survey data, one of Korea (Kleinbaum and Mason 1987) and another of Pakistan (Cochrane et al. 1989), have found that households with fewer children have higher rates of saving.

Household saving may also be subject to scale effects or changes in household size, given the age and sex distribution of the household. To the extent that large families can more effectively pool their risks, they may have less incentive to accumulate savings as protection against unemployment or other adverse economic events.

Third, household saving may vary by the type of household. We are particularly interested in female-headed households and one-person households that may find it difficult to accumulate financial wealth. It is not clear, however, that household type will have any impact on saving beyond that captured by the extensive demographic variables already included in the analysis.

Fourth, we analyze a range of socioeconomic characteristics that capture occupational status and income level of the household. In particular, we estimate variation in saving rates for farm households, distinguishing size of landholdings and distinguishing landowners from renters. For urban households, we distinguish households primarily on the basis of occupation.

The specific form of the equation to be estimated is:

$$\begin{aligned} \ln c = \beta_0 + \beta_1 AGE2 + \beta_2 AGE3 + \beta_3 AGE4 + \beta_4 AGE5 \\ + \beta_5 FEM + \beta_6 OPM + \beta_7 OPF + \beta_8 N1 + \beta_9 N2 + \beta_{10} N3 \\ + \beta_{11} NM4 + \beta_{12} NF4 + \beta_{13} NM5 + \beta_{14} NF5 \\ + \beta_{15} X1 + \cdots + \beta_{14+j} Xj + e \end{aligned}$$

where $\ln c$ is the natural log of the ratio of consumption to disposable income, *AGE*2 to *AGE*5 are dummy variables representing the age of the head,

FEM is a dummy variable that takes the value of 1 for households headed by a woman, *OPM* and *OPF* are dummy variables for men and women living by themselves, *NMk* and *NFk* are the number of male and female household members in selected age categories, *Nk* is the combined male and female population in an age category, and *Xj*'s represent socioeconomic variables. More detailed definitions are provided in Table 4.2.

Description of Survey

Our analysis is based on data from the 1981 Socio-Economic Survey (NSO 1985), conducted throughout the kingdom by the National Statistical Office (NSO) of Thailand during the 12-month period from February 1981 through January 1982. The primary objective of the survey was to assess patterns and levels of household expenditures and income and to relate variations in expenditure patterns to differences in household characteristics.

The survey covered all private, noninstitutional households. Individuals living in transient hotels and rooming houses, boarding schools, military barracks, *wat* (temples), hospitals, prisons, and other such establishments, as well as foreign diplomats and other temporary residents, were not interviewed.

Sampling procedure. Information was obtained from a sample of households selected by a statistical sampling procedure to represent all private, noninstitutional households in each region (the Northern, Northeastern, Central, and Southern) and the Greater Bangkok Metropolitan Area. This procedure was based on a self-weighting, stratified, three-stage sample design.

In the first stage, sample *amphoe* were selected as primary sampling units with probability of selection proportional to their population. The total sample includes 135 *amphoe,* scattered in 63 *changwat.*[3] In the second stage, geographic areas within sample *amphoe* were stratified into three community types representing different levels of urbanization: municipal areas, sanitary districts, and villages. Sample blocks were selected systematically from the municipal area stratum, and sample villages were selected from the sanitary district and village strata, with probability of selection proportional to their populations. In the third stage, all households and vacant units in sample blocks and villages were listed and classified by size and occupation of the household head or as vacant. Within sample blocks, 12 addresses in municipal areas, eight in sanitary districts, and six in villages were selected from these listings. A similar procedure was followed for the Greater Bangkok Metropolitan Area, which includes the Bangkok metropolis, Nontha-

3. *Amphoe* and *changwat* are political units. Thailand has four regions; *changwat* are divisions of regions and *amphoe* are divisions of *changwat.*

Table 4.2. Description of variables used in analysis of consumption

Name	Definition
c	Household consumption ratio
AGEj	Age of household head 1 = Less than 25 2 = 25–39 3 = 40–49 4 = 50–59 5 = 60 and older
FEM	Female head (1 if female head, 0 if male head)
OPM	One-person, male (equal to 1, 0 otherwise)
OPF	One-person, female (equal to 1, 0 otherwise)
Ni	Number of members in age category *i* 1 = 0–2 years of age 2 = 3–12 years of age 3 = 13–19 years of age
NMi	Number of male household members in age category *i*
NFi	Number of female household members in age category *i* 1 = 20–59 years of age 2 = Age 60 and older
V16	Farm operator, small landowner (equal to 1, 0 otherwise)
V17	Farm operator, medium landowner (equal to 1, 0 otherwise)
V18	Farm operator, large landowner (equal to 1, 0 otherwise)
V19	Farm operator, small land renter (equal to 1, 0 otherwise)
V20	Farm operator, large land renter (equal to 1, 0 otherwise)
V21	Farm operator, fishing, forestry, etc. (equal to 1, 0 otherwise)
V22	Entrepreneur, paid employees (equal to 1, 0 otherwise)
V23	Entrepreneur, no paid employees (equal to 1, 0 otherwise)
V24	Professional, technical, and managerial (equal to 1, 0 otherwise)
V25	Laborers, farm (equal to 1, 0 otherwise)
V26	Laborers, nonfarm (equal to 1, 0 otherwise)
V27	Clerical, sales, and service workers (equal to 1, 0 otherwise)
V28	Production workers (equal to 1, 0 otherwise)
V29	Economically inactive (equal to 1, 0 otherwise)

buri, Pathumthani, and Samutprakarn. At the second stage, however, communities were stratified into city core, suburbs, and fringe areas.

The number of blocks and villages selected in the second stage was determined to give a uniform sampling rate within each community type stratum. This second-stage sample size was calculated by the following formula:

$$N_i = \frac{1}{F} \times \frac{1}{N} \times \frac{1}{P_i} \times \frac{M_i}{N_{ij}}$$

where:

N_i = sample size (number of blocks and villages in the ith *amphoe*)
$1/F$ = overall sampling fraction
N = number of sample *amphoe* in subregion
P_i = probability of selecting the first-stage ith *amphoe* in a subregion
M_i = total number of households in the ith sample *amphoe*
N_{ij} = number of sample households in the jth block of village in the ith *amphoe*

The overall sampling fraction $1/F$ varies according to area as follows:

Area	Sampling fraction
Greater Bangkok Metropolitan Area	1/300
Municipal areas in other *changwat*	1/250
Villages in sanitary districts	1/500
Villages	1/1000

A total of 12,250 sample addresses were selected for the survey. They were distributed by region and community type as follows:

Area	Total	Municipal areas	Sanitary districts	Villages
Northern	2,302	600	472	1,230
Northeastern	3,180	612	576	1,992
Central	2,146	468	496	1,182
Southern	1,448	624	176	648
Bangkok*	3,174	2,112	240	822
Total	12,250	4,416	1,960	5,874

*Community types are city core, suburbs, and fringe areas.

The total household sample was divided into 12 regionally representative subsamples, and one subsample of households was interviewed during each month of the year.

Every effort was made to interview all households living in the sample dwelling units. If an interview proved to be impossible, a substitute household from the same size and occupation group was selected and interviewed. Substitutions were made if: (1) after several visits, no responsible member of the household could be found at home; (2) the household members were temporarily away and not expected to return during the survey period; (3) the sample address could not be found because of improper listing; (4) the dwelling could not be reached due to impassable roads or for security reasons; and (5) the household members refused to be interviewed. However, no substitutions were made for vacant dwelling units.

Data collection. One or two weeks prior to the scheduled interview period, interviewers who were permanent members of the field operation divisions working out of NSO provincial branch offices were sent out to list all households residing in sample blocks and villages. From the listing, sample households were selected. To obtain complete information, several visits were made. The first visit was to collect information on household composition, housing facilities, income and work experience of each household member, and expenditure on nonfood consumption. Various reference periods were used for collecting data. For all goods and services, data were obtained for the preceding month. However, for items usually purchased infrequently and for income, data were obtained for the preceding 12 months. During the second half of the month, interviewers visited households every other day over a seven-day period to obtain detailed information about expenditures and consumption of food, beverages, and tobacco.

Quality control. To provide the highest possible quality of collected data, supervisors were expected to reinterview about 10 percent of the sample households each month, and to assist interviewers as problems occurred. In addition, each completed interview was subject to a thorough field edit, followed by a follow-up interview if the information was found to be incomplete or internally inconsistent. In this connection, a household account balance sheet was prepared for each completed interview. This balance compared total money "disbursements" with total money "receipts" for the preceding month. If the account was more than 15 percent out of balance, the interviewer was expected to revisit the household to reconcile the difference.

Data editing. All questionnaires were examined for completeness and consistency. Descriptive information was coded numerically for computer processing. All expenditure and income values were converted to a monthly basis by dividing annual values by 12 and multiplying weekly values by 4.3.

Farm income was calculated as the total annual value of production less operating expenses plus rent received from renting out agricultural equipment or animals (if any). Nonfarm business income was calculated as sales less operating expenses.

Concepts and definitions.

Household was defined as:

- A group of two or more related individuals who make common provision for food and other living essentials; or,
- An individual living with a group of unrelated persons, not exceeding five persons. Even if the individuals shared meals, each was treated as a one-person household; or,

- An individual who makes provision for his/her own food and other living essentials without having common housekeeping or financial arrangements with other persons.

Members of a household may pool their income and have a common budget. They may be related or not. Unrelated boarders or lodgers not paying for living quarters or meals, and servants receiving food, clothing, and housing free or as part of wages were counted as household members. Married children and their spouses were treated as separate households. Unrelated boarders or lodgers and their family members, if any, paying for living quarters or meals were treated as separate households.

Household members. The criteria used to identify household members were:

- Common housekeeping arrangements
- Sharing of principal meals
- Common financial arrangements for supplying basic living essentials
- Recognition of one member as head

If usual members of the household were absent at the time of the interview but were not expected to be away for more than three months, they were counted as members provided their income and expenditures could be recorded.

Head of household. The head of household was the person recognized as such by other members, whether or not that person was responsible for the financial support and welfare of the household.

Household income. The total household income includes:

- Wages and salaries, tips, bonuses, etc.
- Net profits from farming and nonfarming activities
- Property income, such as land rent, royalties, interest, and dividends
- Transfer payments received, such as assistance payments, pensions, scholarships, and grants
- Income-in-kind—the value of goods and services received as part of pay, home-produced and consumed (including rental value of owner-occupied dwelling), or received free from other sources
- Other money receipts such as insurance proceeds, lottery winnings, and other windfall receipts

Household disposable income. Disposable income for the household equals total household income less taxes paid.

Household expenditures. Total household expenditures include:

- The amount spent to purchase goods and services used for living purposes
- The value of goods and services received as part of pay, home-produced and consumed (including rental value of owner-occupied dwelling), or received free from other sources
- The amount spent for contributions, insurance premiums, lottery tickets, interest on debts, and other nonconsumption items

Occupation. This is the type of work performed by a person at their principal job. If, during the previous 52 weeks, the respondent had more than one job, the job with the greatest number of weeks worked was recorded. If the number of weeks worked for each job was the same, the job with the highest income was recorded.

Socioeconomic class. The classification of households into socioeconomic groups was based on the main source of livelihood, economic activity, and occupation. Ten categories are employed:

- Farm operators who own most of the land they work
- Farm operators who rent most of the land they work
- Self-employed trade and industrial workers
- Self-employed professional, technical, and administrative workers
- Professional, technical, and administrative workers who work for pay
- Farm workers
- General workers
- Clerical, sales, and service workers
- Production workers
- Economically inactive households

In general, socioeconomic class is based on the principal source of livelihood and the employment status of the chief income earner, usually the household head. However, if the combined earnings of several members of the household represented the main source of livelihood, the classification is based on the employment status of these members. For example, if a household operated a small farm but the earnings of the household members working off the farm as common laborers exceeded farm profits (including the value of home-produced and consumed products), the household was then classified in the general worker group.

Data and Estimation Procedure

For the analysis of saving, a broad definition of expenditure is used rather than a definition designed to mimic the national income account concept of household consumption. Expenditure includes all household payments, including gifts, insurance premiums, lottery ticket purchases, and interest payments, but the payment of direct taxes is excluded. Expenditure also includes the value of food produced and consumed at home and the rental value of owner-occupied housing. Household income is measured by disposable income and is the sum of all receipts, including earnings, property income, transfers, insurance proceeds, lottery winnings, and non-money income, e.g., foods produced for home consumption and the rental value of owner-occupied housing. From this value, direct taxes are subtracted to obtain disposable income. The ratio of expenditure to disposable income, the household consumption ratio, is the dependent variable analyzed most extensively below.

The household consumption ratio and the household saving ratio (equal to 1.0 less the consumption ratio) differ from their national income accounting counterparts in several ways. First, several transfer items, gifts, lottery tickets and winnings, and interest payments and receipts are included as expenditure and as income. These are included because for individual households such items represent income or expenditures even though for the economy as a whole, they do not. Second, the household consumption ratio or household saving ratio uses total income including taxes in the denominator, whereas this analysis is concerned with the disposition of resources over which the household has control, namely disposable income. Third, national income accounts typically include employer contributions to life insurance and pension plans as household income and as household saving (with operating costs of the insurance or pension plan netted out). Likewise, employer-provided health care is typically included in household income and expenditure. The analysis reported below does not include these items.

The demographic characteristics of households are distinguished in a number of ways. First, the age of the household head is included using a series of dummy variables for age of head: less than age 25, 25–39, 40–49, 50–59, and 60 and older. Second, the demographic composition of household membership is captured using a series of variables assigned a value equal to the number of members who are males or females at selected ages. The following age categories are used for both males and females: 0–2, 3–12, 13–19, 20–59, and 60 and older. The number-of-members variable includes heads as well as other household members.[4] Third, households are distinguished using a dummy variable that takes the value of 1 if the head is a female and zero if the head of the household is male. In addition, one-person male households and one-person female households are also distinguished using dummy variables.

Finally, a series of dummy variables is employed to measure the socioeconomic status of the household. These variables are used in lieu of variables that measure occupation of the head and household assets. Although the occupation of the head is available, it is adequately captured by the socioeconomic status variables. Household assets are not available from the survey. Farm owners are distinguished from farm renters and are further distinguished by the size of their landholdings. Self-employed households are distinguished by whether they have employees or not. A complete description of the socioeconomic variables is provided in Table 4.2.

Table 4.3 contains summary statistics for each of the variables used in the statistical analysis. Items are weighted so as to obtain a representative estimate for Thailand as a whole. (The weighting procedure is described below.)

4. Preliminary analysis yielded no gender differences among children. Results reported below only distinguish adult males and females.

Table 4.3. Descriptive statistics: 1981 Socio-Economic Survey of Thailand

Variable name	Mean	Standard deviation	Minimum value	Maximum value
Consumption ratio[a]	0.9872	0.2519	0.5001	1.5000
Age dummies				
*AGE*1	0.0653	0.2537	0	1
*AGE*2	0.3352	0.4848	0	1
*AGE*3	0.2308	0.4327	0	1
*AGE*4	0.1859	0.3995	0	1
*AGE*5	0.1828	0.3969	0	1
Household type				
FEM	0.2059	0.4153	0	1
OPM	0.0413	0.2045	0	1
OPF	0.0448	0.2125	0	1
Number of members				
*N*1	0.2533	0.5069	0	3
*N*2	1.0960	1.2548	0	7
*N*3	1.4003	2.0211	0	14
*NM*4	1.1886	1.1505	0	12
*NM*5	0.1460	0.3759	0	3
*NF*4	1.3281	1.1933	0	12
*NF*5	0.1873	0.4332	0	4
Socioeconomic status				
*V*16	0.0890	0.2923	0	1
*V*17	0.1069	0.3172	0	1
*V*18	0.1378	0.3539	0	1
*V*19	0.0292	0.1729	0	1
*V*20	0.0253	0.1612	0	1
*V*21	0.0149	0.1245	0	1
*V*22	0.0268	0.1658	0	1
*V*23	0.1426	0.3590	0	1
*V*24	0.0868	0.2891	0	1
*V*25	0.0542	0.2325	0	1
*V*26	0.0203	0.1449	0	1
*V*27	0.1040	0.3134	0	1
*V*28	0.0913	0.2958	0	1
*V*29	0.0712	0.2641	0	1

Source: NSO (1985).

Note: Number of observations = 9,097.

a. Households with $c \leq .5$ or >1.5 were excluded from the sample.

Statistical Analysis

The most serious statistical problem that may influence empirical results is reporting error, because data on consumption and income are notoriously difficult to collect. Despite the care with which the socioeconomic survey data were collected, reporting errors are a serious problem. The calculated consumption ratio varies over an unreasonably wide range and, furthermore, income is systematically underreported as compared with consumption. Thus, the average consumption ratio for the sample exceeds 1.0. National income account statistics, although not strictly comparable, would be consistent with a value in the 0.85 to 0.90 range.

The implications of errors in the dependent variable depends on the nature of the errors. If the error is multiplicative and uncorrelated with independent variables, the log specification employed here yields unbiased regression coefficients. As a further safeguard, the model was estimated using the full sample and using a subsample of households with reported consumption ratios ranging from 0.5 to 1.5. In addition, an alternative and independent measure of consumption was constructed using changes in assets and liabilities collected by the survey. The alternative measure is also crude and probably subject to even greater reporting error, but does provide for a partial cross-check of results. For the most part, the alternative approaches provide a generally consistent picture about the determinants of household saving. The results reported below are based on the sample with a consumption ratio varying between 0.5 and 1.5.

The consumption ratio was regressed on the independent variables described above using weighted least-squares regression. The weights used are those calculated by the World Bank for the 1981 Socio-Economic Survey (NSO 1985), obtained by comparing 1980 census tabulations of the number of households to sample sizes in each sampling unit (World Bank 1985). Because a different weighting scheme is employed than the one used by the NSO, the results are not directly comparable to those in NSO publications.

The statistical analysis can only shed a limited amount of light on the factors that account for differences in the household consumption ratio.[5] All of the independent variables taken together explain less than 4 percent of the variation in the consumption ratio. Demographic characteristics of the household, including the age of head, have a statistically significant impact on the consumption ratio, as does socioeconomic status. None of the variables that measure household type are statistically significant, however.

5. See Appendix A for detailed results.

Household composition and the age of the household head. The statistical results provide convincing evidence that the consumption ratio increases and the saving ratio declines as the number of children in the household increases. Children under 3 years of age have no consistent or reliably estimated effect on saving, but the presence of a child 3–12 years of age increases the consumption ratio by a full percentage point or more, whereas children 13–19 years of age have somewhat less effect.

The model has been estimated for several subsamples as a further gauge of the reliability of the results and in an attempt to determine whether the results can be projected over the entire population. The sample was subdivided based on occupational status of the household. Farm households owning their land are distinguished from those that are land renters, and nonfarm households were divided into two groups: entrepreneurial/professional households and households consisting mainly of employees or unemployed members. Results were also estimated separately for households with a head who had primary education or less, a head with secondary education, and a head with some tertiary education.

The estimated impact of the number of children 3–12 years of age is remarkably constant across all households (Table 4.4). The partial effect of an additional child ranges from 0.010 to 0.020, and is statistically significant for all but two subgroups. The partial effect of an additional child 13–19 years of age varies quite considerably from group to group. In the case of land-renting farm households, the contribution of teenagers to income exceeds their impact on consumption. But among employee households and households headed by more educated adults, teens have a far smaller impact on income than on consumption. This finding is entirely consistent with the widely held view that the economic value of children is greater in agrarian societies because children can be more usefully employed in agriculture. Likewise, households with their own businesses are more likely to be able to employ teenage children.

It is interesting to speculate as well about the difference between land renters and landowners. The economic value of a teenager may vary depending upon whether complementary inputs are relatively abundant or not. It may be that landowners are working with a relatively fixed supply of land whereas land renters can, with lower transaction costs, vary the amount of cultivatable land. If this is the case, the marginal product of additional workers, their children, will be higher, i.e., they will contribute more to farm income.

Teenage employment represents a trade-off between current earning and human capital investment through additional schooling. Teenagers from different backgrounds face different opportunities that will offer differing rewards to investment in education. Thus, teenagers of parents with more education may have a greater incentive to stay in school and postpone em-

Table 4.4. Household composition and the consumption ratio: Number of children

Sample characteristics	Partial effect of a child age			Number of observations
	0–2	3–12	13–19	
Full sample	0.001	0.012*	0.004*	9,096
Landowners	0.015	0.012*	0.005	2,446
Land renters	–0.035	0.013	–0.013*	572
Business persons and professionals	–0.012	0.016*	0.001	2,353
Employees and the unemployed	–0.002	0.010*	0.011*	3,722
Primary education for head	0.002	0.011*	0.003	7,390
Secondary education for head	–0.006	0.013	0.012*	915
College education for head	0.017	0.020*	0.016*	765

* Significant at 0.05 level.

ployment. In addition, the financial advantage to parents themselves will depend on the likelihood that teenagers will remain economically tied when they become adults. Children may be more likely to stay at home in households that own land (to be passed on to a son or daughter). It could be to the advantage of such households to invest more in their children.

Some analyses of aggregate saving data have shown that an increase in the relative number of elderly household members depresses saving. This is an important phenomenon because it implies that, over the demographic transition, age structure changes will have, to some extent, offsetting effects. As the number of children declines saving rises, but at later stages of the demographic transition, saving may decline as the number of elderly increases (Leff 1969).

The analysis of household data distinguishes two ways in which the number of elderly affects saving. The first, the effect of the age of the head, is discussed below. The second, the addition of elderly household members, is summarized in Table 4.5. These results provide no evidence that, controlling for the age of the household head, an additional elderly member depresses saving. Older women have no significant effect on saving one way or another. An additional elderly man actually depresses the consumption ratio and increases the saving ratio. Furthermore, the magnitude of the effect is quite substantial for the entire sample and for many of the subgroups. It is interesting to note, however, that for heads with secondary and college education, the presence of an additional elderly male member depresses saving. The estimated coefficient is not statistically significant, however.

Table 4.5. Household composition and the consumption ratio: Number of adults

	Partial effect of adult			
	Age 20–59		Age 60 and older	
Sample characteristics	Female	Male	Female	Male
Full sample	-0.008*	-0.010*	-0.0001	-0.022*
Landowners	-0.010	-0.000	-0.023	-0.028
Land renters	0.014	-0.015	0.033	-0.034
Business persons and professionals	-0.016*	-0.014*	0.009	0.009
Employees and the unemployed	-0.003	-0.017*	0.008	-0.047*
Primary education for head	-0.006*	-0.011*	-0.002	-0.024*
Secondary education for head	-0.017*	-0.013	0.017	0.053
College education for head	-0.020	0.017	-0.020	0.004

* Significant at 0.05 level.

The number of elderly also influences aggregate saving because an increase in their numbers will raise the number of households with elderly heads. These results, summarized in more detail below, show that the saving ratio declines systematically with the age of the head. Households headed by the elderly save about 1 percent less of their income than those headed by someone 55 to 64 years of age, but nearly 4 percent less than households with a head in the 25 to 39 age range. The net effect of aging, then, is difficult to judge. The impact on saving will depend on the extent to which the elderly establish separate households and the exact nature of changes in the age structure. However, the forecasts to which we turn below provide a convenient way of summarizing the impact of the number of elderly. These show that at least between now and 2015, an increase in the number of elderly will not depress aggregate saving.

Household size and scale effects. The impact of household size, per se, on the consumption ratio is assessed by calculating the change in the consumption ratio were the average number of members in each age and sex category to decrease by a given percentage holding all other variables constant. The impact of such a change is of interest in judging the impact of extended families. One might think of siblings with identical childbearing histories who choose to live in separate households rather than together.[6] To judge the impact of a decline in household size, then, the change in the consump-

6. This is a theoretical construct and not a characterization of extended households in Thailand, which are typically of the stem type (see Chapter 2).

tion ratio accompanying a 50-percent decline in the number of members in each age category was calculated. The calculated impact of such a change is to reduce the consumption ratio by about one-quarter of 1 percentage point. In sum, there is no evidence of scale effects.

Household type. The consumption function is specified so as to distinguish four types of households: family households with a male head, family households with a female head, men living alone, and women living alone.[7] The effect associated with household type is shown in Table 4.6, which gives adjusted mean values for the consumption and saving ratio. The adjusted means give the calculated values if all variables, except those governing household type, are set to the mean value for the entire sample.[8] This allows us to compare, for example, saving by female-headed and male-headed family households were there no difference in household size or composition, per capita expenditures, or socioeconomic status. It is important to understand that this is a theoretical construct intended to identify the effect of household type, per se. Thus, one-person household adjusted means are calculated setting the number of member variables to their sample means even though one-person households cannot have more than one member. But by controlling for household size and other variables in this manner, we can quantify the unique effect associated with one-person households beyond the effect associated with variation in household size observed across all types of households. Thus, any observed differences across household type can be traced to differences in demographic composition or other characteristics that distinguish different types of households.

The statistical results suggest that household type may not be a particularly important determinant of saving. Men living alone have somewhat lower saving rates than calculated for other types of households, and households with single female heads have somewhat higher saving ratios. However, the differences shown are not statistically significant for the full sample or for any of the subsamples.

Age of head. The effect of the age of the household head is estimated by including variables that distinguish five age categories, under 25, 25–39, 40–49, 50–59, and 60 or older. The relationship between household consumption and the age of head is statistically significant. The estimated age profile of saving, calculated by holding all other variables at their sample means, is shown in Figure 4.3. The age profile is hump-shaped, reaching

---

7. Primary-individual households and groups of unrelated individuals are treated as several one-person households by the 1981 Socio-Economic Survey. In the great majority of family households headed by a woman, the husband of the head is not present in the household.

8. The resulting values are adjusted to conform to national income statistics on aggregate household saving.

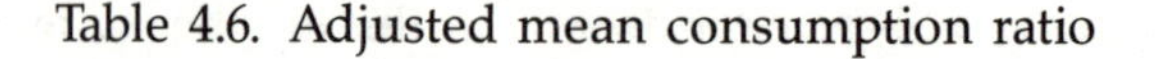

Table 4.6. Adjusted mean consumption ratio

Household type	Consumption ratio	Saving ratio
Intact	0.867	0.133
Single female-headed	0.862	0.138
One-person, male	0.875	0.124
One-person, female	0.867	0.133

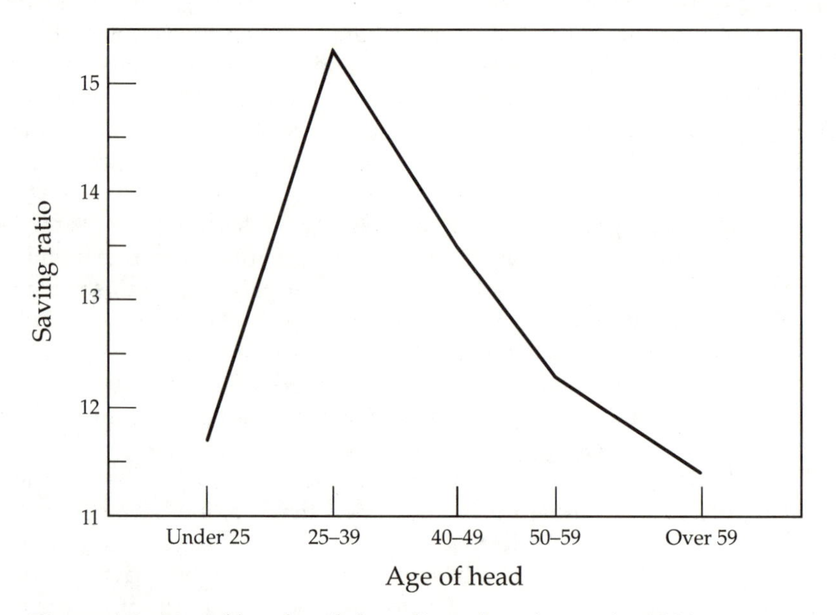

Figure 4.3. Age of head and the adjusted saving ratio: 1981

its peak at 15 percent of disposable income among household heads age 25 to 39. Households with a head under age 25 or over 60 have the lowest saving ratios—in the 11 to 12 percent range.

The impact of the age of head is quite substantial and, by itself, would lead to a decline in the household saving ratio as population aging sets in. However, other demographic factors, namely the compositional effects described above, will offset the age-of-head effect. The net impact on consumption and saving is assessed below using forecasts of aggregate saving.

The effect of control variables. The regression equation also includes a number of control variables that measure different dimensions of socioeconomic status, including residence (farm versus nonfarm), occupation, and wealth (size of farm). The finding that seems to stand out is a positive association between saving and socioeconomic status or wealth. Farm households with large landholdings have higher saving than those with small landholdings; farm renters with large land areas have higher saving than those with small land areas; and entrepreneurial/professional, technical, and managerial households have higher saving than employee households.

FORECASTS

Description of Methodology

The saving ratio is forecast using aggregate level demographic data generated by HOMES (see Chapter 2) and using exogenously supplied assumptions about growth in per capita income. The saving ratio is calculated separately for intact family households, family households with single male and single female heads, male one-person households, and female one-person households. For each household type, forecasts are further broken down by the age of the household head. Of course, the average saving ratio for all households of each type, all households with heads of specified age, and all households combined are also calculated.

Forecast saving ratios are calculated using the estimated consumption equation and three types of independent variables: per capita disposable income, demographic characteristics of the household, and control variables.

Forecasts of the age of head, type of households, and number of male and female members in five-year age groups is a direct output of HOMES. For forecast purposes, however, we require the number of members in age groupings that do not correspond to the five-year schema. Standard demographic procedures for interpolating single-year age data from five-year age groupings are used to obtain the number of members of ages 0–2, 3–12, and 13–19.[9]

The socioeconomic status variables included in the regression equations are treated as control variables for purposes of forecasting. In other words, the proportion of households in each socioeconomic category is held constant at the 1981 level observed for each age of head and household type group. The proportions are obtained directly from the 1981 Socio-Economic Survey (NSO 1985).

Per capita disposable income is not required to forecast changes in the saving ratio, because income is not an independent variable in the consumption function. Forecast income is used in two other ways, however. First, the saving ratio for all households combined will be affected by changes in the distribution of income from high saving to low saving households

9. Sprague multipliers are employed for this purpose.

or vice versa. Second, we also use forecast per capita disposable income to present forecasts in the total amount of national saving in addition to the national saving ratio.

Disposable income is expected to rise as a consequence of general improvements in the standard of living in Thailand and forecasts presented below are based on an assumed rate of growth in per capita income of 4 percent per annum. In addition, household income will be affected directly by changes in household composition, e.g., the forecast decline in the number of young adults per household. These demographic factors have been incorporated into the forecasts using parameter estimates obtained by regressing the log of per capita income on the same set of independent variables used to analyze the consumption ratio. For more details, see Chapter 5.

Number of Members

The average number of members per household is projected to decline from 5.3 members in 1980 to 3.7 in 2005 (Table 4.7).[10] The greatest declines are among households with heads 35–49 years of age. In 1980, for example, households with heads 40–44 years of age averaged 6.4 members as compared with only 4.2 members in 2005. Because the greatest decline is expected among households at the peak of their family size, variation across the life cycle was considerably greater in 1980 than is expected for 2005.

The greatest part of the decline in average household size can be traced to reduced numbers of children per household. Between 1980 and 2005, the number of children under 3 in intact households declines by 50 percent or more depending upon the age of the head's spouse (Table 4.8). Similar percentage declines are registered for older children and teenagers, as well. The decline in the average number of adults per household is quite dependent on the age of the (male) head or his wife. Among older heads, the number of adults 20 to 59 years of age declines by roughly one-quarter. But in the case of households with younger heads, no decline is anticipated. The number of elderly per household is anticipated to remain constant during the period in question.

Forecasting Household Saving

Detailed forecasts for the saving ratio in 1980 and 2005 are presented in Tables 4.9 and 4.10. The average saving ratios for one-person households in each of the five-year age categories do not change over the forecast interval because they experience no change in their demographic composition. But because of changes in the age distribution of heads, the average for

10. These averages do not include primary-individual households and so differ somewhat from projected values presented in Chapter 2.

Table 4.7. Average number of household members: 1980 and 2005

Age of head	1980	2005
Less than 25	3.72	3.17
25–29	4.60	3.48
30–34	5.32	3.69
35–39	6.09	4.11
40–44	6.35	4.22
45–49	6.33	4.05
50–54	5.92	3.76
55–59	5.25	3.41
60–64	4.85	3.27
65–69	4.54	3.10
70–74	4.48	3.18
75 and older	4.54	3.28
Total	5.31	3.72

Note: All values calculated at the mean.

Table 4.8. Age of members, intact households: 1980 and 2005

	Age of spouse of head			
Age of member	25–29	40–44	55–59	70–74
1980				
0–2	0.74	0.36	0.30	0.28
3–12	1.61	1.92	0.81	0.96
13–19	0.18	1.65	0.93	0.41
20–59	2.16	2.62	3.17	1.35
60+	0.08	0.12	0.56	1.98
Total	4.77	6.67	5.77	4.98
2005				
0–2	0.35	0.13	0.10	0.09
3–12	0.95	0.66	0.30	0.35
13–19	0.10	0.85	0.33	0.21
20–59	2.12	2.64	2.51	1.07
60+	0.08	0.14	0.55	1.98
Total	3.60	4.42	3.79	3.70

Table 4.9. Calculated saving ratio: 1980

Age of head	Intact	Single male head	Single female head	One-person male	One-person female	All combined
Less than 25	0.103	0.109	0.102	0.097	0.105	0.103
25–29	0.139	0.156	0.138	0.145	0.160	0.140
30–34	0.136	0.154	0.130	0.154	0.149	0.137
35–39	0.139	0.147	0.133	0.146	0.146	0.139
40–44	0.126	0.123	0.116	0.123	0.136	0.125
45–49	0.133	0.131	0.128	0.110	0.121	0.132
50–54	0.134	0.110	0.121	0.100	0.111	0.131
55–59	0.138	0.123	0.128	0.104	0.099	0.134
60–64	0.124	0.132	0.114	0.097	0.073	0.121
65–69	0.119	0.149	0.110	0.110	0.076	0.118
70–74	0.117	0.127	0.106	0.096	0.088	0.112
75 and older	0.116	0.165	0.094	0.105	0.084	0.109
Total	0.131	0.133	0.120	0.123	0.112	0.130

Table 4.10. Projected saving ratio: 2005

Age of head	Intact	Single male head	Single female head	One-person male	One-person female	All combined
Less than 25	0.105	0.111	0.106	0.097	0.105	0.105
25–29	0.146	0.154	0.142	0.145	0.160	0.146
30–34	0.148	0.154	0.138	0.154	0.149	0.148
35–39	0.155	0.152	0.145	0.146	0.146	0.154
40–44	0.142	0.132	0.128	0.123	0.136	0.140
45–49	0.145	0.140	0.136	0.110	0.121	0.144
50–54	0.141	0.115	0.126	0.100	0.111	0.137
55–59	0.140	0.126	0.130	0.104	0.098	0.136
60–64	0.125	0.135	0.117	0.097	0.073	0.123
65–69	0.122	0.152	0.114	0.110	0.076	0.122
70–74	0.123	0.140	0.112	0.096	0.088	0.119
75 and older	0.122	0.187	0.100	0.105	0.084	0.121
Total	0.142	0.140	0.127	0.124	0.111	0.140

all one-person male households combined rises moderately whereas the average for all one-person female households declines moderately.

The saving ratio for family households is forecast to rise from 13.1 percent in 1980 to 14.2 percent in 2005 for intact households, from 13.3 to 14.0 percent for households headed by single males, and from 12.0 to 12.7 percent for households headed by single females.

Changes in the relationship between age of head and saving is portrayed graphically in Figure 4.4. Saving for every age category of household head increases between 1980 and 2005, but the greatest increases are observed among households with children, i.e., households with heads 25–49 years of age. Saving also increases moderately for households with heads 65 years of age and older. This is also a consequence of declines in the number of children in their households.

One of the interesting implications of the change in the age profile of saving illustrated in Figure 4.4 is that a significantly higher percentage of household saving will originate in households with a head 35–49 years of age than in the past. We estimate that in 1980 a little under 39 percent of all saving originated in these households but by 2005 the figure will increase to almost 45 percent. At the same time, the percentage of saving originating among households with a head under age 35 is forecast to decline by 4.4 percentage points. Such a change would presumably affect the relative demand for alternative financial instruments, e.g., stocks versus bonds, could conceivably affect the term structure of interest rates, and should certainly influence the marketing strategies of financial institutions.

Forecasts at five-year intervals from 1980 to 2015 are presented in Table 4.11. A steady increase in the household saving ratio from 1980 is anticipated to continue through the year 2000. Thereafter, the saving ratio is relatively constant at about 14 percent of disposable income. The beneficial effects of fertility decline apparently will be captured prior to the turn of the century.

The gradual increase in the saving ratio together with rising income combine to boost the absolute amount of domestic resources supplied by households for investment purposes by substantial amounts. Monthly aggregate household saving is calculated to rise from 5.9 billion baht in 1980 to 32.6 billion baht by 2005 and to 55.5 million baht by 2015. Thus, household saving increases tenfold over the 35-year projection period, representing a rate of growth of 6.4 percent per annum. The forecasts elaborated here are conservative in the sense that they are based on statistical analysis of the full sample. But the analysis of subsamples indicates that the more "modern" segments of the population, households with more educated heads and households employed in nonagricultural activities, tend to be more sensitive to demographic change. Of course households with relatively young heads are those particularly likely to participate in the modern sector in

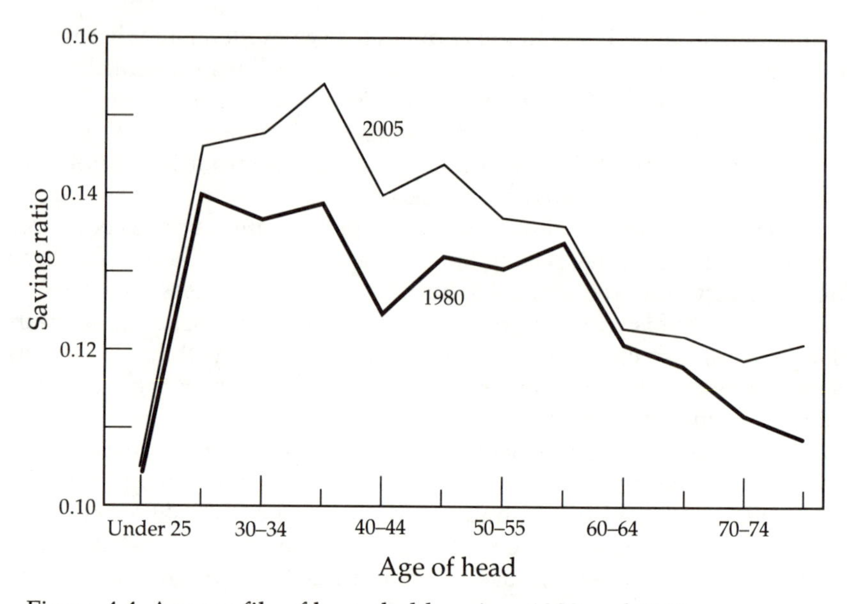

Figure 4.4. Age profile of household saving: 1980 and 2005

Table 4.11. Projected savings: 1980–2015

Year	Saving ratio	Aggregate monthly saving[a]
1980	0.130	5,853
1985	0.132	8,571
1990	0.135	12,393
1995	0.137	17,531
2000	0.139	24,199
2005	0.140	32,628
2010	0.140	42,967
2015	0.140	55,498

a. Millions of baht.

the near future and also the ones who will experience significant declines in the number of children. Thus, a more complete analysis would imply a more significant increase in household saving by 2005. How much greater might the increase be? To obtain an outside estimate of the change, our simulation exercise was repeated using coefficients of the number of children for households with college-educated heads. The result was to increase household saving by an additional 7 to 14 percent depending on the age of the household head, with heads ages 35–49 experiencing the greatest gains. Overall saving is forecast to reach 15 percent by 2005, exceeding the record levels of the 1970s.

An area deserving further scrutiny is the potential effect of changes in the structure of the Thai economy and accompanying urbanization. Our forecasts do not account for these effects, which could be quite significant. High rates of saving are characteristic of four groups: large landowners; employers in fishing, forestry, etc.; entrepreneurs with employees; and professional, technical, and managerial workers. Low rates of saving are characteristic of four other groups: farm laborers, nonfarm laborers, small landowners, and small land renters. Thus, the relative decline of the agricultural sector almost certain to occur over the next two decades may well serve to increase saving. This would be particularly true if agricultural landholdings are not fragmented. These results also suggest that the larger scale entrepreneurial class (entrepreneurs with employees and large landowners) makes a relatively important contribution to national saving. However, it is certainly conceivable that smaller landowners and smaller scale entrepreneurs are investing directly in their enterprises and that this is not captured as fully as more monetized saving and investment.

CONCLUSIONS

Previous research on aggregate saving trends has concluded that a number of Asian countries, Japan and Korea being notable examples, have achieved higher national saving rates as a consequence of declining fertility and shifts in age structure. Although Thailand has experienced rapid fertility decline in recent years, there is no evidence that saving has risen as a result. In fact, the national saving rate has declined markedly over the last 10 years as has the household saving rate.

Analysis of household saving patterns in 1980–81 indicates, however, that declines in child dependency should lead to higher saving in the future. Over the next 15 years, given projected declines in fertility, the household saving ratio is forecast to rise by 1.0 percentage point or by about 8 percent. If actual events bear out these forecasts, household saving rates should approach the record levels achieved during the 1970s. Moreover, the analysis presented here provides some support for an even more significant increase that would reach or surpass the saving rates recorded by households during the 1970s.

5
Consumer Expenditures

by Andrew Mason, Varai Woramontri, and Robert M. Kleinbaum

In this chapter the 1981 Socio-Economic Survey (NSO 1985) is analyzed to determine how rising income and changes in the demographic character of households affect the allocation of resources among alternative goods and services. The resulting statistical analysis is then combined with household projections and alternative scenarios about economic growth to forecast consumer expenditure to the year 2005 and to assess the relative importance of demographic and economic factors as determinants of spending patterns.

Per capita disposable expenditure is expected to rise as a consequence of general improvements in the standard of living in Thailand. The base forecast assumes that per capita expenditure will grow at 4 percent per annum due to general increases in productivity. But in addition to this growth, per capita expenditure per household will change in response to changing demographic characteristics. For example, declines in family size lead to additional increases in per capita expenditure depending on the age and sex of household members.

Overall, per capita expenditure by intact family households is forecast to grow at around 5 percent per annum through 2005, depending on the age of the household head. The greatest increases are among intact households with large families and low per capita expenditures in 1980. For example, in 1980 per capita expenditure for intact households headed by males 45–49 years of age was around 520 baht; by 2005 it is forecast to be around 1,900 baht, representing an annual growth rate of about 5.2 percent. The smallest increases are forecast for households with few children living at home, i.e., households with older heads; those with heads in their late 60s grow at about 4.7 per annum.

Total monthly private expenditures are forecast to rise from a value of about 26 billion baht per month in 1980 to nearly 133 billion baht per month in 2005, representing a growth rate of about 6.5 percent per annum. The most rapid growth of private expenditures, 7.1 percent per annum, is estimated for the 1980–85 interval. By the end of the forecast interval, 2000–2005, the rate of growth will have slowed to 5.9 percent per annum.

The most significant change forecast for 2005 is the dramatic decline in the importance of expenditures on food and nonalcoholic beverages. These expenditures will decrease from over one-half the family's budget in 1980 to only one-third of the budget in 2005. Although in percentage terms expenditures on food and nonalcoholic beverages grow more slowly than do expenditures on other goods and services, the absolute increase is the greatest: monthly expenditures on food rise from about 13 billion baht per month in 1980 to 45 billion baht per month in 2005. Expenditures on housing and household operations are forecast to increase significantly during this period. The percentage of the budget devoted to housing is forecast to increase from 19.4 percent to 22.3 percent between 1980 and 2005.

The share of the household budget devoted to goods and services other than food or housing is also expected to shift significantly—monthly expenditures for these items increase from about 32 percent in 1985 to nearly 43 percent in 2005. The most notable increases are allocations for miscellaneous goods and services (forecast to increase by about 7 percent) and transport and communication (nearly a 5 percent increase). The percentage of the budget allocated for recreation and reading also is expected to increase but by a lesser amount (1 percent). In each of these categories total expenditure is forecast to increase tenfold over the 25-year period. Allocations for apparel and alcohol and tobacco, however, drop significantly by about 3 percent for alcohol and tobacco and by over 4 percent for apparel. Allocations for medical care, personal care, and education each decrease by about 1.5 percent to 2 percent.

Changes in expenditure shares can be attributed to two broad causes: economic growth and demographic change. Analysis of our forecasts demonstrates that expenditures are influenced more by economic growth than by demographic factors. These results are obtained through extensive analysis that involves the following steps: (1) specification of expenditure equations; (2) preparation of survey data; (3) statistical analysis; and (4) forecasting. Each of these steps is described in the following section.

SURVEY ANALYSIS

Specification of Expenditure Equations

Three broad sets of factors can be identified that determine the likely course of consumer expenditures in any country. First, rising income induces changes in expenditure patterns as households devote a smaller share of their resources to necessities and a greater share to luxuries. Second, price changes lead households to substitute items that are less expensive for those that are more expensive. And, third, changing demographic characteristics affect expenditure decisions as households respond to the changing needs of family members.

Ideally, any analysis of consumer expenditure data would incorporate each of these factors. Quite frequently and in the analysis presented here, income and demographic effects are analyzed whereas price effects are not. There are two reasons why price effects are ignored. First, it is difficult to analyze price effects accurately using survey data for a single year because regional price differences may be small and are difficult to measure. Second, even if reliable estimates of price effects are obtained, it is very difficult to forecast price changes. To estimate price changes in a closed economy requires analysis of both the demand and supply side and simultaneous forecasting of prices and expenditures. In an open economy, prices are determined by the world market for which there are no generally accepted price forecasts. Thus, the forecasts presented here are agnostic with respect to price changes, i.e., forecasts are based on the presumption that *relative* prices will not change.

In addition to income and demographic variables, the specification of the expenditure equations also includes control variables that capture important characteristics of the household but do not vary systematically over time. These factors explain differences among households but have an unchanging effect on forecast aggregates.

The general form of the expenditure equation to be estimated is:

$$s_i = \beta_0 + \beta_1 \ln Y/N + \beta_2 (\ln Y/N)_2 + \beta_3 AGE + \beta_4 AGE$$
$$+ \beta_5 FEM + \beta_6 OPM + \beta_7 OPF$$
$$+ \beta_8 N_1 + \cdots + \beta_{7+k} Nk + \beta_{8+k} X_1 + \cdots + \beta_{7+k+j} Xj + e \qquad (1)$$

where s_i is expenditure on category i divided by total expenditure, Y/N is per capita disposable income, AGE is the age of the household head, FEM is a dummy variable that takes the value of 1 for households headed by a woman, OPM and OPF are dummy variables for men and women living by themselves, Nk is the number of household members in age and sex category k, and Xj is a control variable.

The functional form of the expenditure equations is selected so that it does not violate axioms of consumer demand theory and is sufficiently flexible to capture the determinants of expenditures in a variety of settings.[1] An attractive feature of the specification is that it is easy to estimate, to interpret, and to use for forecasting. The choice of specification was based on a number of considerations. The effect of income on the demand for a good is generally measured by income elasticity—the percentage change in expenditure on the good induced by a 1 percent increase in income. Some specifications assume that the income elasticity for each good is constant; however, income elasticity must vary with the household's income for the household's budget constraint to be satisfied. The specification employed here allows for income elasticity to vary with the level of income. The income elasticity, η_i, can be calculated using estimated coefficients from the share equation:

$$\eta_i = 1 + \frac{\beta_1 + 2\beta_2 \ln Y/N}{s_i} . \tag{2}$$

A variety of specifications have been proposed for including demographic effects in expenditure equations (Pollak and Wales 1980, 1981; Deaton et al. 1989). The most widely discussed issue is whether demographic translating or demographic scaling is the most appropriate specification. The idea behind translating is that an additional household member requires certain expenditures that are essentially independent of the overall standard of living of the household. For example, a newborn child costs so much for food, clothing, etc., in the same sense that a particular good costs the same amount irrespective of the characteristics of the household purchasing it. The idea behind scaling, however, is that members have a claim on household resources that varies with their demographic characteristics. For example, a child might "require" 50 percent of the expenditure that an adult would "require" irrespective of the level of income. Thus, the cost of any member will vary in direct proportion to the household's income. The specification employed here uses demographic scaling because the impact on any expenditure category of a change in the number of members of type k varies in direct proportion with total expenditures.

In addition, the specification employed here allows for scale economies. The extent of scale economies can be judged by calculating the impact of an equal percentage increase in the number of members of all types using the estimated coefficients of the number of members.

The age categories used to distinguish household members are based on judgment and preliminary analysis. Small age categories are used to dis-

1. For a comprehensive, general discussion of techniques for analyzing consumer expenditure data, see Deaton and Muellbauer (1980).

tinguish among young members who are undergoing the greatest developmental changes. The analysis reported below uses three age categories for those under age 20, 0–2, 3–12, and 13–19, and only two age categories to distinguish adults, 20–59 and 60 and older. The specification also distinguishes the impact of male and female members, although in the case of Thailand gender differences prove to be relatively unimportant.

The age of the head of the household and its square are included to capture life-cycle effects beyond those captured by including the number of members, including the head, of each age. The clearest rationale for including the age of the head is for households in which the head is the principal earner. In a pure life-cycle model, expenditure shares are determined by lifetime earnings rather than current earnings. Because earnings generally rise with the age of the household head, the difference between current and lifetime average earnings is systematically related to the age of the head. Consequently, for luxuries age of head should be inversely related to the budget share and for necessities age of head should be positively related to the budget share. Or, equivalently, the partial effects on budget shares of per capita income and age of head should be of opposite sign.

It may be that expenditures on some goods are more closely related to lifetime earning than others. An obvious example is housing. In general, one might plausibly expect the life-cycle argument to prove more robust with expenditures on durables than on other goods. Age of head may also capture life-cycle phenomena other than the simple relationship between current and lifetime average earnings. And, in particular, age of head may pick up variation in consumption "needs" associated with the age of household members, particularly because very broad age categories are used to include adult members in the expenditure equations.

The final demographic variables included are ones that distinguish consumption patterns among different types of households, those headed by females, and men and women living alone. The principal motivation for including these variables is the fact that these different types of households are projected separately and, using the results of the analysis, forecasts of consumption patterns by type of household are provided below.

In addition to the factors described above, a number of background characteristics are controlled for in the analysis undertaken here. Particular emphasis is given to occupation, socioeconomic status, and place of residence.

Data and Estimation Procedure

Statistical analysis is based on the 1981 Socio-Economic Survey (NSO 1985), conducted throughout the Kingdom by the National Statistical Office (NSO) during the 12-month period February 1981 through January 1982. The primary objective of the survey was to assess patterns and levels of household expenditure and income and to relate variations in expenditure patterns to differences in household characteristics. A detailed description of the survey is provided in Chapter 4.

Consumer expenditures were divided into 10 broad categories, which with a few exceptions conform to the conventions followed by the NSO. Tobacco products and alcoholic beverages were combined into a single expenditure category and nonconsumption expenditures, e.g., gifts, insurance premiums, lottery tickets, and interest payments, were combined with miscellaneous consumption expenditures. Direct taxes, counted as a nonconsumption expenditure by NSO, were not included as an expenditure item.

Two alternative measures of income are used: per capita disposable income and, as a proxy, per capita expenditure. The advantage of per capita expenditure is that it is less subject to year-to-year fluctuations than income, making it a more reliable measure of permanent income. This is advantageous particularly for farm households or entrepreneurial households, which often experience wide fluctuations in income. Nevertheless, using per capita expenditure for analyzing expenditures on high cost items, e.g., consumer durables, may be ill-advised. Years in which a consumer purchases a car, for example, should have higher expenditure than normal because of the lumpiness of the expenditure. Thus, the use of expenditure as a proxy may lead to a downward-biased estimate of income elasticity. The analysis carried out here uses both per capita expenditure and per capita disposable income as regressors.

Disposable income is the sum of all receipts, including earnings, property income, transfers, insurance proceeds, lottery winnings, and non-money income, e.g., foods produced for home consumption and the rental value of owner-occupied housing. From this value, direct taxes are subtracted to obtain disposable income.

The demographic characteristics of households are distinguished in a number of ways. First, households are distinguished using a dummy variable that takes the value of 1 if the head is a female and zero if the head of the household is male. One-person male households and one-person female households are also distinguished using dummy variables. Second, the demographic composition of household membership is captured using a series of variables assigned a value equal to the number of members who are males or females at selected ages. The following age categories are used for both males and females: 0–2, 3–12, 13–19, 20–59, and 60 and older. The number of members variable includes heads, as well as other household members. Third, the age of the household head and its square are included as regressors.

Finally, a series of dummy variables is employed to measure socioeconomic status of the household. These variables are used in lieu of variables that measure occupation of the head and household assets. Occupation of the head is available but is adequately captured by the socioeconomic status variables. Socioeconomic status is based on a combination of occupation and economic status. (Household assets are not available from the survey.) Farm owners are distinguished from farm renters and are further distinguished by the size of their landholdings. Self-employed households are distinguished by whether they have employees or not. A complete description of the socioeconomic variables is provided in Table 5.1.

Table 5.2 reports summary statistics for each of the variables used in the statistical analysis. Items are weighted so as to obtain a representative estimate for Thailand as a whole. (The weighting procedure is described below.)

The shares of consumer expenditures devoted to each category were regressed on the independent variables described above. Two sets of regressions were estimated: one using per capita expenditures as an independent variable and the other using per capita disposable income. There are no special statistical problems associated with estimating share equations. Although cross-equation information exists (the shares must sum to 1), there is no loss of efficiency from using least-squares regression if the right-hand side variables are the same in all share equations.[2] An additional advantage of ordinary least squares is that calculated budget shares will always sum to 1 as long as the right-hand side variables are identical in all share equations. The estimates presented below are obtained using weighted least-squares regression. The weights used are those calculated by the World Bank for the 1981 Socio-Economic Survey (NSO 1985), obtained by comparing 1980 census tabulations of the number of households to sample sizes in each sampling unit (World Bank 1985). Because a weighting scheme different from that used by the NSO of Thailand is used here, the results are not directly comparable to those in NSO publications.

The dependence of the natural log of per capita expenditure and per capita income on demographic characteristics of the household and socioeconomic status are analyzed using the same independent variables, with the exception of the log of expenditure/income and its square. Again, coefficients are estimated using weighted least squares.

Results of the Analysis

In general terms, the statistical analysis is reasonably successful. Coefficients are estimated with a fairly high degree of accuracy. The independent variables, taken together, explain as little as 3 percent of the variance in the case of medical care expenditures and as much as 40 percent of the variance in the case of food and nonalcoholic beverages. Of the two sets of regressions, a consistently higher percentage of the variation is explained when per capita expenditures, rather than per capita income, is used as

2. See Kmenta (1971) for a discussion of seemingly unrelated regression.

Table 5.1. Description of variables used in expenditure analysis

Name	Definition
s_i	Expenditure on category i as proportion of total expenditures 1 = Food and nonalcoholic beverages 2 = Alcoholic beverages and tobacco products 3 = Apparel and footwear 4 = Housing and household operations 5 = Medical care 6 = Personal care 7 = Transport and communication 8 = Recreation and reading 9 = Education 10 = Ceremonies and miscellaneous items
LNE	Natural logarithm of expenditures per capita
LNE2	Square of *LNE*
LNY	Natural logarithm of disposable income per capita
LNY2	Square of *LNY*
NM_i	Number of male household members in age category i
NF_i	Number of female household members in age category i 1 = 0–2 years of age 2 = 3–12 years of age 3 = 13–19 years of age 4 = 20–59 years of age 5 = Age 60 and older
FEM	Female head (1 if female head, 0 otherwise)
OPM	One-person, male (equal to 1, 0 otherwise)
OPF	One-person, female (equal to 1, 0 otherwise)
V16	Farm operator, small landowner (equal to 1, 0 otherwise)
V17	Farm operator, medium landowner (equal to 1, 0 otherwise)
V18	Farm operator, large landowner (equal to 1, 0 otherwise)
V19	Farm operator, small land renter (equal to 1, 0 otherwise)
V20	Farm operator, large land renter (equal to 1, 0 otherwise)
V21	Farm operator, fishing, forestry, etc. (equal to 1, 0 otherwise)
V22	Entrepreneur, paid employees (equal to 1, 0 otherwise)
V23	Entrepreneur, no paid employees (equal to 1, 0 otherwise)
V24	Professional, technical, and managerial (equal to 1, 0 otherwise)
V25	Laborers, farm (equal to 1, 0 otherwise)
V26	Laborers, nonfarm (equal to 1, 0 otherwise)
V27	Clerical, sales and service workers (equal to 1, 0 otherwise)
V28	Production workers (equal to 1, 0 otherwise)
V29	Economically inactive (equal to 1, 0 otherwise)

a regressor. Because expenditures on durables are small and consumer finance is relatively unimportant, the discussion of results will focus on regressions using per capita expenditures.

The effect of income. The relationship between per capita expenditure and the composition of expenditure is summarized in Table 5.3. The expenditure elasticity is the percentage increase in expenditure on a given item yielded by a 1 percent increase in per capita expenditure. It is calculated using the coefficients of the per capita expenditure terms as explained above.

The impact of increased income (as proxied by expenditure per capita) on the composition of the budget is generally in keeping with the results obtained in studies of other countries. Expenditures on food and beverages increase more slowly than total expenditures and its share of the budget declines as households achieve higher standards of living. By contrast, expenditures on miscellaneous items, transport and communication, recreation, and to a lesser extent, education, medical care, and apparel, consume a larger share of the budget among higher income households. The shares devoted to housing, alcohol and tobacco, and personal care are less strongly influenced by income.

The expenditure elasticities reported in Table 5.3 are calculated at the mean value of per capita expenditure. As per capita expenditure increases over time, the elasticities will change depending on the coefficients of the squared expenditure term. For all expenditure categories but one the coefficient of the squared term is statistically significant but is generally of small magnitude. Thus, even fairly substantial changes in per capita expenditure are not associated with changes in the sign of the partial effect of expenditure on budget share.

Household size and scale effects. The impact of the number of household members on the composition of the budget is assessed by calculating the predicted change in budget shares assuming the average number of members in each age and sex category increases by a given percentage, holding all other variables constant. Budget shares will change as a consequence of scale economies. In general, goods that are jointly consumed are most likely to exhibit scale economies. Housing provides a clear example of a good with scale economies, because at least some rooms and facilities are shared among family members. Thus, if a household has 10 percent more members (and 10 percent more income), expenditures on housing would undoubtedly increase, but by less than 10 percent. Thus, the budget share of housing would decline.

The impact on budget shares of a 10-percent increase in average household size is shown in Table 5.4. Three expenditure categories exhibit scale economies: food, housing, and alcohol and tobacco products. Food and

Table 5.2. Summary statistics: 1981 Socio-Economic Survey of Thailand

Variable name	Mean	Standard deviation	Minimum value	Maximum value
Budget shares				
Food	0.5102	0.1626	0	0.9764
Alcohol and tobacco	0.0369	0.0516	0	0.6408
Apparel	0.0665	0.0837	0	0.6781
Housing	0.1859	0.1128	0	0.9502
Medical care	0.0320	0.0623	0	0.9458
Personal care	0.0226	0.0176	0	0.3256
Transport and communication	0.0539	0.0859	0	0.9294
Recreation and reading	0.0194	0.0411	0	0.6124
Education	0.0105	0.0227	0	0.6001
Miscellaneous	0.0621	0.0953	0	0.9291
Income and expenditure				
LNE	6.3555	0.9040	3.6775	11.5151
LNY	6.4243	0.8078	4.1799	10.8483
Number of members				
NM1	0.1220	0.3531	1	2
NM2	0.5685	0.8428	0	5
NM3	0.6864	1.3349	0	5
NM4	1.1809	1.1513	0	12
NM5	0.1418	0.3747	0	3
NF1	0.1353	0.3749	0	2
NF2	0.5429	0.8322	0	5
NF3	0.7159	1.3405	0	10

NF4	1.3208	1.1832	0	12
NF5	0.1833	0.4341	0	4
Household type				
FEM	0.2057	0.4190	0	1
OPM	0.0380	0.1983	0	1
OPF	0.0459	0.2170	0	1
Socioeconomic status				
V16	0.0983	0.2977	0	1
V17	0.1080	0.3217	0	1
V18	0.1393	0.3589	0	1
V19	0.0337	0.1872	0	1
V20	0.0280	0.1712	0	1
V21	0.0177	0.1366	0	1
V22	0.0308	0.1790	0	1
V23	0.1458	0.3658	0	1
V24	0.0751	0.2733	0	1
V25	0.0563	0.2388	0	1
V26	0.0193	0.1428	0	1
V27	0.0916	0.2990	0	1
V28	0.0828	0.2857	0	1
V29	0.0733	0.2701	0	1

Source: Compiled from data in NSO (1985).

Note: Number of observations = 11,892.

Table 5.3. Effects of income on expenditure: 1981

Expenditure category	Scale elasticity
Food	0.722
Alcohol and tobacco	0.979
Apparel	1.290
Housing	1.085
Medical care	1.299
Personal care	0.884
Transport and communication	1.708
Recreation and reading	1.655
Education	1.242
Miscellaneous	1.762

Source: Data used in calculating this table, and all other tables in this chapter, are from NSO (1985), unless otherwise noted.

Note: All values calculated at the mean.

Table 5.4. Household size and scale effects: 1981

Expenditure category	Scale elasticity
Food	–0.094
Alcohol and tobacco	–0.149
Apparel	0.284
Housing	–0.091
Medical care	0.009
Personal care	0.017
Transport and communication	0.448
Recreation and reading	0.416
Education	0.080
Miscellaneous	0.160

Note: All values calculated at the mean.

housing clearly fit the normal notion of scale economies. That alcohol and tobacco products would exhibit scale economies is somewhat puzzling.

When scale economies are present for some goods, the shares of other goods and services will increase, by definition, with household size. But the presence of scale diseconomies may result in some goods increasing by a greater amount than others. In percentage terms, the largest increases are for transportation and communication and for recreation and reading. Transportation is a particularly interesting category because there is clearly potential for joint consumption if private transportation, e.g., personal automobile or motorcycle, is an important transportation mode, because household members can pool. Offsetting this economy, however, is the possibility that transportation requirements may be greater for larger households because it is more difficult to locate one's residence so as to minimize transportation costs. Thus, if household members rely on public transport, an increase in household size may lead to disproportionate increases in transportation expenditure. Another aspect of increasing household size may account for the disproportionate increase in recreation and reading. To the extent that members of larger families have reduced privacy, the demand for outside recreational activities may increase.

Household composition. Statistical results show that, in general, the age composition of households has an important bearing on expenditure patterns whereas the sex composition does not. The analysis of composition is distinguished from the analysis of changes in the number of members by considering the impact on budget share of a shift in a household member from one age category to another or from male to female. The effect is calculated by taking the difference between the two coefficients that correspond to the two age-sex groups in question.

Table 5.5 provides a fairly complete picture of the impact on the food share of changes in composition. The first four columns quantify changes in the age composition of male or female members and the fifth column quantifies changes in the sex composition. The first row shows the change in the share devoted to food associated with the loss of a male child age 2 or younger and the gain of a male member within the four alternative age groups. The greatest positive impact is for a child in the 3–12 age category—the share devoted to food increases by 0.008. The most intuitive approach to the table is probably to look at the principal diagonal which essentially shows the impact of a household member aging. As a male reaches age 3, food expenditure shifts up substantially, drops back down as he reaches his teens, is unaffected by the transition to adulthood, and rises again as he passes 60 years of age. The effect associated with a 60 year old is not statistically significant, however. The age pattern for females is surprisingly similar to that observed for males. The only substantial difference is that associated with the presence of older women.

The last column in Table 5.5 confirms the observation that the age pattern of consumption is quite similar for male and female members. Except for the unreliably estimated impact of an elderly male member, having a female rather than a male member in the household has no noticeable impact on food expenditure.

The main features of the regression results required for an exhaustive analysis of compositional effects are reported in Appendix 5.1 and are summarized here. The presence of an adult male age 20–59 has a substantial positive

Table 5.5. Household composition and food expenditure: 1980

Age of member lost	Age of member gained				Female of same age
	3–12	13–19	20–59	60+	
Males					
0–2	0.008	0.001	0.001	0.006	0.002
3–12		-0.007	-0.007	-0.002	-0.001
13–19			0.000	0.005	-0.000
20–59				0.005	0.003
65+					-0.011
Females					
0–2	0.006	-0.001	-0.003	-0.006	
3–12		-0.006	-0.009	-0.012	
13–19			-0.003	-0.00	
20–59				-0.003	
65+					

impact on the consumption of alcoholic beverages and tobacco products. The presence of an elderly male or female has a substantial positive impact on expenditures on housing and household operations.

Medical care expenditures are higher in households with young children. Expenditures on education are lower for households with children under 3 and higher with children age 3 to 19. With the exception of alcohol and tobacco, the gender of household members has no apparent bearing on spending patterns.

Household type. The share equations are specified to allow us to distinguish four types of households: family households with a male head, family households with a female head, men living alone, and women living alone.[3] The effect associated with household type, per se, is shown in Table 5.6, which gives adjusted mean values for each of the expenditure categories.

The details of the method by which adjusted means are calculated are not included here, but the interpretation of the adjusted means is perfectly straightforward. The adjusted means give the calculated value of expenditure shares if all variables, except those governing household type, are set to the mean value for the entire sample. This allows us to compare, for ex-

3. Primary-individual households, groups of unrelated individuals, are treated as one-person households by the socioeconomic survey. In the great majority of family households headed by a woman, the husband of the head is not present in the household.

Table 5.6. Household type and adjusted mean expenditures: 1980

Expenditure category	Male head	Female head	One-person male	One-person female	All combined
Food	0.506	0.505	0.560	0.564	0.510
Alcohol and tobacco	0.040	0.023	0.063	0.021	0.037
Apparel	0.065	0.072	0.058	0.076	0.067
Housing	0.184	0.191	0.176	0.198	0.186
Medical care	0.032	0.036	0.015	0.027	0.032
Personal care	0.022	0.025	0.025	0.026	0.023
Transport and communication	0.057	0.051	0.034	0.024	0.054
Recreation and reading	0.020	0.022	0.009	0.014	0.019
Education	0.010	0.013	0.011	0.008	0.010
Miscellaneous	0.064	0.062	0.050	0.042	0.062

ample, food expenditures of female-headed and male-headed family households assuming no difference in household size or composition, per capita expenditures, or socioeconomic status. It is important to understand that this is a theoretical construct intended to identify the effect of household type, per se. Thus, one-person household adjusted means are calculated by setting the number of member variables to their sample's mean even though one-person households cannot have five or six members. But by controlling for household size and other variables in this manner, we can quantify the unique effect associated with one-person households beyond the effect associated with variation in household size observed across all types of households.

Comparison of expenditures by family households headed by a male with those headed by a female shows moderate differences. The share devoted to food is essentially the same for both household types, but male-headed family households spend about 20 percent more on alcohol and tobacco products than do female-headed family households. Female-headed households spend more on apparel, medical care, personal care, recreation, and education whereas male-headed family households spend about 6 percent more on transport and communication.

Other considerations aside, one-person households spend a substantially higher percentage of their budget on food and a substantially lower percentage on medical care, transport and communication, recreation, and ceremonies and miscellaneous items than do family households irrespective of the sex of the household head. Gender differences are, for the most part, similar to those observed for family households but of substantially greater magnitude. Expenditure on alcohol and tobacco products by single males is exceptionally high. Education expenditure, which is somewhat higher for single males than for single females, is the only case in which the gender pattern for one-person households is different from that for family households.

Age of head. The age of the household head and its square are included in the share equations allowing for a nonlinear relationship. For all but medical expenditures, either age or its square and usually both are statistically significant. Table 5.7 summarizes the age-of-head relationship by presenting adjusted means, which control for all variables except the age of the head. Three ages were selected—the mean age for the entire sample or 45 years of age in round numbers; one standard deviation below the mean or 30 years of age; and one standard deviation above the mean or 60 years of age.

One noteworthy feature of these results is the well-behaved nature of the relationship between the percentage share for each expenditure category and the age of head. Despite the flexibility of the function used, the estimated relationship is very nearly linear for every expenditure category over the age range shown. And in no case is there even a hint of a non-monotonic relationship.

The changes in expenditures are moderate but far from inconsequential. Over the 30-year age span shown, expenditures on alcohol and tobacco, housing, medical care, and miscellaneous items increase by 10 percent or more. Expenditures on apparel, personal care, transportation and communication, recreation and reading, and education decrease by at least 10 percent and, in some cases, by substantially more.

The statistical results are not consistent with a single theoretical explanation of the relationship between the age of the head and expenditure shares. There are two distinct reasons why shares should vary with the age of the head. First, per capita income for young heads generally understates lifetime economic prospects because earnings rise with the age and experience of workers. From a lifetime perspective, then, households with young heads will have higher lifetime earnings than households with old heads even though current per capita incomes are identical. Consequently, households with young heads will devote a higher percentage of their expenditures to luxuries (goods with high income elasticities) and a lower percentage to necessities (goods with low income elasticities). The negative relationship between food expenditures and age is inconsistent, then, with the first theoretical explanation. Of the nine expenditure categories with income elasticities substantially different from 1, only four had elasticities consistent with the age-of-head relationship. Clearly, age is not solely a proxy for the difference between current and lifetime resources.

Table 5.7. Age of head and adjusted mean expenditures: 1981

Expenditure category	Age of head 30	45	60
Food	0.519	0.510	0.502
Alcohol and tobacco	0.033	0.037	0.041
Apparel	0.076	0.067	0.057
Housing	0.177	0.186	0.195
Medical care	0.028	0.032	0.036
Personal care	0.026	0.023	0.019
Transport and communication	0.060	0.054	0.048
Recreation and reading	0.021	0.019	0.018
Education	0.012	0.011	0.009
Miscellaneous	0.049	0.062	0.076

A second explanation is that age is capturing demographic effects that are not adequately captured by the extensive number of demographic variables already included. The age of the head is captured to some extent because the head is included as a household member. However, the age category for prime-age adults is very broad (20–59) so that the age of the head may capture age differences within the broad range. One approach to judging this hypothesis is to compare the age relationship to the impact of substituting a member 60 or older for one 20 to 59. If this leads to a decline in the share, one might expect a negative relationship between age of head and share, as well. Again, the impact of changes in adult composition are only partially consistent with the age-of-head relationship. The impact of an elderly male, appropriate because most heads are men, is consistent with the age relationship in only four of 10 cases. On the other hand, the impact of an elderly woman is consistent in seven cases. In four cases, the impact of a 60-year-old man and a 60-year-old woman are the same and, in three of these cases, consistent with the share/age-of-head relationship.

The effect of control variables. The regression equations also include a number of control variables that measure different dimensions of socioeconomic status, including residence (farm versus nonfarm), occupation, and wealth (size of farm). There is no simple way to summarize these findings, and as they are not of central interest here they are not described. Results are reported in Appendix 5.1, however.

The determinants of per capita expenditure. The analysis of the effects of household membership on expenditure described above considers the impact of adding a member given per capita income or per capita expenditure. This approach neglects a second way in which changes in membership affect expenditure—namely, that per capita expenditure itself will be influenced by household membership. For example, the loss of a prime-age male should certainly lead to lower per capita expenditure. Or, the birth of an additional child should lead to lower per capita expenditure.

To determine the indirect impact of changes in household composition on expenditure, the statistical relationship between per capita expenditure and household composition is estimated using the same independent variables used in the share equations above. Of course, neither per capita expenditure nor its square are included as independent variables.

Interpretation of the results of this analysis should be undertaken with some caution, however, because per capita income or expenditure may influence the size and composition of households in a number of important ways. Income may affect childbearing, for example. If, in accord with traditional economic theory, men with higher earnings are likely to have more children, the analysis conducted below will underestimate the impact of a birth on per capita expenditure or income for any particular family. Likewise, if elderly parents are more likely to live with their offspring after they have depleted their economic resources, then coresidence is not a cause of reduced income but a consequence.

Detailed per capita expenditure and per capita income regression results indicate that the coefficients of the independent variables are estimated with considerable accuracy and that virtually every coefficient is significantly different from zero at the 99 percent confidence level. The independent variables, taken together, explain 50 percent of the variation in the dependent variable.

The detailed results presented in Appendix 5.1 are quite interesting in their own right. An increase in family size leads to reduced per capita expenditures irrespective of the sex or age of the member in question. Children have the greatest impact: an additional child under age 3 reduces per capita expenditure by about one-quarter, irrespective of the sex of the child, whereas an additional child between the ages of 3 and 12 reduces per capita expenditure by about 15 percent. The addition of older members reduces per capita expenditures by smaller percentages. An alternative way of looking at the impact of family size is to consider the impact of a 10-percent increase in family size that leaves age composition unaffected. A 10-percent increase in the number of male members leads to a 2.8 percent reduction in per capita expenditure, whereas a comparable increase in female members leads to a 2.5 percent reduction. The type of household also has a very important influence on per capita expenditure. Compared with family households with a male head, per capita expenditures of family households with a female head are 12.3 percent lower. By contrast, one-person male households have a per capita expenditure that is 52 percent higher and one-person female households have a per capita expenditure that is 35 percent higher.

Per capita expenditure bears a nonlinear relationship to age of the head. The peak of per capita expenditure occurs at age 38, when per capita expenditures are about 6 percent higher than for age 20 and about 9 percent higher than for age 60.

The relationship of per capita income to demographic variables is quite similar in all respects to the relationship of per capita expenditure; therefore, the details will not be discussed.

FORECASTS

Description of Methodology

Consumer expenditures are forecast using aggregate-level demographic data generated by HOMES and exogenously supplied assumptions about growth in per capita income. Budget shares are calculated separately for intact family households, family households with female heads, male one-person households, and female one-person households. For each household type, forecasts are further broken down by the age of the household head. Of course, average budget shares for all households of each type, all households with heads of specified age, and all households combined are also calculated.

Forecast budget shares are calculated using the estimated share equations and three types of independent variables: per capita disposable expenditures, demographic characteristics of the household, and control variables.

Per capita disposable expenditure is expected to rise as a consequence of general improvements in the standard of living in Thailand. Alternative scenarios are described that reflect different assumptions about the pace of economic growth. The base forecast, which will be discussed most extensively, assumes that per capita expenditure will grow at 4 percent per annum. But in addition to this growth, per capita expenditure per household will change in response to changing demographic characteristics. Based on regression estimates of per capita expenditure, declines in family size lead to additional increases in per capita expenditure depending on the age and sex of the members.

Forecasts of the age of head, type of households, and number of male and female members in five-year age groups is a direct output of HOMES. For forecast purposes, however, we require the number of members in age groupings that do not correspond to the five-year schema. Standard demographic procedures for interpolating single-year age data from five-year age groupings are used to obtain the number of members 0–2, 3–12, and 13–19 years of age.[4]

The socioeconomic status variables included in the regression equations are treated as control variables for purposes of forecasting. In other words, the proportion of households in each socioeconomic category is held constant at the 1981 level observed for each age of head and household type group.[5] The proportions are obtained directly from the 1981 Socio-Economic Survey (NSO 1985).

Description of Independent Variables

Number of members. The average number of members per household in 1980 is compared with the average number in 2005 in Table 5.8. Overall average household size is projected to decline from 5.3 to 3.7 members over the 25-year interval.[6] The greatest declines are among households with heads 35–49 years of age. In 1980, for example, households with heads 40–44 averaged 6.2 members as compared with only 4.2 members in 2005. Because the greatest decline is expected among households at the peak of their family size, variation across the life cycle was considerably greater in 1980 than is expected for 2005.

The greatest part of the decline in average household size can be traced to the reduced number of children per household (Table 5.9). Between 1980 and 2005, the number of children under 3 in intact households declines by 50 percent or more depending upon the age of the head's spouse. Similar percentage declines are registered for older children and teenagers. The decline in the average number of adults per household is quite dependent on the age of the head or his wife. Among older heads, the number of adults age 20 to 59 declines by roughly one-quarter. But in the case of households with younger heads, no decline is anticipated. The number of elderly per household is not anticipated to change between 1980 and 2005.

Per capita expenditures. Per capita expenditures calculated for 1980 are presented in Table 5.10. One-person households, which for the most part consist of a single earner, have the highest per capita expenditure and men living alone have expenditures that are generally 20 to 25 percent above that of their female counterparts. Total household expenditures for intact households are generally about 10 to 20 percent higher than for households headed by a single female. But because single-female headed households

4. Sprague multipliers are employed for this purpose.

5. This approach may lead to bias in the forecasts to the extent that socioeconomic variables measure more than relative social and economic position.

6. These averages do not include primary-individual households so they differ somewhat from projected values presented in Chapter 2.

Table 5.8. Average number of household members: 1980 and 2005

Age of head	1980	2005
Less than 25	3.72	3.17
25–29	4.60	3.48
30–34	5.32	3.69
35–39	6.09	4.11
40–44	6.35	4.22
45–49	6.33	4.05
50–54	5.92	3.76
55–59	5.25	3.41
60–64	4.85	3.27
65–69	4.54	3.10
70–74	4.48	3.18
75 and older	4.54	3.28
Total	5.31	3.72

are smaller, their per capita expenditures are comparable to those of intact households. For younger female heads, per capita expenditures are substantially greater, whereas for older female heads per capita expenditures are substantially lower.

Younger individuals living alone generally have higher per capita expenditures than do older individuals. Men in their early 30s spend about two-thirds more than do men in their late 60s and women in their early 30s spend about 50 percent more than women in their late 60s. In the case of family households, per capita expenditure is less systematically related to the age of the household head. For intact households with heads between 25 and 74 years of age, per capita expenditure varies from 519 baht per month up to 598 baht per month. The lowest per capita expenditure occurs among households with heads in their 40s whose households are at their peak size. The pattern for single-female-headed family households is somewhat different. Per capita expenditure is highest for women in their late 20s and early 30s, declines to a plateau at around 570 baht for women in their 40s and 50s, and then drops again for women who are 60 or older.

The simulated change in per capita expenditures is dominated by the assumed growth in productivity or living standards expected to occur independently of changes in the demographic composition of the household. As discussed above, per capita expenditures are expected to increase by 4 percent per year. But in addition, per capita expenditures per household are forecast to undergo additional growth in response to declines in the number of household members.

Table 5.9. Age of members, intact households: 1980 and 2005

	Age of spouse of head			
Age of member	25–29	40–44	55–59	70–74
1980				
Males				
0–2	0.38	0.18	0.15	0.15
3–12	0.82	0.98	0.42	0.51
13–19	0.09	0.86	0.47	0.21
20–59	1.08	1.34	1.36	0.67
60+	0.03	0.05	0.53	0.96
Females				
0–2	0.36	0.18	0.15	0.13
3–12	0.79	0.94	0.39	0.45
13–19	0.09	0.79	0.46	0.20
20–59	1.08	1.28	1.81	0.68
60+	0.05	0.07	0.03	1.02
Total	4.77	6.67	5.77	4.98
2005				
Males				
0–2	0.18	0.07	0.05	0.05
3–12	0.48	0.34	0.16	0.19
13–19	0.05	0.44	0.17	0.11
20–59	1.06	1.37	1.04	0.56
60+	0.03	0.06	0.52	0.96
Females				
0–2	0.17	0.06	0.05	0.04
3–12	0.47	0.32	0.14	0.16
13–19	0.05	0.41	0.16	0.10
20–59	1.06	1.27	1.47	0.51
60+	0.05	0.08	0.03	1.02
Total	3.60	4.42	3.79	3.70

Forecasts of per capita expenditures in 2005 are presented in Table 5.11. Because one-person households do not undergo change in demographic composition, the annual growth in forecast expenditures for any age–sex group is equal to 4 percent.

Per capita expenditure by intact family households grows at around 5 percent per annum depending on the age of the household head. The greatest

Table 5.10. Calculated per capita expenditures by household type: 1980

Age of head	Intact	Single male-headed	Single female-headed	One-person, male	One-person, female	All combined
Less than 25	640	864	744	1,989	1,787	709.0
25–29	598	974	686	2,236	2,275	659.0
30–34	553	864	641	2,566	1,830	606.0
35–39	531	711	589	2,275	1,859	572.0
40–44	520	707	570	1,827	1,557	555.0
45–49	519	766	543	1,707	1,592	558.0
50–54	573	640	577	1,704	1,347	605.0
55–59	583	598	570	1,637	1,251	616.0
60–64	586	491	549	1,656	1,170	612.0
65–69	553	466	519	1,528	1,295	610.0
70–74	560	344	516	1,506	1,324	609.0
75 and older	517	154	379	1,392	1,155	500.0
All ages combined	565	636	562	1,950	1,483	610.0

Source: These values are obtained using demographic data from the 1980 census to adjust means from the 1981 Socio-Economic Survey.

Note: All values in baht.

Table 5.11. Forecast per capita expenditures by household type: 2005

Age of head	Intact	Single male-headed	Single female-headed	One-person, male	One-person, female	All combined
Less than 25	1,919	2,639	2,313	5,414	4,863	2,091
25–29	1,990	3,121	2,209	6,078	6,185	2,137
30–34	1,987	2,781	2,187	6,975	4,976	2,114
35–39	1,994	2,252	2,022	6,185	5,054	2,080
40–44	1,953	2,278	1,976	4,967	4,234	2,019
45–49	1,926	2,508	1,897	4,639	4,326	2,004
50–54	2,040	2,162	2,000	4,633	3,662	2,099
55–59	1,980	2,087	1,910	4,451	3,402	2,050
60–64	1,913	1,817	1,869	4,501	3,180	1,999
65–69	1,801	1,865	1,757	4,153	3,521	1,978
70–74	1,829	1,370	1,727	4,093	3,599	1,946
75 and older	1,681	866	1,251	3,783	3,139	1,598
All ages combined	1,965	2,118	1,898	5,249	3,955	2,055

Note: All values in baht.

increases are among households with large families and those with low per capita expenditures in 1980. For example, the growth for households with heads 45–49 years of age is 5.2 percent. The smallest increases are forecast for households with few children living at home, namely households with older heads. Households with heads in their late 60s grow at about 4.7 percent per annum. Per capita expenditures for single-female households are also forecast to grow at about 5 percent per annum, with somewhat less variation in the rate of growth than forecast for intact households. Expenditures by households with older heads are expected to grow at a somewhat slower pace so that in relative terms the situation of older households is forecast to deteriorate slightly over the next 25 years.

Figure 5.1 compares changes in per capita expenditure for the two most important household types, intact and single-female headed. Values are graphed using a log scale so as to emphasize percentage differences in expenditures. In 1980 life-cycle variation in per capita expenditure is quite evident in the dip among households of childrearing age. By 2005 most of the dip, i.e., the life-cycle variation in household expenditure, has disappeared because the number of children per household has declined so substantially. Likewise, for single-female headed households much of the life-cycle variation in per capita expenditure disappears between 1980 and 2005; per household expenditure declines much more slowly with age in 2005.

Forecasting Consumer Expenditures

The most significant change in forecast budget shares is the dramatic decline in the importance of food and nonalcoholic beverages—from over half of the family's budget in 1980 to only one-third of the budget in 2005 (Table 5.12). The resources thus freed up are devoted to a number of areas—the largest increases are in miscellaneous items and ceremonies (up 7 percentage points), transportation and communication (up 4.6 percentage points), and housing and household operations (up 3 percentage points). In percentage terms, expenditures on apparel, medical care, and reading and recreation also increase quite substantially. Expenditures on alcohol and tobacco products are constant at 3.9 percent of the budget and the percentages devoted to personal care and education drop modestly.

Total monthly private expenditures are forecast to reach nearly 133 billion baht per month in 2005 compared with about 26 billion baht per month in 1980—a rate of growth of 6.5 percent per annum (Table 5.13). The forecast aggregates represent a gradual decline in the rate of growth of private expenditures from 7.1 percent during the 1980–85 quinquennium to reach 5.9 percent during the 2000–2005 quinquennium. Although in *percentage* terms, expenditures on food and nonalcoholic beverages grows more slowly than expenditures on any other category, the *absolute* increase is greatest.

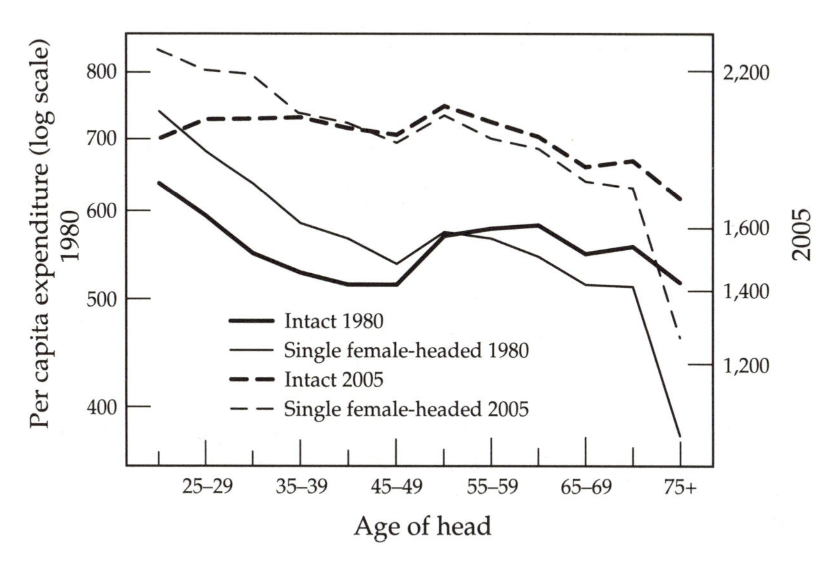

Source: Data were calculated by the authors.

Figure 5.1. Per capita household expenditure: Comparison of 1980 and 2005

Table 5.12. Forecast budget shares: 1980–2005

Expenditure category	1980	1985	1990	1995	2000	2005
Food	0.511	0.476	0.442	0.407	0.373	0.340
Alcohol and tobacco	0.039	0.039	0.040	0.040	0.039	0.039
Apparel	0.066	0.070	0.073	0.075	0.076	0.075
Housing	0.194	0.200	0.205	0.211	0.217	0.223
Medical care	0.035	0.037	0.038	0.040	0.041	0.043
Personal care	0.021	0.021	0.021	0.020	0.020	0.019
Transport and communication	0.050	0.059	0.068	0.077	0.086	0.096
Recreation and reading	0.018	0.021	0.023	0.026	0.029	0.032
Education	0.010	0.010	0.010	0.009	0.008	0.007
Miscellaneous	0.056	0.068	0.081	0.095	0.111	0.127

Monthly expenditures on food rise from 13 billion baht per month in 1980 to 45 billion baht per month in 2005. The greatest increases in percentage terms are anticipated for transportation and communication, recreation and reading, and miscellaneous items. Total expenditure in each category is forecast to rise tenfold over the 25-year period tracked.

Table 5.13. Forecast monthly expenditures: 1980–2005

Expenditure category	1980	1985	1990	1995	2000	2005
Food	13,311	17,717	23,198	29,652	36,979	45,021
Alcohol and tobacco	1,027	1,479	2,102	2,918	3,950	5,222
Apparel	1,721	2,618	3,855	5,476	7,521	10,041
Housing	5,049	7,411	10,774	15,369	21,470	29,387
Medical care	917	1,368	2,006	2,886	4,077	5,624
Personal care	550	779	1,086	1,479	1,965	2,555
Transport and communication	1,316	2,205	3,592	5,652	8,599	12,723
Recreation and reading	460	760	1,223	1,906	2,882	4,246
Education	260	375	512	661	801	916
Miscellaneous	1,468	2,540	4,284	6,997	11,035	16,848
Total expenditure	26,079	37,253	52,633	72,999	99,279	132,583

Note: All values in millions of baht.

Changes in the composition of household expenditure will have an important impact on the Thai economy. Clearly one of the most important changes is the decline in the relative size of the domestic agricultural market (Tables 5.12 and 5.13). Barring a substantial increase in the export of agricultural products or a substantial decline in the productivity of agricultural workers relative to nonagricultural workers, the decline in the demand for agricultural products will be matched by a decline in agricultural employment relative to employment in other sectors of the economy. As "surplus" agricultural workers depress wages relative to those available in the manufacturing and service sectors of the economy, a significant flow of population from rural to urban areas will inevitably result. Increased urbanization will, in turn, have important implications for investment in urban infrastructure, housing needs, and other aspects of the Thai economy that go beyond the scope of this study. Some of these issues are discussed in additional detail in Chapter 3, which focuses on labor force and employment issues.

As a percentage of total expenditures, the most rapidly expanding expenditure category is housing. Complementary analysis reported in Chapter 8 on housing needs details the most important implications of the rapid expansion anticipated in residential construction and so we will not elaborate on the issues here.

Perhaps the most surprising results presented in Tables 5.12 and 5.13 are the relatively slow growth in expenditures on health and education. The overall implications for the Thai economy are difficult to assess, because the public sector is so important in both areas. Thus, overall changes in health and education cannot be judged solely on the basis of household expenditure. These results do suggest, however, that the demand for private education or private health care is not very income sensitive in Thailand. Higher income households apparently do send their children to public schools and seek publicly subsidized health care. Will this change in the future? The answer probably depends as much on government policy about the quality of public sector services as on anything else. If fiscal problems erode public support for either sector, private expenditure will undoubtedly grow more rapidly than forecast here.

Economic growth versus demographic change. Changes in expenditure shares can be attributed to two broad causes—economic growth and demographic change. In the model employed here, economic growth shifts budget shares away from necessities, e.g., food, and toward luxuries or goods with high income elasticities, e.g., transportation and communication. The impact of demographic change is more varied. First, the demographic compositions of households change. Because households are smaller or have different age compositions, their consumption basket changes. Second, the kinds of households change. In particular, the number of households with older heads increases and, less important, the number of one-person, intact, and single-headed households changes. Third, changes in the demographic composition of households affect per capita income. For example, the addition of a young member lowers per capita income which, in turn, induces a shift toward necessities and away from luxuries.

Analyses of forecasts demonstrate that expenditures are influenced more by economic growth than by demographic factors.[7] In particular, the shift in expenditures on food, apparel, medical care, personal care, transportation and communication, recreation and reading, and miscellaneous items can be attributed almost entirely to overall economic growth. Increased expenditure on housing is about equally accounted for by demographic change and economic growth, whereas the decline in educational expenditure is a product of demographic change. The absence of change in the share devoted to alcoholic beverages is a result of demographic change and economic growth having offsetting effects.

These conclusions are based on a simple analysis made possible through repeated simulations. The impact of changes in household membership are assessed by forecasting expenditures allowing changes in household membership while holding the kinds of households and per capita income constant at the initial values used for 1980. A second simulation relaxes the restriction on the kinds of households allowing them to change as originally forecast. A third simulation allows for response in per capita income

7. These results are broadly consistent with analysis of cross-national aggregate spending patterns reported by Eilenstine and Cunningham (1972).

to demographic characteristics of the household, but assumes that exogenous growth in per capita income will be zero.

The detailed decomposition of changes in budget shares is presented in Table 5.14. The dominance of the impact of economic growth is evident. The impact of demographic change is subdued because in most instances changes in consumption related to household membership are offset by changes in per capita income related to household membership. Changes in the kinds of households have only a negligible influence on budget shares.

Reliability

There are a number of different aspects of reliability to be assessed. Of course, the reliability of regression estimates, based on standard errors and the coefficient of determination, is one element of an overall assessment of reliability, which is discussed above. There are other important elements related to forecasting that should also be assessed.

Summation condition. One straightforward issue concerns the requirement that budget shares must sum to 1. If the budget share equations are evaluated at the means of the independent variables, the calculated shares will automatically sum to 1 for any specification used. One advantage of the specification employed here is that the total of the budget shares equals 1 for all forecasts.

Analysis of residuals. A second issue concerns the reliability of forecasts for particular groups. The specification of the expenditure functions employed assumes that subgroups of the population are affected in the same way by changes in the independent variables. For example, the effect of changes in the age of head is the same for intact, female-headed, and one-person households. Income elasticity is the same irrespective of whether the household head is 60 or 20, and so on. As a practical matter it is not possible nor is it desirable to allow for all possible interactions among the independent variables. However, if particular subgroups are of special interest, it is important to ensure that their budget shares are not systematically under- or over-estimated.

The forecasts presented here distinguish households by their type and by the age of their head. For each household group and expenditure category, the residual budget share is calculated as the difference between the calculated share and the observed share.

Dummy variables used in the statistical analysis insure that the budget share for any household type will not be systematically over- or under-predicted. But because a single age-of-head relationship is employed for all four household types, there may be systematic differences associated with age of head.

Table 5.14. Decomposition of budget share changes: 1980–2005

Expenditure category	Demographic effects				Economic growth	Total change
	Household membership	Age and type of households	Income effects	Total		
Food	+0.011	-0.001	-0.036	-0.026	-0.147	-0.173
Alcohol and tobacco	+0.002	—	--	+0.002	-0.002	—
Apparel	-0.006	—	+0.005	-0.001	+0.011	+0.010
Housing	+0.008	+0.001	+0.004	+0.013	+0.017	+0.030
Medical care	-0.002	—	+0.002	—	+0.008	+0.008
Personal care	+0.001	—	+0.000	+0.001	-0.003	-0.002
Transport and communication	-0.007	-0.001	+0.010	+0.002	+0.043	+0.045
Recreation and reading	-0.003	—	+0.003	—	+0.014	+0.014
Education	-0.003	+0.001	—	-0.002	—	-0.002
Miscellaneous	-0.002	+0.001	+0.012	+0.011	+0.060	+0.071

In general, the residual analysis shows that the age relationship for one-person households differs fairly consistently from that for family households. And, in particular, budget shares tend to be more sensitive to age for one-person households. This is not too surprising because family households usually consist of many members with differing ages and, in particular, adult members are not carefully distinguished according to their age in the specification employed.

A comparison of residuals also turns up additional "discrepancies." For example, for female-headed households, expenditures on alcohol and tobacco products rise quite systematically with the age of the head, whereas this does not appear to be the case for male-headed households.

The corrective action required is very clear. When household types have distinctive age-of-head patterns, the statistical analysis should include age of head and its square interacted with dummy variables used to distinguish different types of households. As a general rule, different age patterns for one-person households should be anticipated.

Negative shares. The specification employed does not preclude predicted negative shares and, hence, predicted negative expenditures. For some subgroups of the household population, instances of very small negative shares are encountered for two age categories of one-person female households in 2005. In the particular case at hand, the values are so small that setting them to zero would have no noticeable effect. However, the existence of calculated negative shares is symptomatic of a misspecification of the education share equation. As discussed above, the age pattern for one-person households is frequently quite distinct from that for other households and this is particularly true for education. Use of a more appropriate age specification for education expenditures by one-person households would address the negative share problem in a more rigorous and reliable manner. However, this should be accomplished while maintaining the same independent variables in all share equations.

CONCLUDING REMARKS

There are a number of important respects in which the model can be improved for future applications to Thailand or elsewhere. First, greater attention can be devoted to how modernization and development will affect expenditure patterns. As development proceeds, tastes and the opportunity set available to future Thai generations will differ from that of today. This will not only affect the share devoted to each category by the "average" household, but the relationship between other independent variables and expenditure shares, as well. More detailed investigation of such interactions in Chapter 4 on saving, for example, shows that the impact of the number of children on the household consumption ratio varies considerably depending on the educational attainment of the head and socioeconomic status of the household.

Second, analysis of the impact of prices on consumer expenditure would provide important additional information not available from this study. Price data were not available to support this analysis and, in any case, the use of regional variation in prices to estimate price elasticities suffers from some drawbacks. However, as additional surveys on consumer expenditure for Thailand become available, the analysis of pooled cross-section time series data may yield more reliable estimates of price elasticities.

Third, a number of recent studies have developed new procedures for estimating the "cost" of children. This type of analysis could be usefully combined with HOMES to estimate the cost of children and its variation over the household's life cycle.

Appendix 5.1
ESTIMATION RESULTS FROM EXPENDITURE ANALYSIS

Appendix Table 5.1.1. Detailed expenditure results using per capita in-

Variable	Food and nonalcoholic beverages		Alcoholic beverages and tobacco products	
	Parameter estimate	Standard error	Parameter estimate	Standard error
Intercept	0.764491	0.050501	0.010453	0.017850
LNY	0.020917	0.014796	0.006717	0.005230
LNY2	-0.007287	0.001123	-0.000733	0.000397
NM1	0.009144	0.003808	0.000471	0.001346
NM2	0.006533	0.001654	-0.001429	0.005845
NM3	-0.003854	0.001047	-0.001972	0.000370
NM4	-0.003070	0.001254	0.003398	0.000443
NM5	-0.001645	0.004516	-0.006652	0.001596
NF1	0.008115	0.003583	-0.002983	0.001267
NF2	0.005708	0.001665	-0.001780	0.000589
NF3	-0.005871	0.001028	-0.002361	0.000363
NF4	-0.008821	0.001230	-0.003624	0.000435
NF5	-0.010097	0.003499	0.002564	0.001237
FEM	0.005012	0.003852	-0.016687	0.001362
AGE	-0.002550	0.000540	0.000589	0.000191
AGE2	0.000024	0.000006	-0.000003	0.000002
V17	-0.130398	0.005526	0.000031	0.001953
V18	-0.020594	0.005395	-0.002674	0.001907
V19	-0.013179	0.007864	0.009247	0.002780
V20	-0.026227	0.008518	-0.003375	0.003011
V21	-0.005904	0.010215	0.006945	0.003611
V22	-0.056901	0.008790	0.002483	0.003107
V23	-0.027578	0.005400	0.005439	0.001909
V24	-0.087710	0.006678	0.003163	0.002361
V25	0.004566	0.006601	0.002668	0.002333
V26	-0.005391	0.009815	0.007796	0.003469
V27	-0.036633	0.006064	0.012710	0.002144
V28	-0.013400	0.006069	0.015921	0.002145
V29	-0.044699	0.006472	0.000261	0.002288
OPM	0.028735	0.007301	0.022539	0.002581
OPF	0.030807	0.007099	-0.002487	0.002509
Adjusted *R* square		0.2494		0.0636
No. of observations		11,890		11,890

come as independent variable

Apparel and footwear		Housing and household operations		Medical care	
Parameter estimate	Standard error	Parameter estimate	Standard error	Parameter estimate	Standard error
0.092932	0.029550	-0.078943	0.039279	0.096699	0.022101
0.002282	0.008658	0.056277	0.011508	-0.018298	0.006475
0.000081	0.000657	-0.003166	0.000873	0.001193	0.000491
-0.007599	0.002228	-0.003133	0.002962	0.008869	0.001667
0.000448	0.000968	-0.003867	0.001286	-0.002747	0.000724
0.004330	0.000613	-0.004106	0.000814	-0.002274	0.000458
0.002067	0.000734	-0.006418	0.000975	-0.002442	0.000549
0.000858	0.002642	0.008413	0.003512	0.001708	0.001976
-0.005575	0.002097	-0.000332	0.002787	0.007610	0.001568
0.000811	0.000975	-0.005043	0.001295	-0.000694	0.000729
0.004550	0.000601	-0.004454	0.000799	-0.001317	0.000450
0.002335	0.000720	0.001347	0.000957	-0.001111	0.000538
-0.002326	0.002047	0.005732	0.002721	0.001727	0.001531
0.004271	0.002254	0.009042	0.002996	0.002325	0.001686
-0.001874	0.000316	0.002013	0.000420	0.000192	0.000236
0.000014	0.000003	-0.000016	0.000004	0.000000	0.000003
0.013200	0.003234	0.002390	0.004298	-0.003861	0.002419
0.011584	0.003157	0.000884	0.004196	0.007154	0.002361
0.004313	0.004602	0.009131	0.006117	0.000374	0.003442
-0.000461	0.004984	-0.000162	0.006625	0.015140	0.003728
-0.011647	0.005977	0.015178	0.007945	-0.003131	0.004470
-0.018258	0.005143	0.033499	0.006836	-0.004380	0.003847
-0.166310	0.003160	0.016690	0.004200	-0.002614	0.002363
0.006495	0.003908	-0.000351	0.005194	-0.009374	0.002923
-0.000933	0.003862	-0.006772	0.005134	0.001952	0.002889
-0.001925	0.005743	-0.003947	0.007634	0.006297	0.004296
-0.008847	0.003549	0.004211	0.004717	-0.002665	0.002654
-0.012807	0.003551	-0.003949	0.004720	-0.001222	0.002656
-0.007774	0.003787	0.028573	0.005034	-0.000784	0.002832
-0.008763	0.004272	-0.003167	0.005678	-0.014476	0.003195
0.005908	0.004154	0.008579	0.005521	-0.005285	0.003107
	0.0343		0.067		0.0244
	11,890		11,890		11,890

(continued)

Appendix Table 5.1.1. Detailed expenditure results using per capita in-

Variable	Personal care		Transport and communication	
	Parameter estimate	Standard error	Parameter estimate	Standard error
Intercept	0.043230	0.006017	0.042907	0.029301
LNY	-0.002641	0.001763	-0.015899	0.008585
LNY2	0.000150	0.000134	0.002694	0.000651
NM1	-0.001172	0.000454	-0.004757	0.002210
NM2	-0.000944	0.000197	0.000235	0.000959
NM3	0.000012	0.000125	0.003280	0.000607
NM4	0.000263	0.000149	0.003578	0.000728
NM5	0.001477	0.000538	-0.002145	0.002620
NF1	-0.002185	0.000427	-0.000034	0.002079
NF2	-0.001224	0.000198	0.002151	0.000966
NF3	0.000820	0.000122	0.002547	0.000596
NF4	0.001872	0.000147	0.003715	0.000714
NF5	-0.001269	0.000427	0.004639	0.002030
FEM	0.003106	0.000459	-0.008105	0.002235
AGE	-0.000470	0.000064	-0.000402	0.000313
AGE2	0.000003	0.000001	-0.000001	0.000003
V17	0.000160	0.000658	0.004400	0.003206
V18	0.000218	0.000643	-0.000536	0.003130
V19	0.000852	0.000937	0.001498	0.004563
V20	0.002145	0.001015	-0.000911	0.004943
V21	0.000581	0.001217	-0.002827	0.005927
V22	0.003886	0.001047	0.031246	0.005100
V23	0.003512	0.000643	0.009650	0.003133
V24	0.007163	0.000796	0.049439	0.003875
V25	0.002270	0.000786	0.005042	0.003830
V26	0.004735	0.001169	-0.000569	0.005695
V27	0.007021	0.000723	0.015312	0.003519
V28	0.005947	0.000723	0.005105	0.003521
V29	0.001577	0.000771	0.007536	0.003755
OPM	0.001649	0.000870	-0.013049	0.004236
OPF	-0.000043	0.000846	-0.016855	0.004119
Adjusted *R* square		0.081		0.101
No. of observations		11,890		11,890

come as independent variable *(continued)*

Recreation and reading		Education		Ceremonies and miscellaneous	
Parameter estimate	Standard error	Parameter estimate	Standard error	Parameter estimate	Standard error
0.020828	0.014290	-0.067672	0.007718	0.075075	0.032077
-0.005954	0.004187	0.020506	0.002261	-0.063908	0.009398
0.001108	0.000318	-0.001543	0.000172	0.007503	0.000713
0.000758	0.001078	-0.003588	0.000582	0.001007	0.002419
0.001422	0.000468	0.001837	0.000253	-0.001487	0.001050
0.001563	0.000296	0.002944	0.000160	0.000076	0.000665
0.001048	0.000355	0.000446	0.000192	0.001118	0.000797
0.001568	0.001278	0.000889	0.000690	-0.004471	0.002868
-0.000776	0.001014	-0.003703	0.005476	-0.000136	0.002276
0.000628	0.000471	0.001427	0.000255	-0.001984	0.001058
0.001205	0.000191	0.003487	0.000157	0.001394	0.000653
0.000987	0.000348	0.001235	0.000188	0.002066	0.000781
0.000681	0.000990	0.000107	0.000535	-0.000885	0.002222
0.001338	0.001090	0.002351	0.000589	-0.002653	0.002447
-0.000724	0.000153	0.000088	0.000082	0.003136	0.000343
0.000007	0.000002	-0.000002	0.000001	-0.000025	0.000004
-0.002558	0.001564	-0.001059	0.000845	0.000337	0.003510
-0.004270	0.001527	-0.001705	0.000825	0.009940	0.003427
-0.003396	0.002225	-0.000278	0.001202	-0.008562	0.004995
0.000905	0.002410	-0.003659	0.001302	0.016605	0.005410
-0.000973	0.002895	0.002439	0.001561	-0.000661	0.006488
0.005764	0.002487	0.012667	0.001343	-0.010006	0.005583
0.007464	0.001528	0.007475	0.000825	-0.003406	0.003430
0.012908	0.001890	0.011734	0.001021	0.006834	0.004242
-0.002384	0.001868	-0.000495	0.001009	-0.005913	0.004192
-0.000415	0.002777	0.000360	0.001500	-0.006942	0.006234
0.010989	0.001716	0.010113	0.000927	-0.012212	0.003852
0.003666	0.001717	0.003876	0.000927	-0.003138	0.003855
0.005033	0.001831	0.013743	0.000989	-0.003465	0.004111
-0.009435	0.002066	0.000913	0.001116	-0.004946	0.004637
-0.005283	0.002009	-0.004475	0.001085	-0.010867	0.004509
	0.0686		0.1331		0.1212
	11,890		11,890		11,890

Appendix Table 5.1.2. Detailed expenditure results using per capita expen-

	Food and nonalcoholic beverages		Alcoholic beverages and tobacco products	
Variable	Parameter estimate	Standard error	Parameter estimate	Standard error
Intercept	1.471854	0.060591	-0.040550	0.024140
LNE	-0.124766	0.177505	0.020415	0.007072
LNE2	-0.001606	0.001327	-0.001601	0.000529
NM1	-0.008918	0.003394	0.001055	0.001352
NM2	-0.004882	0.001475	-0.001006	0.000588
NM3	-0.011288	0.000938	-0.001674	0.000374
NM4	-0.009319	0.001119	0.003540	0.000446
NM5	-0.005451	0.004009	-0.006623	0.001597
NF1	-0.007366	0.003190	-0.002429	0.001271
NF2	-0.004887	0.001484	-0.001362	0.000591
NF3	-0.011530	0.000915	-0.002159	0.000364
NF4	-0.012768	0.001094	-0.003489	0.000436
NF5	-0.014674	0.003106	0.002671	0.001237
FEM	-0.002959	0.003422	-0.016272	0.001363
AGE	-0.001731	0.000479	0.000551	0.000191
AGE2	0.000013	0.000005	-0.000003	0.000002
V17	-0.014663	0.004897	-0.000218	0.001951
V18	-0.020589	0.004719	-0.003765	0.001880
V19	-0.013478	0.006980	0.008153	0.002781
V20	-0.007590	0.007557	-0.004585	0.003011
V21	0.004300	0.009054	0.005614	0.003607
V22	0.002938	0.007694	-0.001329	0.003065
V23	0.007260	0.004776	0.003546	0.001928
V24	-0.029944	0.005870	0.003279	0.002339
V25	0.004105	0.005855	0.002410	0.002333
V26	0.000487	0.008702	0.007290	0.003467
V27	0.010004	0.005367	0.010648	0.002138
V28	0.012032	0.005352	0.014335	0.002132
V29	-0.007407	0.005741	-0.001446	0.002981
OPM	0.055975	0.006545	0.022272	0.002607
OPF	0.062878	0.006351	-0.002843	0.002530
Adjusted *R* square		0.4087		0.0629
No. of observations		11,890		11,890

diture as independent variable

Apparel and footwear		Housing and household operations		Medical care	
Parameter estimate	Standard error	Parameter estimate	Standard error	Parameter estimate	Standard error
-0.316912	0.039566	0.053057	0.053143	-0.090898	0.029793
0.113588	0.011591	0.012776	0.015569	0.028581	0.008728
-0.007237	0.000866	0.000292	0.001637	-0.001480	0.000652
-0.003270	0.002216	-0.002996	0.002977	0.011912	0.001669
0.003278	0.000963	-0.004040	0.001294	-0.000593	0.000725
0.006241	0.000613	-0.004095	0.000823	-0.000928	0.000461
0.003428	0.000731	-0.006233	0.000981	-0.001551	0.000550
0.001808	0.002618	0.008527	0.003516	0.002084	0.001971
-0.017762	0.002083	-0.000280	0.002798	0.010347	0.001569
0.003539	0.009693	-0.005260	0.001302	0.001362	0.000730
0.005827	0.005972	-0.004465	0.000802	-0.000270	0.000450
0.003262	0.000714	0.001460	0.000959	-0.000166	0.000538
-0.001887	0.002028	0.006023	0.002724	0.002309	0.001827
0.006776	0.002235	0.008707	0.003001	0.004061	0.001683
-0.002043	0.000313	0.001978	0.000420	0.000342	0.000235
0.000016	0.000003	-0.000016	0.000004	0.000002	0.000002
0.013051	0.003198	0.001097	0.004295	-0.004993	0.002408
0.008630	0.003081	0.005491	0.004139	0.003132	0.002320
0.004139	0.004558	0.008980	0.006122	0.000341	0.003432
-0.006955	0.004935	0.001663	0.006628	0.010176	0.003716
-0.016951	0.005912	0.017584	0.007941	-0.007594	0.004452
-0.034152	0.005024	0.034306	0.006748	-0.018885	0.003783
-0.027313	0.003119	0.019314	0.004189	-0.011057	0.002348
-0.007218	0.003833	0.001330	0.005149	-0.022704	0.002886
-0.001966	0.003523	-0.005352	0.005135	0.000998	0.002879
-0.004642	0.005682	-0.001659	0.007632	0.003747	0.004279
-0.020858	0.003505	0.006307	0.004707	-0.012806	0.002639
-0.021278	0.003495	-0.000830	0.004694	-0.008583	0.002632
-0.179182	0.003749	0.030701	0.005035	-0.008936	0.002823
-0.007741	0.004274	-0.007765	0.005740	-0.017483	0.003218
0.003723	0.004147	0.005461	0.005570	-0.009181	0.003123
	0.0526		0.0654		0.0299
	11,890		11,890		11,890

(continued)

Appendix Table 5.1.2. Detailed expenditure results using per capita expen-

Variable	Personal care		Transport and communication	
	Parameter estimate	Standard error	Parameter estimate	Standard error
Intercept	0.052557	0.008110	-0.055144	0.038585
LNE	-0.003799	0.002376	-0.005829	0.011304
*LNE*2	0.000103	0.000178	0.003460	0.000845
*NM*1	-0.001586	0.000454	0.000127	0.002161
*NM*2	-0.001219	0.000197	0.003398	0.000939
*NM*3	-0.000169	0.000126	0.005276	0.000597
*NM*4	0.000134	0.000150	0.005249	0.000712
*NM*5	0.001431	0.000537	-0.001291	0.002553
*NF*1	-0.002556	0.000427	0.004179	0.002032
*NF*2	-0.001482	0.000199	0.005064	0.000945
*NF*3	0.000677	0.000122	0.004174	0.000582
*NF*4	0.001776	0.000146	0.004785	0.000697
*NF*5	-0.001384	0.004157	0.005868	0.001978
FEM	0.002905	0.000458	-0.006049	0.002179
AGE	-0.000444	0.000064	-0.000651	0.000305
*AGE*2	0.000002	0.000001	0.000003	0.000003
*V*17	0.000193	0.000656	0.004356	0.003119
*V*18	0.000417	0.000632	-0.001174	0.003005
*V*19	0.000872	0.000934	0.001653	0.004445
*V*20	0.002662	0.001012	-0.005878	0.004812
*V*21	0.001004	0.001212	-0.005599	0.005765
*V*22	0.005920	0.001030	0.013290	0.004900
*V*23	0.004435	0.000639	0.000057	0.003041
*V*24	0.008817	0.000786	0.031862	0.003738
*V*25	0.002277	0.000784	0.005219	0.003729
*V*26	0.004885	0.001165	-0.002293	0.005541
*V*27	0.008239	0.000718	0.001883	0.003418
*V*28	0.006647	0.000716	-0.002025	0.003408
*V*29	0.002535	0.000768	-0.002934	0.003656
OPM	0.002605	0.000876	-0.023689	0.004168
OPF	0.000833	0.000850	-0.076845	0.004144
Adjusted *R* square		0.0862		0.1469
No. of observations		11,890		11,890

diture as independent variable *(continued)*

Recreation and reading		Education		Ceremonies and miscellaneous	
Parameter estimate	Standard error	Parameter estimate	Standard error	Parameter estimate	Standard error
-0.009600	0.019181	-0.111011	0.010418	0.046650	0.042423
-0.001290	0.005619	0.032642	0.003052	-0.072318	0.012428
0.001087	0.000420	-0.002380	0.000228	0.009364	0.000929
0.001889	0.001074	-0.003276	0.000584	0.005063	0.002376
0.002091	0.000467	0.001996	0.000254	0.000978	0.001033
0.001995	0.000297	0.003106	0.000161	0.001548	0.000657
0.001485	0.000354	0.000540	0.000192	0.002728	0.000783
0.001887	0.001269	0.000968	0.000689	-0.003340	0.002807
0.000152	0.001010	-0.003417	0.000548	0.003147	0.002234
0.001233	0.000470	0.001591	0.002552	0.000203	0.001039
0.001538	0.000290	0.003551	0.000157	0.002656	0.000640
0.001228	0.000346	0.001325	0.000188	0.002888	0.000766
0.000906	0.000983	0.000125	0.000534	0.000044	0.002174
0.001730	0.001083	0.002571	0.000588	-0.001469	0.002396
-0.000764	0.000152	0.000070	0.000082	0.003000	0.000335
0.000007	0.000002	-0.000002	0.000001	-0.000023	0.000004
-0.002204	0.001550	-0.000742	0.000842	0.001121	0.003429
-0.003432	0.001494	-0.001394	0.000811	0.012685	0.003304
-0.003308	0.002210	-0.000412	0.001200	-0.007941	0.004887
0.000175	0.002392	-0.004093	0.001299	0.014427	0.005291
-0.000883	0.002866	0.001981	0.001557	0.000544	0.006339
0.003509	0.002436	0.011119	0.001323	-0.016717	0.005387
0.005852	0.001512	0.006916	0.000821	-0.009011	0.003344
0.010134	0.001858	0.011168	0.001009	-0.003838	0.004110
-0.002161	0.001853	-0.000440	0.001007	-0.005090	0.004099
-0.000543	0.002755	0.000526	0.001496	-0.007798	0.006092
0.008532	0.001699	0.009680	0.000923	-0.021629	0.003758
0.001648	0.001694	0.003596	0.000920	-0.006842	0.003747
0.003090	0.001817	0.013271	0.000987	-0.010624	0.004019
-0.011353	0.002072	0.001329	0.001125	-0.014149	0.004582
-0.007632	0.002011	-0.004226	0.001092	-0.021329	0.004447
	0.0816		0.1635		0.1588
	11,890		11,890		11,890

6
The Education Sector: Enrollment Rates and Expenditures on Schooling

by Mathana Phananiramai and Andrew Mason

The link between demographic change and the education sector is widely appreciated. Unlike most other government services, education is targeted at a very specific age group. Expenditures on education will vary in direct proportion to the number of school-age children if the proportions enrolled and expenditures per student do not change. This simple demographic relationship has been and will continue to be very important in Thailand. Since 1960 the number of school-age children has been growing rapidly, and trends in educational expenditure have been dominated by efforts to provide schooling for these increased numbers. But as a result of rapid fertility decline, the demographics of schooling have begun to change. The number of children of primary school age is actually beginning to decline, and the number of potential students of secondary and tertiary school age will also begin to decline in the not so distant future.

Future growth in the education sector will depend increasingly on the extent to which Thai students increase their educational attainment as well as how much the quality of schooling (and expenditures on schooling) are raised. These issues are examined in detail below.

Demographically based enrollment projections have been widely used by education researchers and planners for years, and a set of projections presented in this chapter uses these procedures. But this chapter also proposes and implements a new method for forecasting enrollment that has not been used elsewhere. Survey data on school enrollment are analyzed to determine how the individual and household characteristics of potential students affect the probability of their being enrolled. Results from this analysis are combined with projections of the number and demographic characteristics of households, based on HOMES, to forecast enrollment probabilities and to project the number of students at each schooling level.

Data used in this chapter were compiled from several secondary sources in Thai. Data on enrollments and teachers' qualifications were compiled from various editions of the *Final Report on Education Statistics* prepared by the National Statistical Office, Office of the Prime Minister and the Office of the Undersecretary, Ministry of Education; the *Educational Report* prepared by the Institution of Higher Education, Office of University Affairs; education statistics prepared separately by various departments in the Ministry of Education, including the Department of Teacher Training, Department of Vocational Education, Department of General Education, Department of Physical Education, Office of National Primary Education, and the Office of Private Education; and the *Educational Report* prepared by the Bangkok Metropolitan Administration and the Office of Local Education, Ministry of the Interior. Costs of education were compiled from data in the various editions of the *Annual Government Expenditure Report* prepared by the Budget Bureau, Ministry of Finance. Costs by level of education were calculated from the budgets allocated to the government agencies involved in educational activities—the Ministry of Education, the Office of University Affairs, and the Ministry of the Interior.

In this chapter we will first present an overview of Thailand's educational system, enrollment data, a discussion of the private versus the public sector, and information on school inputs. Next we will present results from the analysis of survey data on school enrollment and enrollment projections using HOMES. Those results are then compared to standard enrollment projections. Finally, we analyze education costs and present forecasts for two areas: operating and capital costs borne by the public sector and household expenditure on education.

EDUCATIONAL PERFORMANCE AND POLICY IN THAILAND

Education in Thailand has long been divided into three broad levels: primary, secondary, and tertiary. But the number of years required to complete each level, the availability and emphasis on vocational education, and other educational policies have changed periodically. Between 1935 and 1960, primary education consisted of four years of schooling and was, in principle, compulsory. During that period, educational policy emphasized the extension of public primary education to all children. With the accomplishment of that goal, six years of primary-level schooling were made compulsory in 1978.

In recent years pre-primary education, including kindergarten, has become available to children age 3 to 5. Children enter primary school when they are anywhere between 6 and 8 years of age, depending largely on the locality. Secondary education is divided into lower and upper divisions, each consisting of three years so that, typically, those 12–14 years of age attend lower secondary and those 15–17 attend upper secondary.

Thailand has developed an extensive vocational education program. Vocational training is incorporated directly into the curriculum of primary schools, and both lower and upper secondary vocational programs are offered that emphasize technical training preparing students for specific occupations. Before 1960 the vocational stream was a relatively closed track in that once a student entered it was difficult to transfer to the academic track. Moreover, the track terminated at the secondary level. Since 1960, however, the academic and vocational tracks have become less mutually exclusive and vocational education has been extended to higher education.

Teacher training has been handled as a separate educational stream and has played an important role in Thai education. Before 1960 teacher shortages were met via specialized training equivalent to a secondary education. As the shortages have attenuated, secondary training has been phased out and is no longer available. Training at the associate degree level (equivalent to two extra years of training after secondary school) is provided only to fine arts and physical education teachers. Other teachers are trained to the bachelor's degree level or higher.

The government plays a major role in all aspects of Thailand's educational system. Although private preschools are actively encouraged, the government runs a number of pre-primary schools for demonstration and research purposes and in localities where private organizations do not provide such services. It is the policy of the government to provide primary education free to all children, and more than 90 percent of all primary students attend public schools. Private schools play a somewhat more important role at the secondary and tertiary levels, but the majority of secondary students are enrolled in public schools. Furthermore, all major universities in Thailand are public institutions. And even though the government encourages private tertiary institutions, educational policy and management is strictly controlled by various government agencies.

Pre-Primary and Primary Education

Pre-primary school is not compulsory and, until recently, most students were drawn from urban areas. Although the private sector has played an important role in providing preschool education, the relative importance of the public sector has increased, particularly as preschool enrollment in rural areas has risen. In contrast, the public sector is more dominant at the primary level, where over 90 percent of all students attend public schools. In urban areas, however, private education at the primary level is somewhat more important.

The quality of education, measured either by the student–teacher ratio or by teachers' qualifications, varies across different types of schools. In 1985 the student–teacher ratio was 18 in provincial schools and 19 in municipal schools, but 26 in private schools. The average qualifications of teachers are highest in municipal schools, especially in the Bangkok metropolis. The average qualifications of teachers in rural schools are lowest among public schools but are still higher than the average qualification of teachers in private schools. In fact, the quality of private schools in the academic stream varies widely, ranging from very high quality in a few top private schools to very poor quality as compared with public schools. In general, private school teachers are disadvantaged in terms of economic benefits, social welfare, and professional advancement as compared with those in public schools. Unlike private school teachers, all public school teachers are government officials and receive the security and other benefits accorded by the Civil Service Act.

Secondary Education, Academic Stream

Secondary education is provided primarily by the public sector—88 percent of all secondary students attended public schools in 1985. The quality of education varies considerably at the secondary level. The quality of demonstration schools, measured either by the student–teacher ratio or the average qualification of teachers, is the highest. However, this type of school provides education only to a small group of children who are the sons or daughters of privileged parents. Admission to these schools is usually governed by rules unrelated to the academic achievement of children. Except for a few top schools in Bangkok, the average quality of private schools is the worst as measured by the student–teacher ratio and average qualifications of teachers. Private school teachers at this level are also disadvantaged in terms of professional advancement and job security as compared with public school teachers. Not surprisingly, the role of private education at this level is diminishing over time.

Education in the Teachers' Training Stream

Teachers' training is fully under state control. Before 1980 the Teachers' Training College mainly awarded degrees below the bachelor's level because there was an urgent need for a large number of teachers to meet the rapidly increasing demand related to rapid population growth and the government's policy of expanding compulsory education. As the demand for teachers has slackened, however, teachers' colleges all over the country have terminated evening programs that award teachers' certificates or diplomas and have increasingly emphasized baccalaureate education. Eventually, all programs that offer teacher training at a level lower than the bachelor's degree will be terminated.

Vocational Education

Public and private institutions, which are both under the jurisdiction of the Ministry of Education, share equal responsibility for providing vocational education. Three streams are offered: lower vocational level, equivalent to higher secondary education in the academic stream; upper vocational education, equivalent to the diploma or associate bachelor's degree level; and higher vocational education at the baccalaureate degree level. The curriculum for upper vocational education usually requires two to three years of education after the completion of the secondary level. Hence it is higher than the secondary level but slightly lower than a bachelor's degree. The majority of vocational education in Thailand is at the lower vocational level.

If we judge the quality of education by the student–teacher ratio, public vocational schools seem to be better than private vocational schools on the average. The quality of teachers, as measured by their academic qualifications, is also better in public schools than in private schools.

Higher Education

There are 12 public colleges and universities that provide education at the undergraduate and graduate levels. Admission to these "closed" universities is very competitive, with selection based mainly on academic merit as determined by an entrance examination. These institutions accommodated about one-fifth of the students enrolled in higher education in 1985. Public universities are heavily subsidized by the government, therefore, tuition and fees are quite low.

Most tertiary students are enrolled in open universities. The main objective of the open university is to create equal opportunity for higher education, and all persons who have completed upper secondary school are accepted. In addition to classroom teaching, the open university relies heavily on mass media including television and radio. The first public open university, Ramkhamhang University, was established in 1971. The second open university, Sukhothai Thammathirat, was established in 1978. No classroom training is offered at Sukhothai Thammathirat. Teaching is mainly based on textbooks, self study, and mass media. In 1985 these two open universities accounted for about 82 percent of all students enrolled at institutions of higher education.

Thirteen private colleges award the bachelor's degree in various fields such as the humanities, engineering, law, and nursing, but the majority concentrate on the social sciences. Private colleges accounted for only about 5 percent of tertiary students in 1985.

ENROLLMENT PROJECTIONS

There are two traditional methods for projecting school enrollment: the enrollment-ratio method and the transition-rate method (Jones 1971, 1975;

Robinson 1975; U.N. 1985). The enrollment ratio is calculated as the number of students attending a particular level or grade divided by the population in the age group associated with the particular level or grade. For example, secondary enrollment ratios are calculated as the ratio of the number of secondary students divided by the population 12–17 years of age. School enrollment is projected in two steps. First, enrollment ratios are projected using procedures that vary from econometric models to ad hoc assumptions. Second, the projected enrollment ratios are multiplied by projected population data to yield school enrollment.

The transition-rate method works by using the number of students enrolled in one year in each grade to determine the number of students enrolled in the following year in the next highest grade. In its full implementation, students in each grade are determined using data on the proportion dropping out, the proportion repeating, and the proportion continuing on to the next grade. In Thailand, data on repetition and drop-out rates are not generally available. Hence, this study employs a simpler version based on transition rates that combine repeaters and advancers into a net rate. Enrollment in the first grade is determined by multiplying the population of school entry age by the proportion entering.

Each of these approaches has its advantages. The enrollment-ratio method is the simplest to apply, whereas the transition-rate method is more easily linked to specific school policies, e.g., decisions to reduce the repeater rate or to make a particular level of education compulsory. The major difficulty with both approaches is projecting the relevant rates. Although educational achievement increases, in general, with economic development, neither enrollment ratios nor transition rates always increase in a smooth or consistent way.

It is a common phenomenon for enrollment ratios, particularly at the primary school level, to reach very high levels, even levels exceeding 100, at relatively low levels of economic development. As many countries are trying to extend basic education to those who are beyond the traditional schooling age, the number enrolled may exceed the population at the traditional age. But as the schooling system matures and basic education becomes more widespread, primary school is devoted more exclusively to those in the traditional ages and the enrollment ratio declines.

As schooling becomes more widespread, transition rates tend to increase at the lower levels first. As all children go to primary school, primary continuation rates approach 1.0. But as this occurs, continuation rates may decline at higher levels. If, for example, primary education is made compulsory, the proportion of those who complete primary school and continue on to secondary may decline. This does not mean, of course, that the number continuing on to secondary school will decline. As primary education becomes accepted, however, and the need for secondary education increases, the proportion continuing on to the secondary level will rise.

These peculiarities of enrollment ratios and transition rates imply that simple extrapolations or more complex statistical fitting to quantitative measures of development trends can prove to be quite misleading. This is not to say that these methods cannot yield useful results. Rather, that they must be employed with considerable care.[1]

An alternative approach employed below uses detailed microlevel data to estimate the probability that an individual in a particular age group will be in school and how that probability will vary with individual characteristics, e.g., age and sex, and household characteristics, e.g., household income, educational attainment of parents, and the number and ages of other household members. The resulting regression equations are combined with HOMES-based forecasts of the determining factors to yield estimates of the probability that individuals in each age group will be enrolled in school. These values are multiplied, in turn, by projections of the population in each school-age group to determine the number enrolled.

The remainder of this section applies the transition-rate method and the micro-based (HOMES) method to project school enrollment in Thailand to 2015.

A HOMES-Based Approach to Enrollment Projections

Some efforts have been made to model explicitly the dependence of enrollment on socioeconomic characteristics based on time series and international cross-section data,[2] but we are aware of no enrollment projections based on analysis of household survey data. This section will employ such an approach. The factors affecting school enrollment are statistically analyzed based on the 1981 Socio-Economic Survey of Thailand (NSO 1985). The results are combined with the HOMES model to forecast the probability that children at selected ages will be enrolled and the number of primary, secondary, and tertiary students at five-year intervals.

Modeling school enrollment. Economic models of schooling emphasize education as an investment in human capital. The decision maker weighs the expected financial returns to additional years of schooling against the expected cost and chooses to enroll if the rate of return exceeds the rate available from alternative investments (Becker 1964). Of course, education has value in and of itself beyond its power to enhance the earning potential

1. Examples of interesting analyses include Dresch (1975), Bowen (1981), Ahlburg et al. (1981), and Wachter and Wascher (1984).

2. See, for instance, Schultz (1987).

of its recipient. Thus, individuals may "over-invest" in education in the sense that the rate of return to the last year of schooling will be less than from alternative investments. In some respects, then, education can be seen and modeled as a consumer good, as well as an investment good.

The close association between economic development and increased schooling can be readily explained using the human capital model. As the means of production become more technologically complex and as employment shifts increasingly out of agriculture and into industry, the demand for educated workers increases and their wages are driven upward relative to those of workers with less education. This increases the expected returns to additional schooling and encourages students to extend their schooling while delaying their entry into the labor force. As the supply of educated workers increases, the premium from additional education is reduced but the educational attainment of the work force is maintained at a higher level.

There are additional factors that operate on the cost side. As the economy develops and wages rise, the opportunity cost of additional schooling increases for those who would otherwise be employed. For those who would not be employed, the opportunity cost of schooling will depend on the marginal product of their time in home production. Demographic change, notably the decline in fertility but also changes in household structure, may have substantial effects on the opportunity cost of the time of potential students. Two conflicting factors would seem to operate. If older children care for their younger siblings, fertility decline would reduce the opportunity cost of the time of older siblings. But at the same time, siblings of similar age are substitutes either as producers of child care or in other household activities. Thus, the decline in the number of siblings of similar age should increase the opportunity cost of the time of children.[3]

Some of these determinants can be readily examined using survey data, but it is not clear how adequately other features of the economic model can be captured. With cross-section data individuals face a similar external environment. All potential students, in principle, face the same job opportunities and tuition and fees, for example, so that it is unclear whether cross-section analysis can capture the response to increased demand for educated workers or to increased tuition. In many societies, however, the realistic opportunities that children face may vary substantially from family to family, so that the behavior of children with educated parents or parents employed as professionals, for example, may provide a reliable guide to general behavior when professional jobs become more widely available. Likewise, even if children do face the same opportunities, their perceptions of those opportunities may vary with household characteristics and pro-

3. The number of children and school enrollment may be inversely related because of trade-offs between the quantity and quality of children. See Becker and Lewis (1974) and Willis (1974).

vide a guide to the impact of real changes in opportunities on the demand for schooling.

Other aspects of the determinants of schooling can be readily captured by analysis of survey data. The opportunity cost of time is heavily influenced by both individual and household characteristics that can be tracked over time. To the extent that schooling is a consumer good, the relationship of enrollment to household income can be estimated from cross-section data quite adequately. And to the extent that the taste for education is influenced by parents and their own demand for education, analysis of household data can provide clear evidence about the intergenerational transfer of educational attainment.

The household model of enrollment. School enrollment is expected to decline with the age of students because the opportunity cost of their time increases with age. Males generally have higher enrollment rates than females. Because men, on average, spend more years as members of the labor force, they will receive higher rates of return to schooling.

The age and sex of the household head and a variable that distinguishes intact households from households with single heads is included because they may bear on the opportunity cost of the time of household members. For similar reasons, the number of household members under age 2, age 3 to 5, 6 to 11, 12 to 17, 18 to 24, 25 to 59, and 60 and older is included. As discussed above, additional young household members are expected to discourage enrollment by increasing the opportunity cost of the time of other household members, and additional older members are expected to encourage enrollment by decreasing the opportunity cost of the time of other household members.

A number of variables are included that bear on the expected return to schooling. The natural log of household expenditure per capita and its square are included as proxies for permanent income. Socioeconomic status of the household is included using a series of dummy variables closely tied to the occupation that accounted for the largest share of household income. Finally, the educational attainment of the head is included.

The dependent variable is binary: those who are enrolled in school are assigned a value of 1, those not enrolled are assigned a value of zero. Virtually all children (98 percent) age 9 to 11 are enrolled in school, so their schooling behavior was not analyzed. Because the age of entry varies considerably, the proportion of 6 to 8 year olds who are enrolled is potentially of interest. The factors governing age at entry should, however, be quite different from those governing age at departure. Preliminary analysis of age at entry was not successful and has not been pursued.

Separate estimates, based on the 1981 Socio-Economic Survey of Thailand (NSO 1985), were prepared for three different age groups, 12–14 years, 15–17 years, and 18–24 years, that roughly correspond to lower secondary, upper secondary, and tertiary levels of education. The samples are restricted to members of family households. The numbers of observations for the three age groups are 4,070, 3,712, and 6,875, respectively. The model was estimated using logit procedures because ordinary least squares estimates of binary dependent variables are plagued by well-known statistical problems. (For a detailed description of the survey, see Chapter 4.)

In general, the results are quite consistent with our expectations for all age groups, and the independent variables, taken together, explain a substantial portion of the variation in the dependent variable. The pseudo-R^2 varies from 0.187 for those 12–14 to as high as 0.352 for those 18–24. Among the independent variables, sex, age, head's educational attainment, socioeconomic status, and household composition exhibit statistically significant effects for all three age groups. Income has a significant effect for those 15–17 and 18–24. Sex of the head is statistically significant only for those 18–24 and household type is statistically insignificant for all three groups.

The effects of selected independent variables are summarized in Table 6.1, which presents adjusted means. Adjusted means are the calculated values of the dependent variable with one independent variable set to selected values and all other independent variables set to their sample means. Thus, adjusted means show the partial effect of a variable.

The sex and age of potential students have an important bearing on school enrollment. Calculated at the means of the independent variables, being one year older reduced the probability of school attendance by about 25 percent for those age 12–14 or 15–17 and by 46 percent for those 18–24. Irrespective of the age group, females are considerably less likely to be enrolled than males (Table 6.1).

The most important household characteristic is the educational attainment of the household head. The break between primary and secondary education is particularly important. Children living in households headed by a person who attended secondary school are substantially more likely to be enrolled at all three age groups. The impact of the head's having gone beyond the secondary level could not be estimated with sufficient accuracy to reach any conclusions for the 12–14 and 15–17 age groups.[4] However, the probability that 18–24 year olds will be enrolled is nearly twice as high if their household head has a tertiary education as compared with a secondary education and three to four times as high as compared with a household head with a primary education or less.

The sex of the household head has a statistically significant effect only for 18–24 year olds. Members of female-headed households are more likely to be students. The direction of causality here is rather ambiguous, however.

4. This is not too surprising because only about 2 percent of heads in these age groups had a tertiary education.

Table 6.1. Proportions enrolled, adjusted means: 1981

Independent variables	Age of potential student		
	12–14	15–17	18–24
Gender			
Male	0.823	0.264	0.042
Female	0.742	0.201	0.030
Age of head			
30	0.812	0.212	0.027
40	0.796	0.222	0.032
50	0.778	0.232	0.037
60	0.760	0.243	0.044
70	0.741	0.254	0.052
Education of head			
None	0.772	0.211	0.028
Primary	0.779	0.226	0.033
Secondary	0.859	0.383	0.061
Tertiary	0.875	0.259	0.111

Source: Estimated using data from the 1981 Socio-Economic Survey (NSO 1985).

Members in this age group, especially males, are likely to replace current female heads, once they complete their schooling. Being in school may increase the probability of having a female household head.

Age of head has a mixed impact on enrollment. Household members 12–14 are less likely to be enrolled in school if the head is older, but members 18–24 are less likely to be enrolled if the head is younger.

The household's per capita income (as proxied by per capita expenditure) and socioeconomic status are important determinants of school attendance (see Appendix 6.1 for details). Per capita income has no measurable impact on enrollment among 12–14 year olds, but, calculated at the means, a 1 percent increase in income yields an increase in the probability of being enrolled of 1.3 percent for those 15–17 and 2.8 percent for those 18–24.

Socioeconomic status, looked at in a broad context, has a very consistent impact on school enrollment. For all three age groups, members of farm households and laborer households are least likely to be students. Members of households engaged in urban-type activities, except for those in laborer households, are most likely to be students. Two factors undoubtedly operate here. The opportunity cost of schooling is probably higher among farm households because farm children can be economically productive at an early age. Of course, children can also be economically active in an urban setting working, in particular, as unpaid family workers. Nonetheless, children living in entrepreneurial households have high levels of enrollment. The second factor operating is that the expected returns from additional schooling depend on the student's eventual occupation which, in turn, depends on the employment status of the household. Thus, members of farm households and laborer households have lower expected returns to schooling and, consequently, drop out at a younger age.

Among farm households, socioeconomic status has no consistent effect on schooling across all three age groups. Among farm households that own their land, the size of landholdings does not even have a monotonic relationship to school enrollment. Of those age 15–17 and 18–24, members of large landowner households are least likely to attend school and members of medium-size landowner households are most likely to attend school. Of those 12–14, members of medium-size landowner households are least likely to attend school. This non-monotonic pattern may reflect conflicting income and opportunity cost effects of land size. The opportunity cost of schooling undoubtedly increases with the size of landholdings, but the "affordability" of schooling should increase as well.

Among urban households, the relationship of socioeconomic status to schooling is somewhat surprising. Members of three groups consistently have the highest enrollment ratios: entrepreneurial households without paid workers; clerical, sales, and service worker households; and economically inactive households. It is not entirely clear why professional, technical, and managerial household members would have lower enrollment probabilities. But any interpretation should not neglect that these results quantify partial effects given per capita income. The high rating of economically inactive households is probably a spurious finding in the sense that schooling and employment are competing activities.

The presence of additional household members has a very important effect on school enrollment (Table 6.2). The presence of an additional child under age 12 is estimated to depress school enrollment by other potential students in the household (those 12–24 years of age). This finding is consistent with the view that the presence of a young child will increase the opportunity cost of schooling for older household members. The presence of an additional household member 12 years of age or older is estimated to increase school enrollment by other potential students in the household. This finding is consistent with the view that older household members are substitutes in household production for potential students so that their presence reduces the opportunity cost of school enrollment. It is also possible that economies of scale influence schooling decisions. In a number of areas—such as costs for transportation, lodging, textbooks, information, and transactions—per student costs decline with the number of students.

Enrollment forecasts. The regression estimates described above are used in this section to forecast the proportion enrolled at each age, as well as

Table 6.2. Impact of additional household members on proportions enrolled, adjusted means: 1981

Age of additional household member	Age of potential student		
	12–14	15–17	18–24
None[a]	0.785	0.230	0.035
Under 3	**0.739**	0.225	**0.018**
3–5	0.775	**0.184**	0.028
6–11	0.779	0.215	0.033
12–17	**0.803**	**0.265**	**0.040**
18–24	0.797	**0.251**	**0.046**
25–59	**0.822**	**0.277**	**0.050**
60 and older	**0.844**	0.264	**0.043**

Source: Estimated using data from the 1981 Socio-Economic Survey (NSO 1985).

Note: Boldface values indicate significant differences at the 5 percent level.

a. This category gives enrollment for household members at the mean for the sample.

total enrollments in primary, secondary, and tertiary institutions. Enrollment ratios are calculated by forecasting each of the independent variables separately for households, distinguishing them by age and sex of the head and type of household, using HOMES. Educational attainment of the head is based on projected attainment of men and women combined in five-year age groups consistent with the enrollment projections presented in Table 6.2. Per capita expenditure is forecast using the methods described in Chapter 5, which allow for the impact of changes in household composition and exogenous growth in productivity per worker at 4 percent per annum. Socioeconomic status variables are treated as control variables and held constant at their 1981 means throughout the forecast.

The statistical analysis that serves as the basis for this forecast was restricted to enrollment by members of family households. This excludes one-person households. For forecast purposes, however, enrollment ratios among one-person households were held constant at their 1981 values. The survey did not include persons living in rooming houses and boarding schools, so the unadjusted forecasts would consistently underestimate enrollment to the extent that these students were not covered. Furthermore, definitions of school enrollment for the socioeconomic survey and those applied by various government agencies responsible for administering education undoubtedly differ. One would expect that survey estimates would be the lower of the two because part-time students and those who dropped out would be less likely to report their status as enrolled. All of these factors may particularly affect reported enrollment at the tertiary level. To maintain some consistency, the projections have been adjusted in multiplicative fashion to replicate 1985 enrollment figures reported in the Sixth National Education Plan.

We have forecast enrollment ratios at five-year intervals beginning in 1990 and ending in 2015 (Table 6.3). Among those age 12 to 14, the proportion enrolled increases quite steadily from about 67 percent in 1990 to just under 75 percent in 2005 and to 78 percent in 2015. Among those 15–17, the proportion enrolled increases quite rapidly during the early stages of the projection—from an enrollment ratio of 33 percent in 1990 to a ratio of 42 percent in 2000. Thereafter, the increase slows considerably so that by 2015, just under one-half of those 15–17 are forecast to be enrolled in school. Enrollment ratios for those 18–24 follow a similar pattern, albeit at a much lower level. The proportion enrolled almost doubles between 1990 and 2005, increasing from 12.2 percent to 21.3 percent. But the enrollment rate actually peaks in 2010 and declines very slightly to stand at 21.4 percent in the year 2015.

Enrollment forecasts were prepared by multiplying the proportion enrolled in each age group by the population in the corresponding age group to determine the number of students of ages 6–8, 9–11, 12–14, 15–17, and 18–24. For those under 12 the 1981 enrollment ratios were employed and for those 12 and older, the enrollment ratios presented in Table 6.3 were used. The students were then apportioned among four levels of schooling—primary, lower secondary, upper secondary, and tertiary—in direct relation to their distribution according to the 1981 Socio-Economic Survey (NSO 1985). For example, of those age 15 to 17, 25.1 percent are assumed to be enrolled in lower secondary, 71.2 percent in upper secondary, and 3.6 percent at the tertiary level.[5] The results are reported in Table 6.4.

Primary enrollments are forecast to peak in 1995 at 7.3 million students, which is just barely above the 1990 level. After 1995 primary enrollments are forecast to decline steadily by about two to three hundred thousand every five years. Enrollments at the lower secondary level are forecast to increase somewhat more significantly in percentage terms, from 1.4 million in 1990 to almost 1.6 million in 2000. Thereafter the numbers should hold steady or decline very modestly. Upper secondary enrollments are forecast to increase by 48 percent between 1990 and 2005 when enrollments will peak at 1.8 million students. Tertiary enrollments are forecast to nearly double between 1990 and 2005 and hold steady thereafter.

---

5. An additional source of error is introduced here because level of enrollment is not reported in the 1981 Socio-Economic Survey (NSO 1985). Educational attainment, which we assume was defined by survey workers as the last grade completed, is reported. From this information we inferred the current distribution of enrollments by level of schooling in a somewhat inexact fashion.

Table 6.3. Forecast proportions enrolled: 1990–2015

Year	Age		
	12–14	15–17	18–24
1990	0.673	0.334	0.122
1995	0.700	0.386	0.159
2000	0.724	0.423	0.194
2005	0.744	0.448	0.213
2010	0.762	0.462	0.218
2015	0.777	0.467	0.214

Table 6.4. Forecast enrollments: 1990–2015

Year	Number enrolled (thousands)				
	Primary	Lower secondary	Upper secondary	Tertiary	Total
1990	7,277	1,395	1,236	619	10,526
1995	7,317	1,506	1,505	844	11,172
2000	7,022	1,548	1,740	1,064	11,374
2005	6,746	1,507	1,829	1,195	11,276
2010	6,606	1,493	1,810	1,199	11,108
2015	6,320	1,478	1,786	1,159	10,743

Note: Rows may not sum to totals because of rounding.

The impact of demographic change and its interaction with rising enrollment ratios is clear from Table 6.4. The number of students in the upper educational categories is still increasing rapidly in Thailand. When combined with rising enrollment ratios, the increase in the number of students is dramatic. Between 1990 and 2000, enrollments are forecast to increase at 3.4 percent per annum at the upper secondary level and at 5.4 percent per annum at the tertiary level. Shortly after the turn of the century, however, enrollment levels stabilize with slight increases at the upper levels through 2010 and a slow but steady decrease in enrollments at the primary and lower secondary levels (Table 6.4). Again, the interaction of demographic factors and enrollment ratios accounts for this. At the same time that the size of school-age cohorts is expected to stabilize or decline, the proportions attending school are forecast to stabilize or exhibit only a modest upward trend.

The Transition-Rate Approach

The transition rate is the ratio of students in a grade in one year to the number of students in the previous grade the previous year. In mathematical terms, the transition rate, T_{it}, is represented by:

$$T_{it} = \frac{E_{i+1,\, t+1}}{E_{it}} .$$

where E_{it} is the enrollment in grade i and time t. Current enrollment multiplied by the corresponding transition rate gives an estimate of enrollment in the following period for the next higher grade. Enrollment in the entry grade is estimated by the number of children of entry age multiplied by the proportion entering (assumed to be 1.0 for Thailand).

Transition rates for Thailand from 1978 to 1985 are given in Table 6.5. Typically, transition rates are quite high within any major educational level because students tend to complete programs that they begin. Transition rates between major levels, however, tend to be much lower. For example, only about 40 percent of students who complete primary education continue on to the secondary level ($P6$–$M1$ = 0.4), and only about 50 to 60 percent of lower secondary students continue on to upper secondary school.

On the average, about 40 percent of graduates from lower secondary education continue into the vocational stream (Table 6.5). And of those who complete lower vocational, about 40 percent continue into the upper vocational level. They are joined by a smaller proportion who have completed the academic stream of upper secondary. Table 6.5 also shows proportions continuing into teacher training and university education.

Projection methodology and transition rates. School enrollment is forecast using three pieces of information. The number of new entrants each year is determined using projections of the population age 6 to 8. The size of the entering cohort is calculated as 50 percent of those age 6 plus 25 percent of those age 7 or 8. The number of students beyond the first year of primary school is determined by enrollment in each grade in the previous year and by transition rates. The key data, however, are the transition rates. The assumptions (Table 6.6) that underlie the forecasts presented below are based on the past record, i.e., a continuation of trends and policies promulgated in the Sixth National Education Plan (NEC 1987).

At the primary level, the transition rates $P1$–$P2$ and $P5$–$P6$ are lower than the transition rates for other grades, both because of high drop-out rates and high repetition rates. The Sixth National Education Plan states that the government will try to reduce waste due to dropping out and repetition. Hence, the transition rates $P1$–$P2$ and $P5$–$P6$ are assumed to increase over time: $P1$–$P2$ increases from 0.8685 to 0.95 and $P5$–$P6$ increases from 0.9064 to 0.95 over a 10-year period (Table 6.6).

Table 6.5. Transition rates: 1978-85

School grade	1978-79	1979-80	1980-81	1981-82	1982-83	1983-84	1984-85
Primary							
P1–P2	0.8681	0.8679	0.8703	0.8645	0.8669	0.9091	0.8633
P2–P3	0.9917	0.9789	0.9635	0.9605	0.9620	1.0010	0.9715
P3–P4	0.9256	0.9394	0.9713	0.9707	0.9728	0.9899	0.9627
P4–P5	0.9271	0.9590	0.9754	0.9897	0.9842	0.9931	0.9764
P5–P6	0.8274	0.8495	0.8559	0.8817	0.9043	0.9269	0.9686
Secondary							
P6–M1	a	a	0.4482	0.4301	0.4151	0.4114	0.4002
M1–M2	a	a	0.9660	0.9590	0.9574	0.9664	0.9427
M2–M3	a	a	0.9751	0.9674	0.9661	0.9761	0.9568
M3–M4	a	a	a	0.5699	0.5658	0.5416	0.5130
M4–M5	a	a	a	0.9132	0.9224	0.9242	0.9089
M5–M6	a	a	a	0.9470	0.9650	0.9593	0.9505
Vocational							
M3–LV1	0.3278	0.3368	0.6091	0.4414	0.3915	0.3847	u
LV3–HV1	0.3690	0.4005	0.3926	0.4084	0.5013	0.4470	u
M6–HV1	0.0134	0.0201	0.0272	0.1073	0.1522	0.1784	u
Teacher training							
M6–T1	0.0768	0.0600	0.0834	0.0834	0.0828	0.0438	u
University (closed)[b]							
M6–CU1	0.2256	0.2233	0.2092	0.2059	0.1976	0.2147	u

Source: NSO, *Final Report on Education Statistics* (various editions).

Note: *P*—Primary; *M*—Secondary; *LV*—Lower vocational; *HV*—Higher vocational; *T*—Teacher training; *CU*—Closed university. Numbers indicate the grade within each educational level.

a. Secondary transition rates for 1978–81 cannot be calculated because of changes in the schooling system.

b. The transition rate to open universities is not meaningful because open universities draw a low percentage of new students from recent secondary school graduates.

u—unavailable.

Although the transition rate to lower secondary, *P6–M1*, declined between 1980 and 1985, we suspect this to be a temporary adjustment to the recent extension of compulsory education to six years. The Sixth National Education Plan explicitly targets the continuation rate *P6–M1* for a substantial increase, and we project a rise in the transition rate to 0.7 by the year 2000 from the current level of about 0.4 (Table 6.6).

Transition from lower to upper secondary, both in academic and vocational streams, declined between 1980 and 1985. We believe that both of

Table 6.6. Assumed transition rates for projection

School grade	Assumption employed
Primary	
P1–P2	0.8685 in 1984; increase to 0.95 in 10 years and remain constant
P2–P3	Constant at 0.9717
P3–P4	Constant at 0.9735
P4–P5	Constant at 0.9838
P5–P6	0.9064 in 1984; increase to 0.95 in 10 years and remain constant
Secondary	
P6–M1	0.4114 in 1984; increase to 0.7 in 2000, and remain constant
M1–M2	Constant at 0.97
M2–M3	Constant at 0.97
M3–M4	Constant at 0.54
M4–M5	Constant at 0.92
M5–M6	Constant at 0.96
Vocational	
M3–LV1	Constant at 0.38
LV1–LV2	Constant at 0.96
LV2–LV3	Constant at 0.95
LV3–HV1	0.447 in 1984; increase to 0.5 in 1990 and remain constant
HV1–HV2	Constant at 0.95
M6–HV1	0.1784 in 1984; increase to 0.2 in 1990 and remain constant
HV1–HV2	Constant at 0.95
Teacher training	
M6–T1	0.0809 in 1984; decline to 0.02 in 1990
T1–T2	Constant at 0.95
University	
M6–CU1	0.2147 in 1984; increase to 0.3 in 1990, to 0.4 in 2000

Note: Open university enrollments are assumed to increase by 1 percent annually.

these declines reflect the expansion of lower secondary education and that there is little reason to anticipate further decline. But because further expansion in lower secondary enrollments is anticipated, we do not expect an increase in the *M*3 continuation rates in the foreseeable future. Thus, the rate *M*3–*M*4 is assumed to remain constant at 0.54 and the rate *M*3–*LV*1 to remain constant at about 0.38 (Table 6.6).

Because the Sixth National Education Plan established no explicit policies regarding other levels of education, the assumptions made are based on past trends and our personal judgment. There are two main streams leading to the associate degree, namely higher vocational and technical education and teacher training. The demand for higher vocational and technical education has increased rapidly since 1978. Moreover, technical progress has been increasingly emphasized as a strategy for economic development. Therefore, we anticipate continued demand for workers with higher vocational and technical education and modest increases in transition rates. Transition from lower to higher vocational school, *LV3–HV1*, is assumed to have increased from 0.447 to 0.5 between 1984 and 1990 and to remain constant thereafter. Transition from upper secondary to higher vocational, *M6–HV1*, is assumed to increase from 0.1784 to 0.2 by 1990 and to remain constant thereafter (Table 6.6).

In contrast, teacher training terminating at the associate degree level will be phased out in favor of training at the bachelor's or higher degree level except for teachers of fine arts and physical education. Hence, the transition rate *M6–T1* is assumed to decline from 0.0809 to .02 in 1990 and remain constant thereafter (Table 6.6).

The transition rate from upper secondary education to public and private closed universities, *M6–CU1*, is assumed to increase from 0.2147 in 1984 to 0.30 in 1990 and to 0.40 in 2000. Open university enrollments are assumed to increase by 1 percent annually. This assumption is based on the growth rate during 1984–85, when the number of students in open universities started to pick up after a sharp decline during 1983–84 (Table 6.6).

Projection results. Projection results at five-year intervals are shown in Table 6.7. Between 1990 and 1995 total school enrollment is forecast to increase by about 700,000 students. The increase in schooling is concentrated beyond the primary level, with lower secondary enrollments growing by around 300,000 or by more than 20 percent. Upper secondary enrollment is forecast to increase by about 150,000 students, with about two-thirds of the gain coming in the academic stream. And higher education enrollments are forecast to increase by about 130,000 students with about three-quarters of the increase absorbed by closed universities.

From 1995 onward the effect of declining population growth begins to dominate the effect of increasing transition rates, so that enrollments at each level begin to decline. Total enrollment peaks at 12.1 million in 2005 and declines to 11.4 million by 2015. Total primary enrollments are expected to begin declining from a high of 7.2 million in 1995. Lower secondary enrollments peak at 2.1 million in the year 2000, and upper secondary enrollments peak five years later when enrollment will reach 1.8 million students.

The enrollment ratios implied by the education forecasts are given in Table 6.8. Enrollment ratios are calculated as the number of students in the primary, secondary, and tertiary levels divided by the school-age population (6–11, 12–17, and 18–22 years, respectively). The primary enrollment

Table 6.7. Enrollment projections: 1990–2015 (thousands)

School level	Year					
	1990	1995	2000	2005	2010	2015
Primary	7,110	7,161	6,811	6,555	6,384	6,066
Lower secondary	1,464	1,797	2,126	2,086	2,019	1,966
Upper secondary	1,116	1,279	1,578	1,763	1,666	1,628
Academic	663	762	941	1,051	993	971
Vocational	451	517	638	712	673	657
Higher education	1,111	1,244	1,491	1,675	1,701	1,707
Closed	512	614	829	979	970	939
Open	599	629	662	695	731	768
Total	10,801	11,481	12,006	12,079	11,770	11,367

Note: Closed higher education includes associate degree training for teachers. Columns may not sum to totals because of rounding.

Table 6.8. Projected enrollment ratios by level: 1990–2015

Year	Primary	Secondary	Tertiary
1990	0.938	0.348	0.181
1995	0.956	0.410	0.203
2000	0.961	0.493	0.240
2005	0.960	0.537	0.268
2010	0.960	0.540	0.285
2015	0.964	0.538	0.301

ratio will increase from 0.94 in 1990 to 0.96 in the year 2000 and remain constant thereafter. The secondary enrollment ratio will increase from 0.35 in 1990 to 0.49 in the year 2000 and continue to increase modestly up to 0.54 in 2015. The tertiary enrollment ratio will increase from 0.18 in 1990 to 0.24 in the year 2000 and continue to increase up to 0.30 in 2015.

Reliability and Comparison of Results

A number of factors will influence the reliability of both HOMES and transition-rate forecasts and the extent to which actual enrollments will deviate from forecast values. Primary school enrollments are determined almost entirely by the number of school-age children because primary school attendance is nearly universal. Thus, the reliability of forecasts of primary school enrollment depends almost entirely on the accuracy of population projections. All of those who will be attending primary school in the early 1990s are already born and their numbers can be projected with considerable reliability. But those who will enter primary school in the year 2000 have yet to be born, so that accuracy will depend on the reliability of population and, especially, fertility forecasts. However, anything but an extreme deviation from Thailand's historical trend will result in declining primary school enrollments in the near future.

As we turn to other educational levels, population forecasts become less problematic and transition-rate forecasts become more so. The cohort that will compose the high school graduating class of 2005 is already born, for example, but the proportion that will actually attend and graduate is quite uncertain. Enrollments at the secondary or the tertiary levels could certainly increase more rapidly than forecast if the demand for schooling increases rapidly and the resources are made available to support increased demand. If this occurs, enrollments at the lower and upper secondary level and at the tertiary level may peak at a much later date than forecast. In fact, the forecasts themselves suggest that somewhat higher enrollment ratios can be accommodated early in the next century without requiring substantial capital expenditures or additional teachers. The two greatest uncertainties about the forecasts presented are undoubtedly the division between academic and vocational streams and forecasts of open university enrollments. In fact, the distinction between vocational and academic training in Thailand is becoming increasingly blurred. The National Education Plan of 1987 calls for the incorporation of more vocational training in the academic stream and many general education courses have already been included in the vocational stream. Enrollment in institutions of higher education is particularly difficult to forecast. Our forecasts suggest rapidly increasing enrollments in closed universities up to 2005, but it may be possible to accommodate more students in closed universities after 2005. We have no particularly sound basis by which to forecast open university enrollments and the values presented reflect a simple assumption about open university enrollments.

A comparison of forecasts in Table 6.9 provides some indication about the possible range of enrollments. Because both projections are based on the same underlying population projection, any differences reflect differences in enrollment ratios rather than differences in the school-age population. The HOMES-based approach projects somewhat lower total school enrollment than the transition-rate method. In both 2000 and 2015, total enrollments differ by about 6 percent. At particular school levels, however, the differences are much more substantial. The HOMES-based method projects considerably lower enrollment at the lower secondary level, but significantly higher enrollment at the upper secondary level. In other words, the microanalysis (HOMES) suggests that a lower percentage of primary school graduates will continue on to secondary school, but of those who

Table 6.9. Enrollment projections based on HOMES and the transition-rate method: 2000 and 2015 (thousands)

	2000		2015	
School level	HOMES-based	Transition rate	HOMES-based	Transition rate
Primary	7,022	6,811	6,320	6,066
Lower secondary	1,548	2,126	1,478	1,966
Upper secondary	1,740	1,578	1,786	1,628
Tertiary	1,064	1,491	1,159	1,707
Total	11,374	12,006	10,743	11,367

do, a much higher percentage will continue on to upper secondary school. The HOMES-based method also projects considerably lower tertiary enrollment than the transition-rate method. In both 2000 and 2015, tertiary enrollments are about 30 percent lower using the HOMES-based analysis rather than the transition-rate approach.

THE COST OF EDUCATION

The cost of education can be separated into costs borne by individuals who receive educational services and costs paid by the educational institutions. Costs paid by individuals include tuition and fees, out-of-pocket expenses such as school lunches, uniforms, transportation, board, and textbooks, and the opportunity cost of students' time. The cost paid by institutions is usually divided into two components, namely operating costs and capital expenditures. Operating costs include teachers' salaries and allowances, materials and supplies for instruction, the cost of maintenance and operation of buildings and equipment, etc. Capital expenses are the opportunity cost of durable goods, land and buildings, and other capital employed in the provision of schooling.

The following sections contain forecasts of educational expenditures by public institutions and educational expenditures by individual households. Although these two types account for the great majority of the costs of education, coverage is not complete. The cost of private education not paid by students, e.g., costs covered by endowments, and the opportunity cost of students' time are not forecast.

Government Expenditure on Education

Government expenditure on education as a percentage of total government spending was around 19 percent in 1985. It is one of the highest among developing countries, and demonstrates the government's commitment to education in Thailand. In fact, this category of expenditure is second only to expenditure on economic services and is approximately equal to expenditure on defense (NEC 1985).

In 1985, 57 percent of the public education budget was allocated to primary education. Secondary and tertiary education in the academic stream claim 18.2 percent and 13.4 percent of the total, respectively. Vocational education, at all levels, claims about 8.4 percent and teachers' training claims about 2.2 percent of total expenditure on education.

In 1985 wages and salaries constituted 82 percent of total expenditure in primary and 70 percent in secondary education, but less than 50 percent for vocational schools and universities. The importance of wages and salaries has increased over time for all levels except for vocational education. This trend reflects higher teacher quality and increased government emphasis on the development of human inputs.

Unit costs of education. The calculation of unit costs is based primarily on the budget of the central government. For primary education, the calculated cost is the average cost per student in schools under the Department of General Education and the Office of National Primary Education. Municipal schools, which are under the control of local governments, have not been included; the expenditure forecasts presented below assume that unit costs are identical in all public primary schools. At the secondary level, costs are calculated using budgets of schools under the Department of General Education. Schools under this department constitute the majority of public schools at the secondary level. Due to data deficiency, the costs of demonstration schools and other special schools have not been calculated. For vocational schools, costs include institutions under the Department of Vocational Education and the College of Technology and Vocational Education. For tertiary education, all public universities under the National University Bureau are included.

Operating costs are calculated from the budget for wages, salaries, and maintenance and operation of equipment and buildings in each fiscal year divided by the number of students. Capital expenses per student are calculated as the opportunity cost of durable goods, land, and buildings used in providing educational services divided by the number of students (see Appendix 6.2 for a detailed explanation).

In 1985 the government spent about 3,423 baht per primary student per year and 3,894 baht per secondary student in public schools. Although the operating cost per student in the secondary level was only slightly higher than that in the primary level, the capital expense per student in the secondary level was almost double that in the primary level (Table 6.10).

The cost per student for public vocational schools granting less than a bachelor's degree and for schools granting a bachelor's degree were 8,367 baht and 11,077 baht, respectively, in 1985. Operating costs constituted 81

Table 6.10. Estimated cost per student by type and level of education: 1985 (baht, 1985 prices)

	Number of students	Operating cost	Capital cost	Total cost
Primary	6,057,740	2,917	506	3,423
Secondary	1,638,479	2,956	938	3,894
Vocational (<BA)	304,271	6,780	1,586	8,367
Vocational (BA)	5,025	7,417	3,660	11,077
Teacher training	57,369	13,346	4,494	17,839
Closed university	107,557	34,392	11,897	46,289
Open university	569,869	359	68	428

percent and 67 percent of total costs in these two vocational levels, respectively. The average unit cost for teacher training during the 1978–85 interval of 12,740 baht is employed for cost projections. Of that amount, operating costs constituted about 60 percent.

Cost per student is highest in closed universities and is increasing over time. In 1985 the average cost per student in all public closed universities was 46,289 baht. Operating costs constituted about 74 percent of the total. However, it is well known that the cost per student varies greatly with the field of study. According to a study by the National Education Commission (1985), the cost per student in the medical and natural sciences was at least twice as much as the cost per student in the social sciences. Hence, the cost per student also varies by university because the proportions of the number of students in each field varies. The costs per student in universities that put more emphasis on medical and natural sciences such as Mahidol, Khon Khaen and Chulalongkorn universities are higher than at Thammasat University, which only offers a degree in social sciences.

In contrast to closed universities, the costs per student borne by the government is very low for open universities—about 400 baht, on average. Due to a huge base of students enrolled in open universities and low operating costs, revenues from tuition, fees, proceeds from selling textbooks, and other activities covered most of the costs for open universities.

Forecast of public expenditures. The forecasts of government expenditures on education are based on the transition-rate projections provided in Table 6.7 and the estimated operating costs and capital expenses per student provided in Table 6.10. Transition-rate projections are used because of the more detailed treatment of vocational and teacher training. To isolate the source of changes in the total cost of education, two forecasts are prepared. In the first, unit costs are held constant as of 1985. Hence, any change in public expenditure is due solely to changing enrollments. In the second, unit costs are allowed to increase with anticipated improvements in the quality of education.

Forecast with constant unit cost. If unit costs are held constant, total public expenditure is forecast to increase from 41 billion baht in 1990 to 51 billion baht in 2000 (Table 6.11). Total expenditures will grow by only 2.1 percent per annum between 1990 and 2000. Given expected growth in GDP and government revenues, the fiscal burden imposed by education will decline quite steadily. In fact, if no improvements in school quality are made, public expenditure on education is forecast to decline after 2010.

The relatively slow growth in overall expenditures is forecast despite a fairly substantial shift from low-unit to high-unit cost levels of schooling. The share of expenditures devoted to primary education declines from 54 percent in 1990 to 42 percent in the year 2000, while the share devoted to closed university education rises from 19 percent to reach 26 percent (Table 6.11).

Projection with changing unit costs. The constant unit cost forecasts presented in Table 6.11 are a minimalist approach and surely underestimate future expenditures. The trends in unit costs cited above show that the government has attempted to increase the quality of education at least as measured by expenditures. Undoubtedly, the government will continue to increase expenditure per student in the future. The educational plan calls for improved quality and the constant unit cost forecasts indicate that additional expenditure can be undertaken without undue fiscal hardship.

The forecasts presented in this section allow unit costs to increase in response to changing inputs related to educational quality. For education below the university level, unit costs are related to the student–teacher ratio and the percentage of teachers with a bachelor's degree. In addition, scale economies are captured by relating unit costs to enrollments. At the university level, unit costs are also affected by the field of study—the higher the percentage of social science students, the lower the cost per student.

The following assumptions underlie the forecasts that allow for improved quality: The student–teacher ratios in primary, secondary, and vocational schools are assumed to decline from their 1985 values of 18, 18, and 21, respectively, to 15 for all three levels by 1995, remaining constant until 2015. The percentage of teachers with at least a bachelor's degree is assumed to increase from 40 in 1985 to 80 in 2015 for primary education. For secondary education, the percentage of teachers with at least a bachelor's degree was 78 in 1985, and we assume that all secondary teachers will have college education by the year 2005. For vocational education, the percentage with a college education is assumed to increase from 52 in 1985 to 80 in 2015.

Table 6.11. Projected education costs borne by government, with assumption of constant unit costs: 1990–2015 (millions of baht)

	1990	1995	2000	2005	2010	2015
Total cost	41,370	45,301	50,942	53,575	52,139	50,261
Primary	22,148	22,307	21,217	20,417	19,886	18,895
Secondary	7,296	8,770	10,508	10,752	10,322	10,064
Vocational	3,159	3,690	4,696	5,395	5,215	5,069
Teacher training	745	790	816	843	844	837
Closed university	7,766	9,475	13,422	15,870	15,559	15,067
Open university	256	269	283	298	313	329
Percentage of total						
Primary	53.54	49.24	41.65	38.11	38.14	37.59
Secondary	17.64	19.36	20.63	20.07	19.80	20.02
Vocational	7.64	8.15	9.22	10.07	10.00	10.09
Teacher training	1.80	1.74	1.60	1.57	1.62	1.67
Closed university	18.77	20.92	26.35	29.62	29.84	29.98
Open university	0.61	0.59	0.56	0.56	0.60	0.65

The unit cost projections presented in Table 6.12 are calculated using the regression results reported in Appendix 6.2. The unit costs are applied to students in all public schools. The percentage of students enrolled in public schools is held constant over the entire projection period: primary (91 percent), secondary (88 percent), non-B.A. vocational (56 percent), B.A. vocational (100 percent), teacher training (100 percent), closed university (69 percent), and open university (100 percent). Because variations in unit costs for teacher training and vocational education at the degree level could not be satisfactorily explained via regression analysis, teacher training costs were held constant at their 1985 level, and vocational costs at the degree level were allowed to increase at a constant rate consistent with their historical trend. Among the other levels of education, unit costs increase most rapidly between 1985 and 1995 for secondary education (2.5 percent per annum) and for closed universities (2.0 percent per annum). Unit costs for the open universities actually decline as a result of scale economies.

Given anticipated increases in unit costs, total expenditures are forecast to rise from 46 billion baht in 1990 to almost 54 billion baht in 1995 (Table 6.13). This represents an annual increase in public expenditures of 3.4 percent between 1990 and 1995. Thus, even with anticipated improvements in quality, public expenditures on education may grow at about the same rate or slower than either GDP or government revenues. The forecast annual rate of growth in expenditures between 1995 and 2000 is 3.8 percent,

Table 6.12. Unit costs of education, with assumption of improving quality: 1985–2015

	1985	1995	2005	2015
Primary	3,423	4,004	4,633	5,178
Operating cost	2,917	3,429	4,028	4,550
Capital expense	506	575	605	628
Secondary	3,894	4,988	5,440	5,402
Operating cost	2,956	3,787	4,131	4,131
Capital expense	938	1,201	1,309	1,271
Vocational (<BA)	8,366	9,553	9,422	9,527
Operating cost	6,780	7,897	7,905	7,927
Capital expense	1,586	1,656	1,517	1,600
Vocational (BA)	11,077	11,366	11,556	11,711
Operating cost	7,417	7,417	7,417	7,417
Capital expense	3,660	3,949	4,139	4,294
Teacher training	13,625	13,625	13,625	13,625
Operating cost	9,897	9,897	9,897	9,897
Capital expense	3,728	3,728	3,728	3,728
Closed university	46,289	56,378	66,467	76,556
Operating cost	34,392	43,706	53,020	62,334
Capital expense	11,897	12,672	13,447	14,222
Open university	428	409	389	367
Operating cost	360	345	328	310
Capital expense	68	64	61	57

Table 6.13. Projection of education costs borne by the government, with increasing unit costs: 1990–2015 (millions of baht)

	1990	1995	2000	2005	2010	2015
Total costs	45,611	53,957	64,974	72,033	73,056	73,819
Primary	24,341	26,091	26,971	27,633	28,195	28,854
Secondary	8,341	11,234	14,179	15,021	14,358	13,692
Vocational	3,321	4,044	4,933	5,477	5,346	5,235
Teacher training	745	790	816	843	844	837
University						
Closed	8,612	11,540	17,810	22,788	24,037	24,919
Open	251	258	264	271	276	282

Note: Columns may not sum to totals due to rounding.

but expenditure growth is projected to decline significantly early in the twenty-first century.

Forecast Household Expenditure on Education

So far, our discussion of education costs has dealt exclusively with public expenditures, but part of the cost of education includes expenditures by households for the education of their children. These expenditures include tuition and fees for households sending their children to private schools and expenditures on books, school supplies, uniforms, etc. Data on household expenditures have been collected on an irregular basis as part of the Socio-Economic Surveys; the results reported here are based on analysis of the 1981 Socio-Economic Survey (NSO 1985). (See Chapter 4 for a detailed discussion of the survey and analytic procedures.)

The general approach to forecasting household expenditure is as follows. First, the socioeconomic survey was analyzed to assess the statistical relationship between expenditure on education and household characteristics including per capita income, the age and sex of the head, the number of members in different age groups, and socioeconomic status of the household. Second, the statistical results were combined with forecasts of demographic characteristics of the household and other independent variables generated by the household projection package HOMES to produce forecasts of expenditures per household and total household expenditures on education.

Complete statistical results from the HOMES-based forecast of household expenditures on education are reported in Table 6.14. Average expenditure on education is quite low in Thailand; households devote barely more than 1 percent of their household budget to schooling (Table 6.15). Income has a very negligible effect on the share devoted to education. The impact of family size on education expenditure depends on the age of additional household members. Households with more school-age children, i.e., those age 3–19, devote a larger share of the household's budget to education. On the other hand, the presence of children under age 3 reduces the share devoted to education. Households headed by females and entrepreneurial, professional, technical, and managerial households spend a somewhat greater share of their budget on education than do other households.

Peak expenditure on education occurs among households with a head age 40–44 (Table 6.15). Naturally, these households are particularly likely to have dependent school-age children. There is a "mini-peak" for households with heads age 70–74 because these households are more likely to have grandchildren of school age than are households in nearby age categories.

Total household expenditure on education calculated for Thailand in 1990 is 510 million baht or about 1 percent of total expenditures for that year.

Table 6.14. Analysis of education expenditures by households: Statistical results

Variable name	Parameter estimate	Standard error
Intercept	-0.111011	0.010417
Log per capita expenditure	0.032642	0.003052
Log per capita expenditure squared	-0.002380	0.000228
Males, 0–2	-0.003276	0.000584
Males, 3–12	0.001996	0.000254
Males, 13–19	0.003106	0.000161
Males, 20–59	0.000540	0.000192
Males, 60+	0.000967	0.000689
Females, 0–2	-0.003417	0.000548
Females, 3–12	0.001591	0.000255
Females, 13–19	0.003551	0.000157
Females, 20–59	0.001325	0.000188
Females, 60+	0.000125	0.000534
Age	0.002571	0.000588
Age squared	0.000070	0.000082
Farm operator, medium landowner	-0.000002	8.71E-07
Farm operator, large landowner	-0.000742	0.000842
Farm operator, small land renter	-0.001394	0.000811
Farm operator, large land renter	-0.004093	0.001299
Farm operator, fishing, forestry, etc.	0.001981	0.001557
Entrepreneur, with paid workers	0.011119	0.001323
Entrepreneur, without paid workers	0.006916	0.000821
Professional, technical, and managerial workers	0.011168	0.001009
Laborers, farm	-0.000440	0.001007
Laborers, nonfarm	0.000526	0.001496
Clerical, sales, and service workers	0.009680	0.000923
Production workers	0.003596	0.000920
Economically inactive	0.013271	0.000987
One-person, male	0.001329	0.001125
One-person, female	-0.004226	0.001092

$R^2 = 0.166$

$N = 11{,}890$

Table 6.15. Percentage share of education in household budget and total expenditure on education, by age of head: 1990 and 2005

	1990		2005	
Age of head	Share of household budget (%)	Total (in million baht)	Share of household budget (%)	Total (in million baht)
<25	0.73	35.06	0.57	53.84
25–29	0.83	57.03	0.65	96.08
30–34	1.00	74.88	0.76	135.21
35–39	1.22	91.45	0.88	179.82
40–44	1.23	81.32	0.83	159.79
45–49	1.08	59.72	0.70	112.99
50–54	0.99	49.16	0.63	80.03
55–59	0.82	28.61	0.53	43.04
60–64	0.63	14.90	0.39	21.44
65–69	0.61	8.31	0.37	13.86
70–74	0.77	6.42	0.52	12.54
75 +	0.57	3.24	0.49	7.19
All combined	0.95	510.12	0.68	915.83

Note: All types of households are included.

This figure is expected to grow to over 900 million baht by the year 2005, although the share of total expenditure will actually decline to an average of 0.7 percent. In other words, household expenditure on education is forecast to grow about 30 percent slower than total expenditure between 1990 and 2005.

CONCLUSIONS

Education is one of the most important means by which a country can improve its human resources. The government of Thailand has long recognized the importance of education and has devoted substantial resources to the goals of achieving a highly educated populace. However, because population growth has been so great and resources have been so constrained, most of the government's effort has been devoted to keeping pace with growing primary school enrollments and less on improving quality or on increasing the availability of secondary and post-secondary education.

As population growth has, more or less, been brought under control, new priorities should surface that will affect enrollment, costs, and the allocation of resources among different levels of schooling and between the public and private sectors.

Using the official population projections for Thailand, school enrollments have been forecast through 2015. Total enrollments will increase gradually from 10.4 million in 1985 to reach 11.1 million in 2000. After the turn of the century, the total number of students is projected to decline unless the proportions going on to secondary school increase dramatically.

Although total enrollments will be relatively stable in the foreseeable future, the number of students at some levels of schooling will change more rapidly. The number of primary school students will change only marginally and, after reaching a peak in 1995, will begin to decline. Between 1990 and 2000 secondary school enrollments will grow most rapidly, at about 100,000 students per year. Over the same period the number enrolled in vocational programs is expected to increase by 20,000 a year and the number of students in higher education programs by about 40,000 a year.

This chapter describes an innovative approach to forecasting school enrollment by analyzing the social, economic, and demographic determinants of school attendance using 1981 survey data for Thailand. The most important implication of the survey analysis is that the demand for secondary education may substantially exceed enrollments forecast using the more traditional approach to projecting school enrollment. Enrollment at the upper secondary level seems particularly likely to grow more rapidly if the potential demand is accommodated by educational policy.

Trends in expenditures on education will depend on the extent to which the quality of the educational system is upgraded in Thailand. Given the quality improvements assumed under the scenario described in this chapter, public costs will rise throughout the forecast period. Public cost is estimated at 46 billion baht in 1990, and is forecast to reach 54 billion baht in 1995 and 65 billion baht in 2000. Annual average public costs are forecast to grow at 3.4 percent during 1990–95, 2.9 percent during 1995–2005, and 0.2 percent during 2005–2015. Thus, even if the quality of education is raised, the fiscal burden of Thailand's educational system should not increase and may even decline. This provides an excellent opportunity for Thailand to upgrade the quality of public education over the coming decades.

Although the private sector does not play as important a role in Thailand as it does in some other countries, private expenditure on education is not entirely negligible. In 1981 about 1 percent of household expenditure was devoted to education. The share of the household budget devoted to educational expenditures is forecast to be relatively constant in the foreseeable future. Thus, expenditure per child should increase significantly as total household income increases and the number of children per household declines.

In summary, demographic change in Thailand presents opportunities for expanding the scope and improving the quality of education in Thailand. Public costs need not grow too rapidly even if students choose to spend more years in school, and even if schooling is upgraded by improving the quality of teachers, by reducing the student–teacher ratio, or by investing more in school facilities. Even if public resources are insufficient to achieve all educational objectives, the private sector represents an important and underutilized pool of resources. Current household expenditures per student are quite low. But as incomes rise, and the numbers of children per family decline and higher education becomes increasingly important, public subsidization of education might be usefully focused on areas of critical need and the private sector encouraged to play a more significant role.

Appendix 6.1.
RESULTS FROM SURVEY ANALYSIS

Appendix Table 6.1.1. Definition of variables in logistic model

	Description
Independent variables	
ENR	*ENR* = 1 if attending school = 0 otherwise
Dependent variables	
SEX	*SEX* = 1 if male = 0 if female
AGE	Age of individual, 12–24
HHTYPE 1	*HHTYPE* 1 = 1 if intact household = 0 otherwise
HDSEX	Sex of the head, 1 for male, 0 for female
HDAGE	Age of the head
HDEDEM, HDEDSEC, HDEDCOL	Three dummy variables to represent educational attainment of the head for elementary, secondary, and college level respectively
*LNEXP, LNEXP*2	Log of expenditure per capita and its square, used as proxy of log of income per capita
*SC*2 - *SC*12	Socioeconomic class of household *SC*2 = 1 for farm operator, owning 0–39 rai (0–6.2 hectares) *SC*3 = 1 for farm operator, owning 40 rai (6.4 hectares) or more *SC*4 = 1 for farm operator, renting land *SC*5 = 1 for fishing, forestry, etc. *SC*6 = 1 for entrepreneurs with paid workers *SC*7 = 1 for entrepreneurs without paid workers *SC*8 = 1 for professional, technical, and managerial workers *SC*9 = 1 for laborers *SC*10 = 1 for clerical, sales, and service workers *SC*11 = 1 for production and construction workers *SC*12 = 1 for economically inactive households Referenced group is farm operators, owning less than 9 rai (1.4 hectares)
PiTj	Number of persons age *i* to *j* present in the household
P60UP	Number of persons age 60 or older in the household

Appendix Table 6.1.2. Variable means in the logistic model

Variable names	Age		
	12–14	15–17	18–24
SEX	0.493	0.490	0.457
AGE	12.900	16.007	20.778
HHTYPE 1	0.808	0.797	0.771
HDSEX	0.843	0.840	0.818
HDAGE	46.533	48.034	45.737
HDEDEM	0.778	0.770	0.731
HDEDSEC	0.048	0.048	0.062
HDEDCOL	0.021	0.018	0.030
LNEXP	6.272	6.356	6.461
*LNEXP*2	39.604	40.787	42.194
*SC*2	0.316	0.317	0.277
*SC*3	0.078	0.095	0.081
*SC*4	0.081	0.082	0.072
*SC*5	0.016	0.016	0.015
*SC*6	0.026	0.026	0.025
*SC*7	0.114	0.114	0.107
*SC*8	0.031	0.027	0.042
*SC*9	0.073	0.063	0.076
*SC*10	0.058	0.061	0.084
*SC*11	0.060	0.070	0.087
*SC*12	0.044	0.040	0.040
*P*0*T*2	0.182	0.156	0.328
*P*3*T*5	0.274	0.206	0.202
*P*6*T*11	1.133	0.900	0.516
*P*12*T*17	1.942	2.015	0.849
*P*18*T*24	0.613	0.829	1.786
*P*25*T*59	1.906	1.875	1.564
*P*60*UP*	0.192	0.229	0.277

Appendix Table 6.1.3. Logistic estimates of school enrollment

Independent variables	Age 12–14	Age 15–17	Age 18–24
Intercept	19.111*	-23.689*	-38.924*
SEX	0.480*	0.354*	0.357*
AGE	–1.222*	–0.289*	–0.471*
HHTYPE 1	0.337	0.103	-0.052
HDSEX	-0.337	-0.077	-0.360*
HDAGE	–0.010*	0.006	0.017*
HDEDEM	0.038	0.085	0.176
HDEDSEC	0.590*	0.841*	0.810*
HDEDCOL	0.728	0.266	1.470*
LNEXP	–1.469	6.659	11.595*
LNEXP2	0.168	-0.416*	-0.751*
SC2	–0.347*	0.038	0.068
SC3	–0.409*	-0.222	-0.678*
SC4	–0.591*	-0.068	0.232
SC5	0.336	0.444	-0.725
SC6	0.449	1.297*	1.479*
SC7	0.359*	0.873*	1.033*
SC8	0.597	2.032*	1.430*
SC9	–0.537*	-0.295	-0.335
SC10	0.784*	1.464*	1.261*
SC11	0.323	0.392	0.437
SC12	1.086*	1.442*	1.763*
P0T2	–0.251*	-0.027	-0.677*
P3T5	-0.058	-0.282*	-0.240
P6T11	-0.034	-0.088	-0.042
P12T17	0.113*	0.187*	0.133*
P18T24	0.075	0.113*	0.291*
P25T59	0.241*	0.247*	0.371*
P60UP	0.394*	0.182	0.212*
Likelihood ratio	952.27	1,008.92	1,901.01
Sample size	4,070	3,712	6,875
Pseudo-R^2	0.187	0.214	0.352

* Indicates significance at 5 percent.

Appendix 6.2.
COSTS OF EDUCATION

Calculating Unit Costs of Education

To obtain operating costs per student, the budget for wages, salaries, and for the maintenance and operation of equipment and buildings in each fiscal year has been deflated using the consumer price index and divided by the number of students.

The annual budget for new durable goods and the development or purchase of new land and new buildings cannot be used directly because it does not reflect the opportunity cost in each period. To calculate the opportunity cost, the value of capital stock possessed by each educational institution must be assessed. The imputed rent is then used as a measure of the opportunity cost of capital for providing educational services. Unfortunately, the data on the value of capital stock are not available. This study therefore estimates the value of capital stock using historical data on capital expenditures. Durable goods are assumed to have a useful life of five years and buildings a useful life of 20 years. A linear depreciation rate is employed. Land is assumed to appreciate by 10 percent each year. Hence the value of durable goods at any time period t is

$$D_t = \sum_{j=1}^{5} ED_{t-j}^{1-0.20j}$$

where D_t is the value of durable goods at time t in 1985 prices; and ED_t is the expenditure on durable goods at time t in 1985 prices.

Similarly, the value of buildings at any point in time is

$$B_t = \sum_{j=1}^{20} EB_{t-j}^{1-0.05j}$$

where EB_t is expenditure on new buildings at time t in 1985 prices.

The value of land at time period t is

$$L_t = \sum_{j=1}^{20} EL_{t-j}^{1.10j}$$

where EL_t is expenditure on new land at time t.

The value of capital stock is calculated as

$$K_t = D_t + B_t + L_t$$

The imputed rent of capital is assumed to be 10 percent of the value of the capital plus depreciation. Imputed rent is calculated by

$$R_t = \frac{K_t r}{(1+r)^T - 1} + K_t r$$

where r is assumed to be 0.1, K_t is the value of capital in year t, and T is the life span of usage, assumed to be five years for durable goods and 20 years for buildings. Since land does not depreciate, the imputed rent for land is calculated by $0.1 \times L_t$ where L_t is the value of land in period t. This method of calculation may underestimate actual costs because it does not include opportunity costs of land and buildings that educational institutions have received through donations or other sources. Moreover, the life span of many buildings may be longer than 20 years. Because no data are available prior to 1958, the value of capital stock more than 20 years old cannot be determined.

Determinants of Unit Costs of Education

The unit cost of education below the university level is affected by the number of students, the student–teacher ratio, and the percentage of teachers with at least a bachelor's degree. At the university level, for each type of teaching arrangement (closed or open university), unit cost is also expected to be affected by field of education. The cost per student in the natural sciences is, on average, higher than the cost per student in the social sciences. Therefore, the higher the percentage of social science students, the lower the average cost per student should be. Theoretically, the relationship between the number of students and the average cost of education per student at a given standard of quality can be either positive or negative, depending on whether the scale of educational services provided by the government has gone beyond the optimal level. The student–teacher ratio is expected to have a negative effect on both operating and capital costs per student. The percentage of teachers with a bachelor's degree or higher is another proxy for the quality of education. Intuitively, higher quality teachers would be paid higher salaries and hence this variable should have a positive effect on operating cost per student. However, teachers' salaries depend to a great extent on the number of years they have served in government. Hence, new teachers will usually receive lower salaries than the older group of teachers even if they have more education. Therefore the direction of the effect of this variable is indeterminate *a priori*.

Regression estimates of unit operating costs and capital expenses by level and stream of education are given in Appendix Table 6.2.1. Unit operating cost at the primary level is negatively related to the number of students and the student–teacher ratio, and positively related to the percentage of teachers with a bachelor's degree or higher. For the equation on unit capital expenses, the effect of the percentage of teachers with a bachelor's degree is not statistically significant. The direction of the effects of the other two variables on unit capital expenses is the same as in the case of unit operating costs.

At the secondary level, unit operating cost is significantly affected by the student–teacher ratio and the percentage of teachers with a bachelor's degree. For unit capital expenses, the percentage of teachers with a bachelor's degree is not statistically significant. It should be noted that, whereas further increases in the number of students may slightly reduce unit costs at the primary level, this is not so at the secondary level. According to the regression results, further increases in the number of students at the secondary level will slightly raise unit capital costs.

Both operating costs and capital expenses per student for vocational education below the bachelor's degree level are significantly affected by the number of students and the student–teacher ratio. An increase in the number of students will reduce the unit cost of education. The coefficient of the student–teacher ratio is negative, as expected.

The cost of capital expenses per student in vocational education at a bachelor's degree level is explained relatively well by the three explanatory variables used in previous equations. However, for operating unit cost, no satisfactory result can be obtained. Hence, a constant operating unit cost as of 1985 is used for forecasting.

Because of a recent, rapid decline in the number of students in the teacher training stream, the regression estimates based on the three independent variables used above do not seem to explain variations in costs satisfactorily. Hence, for this stream of education, constant cost as of 1985 will be used for forecasting.

For closed universities, the only factor that affects the cost significantly is the proportion of students in social sciences. As expected, a decline in this proportion will raise both operating costs and capital expenses per student. For open universities, the only factor that has a significant effect on costs is the number of students. A larger number of students will result in lower unit costs as expected.

Appendix Table 6.2.1. Regression equation of unit costs

Dependent variable	Independent variables						
	Intercept	No. of students (thousands)	Student–teacher ratio	Teachers with B.A. (%)	Proportion of social science students to total	R^2	F
PROPC	9,007.13 (3.83)	−0.73 (−2.50)	−108.69 (−4.48)	14.75 (2.69)		0.99	102.69
PRCE	1,272.98 (5.68)	−0.05 (−1.58)	−23.41 (−13.36)			0.97	91.29
SCOPC	3,407.75 (3.14)		−160.23 (−3.14)	31.27 (5.44)		0.92	30.67
SCCE	1,383.11 (6.27)	0.21 (3.61)	−44.05 (−5.01)			0.95	43.60
VLOPC	16,639.84 (10.23)	−0.79 (−0.44)	−562.30 (−5.50)			0.90	23.11
VLCE	3,432.29 (8.03)	−3.02 (−6.47)	−51.18 (−1.93)			0.94	41.17
VHCE	3,030.75 (11.7)	−0.44 (−7.09)	−71.14 (1.28)	19.07 (3.22)		0.93	19.30
CUOPC	202,190.10 (4.96)				−2,794.21 (−4.24)	0.82	17.95
CUCE	25,854.02 (2.83)				−232.53 (1.57)	0.38	2.56

OUOPC	503.25	−0.25	0.30	2.56
	(5.21)	(−1.60)		
OUCE	98.91	−0.05	0.73	16.02
	(12.97)	(−4.00)		

Note: Figures in parentheses are *t*-ratios. Dependent variables are defined as follows.

The first two letters indicate level or stream of education: *PR* = primary; *SC* = secondary; *VL* = vocational, lower than bachelor's degree; *VH* = vocational at bachelor's degree level; *CU* = closed university; *OU* = open university.

Notations indicating type of cost: *OPC* = operating cost per student; *CE* = capital expense per student.

7

Forecasts of Health Care Costs

by Naohiro Ogawa, Nipon Poapongsakorn, and Andrew Mason

When the characteristics of populations change, shifts in the demand for goods and services from both the private and public sectors inevitably occur. Although the importance of demographic factors varies substantially from sector to sector, the health sector is one of those that is particularly sensitive to demographic change. And because human resources play such a vital role in economic development, the health sector attracts substantial government involvement in virtually all developing countries. Demographic changes in these countries, therefore, directly affect government health programs and expenditures.

In Thailand, the government has played an almost exclusive role in providing health services. The Ministry of Public Health (MOPH) has been the main supplier of health services. The exception is in the Bangkok metropolis where the private sector also plays a significant role.

Total government health care expenditures in Thailand were 1.17 percent of real GNP in 1979, growing to 1.43 percent in 1983. On a per capita basis, expenditures rose from 212 to 263 baht (in 1983 prices) over the period in question. In the years 1979 to 1983, total expenditures (in 1983 prices) by the MOPH rose from 6,010 million to 7,902 million baht, but the ministry's share of total public health expenditures remained almost unchanged at 61 percent. The recurrent component of MOPH expenditures increased substantially from 75.8 to 86.3 percent over that period, while the investment component fell from 25.3 to 13.7 percent. In addition, the allocative pattern of expenditures changed, shifting from urban and hospital expenditures to rural and primary health care expenditures.

In recent years the proportion of total health care expenditures paid from public funds has declined slightly and real government health costs per capita have been decreasing (Sussangkarn, Ashakul, and Myers 1986). Despite this recent trend in public spending on health care, the MOPH and other health-related government agencies have been providing services to an increasing number of families and communities, particularly in rural areas, thus improving the government's ability to satisfy basic health needs (Robinson 1986).

In the past two decades or so, several major studies of the Thai health sector have been undertaken, (e.g., Jones and Boonpratuang 1972; Myers et al. 1985; Robinson 1986). Our study is distinguished from these in that we attempt to assess, by utilizing HOMES, the impact of both population growth and household structural transformation on the future financial requirements of the MOPH. A second distinction is our use of micro-level analysis of household health care expenditure data drawn from the 1981 Socio-Economic Survey (NSO 1985).

METHODOLOGICAL APPROACH AND DATA

Changes in the rate of growth and age structure of the population affect both total health service requirements and the types of health services needed. Because the structural pattern of illness varies markedly with age, the number of medical cases by type of illness shifts with changes in the age structure. Moreover, treatment cost varies considerably with type of illness and, hence, with age. Because costs rise with age, total medical care expenditures will grow rapidly even when population growth is slowing, as in Thailand.

The following methodology is used to quantify the impact of demographic change on total health expenditures by the MOPH. Outpatient and inpatient expenditures are calculated separately. Total expenditures for outpatients are calculated as the product of the three factors shown below:

$$\begin{bmatrix} \text{Population} \\ \text{by age, sex, and} \\ \text{household type} \end{bmatrix} \times \begin{bmatrix} \text{Age- and sex-specific} \\ \text{use of MOPH outpatient} \\ \text{medical care} \end{bmatrix} \times \begin{bmatrix} \text{Age-specific} \\ \text{MOPH outpatient} \\ \text{cost per use} \end{bmatrix}$$

The data for the first factor are obtained from the HOMES projections, the details of which are described in Chapter 2. Data for the second matrix were tabulated from the 1981 Health and Welfare Survey undertaken by the National Statistical Office of Thailand. We are assuming that the age- and sex-specific incidence of outpatient medical care is the same in the same age–sex group regardless of their household type.[1] Because the total num-

1. This assumption is necessary because the data on household structure in the 1981 Health and Welfare Survey will not support analysis of the effect of household type.

ber of outpatients treated at government health facilities estimated from this sample survey is considerably lower than the number reported by the MOPH, the National Statistical Office's estimated age-specific number of outpatients has been adjusted to match the ministry's records.

Age- and sex-specific outpatient rates were computed by dividing the total number of outpatients for each age and sex group by the corresponding 1981 population (see Table 7.1). For both sexes, the outpatient rates show a U-shaped pattern with regard to age, except for the age group 5–14.[2] There are substantial differences between males and females, particularly for those 15–54 years of age, because women in these age groups require health services connected with childbearing and, to a lesser extent, family planning services.

Serious data problems make it difficult to estimate outpatient costs. Only data by age of patient, not sex, are available. Moreover, the MOPH does not collect age-specific outpatient cost data; therefore, age-specific costs had to be estimated.[3]

Inpatient costs were forecast in a similar fashion to outpatient costs. Three factors drive these forecasts:

$$\begin{bmatrix} \text{Population} \\ \text{by age, sex, and} \\ \text{household type} \end{bmatrix} \times \begin{bmatrix} \text{Age- and sex-specific} \\ \text{use of MOPH inpatient} \\ \text{services} \end{bmatrix} \times \begin{bmatrix} \text{Age-specific} \\ \text{MOPH inpatient} \\ \text{costs per use} \end{bmatrix}$$

Again, data for the first factor are based on the HOMES projections. The extent of inpatient use is estimated from the same data as outpatient use. Inpatient rates are considerably lower than outpatient rates for both sexes and for all age groups (Table 7.2). The inpatient and outpatient age profiles have, however, a similar shape with one exception—inpatient rates for the school-age population are especially low.

The reliability of projections will depend, in large part, on the stability of the patterns of utilization. Conflicting forces are operating that will affect use. As health conditions improve, the extent of illness should decline

2. One of the most obvious explanations for the irregular pattern of this young age group is the fact that those belonging to this age group are exposed to numerous childhood diseases. The other explanation is related to the fact that they receive on a periodic basis both physical and mental examinations through the school health service program and if they are found in need of medical care services, they are referred to hospitals and clinics for treatment (MOPH 1985). Another explanation is that those age 5 to 14 require more dental care than the population at large.

3. Average outpatient cost is calculated using independent estimates of the average cost per patient for specific causes (Pichaisanit et al. 1984) and the distribution of age- and cause-specific outpatient utilization rates. Because other data were not available, the relative outpatient distributions were set equal to inpatient distribution for Bangkok for each age group (MOPH 1981). The resulting estimates were adjusted to reproduce MOPH estimates of the average cost of providing outpatient services.

Table 7.1. Age- and sex-specific outpatient rates: 1981

Age	Male	Female	Total
0–4	0.752	0.769	0.760
5–14	0.834	0.811	0.822
15–24	0.345	0.442	0.393
25–34	0.403	0.563	0.483
35–44	0.398	0.542	0.470
45–54	0.452	0.627	0.542
55–59	0.468	0.514	0.491
60+	0.560	0.571	0.566

Note: Age- and sex-specific outpatient rates are derived by dividing the number of outpatient cases for each age and sex group by the total population in the same age and sex group on an annual basis.

Table 7.2. Age- and sex-specific inpatient rates: 1981

Age	Male	Female	Total
0–6	0.0559	0.0487	0.0523
7–10	0.0266	0.0291	0.0278
11–14	0.0236	0.0238	0.0237
15–19	0.0246	0.0387	0.0315
20–24	0.0364	0.0807	0.0584
25–29	0.0474	0.0890	0.0682
30–34	0.0453	0.0831	0.0641
35–39	0.0518	0.0722	0.0620
40–49	0.0475	0.0493	0.0484
50–59	0.0681	0.0644	0.0662
60+	0.0836	0.0620	0.0718

Note: Age- and sex-specific inpatient rates are derived by dividing the number of inpatient cases for each age and sex group by the total population in the same age and sex group on an annual basis.

in Thailand. However, as Thais achieve higher standards of living and are better educated, those who are ill will be more likely to rely on the health sector for services.

One means of assessing the likely course of utilization patterns is to compare the Thai profile with that of higher income countries. Japan's experience, as the most developed Asian country, is particularly relevant. Rates of utilization are much lower in Thailand than in Japan as of 1984. Moreover, the shapes of the age profiles are considerably different. In Japan, health

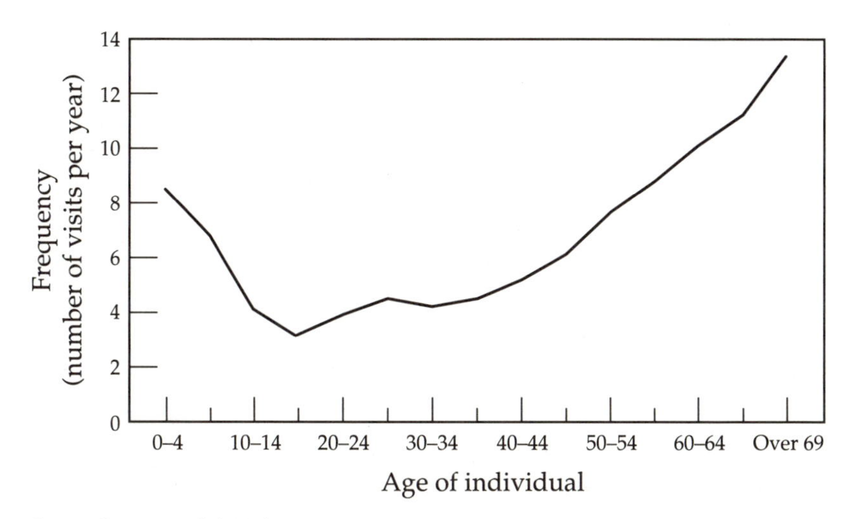

Source: Ogawa et al. (1986).

Figure 7.1. Age-specific patient rates: Japan, 1984

care needs are dominated by the very young and the old (Figure 7.1). In Thailand, the young are heavy health care users, but among adults, utilization rates rise very modestly with age. Maternal health care, provided to women in their prime childbearing ages, is a major component of inpatient services (Figure 7.2). The Japanese experience suggests that important changes in patterns of health care use are likely to occur in Thailand. This is an issue that is explored from a variety of angles below.

Inpatient costs per use are estimated using the same statistical procedures employed for estimating outpatient costs. Total inpatient costs are calculated as the product of the number of persons, utilization rates, and costs per use.

Total inpatient costs estimated in this way for the base year, 1980, are considerably lower than the total recurrent inpatient costs reported by the MOPH. For this reason, the computed age-specific costs for both outpatients and inpatients have been inflated so that both calculated and reported costs are equalized. The adjusted age-specific cost profiles for both outpatients and inpatients are presented in Figures 7.3 and 7.4. The cost differentials among older age groups are relatively small.

The age profiles of outpatient and inpatient costs in Thailand are somewhat different from the age-specific pattern of medical costs for Japan in 1984 shown in Figure 7.5. This may be partly attributable to differences in the pattern of illness and in the quality of medical services between these two countries.

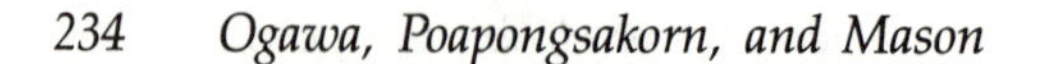

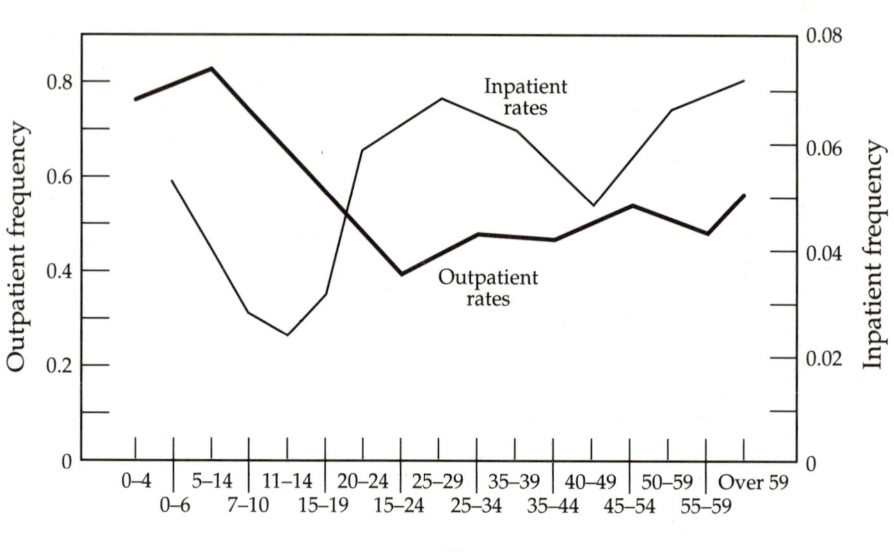

Source: Tables 7.1 and 7.2.

Figure 7.2. Age-specific outpatient and inpatient rates: Thailand, 1981

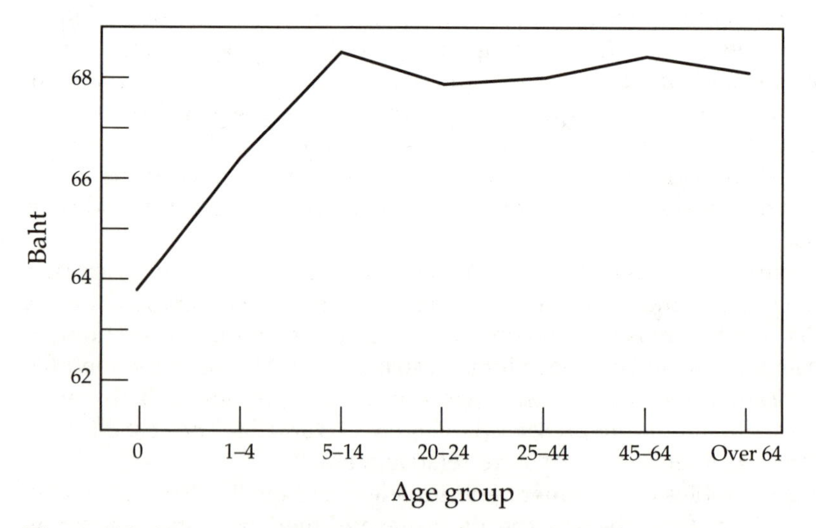

Figure 7.3. Average cost per outpatient visit: Thailand, 1980

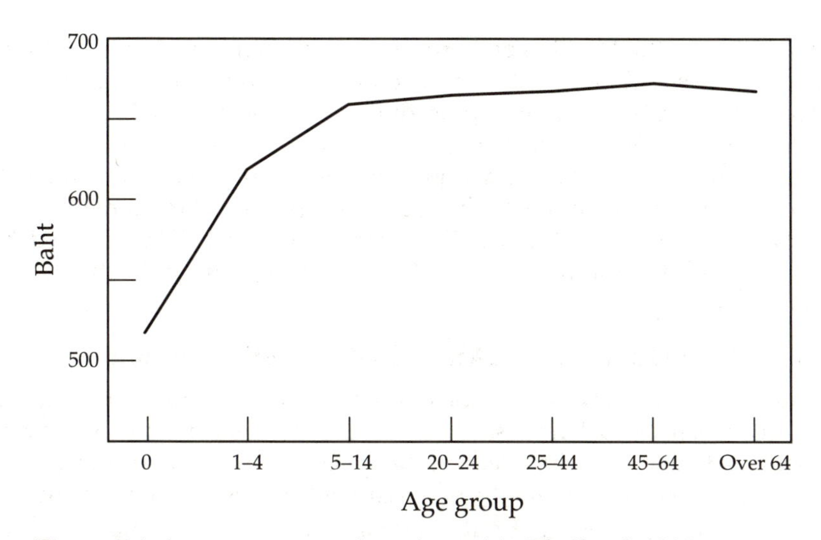

Figure 7.4. Average cost per inpatient visit: Thailand, 1980

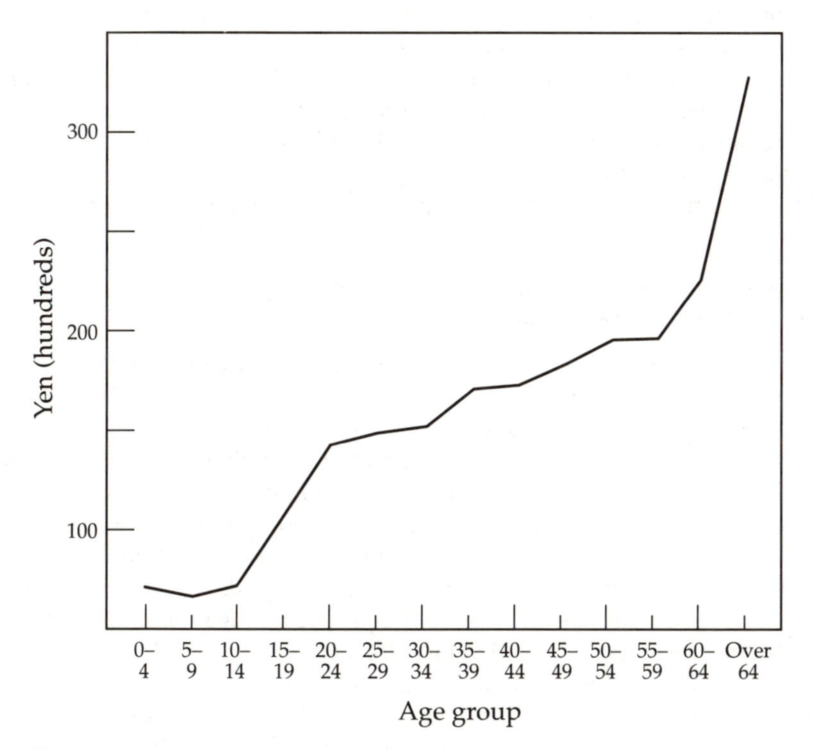

Note: 100 yen = 11.64 baht in 1984.

Figure 7.5. Average cost per patient per use: Japan, 1984

In addition to the MOPH's operating costs, an attempt was made to forecast capital costs. Various statistical methods were tried, but none worked out satisfactorily. For example, a procedure used in Malaysia (Ogawa 1985), which related investment costs to the number of inpatients or outpatients by using time-series data, yielded poor results. Thus, a constant value of 19.03 percent, corresponding to the average proportion of investment costs to total expenditures by the MOPH observed during 1980–86, is used in the present study. (For the period 1980–86, however, observed values were employed.)

MOPH HEALTH CARE PROGRAMS, 1980–2015

A number of important assumptions underlie our preliminary projections. First, a 4 percent annual increase in per capita outpatient and inpatient costs is assumed to allow for the effect on the quality of medical services of the 4 percent real economic growth rate assumed throughout this volume.

Second, the age profiles of outpatient and inpatient rates are assumed to remain unchanged throughout the projection period. Clearly, this simplifying assumption overlooks a number of important possibilities alluded to above. Much of the analysis presented later in this chapter considers alternative patterns of health care use. The projections presented here are clearly deficient in that the data on which they are based predates AIDS.

Third, all demographic projections are based on HOMES projections that use the medium variant of population projections prepared by NESDB. Finally, all monetary values are expressed in 1980–81 prices and do not incorporate inflationary effects.

Base Forecast of the Number of Patients and MOPH Health Expenditures

Using HOMES and the assumptions outlined above, we prepared base forecasts of outpatient services and costs (Table 7.3). The total number of outpatients increases monotonically over the projection period, rising from 28.0 million in 1980 to 36.2 million in 2000 and to 40.4 million in 2015. The ratio of male to female outpatients was 0.90 in 1980 and declines slightly over time—to 0.86 in 2000 and to 0.85 in 2015, reflecting a gradual increase in the sex ratio (in favor of males) in the underlying population.

Due to the aging of the Thai population, the age distribution of outpatients varies substantially with time. The proportion age 0 to 14 diminishes steadily from 53.5 percent in 1980 to 30.6 percent in 2015. Consequently, the index of aging (the number age 35 and over divided by the number age 0 to 14 multiplied by 100) increases from 39.6 to 142.8 during the corresponding period. As a result, the disease-specific pattern of outpatient services will differ in the future, which will bring about important changes in the types of medical care services provided.

Table 7.3. Projected number of outpatient cases treated under the MOPH health care system and projected total outpatient costs covered by MOPH: 1980–2015

Year	Number of outpatient cases (million persons)			Age structure and aging index (%)		Total expenditures for outpatient services (million baht)	Distribution of expenditure by age structure and aging index (%)	
	Male	Female	Total	0–14	35+/0–14		0–14	35+/0–14
1980	13.279	14.701	27.981	53.5	39.6	2,023	49.8	53.2
1985	14.294	16.066	30.360	49.8	45.2	2,953	46.1	60.6
1990	15.231	17.333	32.564	46.3	53.5	4,161	42.6	71.8
1995	16.044	18.455	34.500	42.7	65.3	5,637	38.9	87.6
2000	16.774	19.475	36.249	39.1	80.9	7,806	35.2	108.4
2005	17.456	20.405	37.861	35.9	99.7	10,733	32.0	132.9
2010	18.072	21.205	39.277	33.3	119.7	14,709	29.3	160.1
2015	18.546	21.822	40.368	30.6	142.8	20,130	26.3	194.9

Aging index—the number age 35 and over divided by the number age 0 to 14 multiplied by 100.

In parallel with the growth of the number of outpatients, total expenditures for outpatient services provided by the MOPH will grow monotonically from 2,023 million baht in 1980 to 7,806 million baht in 2000, and to 20,130 million baht in 2015. Again, the proportion of outpatient costs incurred on behalf of those age 0 to 14 falls gradually from 49.8 percent in 1980 to only 26.3 percent in 2015.

The general trends for inpatient care are similar to those for outpatient care. (The base forecast for inpatient care is provided in Table 7.4.) The total number of inpatients is expected to rise from 2.3 million in 1980 to 3.4 million in 2000 and to 4.0 million in 2015. Aging of inpatients also occurs over the projection period, and is even more rapid than it is for outpatients.

Expenditures for inpatient services are forecast to increase from 1,483 million baht in 1980 to 6,337 million baht in the year 2000 and to 16,695 million baht in 2015. As compared with outpatient expenditures, inpatient expenditures are consistently lower over the period in question, but the relative difference between these two types of expenditures shrinks steadily over time (as observed in most other countries). In 1980 inpatient expenditure was 26.7 percent lower than outpatient expenditure, but it will be only 17.1 percent lower in 2015. This is attributable to the aging of the Thai population and the somewhat higher average inpatient costs for older persons. Thus, expenditures by the MOPH will shift from the young to the old and from outpatient to inpatient services.

The sum of outpatient and inpatient expenditures yields the total recurrent cost of health care for the MOPH. Total recurrent costs increase at a rate of 7.0 percent a year, or by 10.5 times during the 35-year period, from 3,506 million baht in 1980 to 36,825 million baht in 2015 (Table 7.5). Total investment costs also grow at a rate of 6.4 percent per annum, or by 8.7 times during the same time period, from 989 million baht in 1980 to 8,653 million baht in 2015. And the total health expenditure for the MOPH increases by a factor of 10.1 in 35 years' time. On an annual basis, it grows, on the average, at a rate of 6.8 percent.[4]

As a percentage of GDP,[5] both recurrent and total expenditures will increase steadily between 1980 and 2015 (Table 7.6). Because of the aging of the Thai population an increasing share of national resources and, unless the government's share in GDP increases, an increasing share of the government's budget will be required for medical expenditures just to keep the quality of care provided constant. And this is not considering the impact of AIDS. More likely, expenditures on medical care will be much greater

4. This annual growth rate is slightly lower than the corresponding figure for Malaysia (8.14 percent) over the period 1975–80 (Ministry of Health, Malaysia, 1982).

5. GDP data are actual through 1985; GDP estimates for 1986–2000 are based on NESDB forecasts; GDP is assumed to grow at 6 percent from 2000 to 2015.

Table 7.4. Projected number of inpatient cases treated under the MOPH health care system and projected total inpatient costs covered by MOPH: 1980–2015

Year	Number of inpatient cases (million persons)			Age structure and aging index (%)		Total expenditures for inpatient services (million baht)	Distribution of expenditure by age structure and aging index (%)	
	Male	Female	Total	0–14	35+/0–14		0–14	35+/0–14
1980	1.020	1.267	2.287	31.3	97.2	1,483	29.7	105.5
1985	1.135	1.436	2.570	28.2	111.3	2,240	26.6	120.9
1990	1.253	1.603	2.856	25.1	133.3	3,252	23.7	144.8
1995	1.364	1.748	3.112	22.3	164.4	4,499	21.0	178.2
2000	1.477	1.880	3.357	19.9	202.2	6,337	18.7	219.2
2005	1.593	2.002	3.595	17.9	248.2	8,857	16.8	269.2
2010	1.701	2.099	3.801	16.2	299.8	12,223	15.1	325.0
2015	1.801	2.176	3.977	14.5	361.0	16,695	13.6	391.1

Table 7.5. Projected recurrent, investment, and total costs for the MOPH: 1980–2015

Year	Recurrent costs (million baht)	Investment costs (million baht)	Total expenditure (million baht)	Distribution of total expenditures by age structure and aging index (%)	
				0–14	35+/0–14
1980	3,506	989	4,495	41.3	69.1
1985	5,193	1,056	6,250	37.7	78.9
1990	7,413	1,742	9,155	34.3	93.9
1995	10,136	2,382	12,518	30.9	114.8
2000	14,144	3,324	17,476	27.8	141.8
2005	19,590	4,603	24,193	25.1	174.1
2010	26,932	6,329	33,261	22.8	209.7
2015	36,825	8,653	45,478	20.6	253.6

Table 7.6. Projected MOPH costs relative to GDP and GDI: Basic forecast and Japanese profile, 1980–2015 (%)

Year	MOPH recurrent costs/GDP	MOPH total costs/GDP	Japan profile total costs/GDP	MOPH investment costs/GDI	Japan profile investment costs/GDI
1980	1.20	1.53		1.33	
1985	1.35	1.63	1.65	1.35	1.37
1990	1.46	1.81	1.85	1.65	1.69
1995	1.50	1.86	1.94	1.68	1.75
2000	1.56	1.94	2.06	1.71	1.82
2005	1.62	2.00	2.17	1.73	1.87
2010	1.67	2.06	2.26	1.73	1.90
2015	1.70	2.10	2.35	1.73	1.93

Source: Ogawa et al. (1986).

GDP—gross domestic product.

GDI—gross domestic investment.

than these forecasts show. If economic growth were to move Thailand toward the Japanese age–medical cost profile, the greater relative outlays at later life-cycle stages would have a significant impact on the share of medical expenses in GDP after the year 2000.

The share of investment expenditures by the MOPH in gross domestic investment (GDI) is also forecast to increase continuously through 2015. The effect of moving to the Japanese profile would be to raise the relative demands of new health facilities on the country's capital resources noticeably after the year 2000.

Base Forecast of MOPH Patients and Health Expenditures by Type of Household

Projections of the number of outpatients by five types of households, cross-classified by age of the household head are provided in Table 7.7.[6] The percentage distribution of outpatients among most household types remains virtually unchanged throughout the projected period. This is consistent with one of the primary results for the HOMES household projection for Thailand: that no significant changes are anticipated in the distribution of households by type.

In 1980, for instance, 83.8 percent of the outpatients belong to intact households, 4.1 percent to single male-headed households, and 11.6 percent to single female-headed households. In 2015 the corresponding figures are 83.3 percent, 4.1 percent, and 11.6 percent, respectively. Although the number of outpatients belonging to both one-person male and female households is extremely small, their percentage shares almost double during 1980–2015.

The composition of outpatients by age of the household head varies considerably among household types. In 1980, for example, for household members in households with heads below age 40, more than 90 percent of those who received outpatient services under the MOPH health care system came from intact households. In contrast, for households with heads over age 65, more than half of outpatients belonged to nonintact households (e.g., single male-headed and single female-headed households). The household composition of outpatients, however, changes only marginally throughout the projection period.

Despite the stable household structure forecast for the next 35 years, the composition of outpatients by age and type of the household head varies markedly over time for all household types. In 1980, 54.4 percent of outpatients from intact households had household heads below age 40. This is the case for 25.2 percent of single male-headed households, 19.2 percent

6. The numbers reported here are slightly smaller than those reported in Table 7.4 because primary-individual households are excluded in Table 7.7.

Table 7.7. Percentage distribution of outpatients by type of household and age of household head: 1980 and 2015

Age of household head	Intact (%)	Single male-headed (%)	Single female-headed (%)	One-person male (%)	One-person female (%)	Total outpatients (thousands)
1980						
<35	93.53	2.30	3.68	0.32	0.17	9,661.50
35–49	88.35	2.40	8.99	0.15	0.11	11,274.99
50–64	70.22	6.94	22.12	0.30	0.41	5,236.30
65+	39.72	16.52	41.25	0.67	1.83	1,707.99
Total	83.76	4.08	11.59	0.27	0.29	27,880.78
2015						
<35	94.35	1.88	3.13	0.42	0.22	11,984.82
35–49	88.36	2.55	8.57	0.30	0.21	16,395.00
50–64	72.13	6.23	20.26	0.60	0.79	9,064.38
65+	42.86	15.13	37.39	1.29	3.34	2,798.94
Total	83.32	4.06	11.59	0.47	0.56	40,243.14

of single female-headed households, 46.8 percent among one-person male households, and 26.6 percent among one-person female households. In 2015 these percentages change as follows: 49.0 percent for intact households, 19.8 percent for single male-headed households, 15.7 percent for single female-headed households, 32.4 percent for one-person male households, and 17.3 percent for one-person female households. Examination of these intertemporal changes in the percentage distribution shows that the impact of the aging of outpatients is most pronounced among one-person households.

By and large, these same observations hold true for the projected results for the inpatient case shown in Table 7.8. There are minor differences in numbers, but none that would change the general conclusions reached.

The projections given in Tables 7.7 and 7.8 indicate that, although the number of both outpatients and inpatients treated at MOPH hospitals and health centers is expected to rise rapidly during 1980–2015, the household composition of these patients is likely to remain stable. Nevertheless, even at the present time, the majority of older patients belong to non-intact households. It is often the case that compared with younger patients, these older patients suffer from more serious illnesses, thus requiring intensive family and hospital care. The majority of older patients (those in non-intact households) do not have spouses, normally the main caregivers at home. And, as discussed in Chapter 2, the average size of households is expected to

Table 7.8. Percentage distribution of inpatients by type of household and age of household head: 1980 and 2015

Age of household head	Intact (%)	Single male-headed (%)	Single female-headed (%)	One-person male (%)	One-person female (%)	Total inpatients (thousands)
1980						
<35	92.88	2.78	3.54	0.53	0.27	800.64
35–49	87.89	2.53	9.18	0.23	0.17	813.01
50–64	70.77	6.72	21.56	0.41	0.55	501.19
65+	41.36	15.76	39.50	0.91	2.47	160.97
Total	82.58	4.48	12.07	0.42	0.45	2,275.81
2015						
<35	93.85	2.25	2.98	0.60	0.32	1,126.24
35–49	88.10	2.66	8.64	0.35	0.25	1,497.29
50–64	72.75	6.06	19.64	0.67	0.89	1,025.64
65+	44.04	14.65	36.08	1.46	3.77	314.47
Total	82.26	4.37	12.05	0.59	0.71	3,963.63

fall as a consequence of reduced fertility. This implies that elderly patients, regardless of their household types, will find it increasingly difficult over time to secure care from their sons and daughters. Hence, these forecasts suggest possible growth in the relative importance of inpatient care as the number of potential caregivers falls off.

The allocation of the MOPH's recurrent costs for outpatient and inpatient services by type of household, as well as by age of the household head, closely follows the percentage distribution of inpatients by the same categories. Thus, there is little reason to repeat the details here since the conclusions are basically the same.

Both outpatient and inpatient services provided by MOPH hospitals and health centers are heavily subsidized. Our forecasts show that the incidence of MOPH medical care subsidies will vary considerably among household types. A finding of this nature provides useful information to MOPH policymakers in formulating health policies for the years to come.

Suppose a cost containment policy to curb the MOPH's rapidly growing expenditures is planned. Officials will be able to assess, prior to the policy's implementation, the financial impact on different types of households. For example, if the proposed policy is designed to reduce MOPH expenditures on elderly patients, the adverse effect is likely to be more serious among non-intact households than among intact households.

In this context, Japan's recent experience is instructive. To bring down accelerating public medical expenditures, Japan abolished the free medical service program for those age 70 and over in 1983. In the following year, the government's free physical examination program for those age 40 and over was implemented. As in Thailand, the age structure of each household type was considerably different in Japan, so these age-specific policy changes changed the allocation of public financial resources among various types of households and generated much controversy.[7]

MOPH Requirements for Health Personnel and Facilities

The results presented thus far clearly point to a rapid increase in the financial requirements of the MOPH. In addition, the need for medically trained manpower is also likely to increase markedly throughout the projected period. The growth in the number of inpatients will also require a greater number of MOPH facilities.

With these considerations in mind, the future requirements of the MOPH for health personnel and facilities are projected. For the sake of simplicity, only the following three major indicators of health personnel and facilities are forecast: medical doctors, nurses, and hospital beds. These indicators are used because they are sensitive to population changes.[8]

For comparative purposes, two different projections are given. In the first case, it is assumed that the ratios of medical doctors and nurses to the total number of outpatients and inpatients remain unchanged at the 1984 level. According to the Survey of Health Resources for 1984 conducted by the MOPH, there were 7,924 medical doctors and 31,827 nurses attached to its hospitals and health centers in the whole kingdom. Because the total number of patients treated under the MOPH health care system for the corresponding year was estimated at 32.41 million, the service ratios for doctors and nurses per 100,000 patients were 24.45 and 98.20, respectively. The constant service ratio approach has also been employed to estimate the number of beds required. In 1984 there were 70,960 beds at MOPH hospitals and a total number of 2.51 million inpatients treated. Thus, the computed service ratio for beds per 100,000 inpatients was 2,823.

For the second projection, service ratios for doctors, nurses, and hospital beds are computed from the data for Bangkok only. Because the ratios for the Bangkok metropolis are considerably higher than those for the whole

7. The foregoing discussions have been based upon the medium variant of NESDB's population projections. For comparative purposes, we also made HOMES projections on the basis of alternative population projections, i.e., low and high variants. The numerical results produced from these alternative projections are only marginally different from those discussed above.

8. Resource requirements for some health programs such as preventative health measures and sanitation schemes are largely independent of population growth (Jones and Boonpratuang 1972).

country, this second projection gives an indication of what care at the Bangkok quality level would entail. According to the 1984 data for Bangkok, the ratios per 100,000 patients were 107.93 for doctors, 326.00 for nurses, and 31,656 for beds. In this alternative projection, it is assumed that the service ratios for the entire country will be raised to those for Bangkok by the year 2015.

Estimates for these two scenarios over the period 1980–2015 are presented in Table 7.9. The growing requirements for medical doctors, nurses, and hospital beds are clear. Under the low scenario, the total number of medical doctors required will increase from 7,400 in 1980 to 9,680 in the year 2000, and to 10,840 in 2015. The corresponding figures for the Bangkok case are 7,400 in 1980, 28,580 in 2000, and 47,680 in 2015. Similar growth patterns are observable with regard to the total number of nurses and hospital beds for both scenarios.

The projections for the first scenario indicate that the numbers of both medical doctors and nurses are "required" to grow, on average, at a rate of 1.1 percent per annum to maintain national service levels. The number of hospital beds must grow at an annual rate of 1.6 percent throughout the projected period to achieve the same end. The higher required growth rate for hospital beds, compared with those for health personnel, is explained by the fact that the number of inpatients is expected to grow more rapidly in the future than that of outpatients.

The annual growth rates of medical personnel and facilities "required" to meet Bangkok standards are substantially higher. They are 5.5 percent for medical doctors, 4.6 percent for nurses, and 8.9 percent for hospital beds.

During 1978–84, the actual growth rates were 4.4 percent for medical doctors, 11.6 percent for nurses, and 1.4 percent for hospital beds (MOPH 1985). Thus, comparison of observed and projected growth rates suggests the low scenario is easily obtainable, whereas the high scenario, except for nurses, may present a formidable challenge.

These conclusions are further confirmed by comparing the forecast growth in demand for medical personnel with the forecast growth in the labor force.[9] If current national standards prevail, the shares of nurses and of nurses plus doctors in the total labor force will actually decline (see Table 7.10). However, the goal of meeting Bangkok standards in the future would entail more than a tripling of the share of nurses in the labor force and more than a doubling of the share of all medical personnel. Although in absolute terms the share would remain low (less than 1 percent), the challenge, given the training costs and long lead times necessary, in meeting the relative growth of demand for medical personnel would be considerable. This

9. These data are from Chapter 3.

Table 7.9. Projected demand for doctors, nurses, and beds under two different assumptions: 1980–2015 (in thousands)

Year	Doctors	Nurses	Beds
Low scenario			
1980	7.40	29.72	64.57
1985	8.05	32.34	72.57
1990	8.66	34.78	80.63
1995	9.20	36.93	87.87
2000	9.68	38.89	94.79
2005	10.14	40.71	101.49
2010	10.53	42.30	107.30
2015	10.84	43.55	112.29
High scenario			
1980	7.40	29.72	64.57
1985	11.98	43.05	178.43
1990	17.11	57.84	315.92
1995	22.65	73.65	472.43
2000	28.58	90.45	647.96
2005	34.86	108.16	841.85
2010	41.36	126.41	1,046.56
2015	47.86	144.57	1,259.04

Table 7.10. Estimates of demand for nurses and doctors as a percentage of the total labor force: 1980–2015 (%)

	Low scenario		High scenario	
Year	Nurses	Doctors + nurses	Nurses	Doctors + nurses
1980	0.13	0.16	0.13	0.16
1985	0.12	0.15	0.16	0.21
1990	0.11	0.14	0.19	0.25
1995	0.11	0.13	0.21	0.28
2000	0.10	0.13	0.24	0.31
2005	0.10	0.12	0.26	0.35
2010	0.10	0.12	0.29	0.38
2015	0.09	0.12	0.31	0.41

is especially so considering the large expected aggregate excess demand for labor from the year 2000 on.

In sum, these results suggest that the MOPH's medical personnel and facilities will need to expand considerably in the years to come, if private care is not substituted for public. Further, the difference in the two scenarios shows that the distribution of health personnel and facilities between Bangkok and the rest of the country is considerably skewed. If the MOPH decides to bring the quality of its medical services outside the Bangkok metropolis up to the Bangkok level by the year 2015, it will have to allocate far greater resources for training and investment programs than it has in recent years.

When these forecasts are interpreted, caution must be exercised in several respects. First, because of attrition of personnel and depreciation of facilities, the numbers of medical doctors, nurses, and hospital beds to be added by the MOPH for each year will be larger than the net increase projected. Because of the potential shift of doctors and nurses from public to private sectors, which has recently been particularly pronounced in Bangkok, attrition rates could be quite high. Second, it is realistic to plan for differential improvement in service ratios for health personnel and facilities, after assessing their relative strengths and weaknesses in the base year. This refinement may lead to a considerably different pattern of the future requirements than discussed. Third, because the AIDS epidemic emerged after the surveys on which these analyses are based, the projections do not incorporate its impact on health care utilization or expenditures.

Number of Patients by Type of Illness

Changes in the age structure of Thailand's population will affect not only the extent of use but disease patterns and the kinds of medical care required. The impact of age structure on disease patterns draws heavily on morbidity data reported by the National Epidemiology Board of Thailand (NEBT). These data were gathered mainly from outpatient and inpatient records compiled by all government hospitals and other health institutions, not just MOPH facilities.

Before proceeding, the limits of analysis of the impact of age structure should be clearly stated. With improvements in health resulting from economic development, improved infrastructure, public health programs, and increased public awareness about healthful behavior, the pattern of disease in any country changes dramatically. Some changes are related to specific programs. For example, inoculation programs have reduced smallpox and improved infrastructure has reduced the incidence of waterborne diseases, e.g., diarrhea. Other diseases may be relatively responsive to economic development. But, in general, the incidence of infectious and parasitic disease has declined with development, and the incidence of degenerative diseases has increased.

Analysis of changes in age structure examines only a particular piece of this process—changes in disease that are related to compositional changes in the population. Most important, increases in the incidence of degenerative diseases that occur because people are living long enough to contract these diseases are captured. But general improvements in health, which are quite selective on particular health problems, will occur quite independently of changes in age structure.

Data on outpatients for 1982 show that the five leading groups of illnesses are diseases of the respiratory system, symptoms and ill-defined conditions, diseases of the digestive system, infectious diseases, and accidents, poisoning, and violence. During the four-year period from 1982 to 1985, the three leading causes of morbidity for outpatients remained unchanged (NEBT 1987). For inpatients, enteritis and other diarrheal diseases, malaria, and motor vehicle accidents were three major causes of morbidity over the period 1983–84.

Over the last decade or so, however, outpatient and inpatient illness patterns have been changing markedly as acute infectious diseases have declined in both number and severity, while most noninfectious diseases have been steadily increasing. Among the latter, cancer has recently emerged as the third major cause of mortality in Thai society (NEBT 1987). In 1971, the incidence rate of cancer from all causes was 12.6 per 100,000 population with the death rate of 4.2 but the corresponding rates for 1981 were 31.0 and 11.4 respectively.[10]

The incidence of illness varies considerably with age (see Table 7.11). For instance, the age-specific incidence rate of cancer rises almost monotonically with age; in 1980 it was only 2.55 cases per 100,000 population for the age group 0–14, but 65.64 cases for those 40–44 years of age, and 351.25 cases for those at ages 70–74. In addition, there are sex differences; the 1981 data show that the overall incidence rate of cancer was 28.37 for males and 33.72 for females (NEBT 1987).

The incidence rates for the 10 leading communicable diseases also vary substantially with age (Table 7.12). Acute diarrhea is tops on the list in virtually all age groups, but varies markedly by age; in 1984 cases per 100,000 population were 6,262 for infants, as opposed to 473 for those age 15 through 34. Measles, dengue hemorrhagic fevers (DHF), and chicken pox are important only among the young population age 0 to 14. In contrast, tuberculosis and hepatitis are common diseases among adults and the elderly. Incidence of tuberculosis, in particular, increases with age. Malaria, hemorrhagic conjunctivitis, influenza, and pneumonia appear on the top 10 list in every age group (Table 7.12).

10. Improvements in the cancer registration system as well as improved diagnosis have contributed to this trend.

Table 7.11. Age- and cause-specific distribution of patients treated at MOPH health facilities in 1981

	Type of case					
Age	Infective	Digestive	Respiratory	Delivery and obstetric	Others	Total
0	0.114	0.017	0.135	0.276	0.458	1.0
1–4	0.045	0.016	0.181	0.0	0.758	1.0
5–14	0.010	0.061	0.066	0.001	0.862	1.0
15–24	0.001	0.019	0.002	0.044	0.933	1.0
25–44	0.001	0.020	0.004	0.034	0.941	1.0
45–64	0.005	0.040	0.027	0.0002	0.928	1.0
65+	0.001	0.034	0.044	0.0	0.911	1.0
Cost per visit (baht)						
Outpatient	74.33	101.83	66.88	66.23	78.04	
Inpatient	1,424.90	1,464.66	684.27	552.02	1,417.46	

Using these age-specific rates, the number of patients for 14 selected illness over the period 1980–2015 have been projected. The results are summarized in Figure 7.6, which compares the projected growth rate less the overall growth rate of disease. Three, cancer, tuberculosis, and, to a lesser extent, hepatitis, will grow more rapidly as a result of the aging of Thailand's population. Four others, dengue hemorrhagic fever, measles, chicken pox, and, to a lesser extent, pneumonia will decline in importance.

No doubt, these compositional changes in patients by type of disease will affect the medical supply side. That is, fewer resources will be required for childhood immunization, but greater medical services will be needed for radioactive treatment or chemotherapy for cancer patients. These structural variations in medical needs, which are likely to arise in the years ahead, will surely call for a gradual change, not only in the quantity of medical personnel but also their composition; for instance, more cancer specialists will be demanded, whereas fewer doctors specializing in maternal and child health will be necessary. These likely future variations will also affect the pattern of allocation and utilization of health facilities such as hospital beds. In any case, to provide efficient and effective medical care services for consumers, these future possibilities should be taken into account by government planners in the process of formulating long-run health care plans.

Table 7.12. Ranking of 10 leading communicable diseases by morbidity rate for various age groups: 1984 (per 100,000 population)

Under age 1		*Ages 1–4*	
Acute diarrhea	6,262.28	Acute diarrhea	2,059.64
Pneumonia	970.18	Pneumonia	548.62
Dysentery	443.38	Measles	458.82
Measles	359.79	DHF	290.33
H. conjunctivitis	298.68	Dysentery	276.41
Influenza	183.58	Malaria	168.35
DHF	88.46	H. conjunctivitis	161.08
Malaria	82.42	Influenza	141.47
Pertussis	45.78	Chicken pox	30.82
Tetanus	44.93	Pertussis	25.33
Ages 5–14		*Ages 15–34*	
DHF	401.62	Acute diarrhea	472.92
Acute diarrhea	370.32	Malaria	408.84
Malaria	208.28	VD	231.40
H. conjunctivitis	168.93	H. conjunctivitis	221.09
Measles	136.19	Influenza	140.96
Influenza	102.39	Dysentery	79.87
Pneumonia	94.31	Hepatitis	39.17
Dysentery	53.69	Enteric fever	35.44
Enteric fever	46.09	Tuberculosis	23.61
Chicken pox	35.63	Pneumonia	20.49
Ages 35–64		*Age 65 and over*	
Acute diarrhea	656.06	Acute diarrhea	1,216.46
Malaria	218.12	Tuberculosis	271.67
H. conjunctivitis	181.99	Dysentery	164.10
Influenza	147.75	Pneumonia	149.15
Dysentery	115.09	H. conjunctivitis	141.28
Tuberculosis	107.42	Influenza	140.13
Pneumonia	47.41	Malaria	90.92
VD	35.13	Enteric fever	22.28
Hepatitis	24.29	Hepatitis	19.73
Enteric fever	24.17	Leprosy	15.44

Source: NEBT (1987:86).

DHF—dengue hemorrhagic fever.

H. conjunctivitis—hemorrhagic conjunctivitis.

VD—venereal diseases.

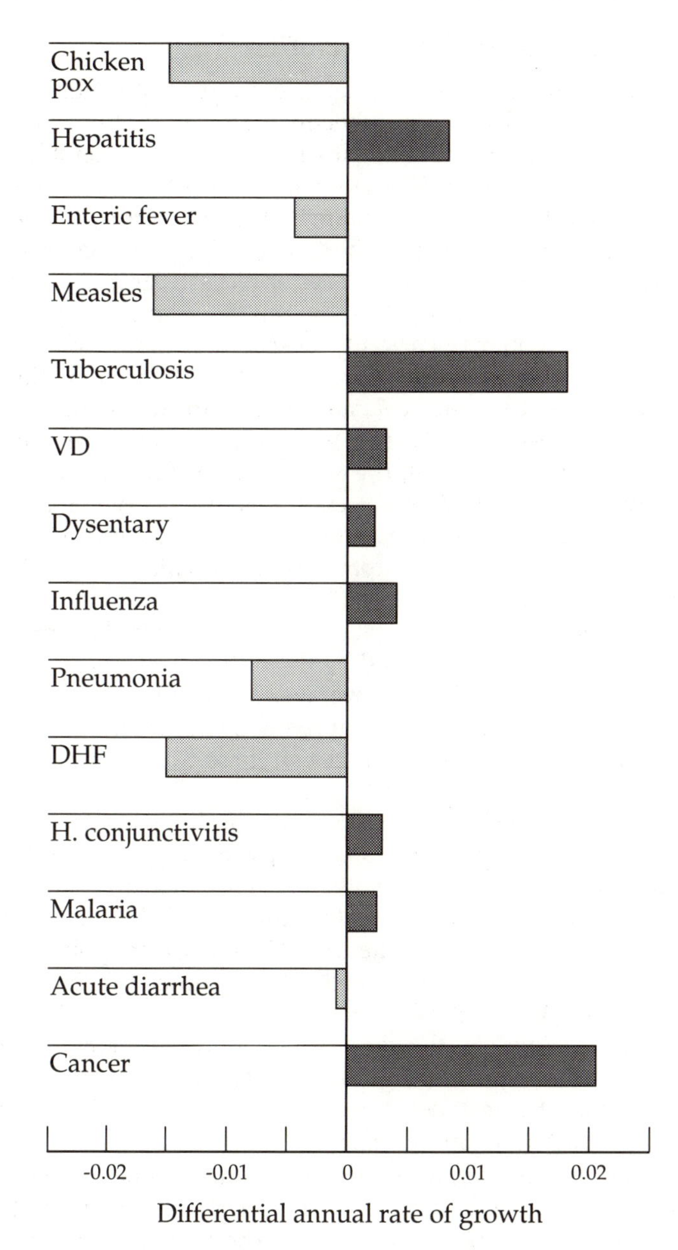

Figure 7.6. Projected differential growth rate in occurrences of 14 illnesses in the total population: 1980–2015

Application of Bangkok Health Profiles

Because of higher per capita income, greater awareness of health problems, and better access to a variety of public medical care facilities in Bangkok, the health-seeking behavior of Bangkok residents is considerably different from that of the population residing outside Bangkok. For example, outpatient rates for MOPH health services are higher in Bangkok than in the rest of the country, and the opposite is the case for inpatient rates. Also, as discussed earlier, in Bangkok the private sector plays a significant role in supplying medical care services. Thus, in this alternative projection, it is assumed that the patterns currently observed in Bangkok will prevail throughout the kingdom by the year 2015. Table 7.13 contains the results, showing the demand for medical care services in the "Bangkok" case.

A careful comparison of this table with Tables 7.3 to 7.5 reveals two interesting differences. First of all, the total number of outpatients increases more rapidly in this alternative projection than in the original forecast. By contrast, the number of inpatients declines over time in this alternative scenario. However, the sum of outpatients and inpatients is greater in this projection than in the base forecast.

Second and more important, total expenditures are fairly comparable to the base forecast. This is explained by the difference between outpatient and inpatient costs per capita. The average cost per outpatient is considerably lower than the average cost per inpatient, so the difference in the numbers of outpatients and inpatients between these two projections is offset in the total expenditure.

These projected results suggest that a gradual shift of patterns of use for the whole country to that observed currently in Bangkok would lead to a substantial change in the composition of patients, but to only a minor difference in the total financial requirements of the MOPH. Moreover, were this alternative scenario adopted by the MOPH as its future policy direction, its facilities for outpatients would need to be expanded, as compared with the base forecast, whereas those for inpatients such as hospital beds would be underutilized. However, the seriousness of these problems may be alleviated to a certain degree through close cooperation between the MOPH and private clinics. For instance, the use of the idle MOPH hospital facilities by private doctors is one possibility.

It should also be borne in mind that this scenario is based upon the assumption that medical care services by the private sector outside Bangkok will grow rapidly in the next few decades. The feasibility of such growth depends heavily upon how fast the Thai rural economy develops in the future.

Table 7.13. Projected number of patients treated under the MOPH health care system and projected expenditure for MOPH, 1980–2015: An application of Bangkok profiles

Year	Number of patients (million persons)			Recurrent costs (million baht)	Investment costs (million baht)	Total expenditure (million baht)
	Outpatients	Inpatients	Total			
1980	27.981	2.287	30.268	3,056	989	4,495
1985	31.141	2.279	33.420	5,397	1,098	6,495
1990	34.131	2.209	36.340	7,880	1,959	9,839
1995	36.819	2.056	38.875	10,853	2,699	13,552
2000	39.252	1.839	41.091	15,022	3,736	18,758
2005	41.541	1.561	43.102	20,320	5,053	25,373
2010	43.619	1.220	44.839	26,888	6,686	33,575
2015	45.281	0.827	46.108	34,819	8,659	43,478

Varying Inpatient Rates

The base projections of inpatient and outpatient cases is strictly a demographic procedure. The demand for health services changes in response to changes in the age composition of the population, but no account is taken of how social or economic trends might, on the one hand, affect health care needs and, on the other hand, the demand for health care services.

Some factors lead to good health by encouraging more extensive use of formal health care services. For example, higher per capita income may contribute to health both by raising nutritional levels and by enabling more extensive and higher quality health care. Improved educational attainment may lead to a wider understanding of basic nutrition and hygiene, but also may lead to greater demand for health care services. Reduced fertility obviously will lead to a lower demand for health services by women of childbearing age, but what of children? Close child spacing is known to adversely effect health, so one would expect lower fertility to reduce the demand for health services.

These issues are explored through analysis of the 1981 Health and Welfare Survey which interviewed 21,860 households about their health-seeking behavior and the basic socioeconomic characteristics of the household. These data are used to examine the use of inpatient services for five groups that make the most extensive demands on the health care system: boys and girls age 6 or younger, women of childbearing age (20–49), and men and women 50 or older. The number of observations for each group are: 7,854 boys and 7,572 girls age 6 or younger; 22,972 women of childbearing age, and 6,424 men and 7,506 women age 50 or older.

For all regressions the dependent variable is dichotomous, equal to 1 if the individual was admitted to a public hospital during the 12 months preceding the survey. The independent variables vary somewhat depending on the group analyzed. A detailed description of variables and statistical results are reported in Appendix 7.1.[11]

Socioeconomic characteristics explain only a small portion of hospital use. The coefficient of determination varies from 0.07 for women of childbearing age down to 0.01 for the elderly. This comes as no surprise because there is an enormous random element in serious illness and resulting hospitalization. Moreover, many of the parameters are not estimated with sufficient precision to constitute conclusive evidence. Again this is to be expected with the analysis of a relatively rare event, e.g., hospitalization.

11. Equations were estimated using ordinary least squares. Because the disturbances are heteroskedastic the standard errors are biased. The extensive use of dichotomous independent variables minimizes some of the problems associated with the application of ordinary least squares to a dichotomous dependent variable (Gunderson 1974).

For boys and girls hospitalization declines substantially with age but age has no discernible impact on hospitalization among childbearing women or the elderly. The result for the elderly is somewhat surprising, but generally consistent with the aggregate age-specific inpatient results presented in Table 7.2. For elderly men an additional year of age is estimated to increase the probability of hospitalization by only 0.0006 and, for women, by only 0.0003.

Although one would expect urban residents to use hospitals more extensively because of their proximity, statistical evidence provides no support for this thesis.

Educational attainment is often cited as one of the most important determinants of good health. The statistical evidence generally supports the view that improved education also leads to increased hospitalization, suggesting that the educated are more likely to respond effectively to major illness not that they are necessarily more successful at avoiding it. The elderly in Thailand fall into two educational categories: those who did not graduate from primary school and primary school graduates who did not complete any higher level of education. For both elderly men and women, primary graduates were more likely to have experienced hospitalization in the previous year.

Analysis of hospitalization among children focuses on the educational attainment of parents. In general, the children of more educated mothers were more likely to experience hospitalization. The educational attainment of the household head had an inconsistent and statistically insignificant impact on hospitalization. Hospitalization among childbearing women was not consistently related to educational attainment.

For all five groups, the impact of the demographic composition of the household is estimated by including the number of members in seven age categories. Hospitalization among the elderly bore no systematic relationship to household membership. Women of childbearing age with a child under age 2 were much more likely to have experienced hospitalization during the previous 12 months. The explanation is obvious—roughly half of these women would have experienced a birth in the previous 12 months.

The impact of additional family members in other age groups is interesting. Neither additional teenagers nor elderly had a statistically significant impact on hospitalization. But an additional child age 2 to 5 reduced both use by women of childbearing age and use by children under the age of 6. Moreover, an additional adult age 25 to 59 depresses hospitalization among the three groups of users. The explanation for these effects is not clear. It may be that household size is serving as a proxy for per capita household income. Statistical analysis of per capita household income (see Chapter 5) shows that per capita income is lower in households with more members in these age groups. No firm conclusion is warranted without further study.

The analysis of hospital utilization suggests that as economic, demographic, and social change proceed in Thailand, the extent of use of inpatient services will change. Although the impact of increased income per se, cannot be estimated, improvements in educational attainment and changes in household size will affect the use of inpatient services by key user groups.

The extent of the change in the demand for inpatient services is forecast by combining the estimated regression equations with projections of educational attainment, urbanization, and household membership.[12] Hospital admissions for those under age 7 and those 50 and older are forecast to increase steadily but gradually over the foreseeable future. For males ages 0–6, for example, the inpatient rate increases from 0.056 in 1980 to 0.064 in 2015. For females, the rate rises from 0.049 to 0.060 during the same period. The increases for the elderly are similar. The inpatient rate for women of reproductive age declines by a substantial amount, from 0.075 to 0.046 between 1980 and 2015.

Table 7.14 presents projections of the number of inpatients and compares the results with projections based on the constant inpatient rate assumptions. The greatest decline is in the use by women of reproductive age. The standard projection forecasts a steady increase to 1.3 million cases by 2015; the varying rate projections forecast a peak at 0.85 million cases in 2005 and a decline to 0.81 million by 2015. The varying rate projection is 30 percent below the constant rate projection in 2015.

For the four other groups of users, the use of varying rates results in an upward revision. By 2005 the number of inpatients is projected to be 11 percent higher for boys, 21 percent higher for girls, 8 percent higher for older men, and 6 percent higher for older women. These increases are not sufficient, however, to offset the great decline in inpatient services demanded by women of reproductive age. The varying rate projections are consistently below the constant rate projections in all years. By 2005 the total number of cases is lower by 8 percent than in the baseline projection.

Refinement of the projection methodology to accommodate changes in utilization rates does not lead to substantial differences in the total caseload of public hospitals. However, the mix of services required and the age profile of patients served is likely to be considerably different than found using the constant utilization rate methodology. In particular, the inevitable decline in obstetric services associated with fertility decline is more adequately captured using the refined methodology.

12. The details of the methods for projecting these variables are provided in Chapters 2, 5, and 6.

Table 7.14. Comparison of sex-specific number of inpatients among selected age groups between changing inpatient rate case and constant inpatient rate case: 1980–2015 (in thousands)

	Male		Female			
Year	0–6	50+	0–6	20–49	50+	Combined[a]
1980	252 (252)	183 (183)	211 (211)	655 (655)	172 (172)	2,287 (2,287)
1985	258 (253)	217 (213)	225 (215)	727 (749)	206 (203)	2,544 (2,570)
1990	261 (249)	260 (250)	233 (211)	770 (906)	247 (238)	2,771 (2,856)
1995	252 (235)	304 (289)	227 (198)	810 (1,027)	286 (273)	2,968 (3,112)
2000	249 (227)	363 (340)	226 (191)	846 (1,126)	335 (317)	3,176 (3,357)
2005	246 (221)	442 (409)	224 (185)	849 (1,199)	403 (381)	3,364 (3,595)
2010	236 (209)	538 (497)	214 (174)	839 (1,239)	484 (461)	3,528 (3,838)
2015	221 (194)	650 (602)	201 (162)	814 (1,322)	571 (550)	3,674 (3,977)

Note: Values in the parentheses have been computed on the basis of constant inpatient rates.
a. Includes age groups for which only constant rate projections have been calculated.

HOUSEHOLD EXPENDITURE

To this point, analysis of the health sector has focused exclusively on the public sector. This limits the scope of the study to the extent that the private sector is an important provider of health care services in Thailand. Estimates based on the 1981 Socio-Economic Survey of Thailand, reported in Chapter 5, indicate that monthly expenditure on medical care in 1980 was just over 900 million baht or nearly twice the MOPH budget. Thus, trends in MOPH costs may be a poor guide to overall trends in the health care industry.

A second limitation of the MOPH analysis is the reliance on methods that identify the impact of changing age structure but do not shed light on how other socioeconomic characteristics of the population are likely to affect the demand for health care services. Analysis of use data described earlier provided some insights about changing inpatient rates that are broadly consistent with changing expenditures.

Analysis of household expenditure, including expenditure on health care, presented in Chapter 5 examines the impact of rising standards of living and changing demographic characteristics of the household. Two aspects of that analysis are particularly relevant here. First, medical expenditures are income elastic in Thailand. At the mean for the sample, the expenditure elasticity is estimated at 1.3. Thus, a 1 percent increase in income is calculated to generate a 1.3 percent increase in medical expenditure. At higher levels of income, the expenditure elasticity is somewhat lower. But even at an income twice the mean, the expenditure elasticity is about 1.2.

A combination of factors may account for the high income elasticity of medical care. High income families may be demanding more care, actually visiting the doctor more frequently or spending more days in the hospital; or they may be seeking higher quality care, paying for a specialist, for example. On the other hand, high income families may be substituting private for public (subsidized) health care. But, in any case, improvements in the Thai standard of living should lead to increased expenditure on health care by the typical family.

What does the analysis of Thai data say about the impact of changes in the demographic composition of the household? In general, the statistical results are consistent with the U-shaped profile one would expect for medical care expenditures. Additional household members, whether male or female, between the ages of 13 and 60 lead to reduced expenditures on medical care. Additional members age 60 and older or under 13 lead to higher medical expenditures. But the effects are statistically significant only in the case of children under the age of 3. Either an additional boy or girl increases the share of the household budget devoted to health by a full percentage point.[13] This result is quite consistent with the finding above that utilization of health services by women of childbearing age is much higher in households with young children. No doubt, the presence of young children is picking up expenditures associated with childbirth.

In general, aggregate trends in household expenditure are consistent with the aggregate trends forecast for MOPH utilization and costs. Aggregate household expenditures (see Chapter 5) are forecast to grow at 9.6 percent per annum between 1980 and 2015, as the share of household expenditure devoted to medical care increases from 3.5 percent to 4.3 percent. The forecast rate of increase in household expenditures is very nearly identical to that forecast for inpatient costs but significantly higher than the rate of growth forecast for MOPH outpatient costs (see Figure 7.7).

13. This is a partial effect that assumes per capita household income is constant. If, as an alternative, household income is constant the partial impact is reduced because an additional child reduces per capita income. In this case, an additional male would increase the share by 0.08 and an additional female would increase the share by 0.075.

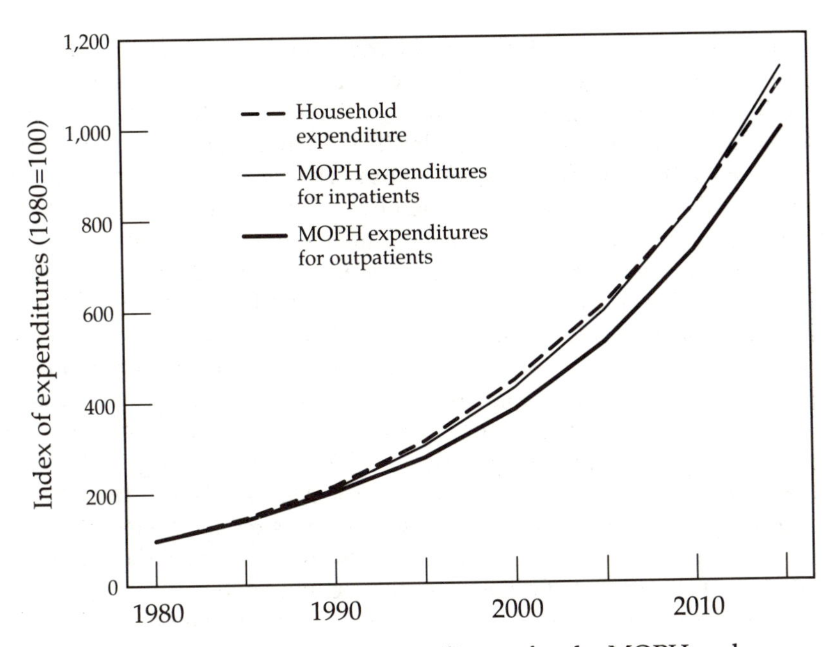

Figure 7.7. Projected medical expenditures for the MOPH and households: 1980–2015

Although it seems reassuring that two divergent approaches provide similar results, it may be mere coincidence. In fact, one would expect the rate of growth of household expenditure to exceed the rate of growth of the MOPH budget if improved standards of living are inducing households to substitute private for public health care.

Additional analysis of the consumer expenditure survey sheds some light on this issue. The survey includes separate categories on payments to government hospitals and clinics (20 percent of all medical expenditures) and payments to private hospitals and clinics (29 percent of medical expenditures). The estimated expenditure elasticities are 1.5 for government hospitals and clinics and 2.6 for private hospitals and clinics. This suggests some tendency to substitute private for public care, but the demand for both public and private medical services should rise over time.

CONCLUDING REMARKS

The results suggest four broad changes in the health sector: overall growth that exceeds the growth of the economy, but not by a substantial margin; a shift in medical services toward outpatient and away from inpatient care; a change in the demographic profile of the typical patient, from young to old; and, a relative decline in the demand for obstetric services.

Demographic change will also affect the provision of care. Owing to reduced fertility, average household size will fall substantially, undermining family support for the aged. Such difficulties are likely to be more pronounced among non-intact households than among intact households, partly because the process of aging will be faster for the former than for the latter, and partly because older members of non-intact households do not have spouses, who are normally the main caregivers at home. These forecast results suggest that the ministry should pay attention to the changing needs for different types of health care among different types of households. They also suggest that the importance of inpatient care might accelerate over time, as a result of a decrease in potential caregivers at home.

The forecast results show that compared with the recent growth trend, the constant ratio growth rates of doctors, nurses, and hospital beds are not too challenging, whereas growth rates based on the Bangkok level of care would present a serious challenge to the MOPH. The differences in the required growth rates between these two cases reflect the fact that the current distributions of MOPH health personnel and facilities between Bangkok and the rest of the country differ considerably.

These findings imply that health care and training provided by the MOPH need to be redirected away from pediatrics toward a greater emphasis on geriatric medicine. Thus, the pattern of demand for medical doctors by specialized fields will vary over time, and the level of needs for hospital beds allocated for each specialized field will also be affected.

The projected results point to the possibility that, although there will be only a minor difference in the MOPH's financial requirements between the "Bangkok" scenario and the base forecast, the composition of patients will be markedly different between the two cases. In the "Bangkok" scenario there will be more outpatients and fewer inpatients compared with the base forecast, requiring a major shift in the allocation of health resources.

The computed expenditure elasticities suggest that expenditures on both types of medical care services will increase faster than total expenditures, and that their shares in the household budget will rise as households achieve higher standards of living.

These projected figures for private medical services are substantially higher than those for medical services provided by the public sector, thus indicating that a growing proportion of Thailand's medical care services are likely to be provided by the private sector.

The most serious limitation of this study is its failure to assess the impact of AIDS on the demand for health sector services. The first AIDS patient in Thailand was reported in 1984, three years after the survey which is the primary source of data for this study. Although estimates of the extent of AIDS vary widely, it is believed that between 200,000 and 400,000 Thais were HIV positive by October 1991 (Wibulpolprasert 1991:11). Because of the long incubation period, only a few hundred Thais are currently being treated for AIDS-related complex and full-blown AIDS. But the number requiring treatment will grow extremely rapidly during the 1990s. One recent projection anticipates 160,000 deaths and an additional 180,000 ill in the year 2000 (Wibulpolprasert 1991:11).

A number of other data problems have been encountered. For example, due to the limitation of data, the effect of the changing pattern of illness and changes in medical technology upon health expenditures could not be incorporated in a satisfactory manner. Although the implications of the present analysis provide a very helpful first step in health policy formulation, these data limitations suggest that caution should be exercised in using the findings of this study for policy purposes.

Appendix 7.1
DETAILED RESULTS:
STATISTICAL ANALYSIS OF HEALTH CARE USE, 1981 SOCIO-ECONOMIC SURVEY OF THAILAND

Appendix Table 7.1.1. List of variables

Variable	Description
AGE	Age
AGE2	Age squared
URBAN	1 if a person is in the municipal area; 0 otherwise
SMOKER	1 if a person is a smoker; 0 otherwise
MSEM	1 if a woman is married or ever married; 0 otherwise
P0T1	Number of family members 0–1 years of age
P2T5	Number of family members 2–5 years of age
P6T11	Number of family members 6–11 years of age
P12T17	Number of family members 12–17 years of age
P18T24	Number of family members 18–24 years of age
P25T59	Number of family members 25–59 years of age
P60UP	Number of family members age 60 and older
MOMWRK	1 if a mother is working; 0 otherwise
Education	
EDPRIM	1 if a person has primary education; 0 otherwise
EDSEC	1 if a person has secondary education; 0 otherwise
EDCOL	1 if a person has tertiary education; 0 otherwise
HDEDPRIM	1 if a household head has primary education; 0 otherwise
HDEDSEC	1 if a household head has secondary education; 0 otherwise
HDEDCOL	1 if a household head has tertiary education; 0 otherwise
MOMEDPRI	1 if a mother has primary education; 0 otherwise
MOMEDSEC	1 if a mother has secondary education; 0 otherwise
MOMEDCOL	1 if a mother has tertiary education; 0 otherwise
	(No education is the reference group)

Appendix Table 7.1.1. List of variables *(continued)*

Variable	Description
Occupation	
PROF	1 if a person is a professional worker; 0 otherwise
MANAG	1 if a person is a managerial worker; 0 otherwise
CLERK	1 if a person is a clerical worker; 0 otherwise
SALESMAN	1 if a person is a salesman; 0 otherwise
FARMER	1 if a person is a farmer; 0 otherwise
TRANSP	1 if a person is a transportation worker; 0 otherwise
CRAFT	1 if a person is a production worker; 0 otherwise
SERVICE	1 if a person is a service worker; 0 otherwise
HDOCCUP1	1 if a household head is a professional worker; 0 otherwise
HDOCCUP2	1 if a household head is a managerial worker; 0 otherwise
HDOCCUP3	1 if a household head is a clerical worker; 0 otherwise
HDOCCUP4	1 if a household head is a salesman worker; 0 otherwise
HDOCCUP5	1 if a household head is a farm worker; 0 otherwise
HDOCCUP6	1 if a household head is a mining worker; 0 otherwise
HDOCCUP7	1 if a household head is a transportation worker; 0 otherwise
HDOCCUP8	1 if a household head is a production worker; 0 otherwise
HDOCCUP9	1 if a household head is a service worker; 0 otherwise
	(Unemployed is the reference group)
Type of employer	
GOVT	1 if a person is a government worker; 0 otherwise
PRIV	1 if a person is a private worker; 0 otherwise
	(Unemployed, unpaid family workers and self-employed workers constitute the reference group)

Appendix Table 7.1.2. Regression results

	Males 0–6 years of age			Females 0–6 years of age		
Variables	Parameter estimate	Standard error	*T*-value	Parameter estimate	Standard error	*T*-value
INTERCEPT	0.1133	0.0160	7.063	0.0758	0.0149	5.095
AGE	-0.0125	0.0015	-8.216	-0.0098	0.0014	-6.882
URBAN	-0.0038	0.0073	-0.523	0.0077	0.0066	1.160
P0T1	-0.0034	0.0053	-0.642	0.0007	0.0048	0.139
P2T5	-0.0099	0.0033	-2.974	-0.0098	0.0030	-3.221
P6T11	0.0020	0.0027	0.748	-0.0024	0.0025	-0.938
P12T17	-0.0041	0.0028	-1.464	-0.0016	0.0026	-0.599
P18T24	0.0009	0.0029	0.312	-0.0001	0.0027	-0.032
P25T59	-0.0064	0.0021	-2.335	-0.0069	0.0025	-2.778
P60UP	-0.0008	0.0050	-0.151	0.0012	0.0047	0.250
MOMWRK	-0.0093	0.0065	-1.428	0.0017	0.0061	0.285
HDEDPRIM	-0.0094	0.0083	-1.131	0.0133	0.0077	1.724
HDEDSEC	-0.0082	0.0118	-0.696	0.0162	0.0111	1.458
HDEDCOL	-0.0193	0.0197	-0.981	0.0084	0.0179	0.467
MOMEDPRI	0.0135	0.0090	1.491	0.0160	0.0084	1.896
MOMEDSEC	0.0185	0.0131	1.419	-0.0019	0.0123	-0.156
MOMEDCOL	0.0497	0.0178	2.787	0.0286	0.0166	1.723
HDOCCUP1	0.0039	0.0203	0.193	-0.0014	0.0192	-0.073
HDOCCUP2	-0.0111	0.0146	-0.758	-0.0209	0.0136	-1.537
HDOCCUP3	0.0021	0.0180	0.117	-0.0072	0.0165	-0.438
HDOCCUP4	0.0123	0.0117	1.044	0.0024	0.0109	0.222
HDOCCUP5	0.0062	0.0103	0.596	-0.0028	0.0094	-0.298
HDOCCUP6	-0.0473	0.0899	-0.527	-0.0560	0.0818	-0.685
HDOCCUP7	0.0157	0.0137	1.149	-0.0041	0.0124	-0.332
HDOCCUP8	0.0139	0.0115	1.213	-0.0189	0.0105	-1.795
HDOCCUP9	0.0189	0.0151	1.257	0.0006	0.0143	0.040
	Adjusted *R*-square = 0.0143			Adjusted *R*-square = 0.0144		

Variables	Females 20–49 years of age		
	Parameter estimate	Standard error	*T*-value
INTERCEPT	0.0919	0.0352	2.608
AGE	-0.0011	0.0021	-0.526
AGE2	-0.0000	0.0000	-0.093
URBAN	0.0036	0.0053	0.680
SMOKER	0.0081	0.0088	0.928
MSEM	0.0691	0.0051	12.118
P0T1	0.1406	0.0040	34.832
P2T5	-0.0090	0.0026	-3.473
P6T11	-0.0016	0.0019	-0.831
P12T17	-0.0023	0.0018	-1.302
P18T24	-0.0058	0.0018	-3.219
P25T59	-0.0049	0.0017	-2.937
P60UP	-0.0046	0.0032	-1.457
EDPRIM	0.0116	0.0070	1.662
EDSEC	0.0052	0.0091	0.575
EDCOL	-0.0170	0.0112	1.516
HDEDPRIM	-0.0058	0.0052	-1.106
HDEDSEC	-0.0137	0.0070	-1.975
HDEDCOL	-0.0036	0.0091	-0.398
PROF	0.0149	0.0130	1.141
MANAG	-0.0027	0.0181	-0.148
CLERK	0.0119	0.0117	1.023
SALESMAN	-0.0388	0.0057	-6.791
FARMER	-0.0518	0.0063	-8.264
TRANSP	-0.0175	0.0298	-0.586
CRAFT	-0.0351	0.0084	-4.172
SERVICE	-0.0470	0.0103	-4.582
GOVT	0.0026	0.0110	0.240
PRIV	-0.0077	0.0069	-1.109
	Adjusted *R*-square = 0.0658		

(continued)

Appendix Table 7.1.2. Regression results *(continued)*

	Males age 50 and older			Females age 50 and older		
Variables	Parameter estimate	Standard error	*T*-value	Parameter estimate	Standard error	*T*-value
INTERCEPT	0.0774	0.0421	1.836	0.0493	0.0282	1.747
AGE	0.0006	0.0006	0.918	0.0003	0.0004	0.733
URBAN	0.0051	0.0082	0.620	-0.0017	0.0065	-0.267
P0T1	0.0052	0.0086	0.606	-0.0035	0.0069	-0.506
P2T5	-0.0027	0.0056	-0.482	0.0047	0.0046	1.023
P6T11	0.0034	0.0040	0.862	-0.0007	0.0034	-0.206
P12T17	-0.0022	0.0034	-0.642	-0.0003	0.0030	-0.094
P18T24	-0.0015	0.0031	-0.478	-0.0012	0.0028	-0.431
P25T59	-0.0053	0.0031	-1.733	-0.0013	0.0024	-0.556
P60UP	-0.0039	0.0060	-0.655	-0.0019	0.0044	-0.422
EDPRIM	0.0197	0.0077	2.541	0.0118	0.0063	1.866
EDSEC	0.0071	0.0134	0.525	-0.0159	0.0171	-0.927
EDCOL	-0.0028	0.0225	-0.125	-0.0036	0.0333	-0.109
PROF	-0.0562	0.0268	-2.095	-0.0469	0.0364	-1.289
MANAG	-0.0505	0.0177	-2.850	-0.0472	0.0356	-1.324
CLERK	-0.0631	0.0268	-2.355	0.0801	0.0500	1.603
SALESMAN	-0.0652	0.0127	-5.150	-0.0118	0.0089	-1.326
FARMER	-0.0532	0.0105	-5.082	-0.0203	0.0078	-2.586
TRANSP	-0.0724	0.0219	-3.300	-0.0680	0.1038	-0.655
CRAFT	-0.0605	0.0166	-3.648	-0.0246	0.0185	-1.328
SERVICE	-0.0438	0.0224	-1.957	-0.0101	0.0251	-0.404
GOVT	0.0358	0.0168	2.134	0.0288	0.0311	0.920
PRIV	-0.0066	0.0141	-0.468	-0.0323	0.0176	-1.836
	Adjusted *R*-square = 0.0090			Adjusted *R*-square = 0.0012		

8

Housing Demand and Required Residential Construction

by Burnham O. Campbell
and Nipon Poapongsakorn

The amount of housing available per capita and the quality of a nation's housing stock are key determinants of national welfare. Whatever the current level of satisfaction derived from the housing stock, as the population grows and changes in composition and as existing units wear out or are destroyed, maintaining existing per capita standards will require the construction of new dwelling units. And additional construction may be needed to raise the average quality of the housing stock, either in response to market demand as real incomes rise or to government programs designed to fulfill unmet social standards.

Regardless of the motivation behind it, new construction employs land, labor, and capital resources that could be used for other purposes. Determining how important this is will depend on the national saving ratio, on the opportunities for external financing, on the expected returns from capital accumulation other than in residential construction, and on the political, social, and economic pressures for maintaining or improving housing standards. These circumstances are likely to differ considerably among countries. Nevertheless, being able to estimate the additional units needed in the future to maintain existing standards is useful in any country for purposes of economic analysis and forecasting and for decision makers in both the government and the private sector.

Supplied with such forecasts and with estimates of the income elasticity of housing demand and knowledge of supply constraints in the construction industry, various possible scenarios can be projected. These projections will help reduce the uncertainties facing the private sector and will aid in the government's sectorial and general economic policymaking. Moreover, given the considerable evidence in many countries of a construction cycle rooted in underlying demographic changes, demographically based time series forecasts of housing requirements and related residential construction activities will be helpful in understanding the cyclical forces at work nationally.

Evaluating both the potential cyclical impact of demographic changes through their effect on residential construction and the national and sectorial allocative implications of such changes is facilitated by the fact that the basic demographic profile of the housing population is known with considerable certainty for the next 15 years. In fact, because the number of household heads among the population 15–24 years of age is relatively small, this profile is likely to be relatively accurate for the next 25 years. After 25 years, forecasts of birth rates, which are more difficult to make, begin to play an increasingly important role.

This chapter presents demographic forecasts (and backcasts) of housing requirements for Thailand based on HOMES estimates of the number of households[1] for quinquennial (five-year) periods from 1950 to 2015. They show the number of dwelling units that would have to be added to the housing stock from 1980–85 on to maintain the 1980 household composition and the number of units that would have had to have been added from 1950 to 1980 to maintain the 1970 household composition. Base estimates of demand by tenure type, founded on the sssumption that the distribution of housing demand by tenure type (owner occupancy, renter occupancy, etc.) by heads in different age groups remains at the 1970 level, are also provided.

Our base forecasts of additional housing units required by ongoing demographic changes assume no future changes in the economic circumstances (e.g., per capita incomes, relative prices of housing) and tastes that determined age- and sex-specific headship rates in 1980.[2] The backcasts make the same assumption about the 1970 determinants of such headship rates. Thus they provide a benchmark against which the impact of other and less easily predicted variables can be measured. Similarly, the estimates of demand by tenure type hold all determinants of such demand other than demographic changes at the 1970 per capita level.

The base forecasts are then adjusted for expected withdrawals from the housing stock and for minimal or "frictional" vacancies to give forecasts

1. See Mason (1987) for a description of the HOMES methodology followed.

2. Controlling for the effect of demographic factors, there is no evidence of significant changes in living arrangements due to economic growth or changes in tastes between the 1970 and 1980 census. However, if growth, urbanization, and industrialization continue at their present pace in Thailand, such changes may well occur at some point in the next 30 years.

of the housing starts required. The forecasts of housing starts are turned into base estimates of real residential construction by assuming that the present average value of a dwelling unit occupied by heads in each age group will remain unchanged in the future. Essentially, this amounts to assuming that the household income elasticity of the quality and number of housing units demanded is zero.[3]

Finally, implicit in forecasts of residential construction based only on demand considerations is the assumption that the supply of new dwelling units of all qualities is perfectly elastic at the present relative price of housing. Although there is evidence to support the assumption of a highly elastic supply of new dwelling units in Thailand in the past, future labor requirements relative to labor force growth will have to be evaluated to determine how reasonable this assumption will be in the future.

Together these assumptions ensure that our estimates serve roughly as a lower bound to the likely range of future outcomes. They thus provide a conservative benchmark from which the effect of the variables initially left out can be quantitatively or qualitatively evaluated. Especially important in this context are the effects of internal migration, clearly expected if industrialization continues, and of feedbacks from growth in per capita income to household formation and to the quality and type of housing demanded. Also potentially important are the future effects of existing backlogs of demand and of changes in the relative prices of housing that may occur as a result of changing supply conditions or changes in real exchange rates.

PROJECTIONS OF HOUSING DEMAND

Methodology

Estimates of the housing stock required by the Thai population are derived as follows:

$$HK^t = HH^t (A_f)(1 + A_{v1} + A_{v2})$$

where: HK^t = the housing stock in year t

HH^t = the number of households in year t

A_f = the occupied housing stock or households in base year (1970 or 1980)

A_{v1} = frictional vacancies as a percentage of the occupied housing stock in base year

A_{v2} = cyclical vacancies as a percentage of the occupied housing stock in base year (assumed to be zero in making forecasts)

---

3. This is a very conservative procedure not only because of the zero elasticity assumption but also because new units and replacement units can be expected to be priced considerably above the average value for the entire stock.

The household forecasts used are based on the HOMES methodology described in Chapter 2 of this volume. HOMES' household estimates for periods before 1980 are based on 1970 census data for Thailand (NSO 1970); estimates from 1980 onward are based on the 1980 census (NSO 1980).

The "doubling rate"—the ratio of occupied housing units to the number of households—is derived from the census and the 1976 Housing Survey (NSO 1977) covering both the numerator and denominator of the ratio.[4] The considerations used in defining upper and lower bounds on this ratio for purposes of sensitivity analysis and the adjustments made for changes in the urban–rural population split are discussed in Appendix 8.1. The latter adjustment is required because there is considerable worldwide evidence that "doubling" is greater in urban than in rural areas.

The expected level of vacancies is more difficult to derive. Simplifying somewhat, vacancies can be considered to be of two kinds, frictional or normal and cyclical vacancies. Both reflect the fact that, like most nonauction markets, the housing market involves information costs and so does not clear continuously. Housing remains vacant while buyers and sellers of housing services adjust their expectations and discover their transaction prices.

Roughly, the greater the mobility between geographic regions and housing neighborhoods and the more rapid the secular change in the market, the higher the ratio of frictional vacancies to the housing stock. As national or regional economic activity declines or as builders respond to the short-run equilibrium price in typical cobweb fashion, cyclical vacancies arise. Essentially, normal vacancies reflect the irreducible minimum of vacancies at any time and cyclical vacancies involve vacancies above the minimum. In the forecasts and estimates presented, the second or cyclical component of vacancies is ignored, there being no empirical basis for trying to "guess" its variation. However, an adjustment is made for normal vacancies. Based on the considerations noted in Appendix 8.2, these are taken to be 2 percent of the occupied housing stock for Thailand.

The change, then, in the estimated housing stock between two five-year periods (quinquennial intervals are used) gives the number of additional units required by changes in demographic factors only or "required additions" (RA^t) during the interval. This number can, of course, be negative as well as positive, and constitutes a base estimate of the change in demand occurring in housing markets from one five-year period to the next.

Required additions are defined in symbols as follows:

$$RA^t = HK^t - HK^{t-1}$$

4. Relatively complete data for the number of households are available in the censuses of 1970 and 1980. The Ministry of Industry of Thailand has been reporting the occupied housing stock since the 1960s and the United Nations made a similar estimate for 1970.

Forecasts of required additions will correctly measure the change in housing demand given two conditions. First, population factors must be the only determinants of housing demand that change over time. Second, there must be no constraints on the supply side that prevent the stock from adjusting to whatever new level is required without any change in relative prices. Thus, they would be expected to underestimate the change in the demand for dwelling units when per capita incomes are growing, especially if income distribution is shifting in favor of younger workers. And the forecasts would be expected to underestimate the change when the relative price of housing falls because of exchange rate depreciation[5] and when industrialization increases the opportunities for urban employment since household size is generally smaller in urban areas.

The number of new units required is not the same as the change in housing demand. Over time the housing stock declines due to aging, natural disasters, or the switching of residential land to other uses; the units lost must be accounted for in estimating required new units or, as used hereafter, required housing starts. The procedure for doing so, with a range of possibilities based on experience elsewhere in the region is given in Appendix 8.3. Required housing starts (RHS^t) are then defined as follows:

$$RHS^t = RA^t + A_w (HK^{t-1})$$

where: A_w = the ratio of withdrawals over five years to the housing stock at the beginning of the base period.

In addition to the reasons already noted for the actual change in the housing stock differing from the forecast or required change, actual housing starts may differ from required housing starts if the movement of households between geographic submarkets cannot be matched by the movement of dwelling units in the same direction. Although there are exceptions, construction usually depends on the sum of excess demands in the geographically segregated submarkets, ignoring excess supply submarkets, rather than on national totals netting out excess supply against excess demand submarkets. So internal migration will generally lead to actual housing starts in excess of required housing starts.[6] Accounting for this source of new construction is only possible in qualitative terms and the lack of such accounting in numerical terms underscores the base or minimum nature of our estimates.

---

5. Baht depreciation will generally raise the demand for non-traded goods and services such as housing, while baht appreciation will have the opposite effect.

6. Although both the rural and urban populations have continued to grow in Thailand, future movement of population out of the northeast and possibly parts of the south could have this effect.

Actual housing starts may differ from required housing starts as well because of supply side constraints and developments. Among other reasons, when government constraints on residential construction (via resource allocations, price controls, etc.) are added or subtracted, housing starts will not equal required housing starts. And where, even over five-year periods, the supply curve of new housing is considerably less than infinitely elastic, the relative price of housing and so the effective demand for housing will depend on the size of required housing starts. Or, if there is a speculative response to excess demand in the short run (when relative prices are more likely to change), which is fed by the usual cobweb adjustment, then actual starts can be expected to differ from required housing starts. All of these factors (and others) cannot be adequately incorporated into the base estimates presented, but, like internal migration, must be considered qualitatively in using these estimates.

Required Housing Stock

Using the methodology described above, we estimated the occupied and total housing stock in Thailand from 1950 to 2015 (Table 8.1). The number of households in Thailand will continue to increase through 2015. The occupied housing stock, derived by adjusting the number of households for the "doubling up" of some households, will also increase through 2015, but at a slightly slower pace since the doubling rate is assumed to decline marginally over time. The required housing stock—that is, the stock of housing required by demographic changes only, which is derived by adjusting the occupied housing stock by a constant percentage for "normal" vacancies—will mirror the increase in the occupied housing stock.

The end result suggests that 20.54 million dwelling units will be required in 2015 or an increase of 111 percent over the 1985 level of 9.74 million dwellings. Since the assumptions made are quite conservative, especially that headship rates will not increase and that undoubling will not pick up as real incomes increase,[7] it is almost certain that the actual demand for housing in Thailand in 2015 will be considerably larger than the required housing stock.

Only government intervention to restrict the supply of new units could prevent the shift of resources to fill this "excess demand" and then only at the expense of rapidly increasing housing prices and speculation or

7. Experience in the United States and Europe also points to the possibility of a significant headship rate effect of growth in per capita income. Japan's experience seems to have differed in that headship rates have fallen off at early life-cycle stages as income has increased. This probably reflects the fact that in Japan, unlike in the United States and Europe, housing costs in most urban areas, especially land costs, have increased more rapidly than nominal income. The relatively abundant supply of land in Thailand suggests the situation there will be more like that in the United States and Europe than Japan.

Table 8.1. The housing market: 1950–2015 (thousands)

Year	No. of house-holds	Occupied stock	Total stock	Period	New house-holds	Required additions	With-drawals	Required housing starts
1950	3,449	3,251	3,316					
1955	4,046	3,814	3,890	1950–55	597	574	332	906
1960	4,734	4,462	4,552	1955–60	688	661	389	1,050
1965	5,423	5,105	5,207	1960–65	689	655	455	1,110
1970	6,211	5,838	5,955	1965–70	788	748	521	1,269
1975	7,354	6,902	7,040	1970–75	1,143	1,085	596	1,680
1980	8,689	8,140	8,303	1975–80	1,335	1,305	700	2,005
1985	10,215	9,552	9,743	1980–85	1,526	1,440	830	2,270
1990	12,001	11,200	11,424	1985–90	1,787	1,681	974	2,655
1995	13,977	13,014	13,274	1990–95	1,976	1,851	1,142	2,993
2000	16,030	14,891	15,188	1995–2000	2,053	1,914	1,327	3,241
2005	18,091	16,761	17,096	2000–05	2,060	1,908	1,519	3,427
2010	20,074	18,545	18,915	2005–10	1,983	1,819	1,710	3,529
2015	21,870	20,142	20,545	2010–15	1,796	1,629	1,892	3,521

Source: Based on NSO (1970, 1980), HOMES forecasts (Chapter 2), and Appendices 8.1, 8.2, and 8.3.

rationing and their attendant misallocations. Whether or not the government would have an incentive to intervene would, however, depend on the opportunity costs of more than doubling the housing stock over the next 30 years. In addition to the social and political costs of not maintaining (or improving) existing standards, the government's decision will in part depend on how rapidly the economy grows and whether the required growth in the housing stock implies a larger or smaller share for residential construction in GDP and gross domestic investment.

Required Additions

The level of new housing units required by the forecast changes in the required Thai housing stock will increase at a decreasing pace to a peak in 1995–2000 and decline thereafter (Figure 8.1). At the peak, required additions will be 33 percent above the 1980–85 level. By 2010–15 they will have declined to only 13 percent above the 1980–85 level.

Even more interesting is the age composition of the growth in housing demand in Thailand. There are systematic differences in the quality, size, location, and tenure of housing demanded by different age groups, resulting in much less than perfect substitutability between the average unit occupied by different age groups. Thus, the variation in net demand by age group can be very important. Relative prices can change to offset excess supply or demand in different segments of the housing market but they are sticky (at least downward) and there are likely to be large differences between the short- and long-run response. Meanwhile, construction will be encouraged in the excess demand segments.[8]

Most impressive in this context is the coming growth in housing demand by middle-aged (35–59) heads (see Table 8.2). By 2015 the dwellings required for this age group in Thailand will be 253 percent of the 1985 level. Heads in this age group generally have less postponable housing demand and require better quality or at least larger housing. They also tend to spend more on furnishings and other housing appurtenances and are more often homeowners than are heads in the other age groups. Thus, the significance of the huge growth forecast for the 35–59 age group is apparent. Enroute to this much increased required housing stock, beginning in 1985–90 (see Figure 8.2) the net new units required for the 35–59 age group will increase continuously to a peak in the first five years of the next century. At that time, the demographically based demand for new units in this age group will be 235 percent of the 1985–90 level!

8. The story told by required additions by age of head does not take account of withdrawals, which could be concentrated in one or more age groups rather than being fairly evenly distributed among the age groups. If, however, withdrawals even roughly follow the distribution of the housing *stock* by age group, required construction will have to be tailored to the changing housing characteristics suggested by the variation in required additions by age group.

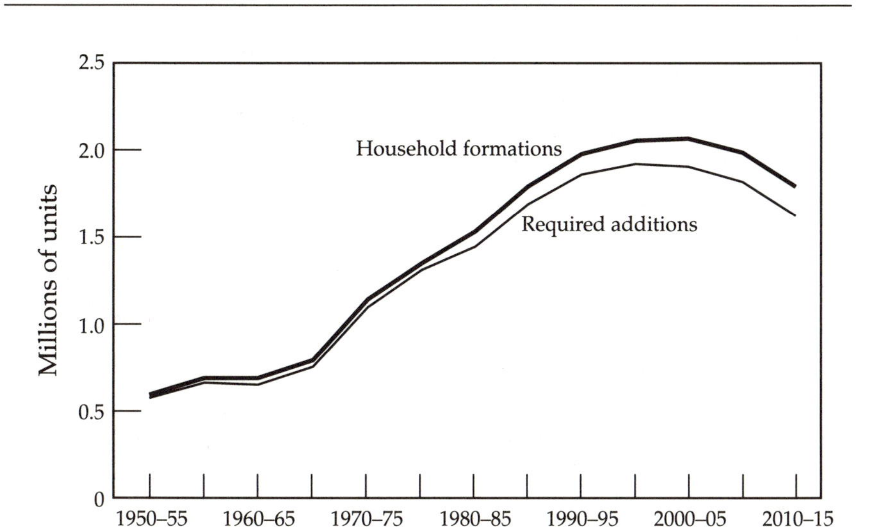

Source: Table 8.1.

Figure 8.1. Projected household formations and required additions to the housing stock: 1950–55 to 2010–15

Table 8.2. Required housing stock by age group: 1950–2015

Year	Age group 15–34	35–59	60+	Total
1950	1,374,401	1,738,915	339,732	3,453,048
1955	1,625,394	2,012,980	413,160	4,051,534
1960	1,916,124	2,338,487	517,092	4,771,703
1965	2,133,695	2,679,025	593,092	5,405,812
1970	2,375,688	3,084,556	702,355	6,162,599
1975	2,900,162	3,530,440	829,327	7,259,929
1980	3,392,016	4,253,880	1,043,257	8,689,153
1985	4,102,419	4,922,158	1,190,146	10,214,723
1990	4,798,926	5,788,625	1,414,127	12,001,678
1995	5,400,843	6,884,043	1,692,355	13,977,241
2000	5,838,852	8,176,692	2,014,792	16,030,336
2005	6,027,772	9,748,547	2,314,498	18,090,817
2010	6,194,231	11,266,288	2,703,715	20,164,234
2015	6,071,205	12,499,959	3,298,558	21,869,722

Source: Based on NSO (1970, 1980) and Appendix 8.4.

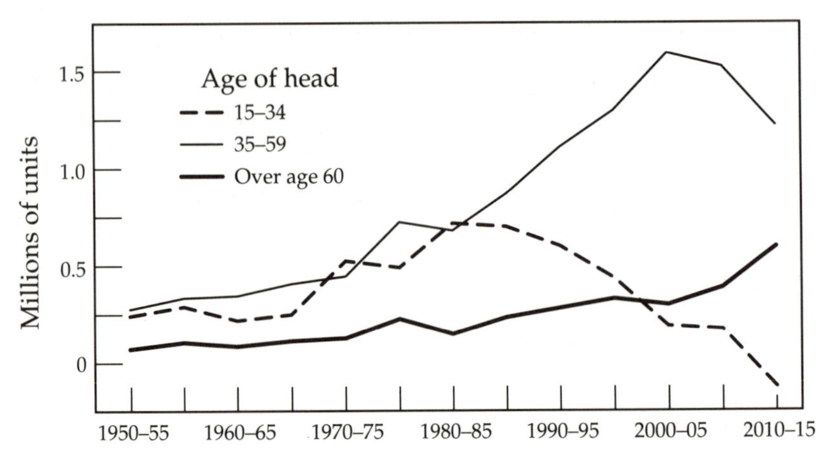

Source: Table 8.2.

Figure 8.2. New housing required by age of head: 1950–55 to 2010–15

The much slower growth through 2010 and decline thereafter in the housing units required for the 15–34 age group in Thailand is also interesting. Heads in this age group can postpone demand if necessary and tend to have specialized housing needs, especially in urban areas. The requirement for new housing units for the 15–34 age group peaked during 1980–85 and then declines steadily. There is very definitely the possibility that the characteristics of the housing being produced are out-of-line with the characteristics of housing demanded. From now on the required number of new units designed for the specialized needs of younger household heads will decline sharply, reaching negative levels in 2010–15. Only a major—but not impossible—upward shift in headship rates could change this conclusion.[9]

Finally, the total housing required for household heads 60 years of age or older in Thailand will remain considerably smaller than for the other two age groups, with required additions for this age group moving up relatively slowly through the first five years of the twenty-first century. Then they will almost double in the following 10 years! The increase at that time to 329.8 percent of the 1980–85 level will offer both an opportunity to the Thai building industry and provide a considerable challenge.

9. These developments reflect the underlying population changes and will also show up in the age structure of the labor force. The relative shortage of younger workers could easily raise the relative incomes of these workers as economic growth continues. A sharp increase in real incomes for young workers has had a significant upward impact on the headship rates of young people in other countries.

In sum, after increasing until the end of this century, the resources required by the housing sector to satisfy the growth in demand based on population changes only will fall off in the early twenty-first century. This will be especially true of resources now directed into housing for younger households. To adequately analyze the potential importance and economic effect of demographic changes on housing markets, however, the estimates of required additions must first be adjusted for the effect of withdrawals and replacement demand and then valued to derive forecasts of real residential construction.

Briefly turning to the sensitivity of the results presented so far to the assumptions made, in Figure 8.3 we show the required additions based on three sets of doubling rates and, for the medium doubling rate, two sets of vacancy rates. The 10 percent or high doubling rate is close to that found in the urban areas in other developing countries and the 0 percent rate is similar to the very low levels found in many highly developed countries. Neither this variation nor the variation of "normal" vacancy rates in the range found in the Asian developing countries (between 2 and 4 percent) for which data were available, significantly changes the general level of or general movement in required additions. But if doubling should fall to zero, required additions in Thailand would be increased by 10 to 11 percent above the basic level forecast over the next six quinquennia.

Required Housing Starts

Required housing starts include the new units required by demographic changes (required additions) and the replacement of units required by withdrawals from the existing stock. There is considerable uncertainty surrounding any forecast of withdrawals since they are influenced by a variety of unrelated variables, e.g., natural disasters, the age composition of the housing stock, the rate of economic growth, urbanization. There is, however, some evidence available from other countries as well as inferential evidence from past Thai housing inventories that will help set the likely range of outcomes (Appendix 8.3).

After sifting through the various possibilities, we used a withdrawal rate of 2 percent of the housing stock per annum for the base estimate.[10] At this basic rate, Thai housing starts (see Figure 8.4) will exceed required additions by increasing amounts and continue to increase, although slowly, to a 2005–10 peak. Housing starts will then remain near this peak through

10. Rates of 1 percent and 3 percent are used to demonstrate the impact of "extreme" values. The basic 2 percent rate implies that 92.5 percent of the Thai housing stock in the year 2015 would have been built after 1985, compared with 60.0 percent if there are no withdrawals at all. The 1 percent extreme implies that 66.0 percent of the 2015 stock would have been built after 1985 and the 3 percent rate that 100 percent would have been built after 1985.

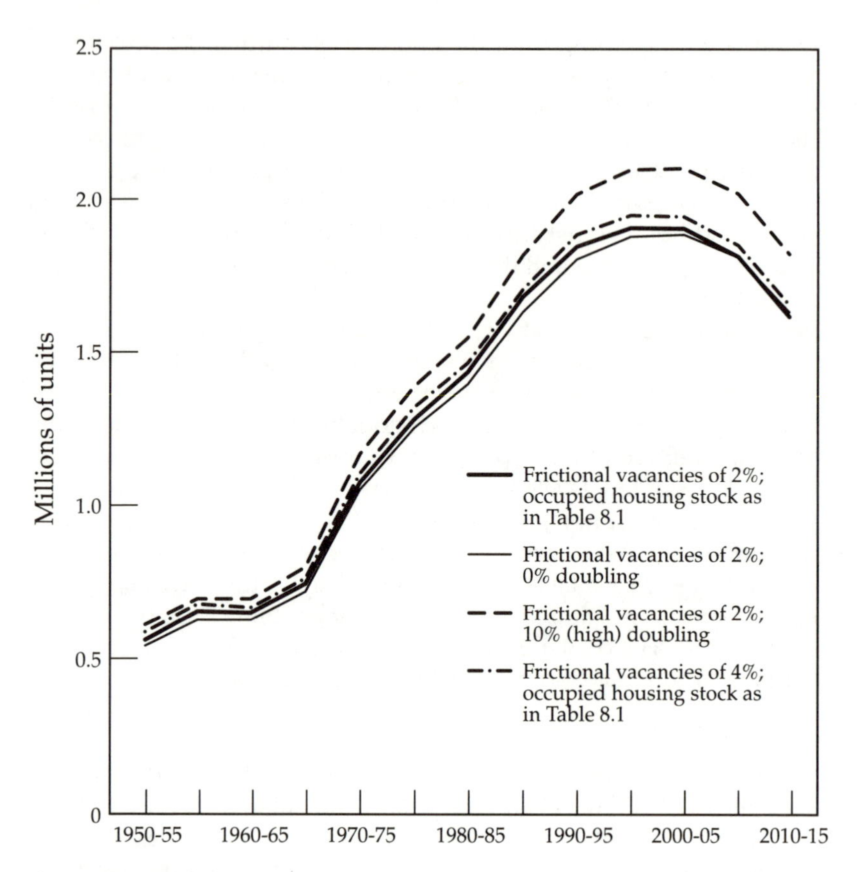

Source: Derived from data in Table 8.1 and indicated variations in vacancy and doubling rates.

Figure 8.3. Required additions: Sensitivity to doubling and vacancy rate assumptions: 1950–55 to 2010–15

the final quinquennium as required additions fall off. Thus, measured by the number of new dwelling units started, the housing sector in Thailand is expected to continue to expand through most of the period covered. For a time at least, this expansion will be by relatively large amounts. The infrastructure servicing residential dwellings and the capacity needed to produce the furniture and household appliances complementary to residential dwellings would then also have to expand just to maintain current service and well-being levels.

The importance of withdrawals to this result is clear. In fact, during 2010–15, withdrawals will exceed population change as a source of hous-

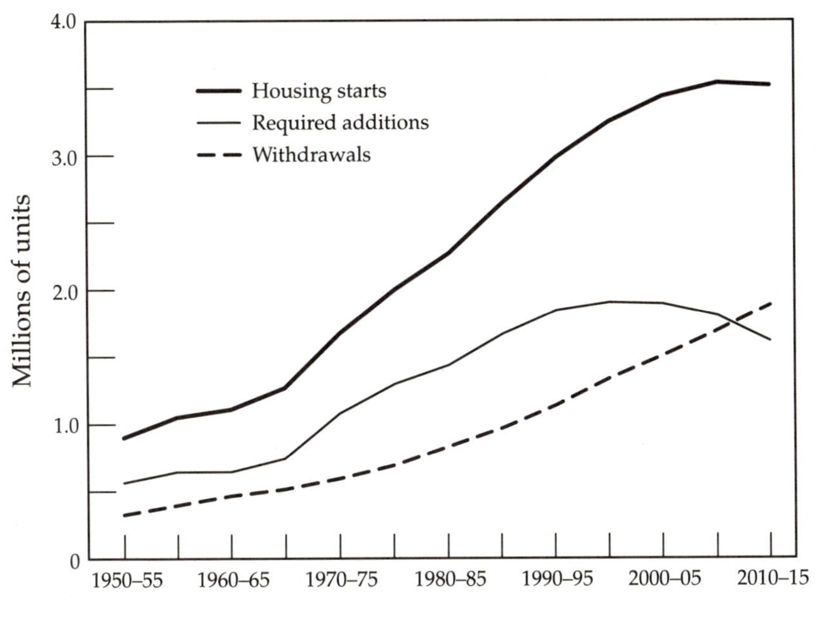

Source: Table 8.1.

Figure 8.4. Housing starts, required additions, and withdrawals: 1950–55 to 2010–15

ing starts in Thailand. Although withdrawals account for fewer housing starts in earlier quinquennia and their relative importance falls off in the 1980s and 1990s when demographic pressures have their maximum impact, they are a very important source of required new construction throughout the period studied. Withdrawals must be considered in any attempt to evaluate the economic impact of population changes on residential construction.

This point is demonstrated still more vividly in Figure 8.5 where the range of outcomes derived from the different withdrawal rate assumptions is shown. Whereas Thai housing starts based on zero withdrawals trace out a cyclical swing, starts based on the 1 percent assumption simply flatten out at a high level and those based on the basic 2 percent and on the 3 percent assumptions go on increasing by significant amounts, the latter reaching a level 73 percent above the 1 percent withdrawal level in 2010–15. Varying the withdrawal assumption can have a large and increasing effect on housing start forecasts. Better data on actual withdrawals would be very useful in putting together forward-looking business or government policies in the residential construction sector.

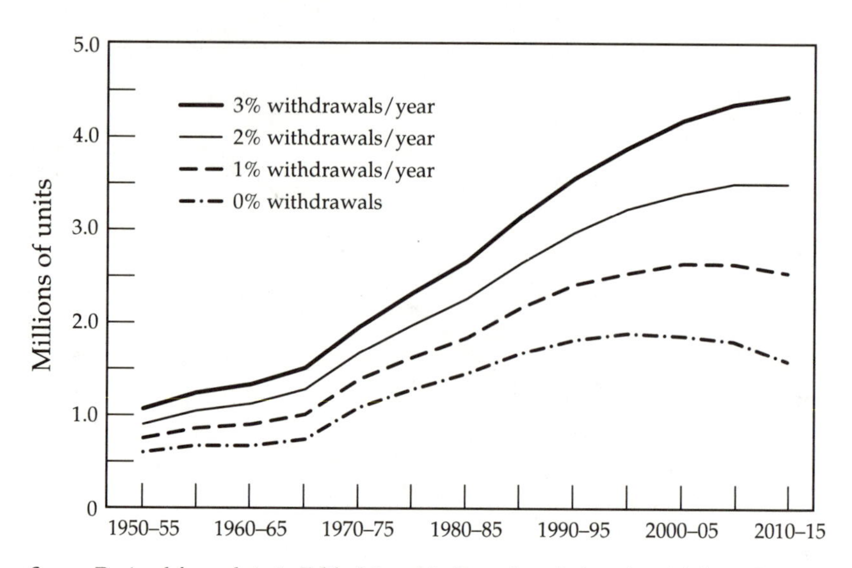

Source: Derived from data in Table 8.1 and indicated variations in withdrawal rates.

Figure 8.5. Effect on housing starts of varying withdrawal rates: 1950–55 to 2010–15

Tenure Composition

The distribution of demand between renter- and owner-occupied housing is important for several reasons. First is the fact that dwelling units in the rental and the owner-occupied markets are generally far from perfect substitutes. For example, although the differences have been blunted by the development of the condominium form of ownership, the average size of the dwelling and so the average price and the amount of land occupied per unit often differ significantly between renter and owner-occupied units. Differences also occur in infrastructure requirements and in the problems associated with population density. Finally, rental units are more likely to be built in anticipation of demand; therefore, the extent of over building as housing demand fluctuates depends on the relative share of rental demand.

National estimates of required additions by tenure class were derived by multiplying our basic forecasts of households by age of head by owner or renter occupancy rates by age of head (NSO 1970). Such estimates assume either that the variation between age groups is the same in different housing markets or that the distribution of the population between markets is relatively constant. Neither of these conditions is met in Thailand, with the proportion of renter occupancy being much higher in most age groups in urban areas (Table 8.3) and with the urban population likely to grow significantly relative to the rural population over the period covered. Thus, national estimates will almost certainly underestimate future renter demand in Thailand.

Another development pointing toward the same bias is the forecast of declining household size discussed in Chapter 2. Smaller households are more likely to rent (or become condominium owners) and by 2005 households are expected to average 3.7 members compared with the almost six members each in the 1970 base year. Working in the same direction will be the reduced number of children per family.

With these caveats, owner-occupied required additions (ORA^t) are forecast using the following relations:

$$ORA^t = \sum A_{oi}(HH_i^t - HH_i^{t-1}) = \sum A_{oi}(HHF_i^t)$$

where A_{oi} = heads in the *i*th age group in owner-occupied housing/total heads in the *i*th age group in the base period

HHF_i^t = net households formed in the *i*th age groups in year t[11]

The extension to renter-occupied required additions (RRA^t) is direct.

To place a "boundary" on the likely underestimation of rental demand introduced by the biases discussed, two categories of forecasts are given for the number of required additions by the two broad tenure classes—owner-occupants and nonowner-occupants (renter-occupants, rent-free occupants, and unknown tenure type)—for which data are available.[12] The first forecast category gives future rental and owner-occupied required additions based on the tenure rates that applied nationally in 1970 in Thailand and the second gives the same distribution on the assumption that the urban tenure rates in 1970 become the national rates. Since a continued trend toward urbanization of the population is likely, especially if the current successful growth story continues, the actual outcome will be somewhere between the two extremes shown.

In the absence of further movement into urban areas, the growth in Thai housing demand will be concentrated on owner occupancy and located largely in rural areas (see Figure 8.6). Rental required additions, as suggested by the variation in the age composition of demand discussed above will decline after 1990–95. This decline holds for both the national and the

11. Because there is no basis for dividing normal vacancy rates or doubling rates among tenure categories, there is little reason to present estimates of required additions by tenure type adjusted for these factors. The same conclusion holds for the allocation of withdrawal rates and estimates of housing starts by tenure type.

12. The procedure used assumes that rents paid by heads in each age group accurately reflect the rents correctly imputed to owned housing in each age group. This probably is most misleading at the later life-cycle stages.

Table 8.3. Tenure rates by age of head, total and urban: 1970 (%)

Age group	Total owner-occupancy rate	Urban owner-occupancy rate	Total nonowner-occupancy rate	Urban nonowner-occupancy rate
15–19	68.04	19.55	31.96	80.45
20–24	78.10	21.51	21.90	78.49
25–29	81.65	29.23	18.35	70.77
30–34	84.62	38.23	15.38	61.77
35–39	87.50	43.52	12.50	56.48
40–44	88.40	47.46	11.60	52.54
45–49	89.78	52.16	10.22	47.84
50–54	91.31	53.29	8.69	46.71
55–59	91.34	55.53	8.66	44.47
60–64	92.07	58.92	7.93	41.08
65–69	92.64	63.77	7.36	36.23
70–74	93.06	68.29	6.94	31.71
75–79	94.33	72.43	5.67	27.57
80–84	95.49	73.88	4.51	26.12
85+	94.55	76.10	5.45	23.90

Source: NSO (1970).

urban forecasts. However, if urban growth does in fact adjust national tenure rates to something near the current urban ratios by 2015, there would be a very large boom in rental (or condominium-type) housing rather than a decline. Since the necessary urban growth is a possibility with unknown probability, these results primarily demonstrate how the methodology described could be used to forecast the tenure composition of housing demand.

To the extent that condominium growth occurs, the key differences noted between rental and owner-occupied units will be blurred and it is more directly relevant to use HOMES to forecast the distribution of households among dwelling units by size and type (stand-alone, row, high-rise) rather than by tenure class. There are sample data that make such forecasts possible, but the differences between rural and urban areas are even more striking and so the relative future growth in the urban and rural population is even more important for housing characteristics than for tenure. Thus, only the tenure-type forecasts are presented.

If the needed population estimates become available, however, the methodology for estimating future demand by the characteristics of housing involves a straightforward adjustment of the relations shown above for

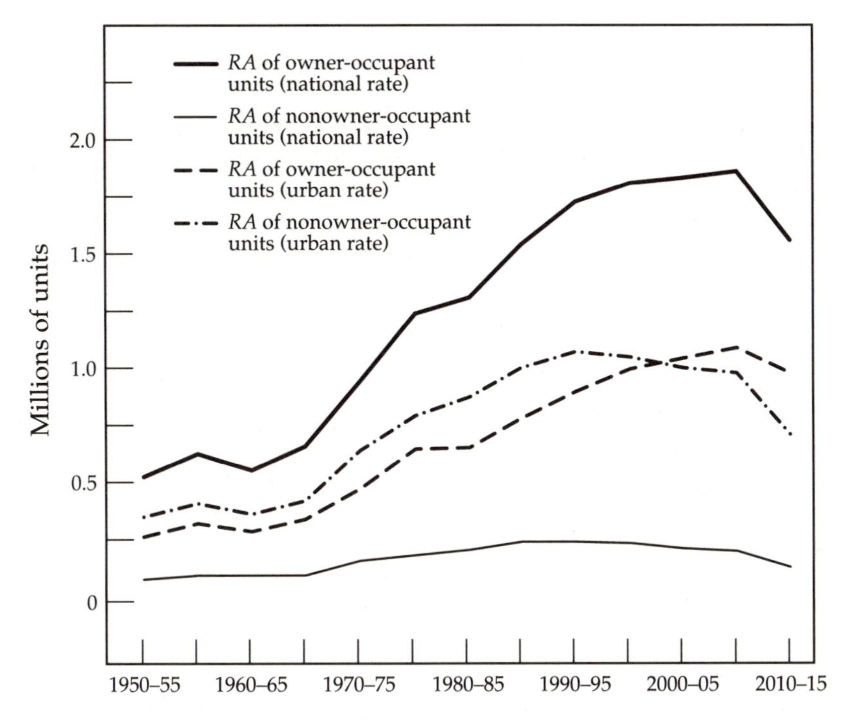

Source: Derived from Appendix Table 8.4.1 and Table 8.3.

Figure 8.6. Tenure composition of required additions (*RA*) based on 1970 national and urban rates: 1950–55 to 2010–15

owner-occupied housing. Rates of occupancy by age of head and by housing characteristics, say number of rooms, would take the place of owner-occupancy rates. Again, the theoretical basis for using such estimates is that dwelling units with different characteristics are not perfect substitutes and that as relative demands change the adjustment in their relative prices will leave new construction profitable in the submarket for one or more of the characteristics.

Summary

Briefly reviewing some of the key results presented in Chapter 2, HOMES forecasts show the number of Thai households increasing by 2.5 percent per year from 1985 to 2015, growing from 10.2 to 21.9 million. Over the same period, the Thai population growth rate is expected to be only 1.3 percent per year, suggesting a significant decline in the average size of households. Along with the accompanying aging of the population, these demographic developments have significant implications for all sectors of the economy as well as for saving and human resource development.

For housing, they imply, as this section has shown, that the stock of dwelling units required to maintain housing stock/household standards in Thailand will increase from 9.7 to 20.5 million between 1985 and 2015. The peak in the number of new units needed to meet this growth in demand will not come until 1995–2000 and 2000–2005. In each of these periods 1.91 million additional units will be required or 33 percent more than were required during 1980–85. However, by 2010–15 the additional units needed will have fallen back to 13 percent above the 1985–90 level. Taken alone, the demographic determinants of the new units required will trace out a long cycle over the next 30 years. If these were the only factors at work, the Thai house building industry would use about one-third more resources annually during 1990–2010 than it currently absorbs.

However, in addition to providing housing units for the net growth in households, new dwelling units are required over time to replace the dwellings withdrawn due to aging, natural disasters, city development, etc. If such withdrawals from the housing stock run at the conservative rate of 2 percent per annum, then required housing starts (the sum of withdrawals plus the above estimates of required additions) will continue to increase, though by smaller and smaller amounts. Required housing starts will reach 3.87 million during 2010–15, a 55 percent increase from the 1980–85 period. If withdrawals are included, the resources required for residential construction in Thailand are substantially increased and the direct cyclical effect of demographic changes disappears.

In sum, these outcomes imply that increasing amounts of resources will be absorbed by the Thai residential construction sector through the next two decades before this sector declines early in the twenty-first century. In addition, a greater land area will be absorbed for housing purposes (over twice as much as currently) by the larger required inventory.[13] The projections do not account for the increased infrastructure necessary to service the additional land and new housing required or the greater ongoing expenses required to maintain the larger infrastructure and the housing stock. From the perennial issue of the transportation system on down the line, growth in Thailand's housing requirements raises many difficult questions. These questions become both more pressing and more difficult if the effect of increasing real per capita incomes on the number, quality, and location of dwelling units demanded is considered.

13. It may be that construction of new units goes up rather than out, requiring different but no less expensive capital and current support expenditures.

RESIDENTIAL CONSTRUCTION EXPENDITURES

Benchmark Estimates

To turn the projections made of required housing starts into required residential construction expenditures, estimates of the average value of housing occupied by heads in different age groups in Thailand were made. These were based on the distribution of rents paid by age of head (see Appendix 8.5) for 1970, the only year for which the requisite data are available. Then, assuming that the average value of the units occupied by heads in different age groups remains at the 1970 level, the value of the required housing stock at different past and future dates was computed by multiplying this average value by the number of heads in each age group at the same dates. Net real residential construction is then equal to the change in the value of the required housing stock. Assuming the withdrawal rate is the same in each age group, this procedure gives the following definition of required gross residential construction (RRC^t):

$$RRC^t = \sum A_{pi}{}^t(HK_i{}^t) - \sum[A_{pi}{}^{t-i}(HK_i{}^{t-1})\ (1 - A_w)]$$

where $A_{pi}{}^t$ = the average value of housing occupied by heads in the *i*th age group in time *t*

$HK_i{}^t$ = housing stock required by the *i*th age group at time *t*

All the sources of difference between required and actual housing starts apply to required and actual residential construction. In addition, the necessity of assuming that the withdrawal, "doubling," and frictional vacancy rates are the same for the housing occupied by all age groups biases the results in unknown ways. Also contributing an unknown bias is the implicit assumption that the average value of houses withdrawn from each age group is the same as the average value of remaining houses.

It is important to recall that underlying all of our residential construction estimates is the assumption that the supply of new dwelling units is perfectly elastic at current prices. This is, of course, an oversimplification under any circumstances, but perhaps less so in Thailand where the supply of labor for residential construction from the agricultural sector (especially in the monsoon off-season) may be very wage elastic.

In addition, whether the pattern of rents paid by different age groups in 1970 provides a reasonable basis for investigating the value of housing that will be required by heads of different ages in future decades is subject to question. The 1970 data (see Appendix 8.5) unexpectedly show rents paid peaking for heads at the early life-cycle stages. They also show an equally unexpected downward shift in rent paid in the later life-cycle stages (from 55–59 on).

It is possible that this pattern reflects the movement of younger household heads into the modern sector and the impact of this movement on their incomes, tastes, and housing expenditures. It may also reflect the fact that renters at the last life-cycle stages are mostly at the lower end of the income distribution. For both reasons, our forecasts will tend to underestimate the value of the dwellings occupied, especially as the proportion of the population in the later life-cycle stages increases and as the effects of industrialization become more fully reflected throughout the housing life cycle.

Finally, the average price (quality here) of housing demanded is likely to be affected by the changes forecast in the nature of Thai households, especially the decline in average size and the decrease in the number of children per household. Both changes would be expected to raise the relative demand for rental or condominium-style housing and so to reduce, relatively, the average construction cost of new dwellings. However, some of the saving on land and dwelling unit size may be put back into higher quality of housing per square meter. And, in fact, consumer expenditure data suggest that at the same income smaller households spend a larger share of their income on housing. They also imply that older households, which will increase relatively in the future, do the same. Thus, the net effect on measured income elasticity of demand of these demographic developments should be small.

Benchmark estimates of the value of required additions in Thailand based on the assumptions and given the caveats discussed trace out a long cycle similar to the one already seen in required additions (Table 8.4). Changes in the age composition of demand accentuate this cyclical movement because the average value per occupied housing unit is lower in the older age groups and the heads in these age groups first fall and then increase in relative importance (see Figure 8.7). The economic effect of residential construction cannot, however, be fully evaluated without considering withdrawals. Adding replacement demand greatly increases the estimates of residential construction but continues the cyclical pattern described. Replacement demand also pushes the peak projected level of residential construction forward in time (to 2000–05).

Income-Adjusted Estimates of Residential Construction

Although the assumption that the demand for housing quality has zero income elasticity provides a bottom line measure of the effects of demographic changes only, it is not a realistic assumption. In fact, evidence on consumer expenditures presented in Chapter 5 suggests that the income elasticity of expenditures on housing in Thailand is slightly over 1.0. Therefore, to adjust the quality of housing demanded for the expected growth in per capita income we assume that the demand for housing quality has

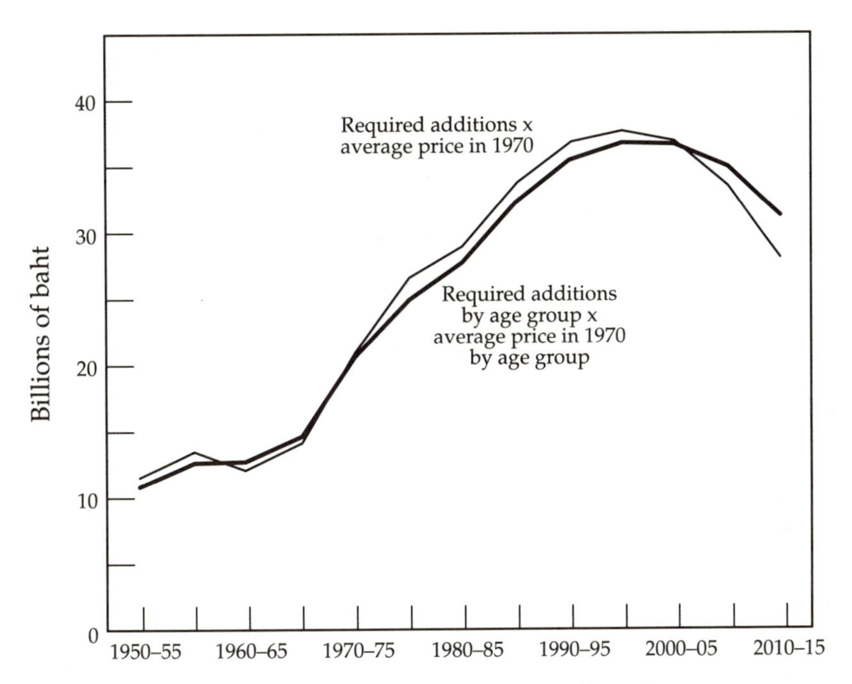

Source: Derived from data in Appendix 8.5 and Appendix Table 8.4.2.

Figure 8.7. Age composition and the value of required additions: 1950–55 to 2010–15

an income elasticity of 1.0 in all age groups and that real income increases by the forecast national growth rate in all age groups, i.e., that the income distribution by age group remains unchanged.

The procedure followed in adjusting the benchmark forecasts of residential construction expenditures for income growth assumes that the quality of newly constructed units (both required additions and withdrawals) increases with income. This ignores the income responsiveness of the modernization of existing units and so gives a relatively conservative forecast of housing expenditures. It also ignores the possible income elasticity of the quantity of housing demanded, either because of induced household formations or the ownership of more than one house for their own use by individual households.

In symbols, the income adjusted estimates of real residential construction are defined as follows:

$$RCy = [(dHH_{di}) \times (AV_i+AV_{i-1})/2] + [(WD_{di}) \times (AV_i+AV_{i-1})/2]$$

where: RCy = Residential construction based on upgrading newly constructed units with income increases

Table 8.4. Benchmark and income-adjusted estimates of real residential con- per capita income: 1950–55 to 2010–15 (millions of baht at 1970

Period	Value of required additions (1970 prices) [1]	Value of required additions (adjusted prices) [2]	Change in the value of housing stock (adjusted prices) [3]	Value of withdrawals (1970 prices) [4]
1950–55	11,491	6,747	9,823	6,622
1955–60	13,676	8,816	13,331	7,683
1960–65	12,067	9,427	22,028	9,116
1965–70	14,213	14,213	37,028	10,302
1970–75	20,968	24,966	47,566	11,994
1975–80	26,715	40,593	86,449	13,902
1980–85	28,900	52,203	98,951	16,714
1985–90	33,774	73,598	147,450	19,573
1990–95	36,784	99,258	218,152	22,710
1995–2000	37,627	121,699	264,127	26,105
2000–05	36,980	144,669	350,270	29,456
2005–10	33,580	160,586	456,696	31,810
2010–15	28,153	166,250	586,194	32,481

Source: Based on Appendices 8.4 and 8.5 and Table 8.1.

Note: Adjusted prices are based on an income elasticity of demand of 1.0 and growth in total real income of 4 percent per annum. The aggregate income growth data were converted to per capita income by dividing the forecast real income by the forecast households in each year.

u—unavailable.

dHH_{di} = Change in households between years i and $i-1$.

AV_i = Average value of the occupied dwelling units in year i or $[(HH_i \times AV_{70} \times Y_{ai})/HH_i]$

where Y_{ai} = Adjustment of housing value to account for income elasticity and per capita income growth between 1970 and year i (based on the assumed income elasticity and growth rate in each instance)

WD = Withdrawals (estimated as described)

Using this methodology yields the results given in Table 8.4 and shown in Figure 8.8. The growth in residential construction expenditures based on an income-induced quality response that is limited to newly constructed units is impressive. These conservative estimates of the effect of income struction adjusted for income elasticity of housing demand and growth in prices)

Value of withdrawals (adjusted prices) [5]	Residential construction constant quality [1] + [4]	Residential construction (adjusted prices: new units only [2] + [5]	Residential construction (adjusted prices: entire housing stock) [3] + [5]	Actual residential construction
3,888	18,114	10,635	13,712	u
4,953	21,360	13,769	18,284	u
7,122	21,183	16,549	29,150	15,224
10,302	24,515	24,515	47,330	20,965
14,281	32,962	39,248	61,848	23,854
21,123	40,617	61,716	107,572	31,332
30,097	45,703	82,300	129,048	52,082
42,651	53,347	116,250	190,101	u
61,281	59,494	160,539	279,433	u
84,433	63,731	206,131	348,560	u
115,234	66,435	259,903	465,504	u
152,122	65,391	312,708	608,818	u
191,806	60,634	358,056	778,000	u

growth yield expenditures and resource requirements almost six times higher in 2010–15 than the forecasts based on demographic changes only! If the required expenditures on infrastructure, furnishings, and other housing-related costs are also considered, the impact on the Thai economy could be great.

Moreover, these forecasts ignore the apparent backlog from the last two decades (Figure 8.9). The backcasts give residential construction estimates that are about the same as actual construction in 1960–65 and then pull away from the actual rate. If the assumptions underlying these estimates are correct, then a considerable quality backlog has built up over the last two decades, with supply side constraints, including financial constraints, limiting the adjustment (through direct interventions or price rationing). The key questions to answer are: What exactly did keep supply from meeting the implied demand and when will the market begin to remove the backlog? And if this happens will speculation take over the resulting residential construction boom? Partial answers are already available as a housing boom involving considerable speculation occurred in the second half of the 1980s.

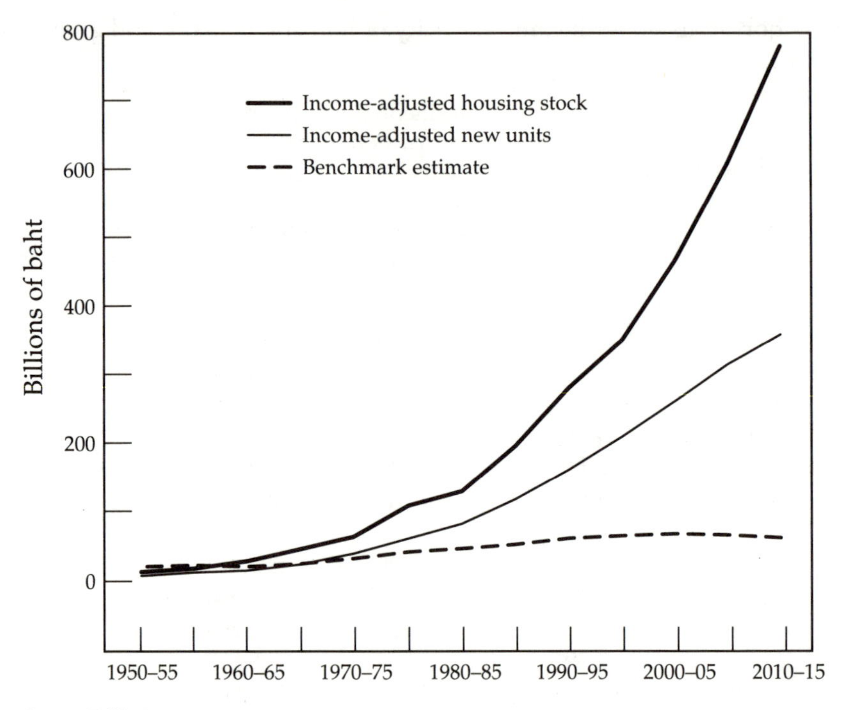

Source: Table 8.4.

Figure 8.8. Income-adjusted and benchmark residential construction forecasts: 1950–55 to 2010–15

When estimated withdrawals are included in the forecast, net residential construction expenditures by broad age groups are roughly distributed in proportion to the share of the housing stock occupied by heads of different ages (Figure 8.10). A major and continuing boom in residential construction in Thailand of dwellings designed for household heads in their middle ages (35–60) seems likely even given the many uncertainties surrounding our estimates. Since expenditures by this age group are less postponable, the result is even more significant. However, expenditures by younger heads (15–34), which peaked in 1980–85 and remained relatively high in 1985–90, will drop quickly thereafter and by 2010–15 become negative. To the extent that housing is geared to the needs of different age groups, difficult times may be ahead for the builders and owners of properties designed for younger households in Thailand. Finally, the market for dwellings for older households will increase relatively slowly until 2005–10 when it will begin a steady increase.

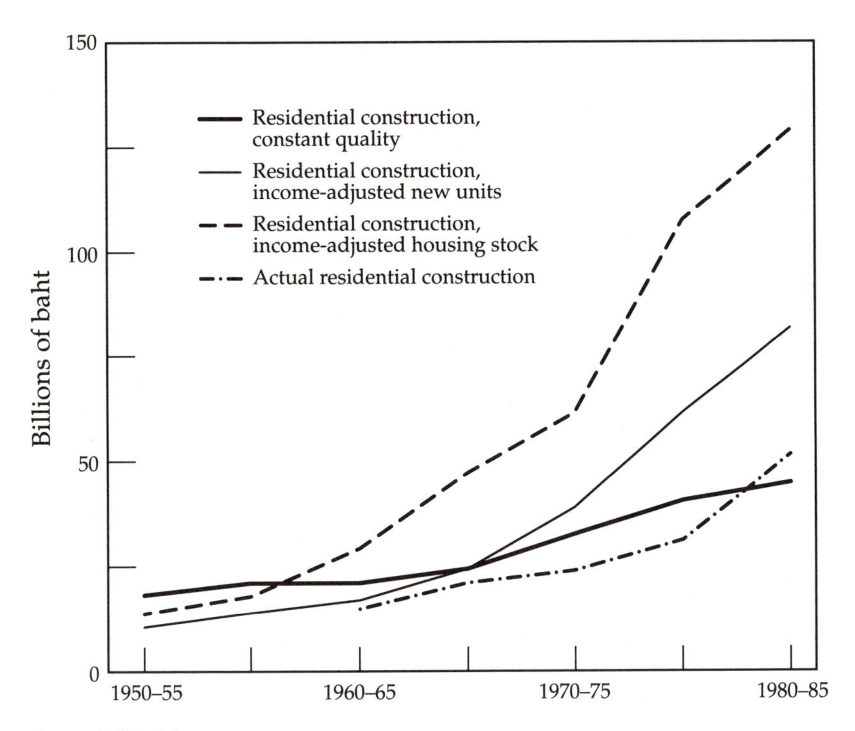

Source: Table 8.4.

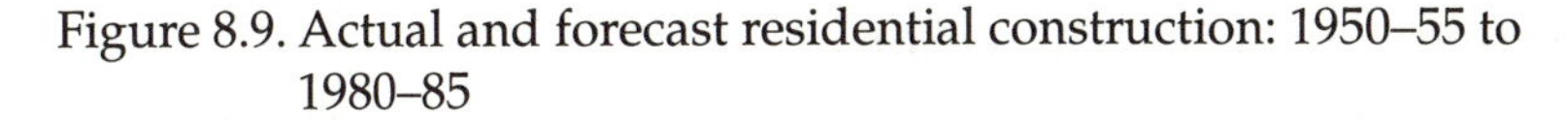

Figure 8.9. Actual and forecast residential construction: 1950–55 to 1980–85

Given the importance of the income growth and elasticity assumptions, it is relevant to test the sensitivity of our results to variations in the assumed income elasticity and to the forecast growth rates. Estimates based on an assumed income elasticity of 0.5 and the actual and forecast growth rate, on an assumed income elasticity of 1.0 and a growth rate of 2 percent per annum in per capita income, and on the combination of the 0.5 and 2 percent per annum growth assumptions are compared in Figure 8.11 with the forecasts already presented.

Shifting the income elasticity and growth rate assumptions as indicated does change the results. All the changes made in the underlying assumptions restore the long cycle in residential construction observed on the basis of zero elasticity of demand and greatly reduce the forecast future levels of construction. But all the forecasts, when compared with the actual level of residential construction, suggest a large and growing quality backlog in Thailand.

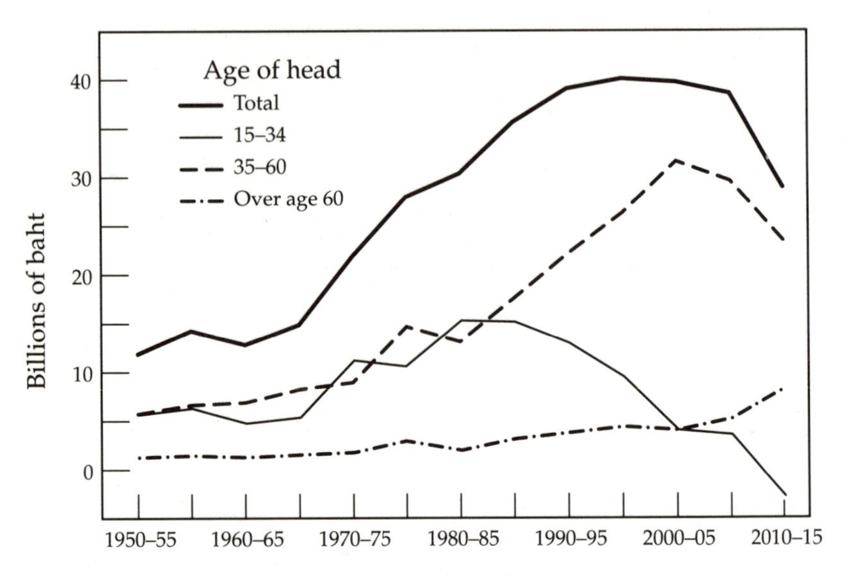

Source: Based on Appendix Table 8.4.2.

Figure 8.10. Net residential construction expenditures (income-adjusted new units) by age of head: 1950–55 to 2010–15

Relation to Gross Domestic Product, Gross Domestic Investment, and the Labor Force

To fully evaluate the impact on the Thai economy of the forecast growth in residential construction, the relation between real residential construction and the forecast growth in real gross domestic product (GDP), in real gross domestic investment (GDI), and in the labor supply in Thailand needs to be investigated.

Basing this analysis on income adjustment of adjusted new units only, the share of residential construction in GDP will slowly rise to a peak in 1995–2000 and fall off thereafter (Figure 8.12). Still, the share will remain above the 1980–85 level until 2005–10. Thus, there will be a substantial increase over current levels in the share of residential construction in national output in Thailand for some time to come. In other words, real resources will be attracted to the residential building sector from other sectors if our projections prove correct. Given the very conservative nature of the forecasting procedures followed, the residential building boom of 1985–90 in Thailand is not surprising.

The forecast share in GDI of residential construction with income adjustment for new units only tells a similar story, but with the peak share arriving sooner. The share of residential construction in GDI in Thailand grew

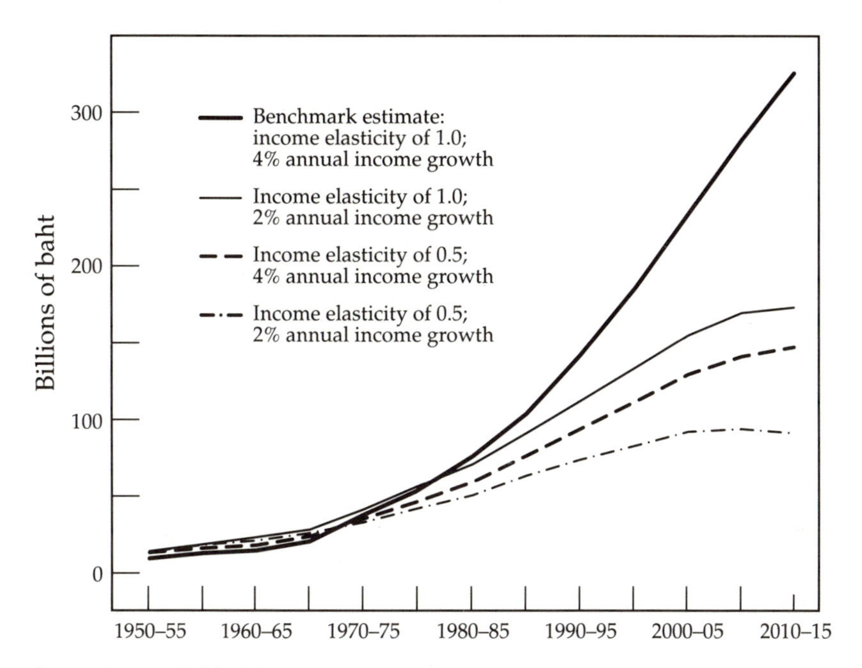

Source: Same as Table 8.4.

Figure 8.11. Required residential construction: Sensitivity analysis comparing estimates based on differing assumptions about income growth and income elasticity, 1950–55 to 2010–15

most rapidly in 1980–85 with the peak share coming in 1990–95 (Figure 8.13). Although residential construction's slice of GDI declines after 1995, it remains slightly above the 1980–85 level through 2000–05. For most of the next three decades then, residential construction will use up a larger share of Thailand's domestic saving and foreign borrowing than it has in the recent past, with obvious growth implications.

Another way of looking at the relative impact of residential construction on the economy is to compare the real growth in this sector with growth in the labor force. Table 8.5 gives indices of labor requirements for the projected levels of residential construction using a 1970–75 productivity base.[14] Indices of the labor supply (based on a constant participation rate) are also given in Table 8.5. The growth in requirements shows that 9.12 times

14. The authors divided real residential construction (number of residential units built between 1970 and 1975) by the 1970 construction labor force to obtain the average product of construction workers. Estimates were made from partial data obtained from the National Statistical Office and the National Economic and Social Development Board.

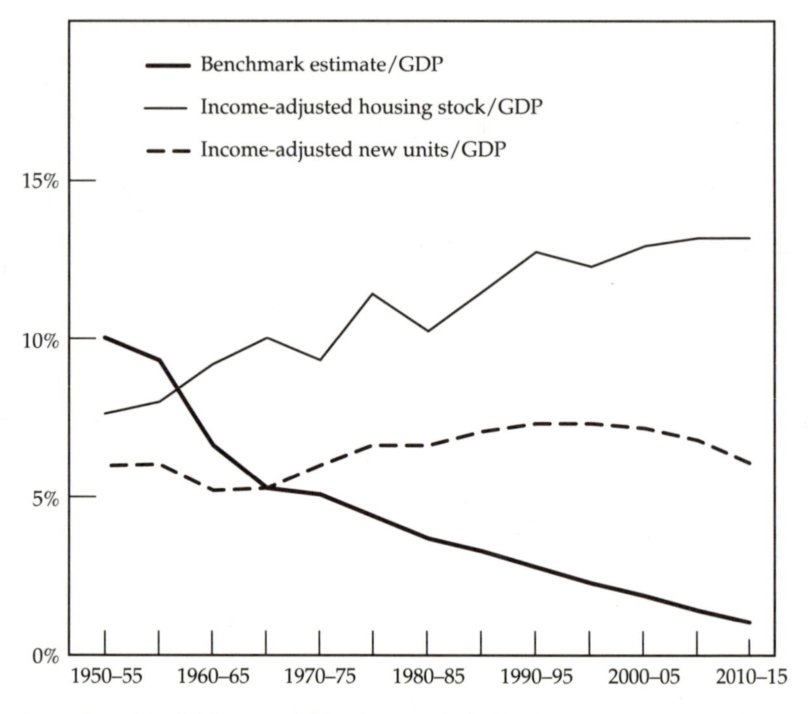

Source: Based on Table 8.4 and GDP forecast described in text.

Figure 8.12. Share of residential construction in GDP: 1950–55 to 2010–15

as much labor will be required in 2010–15 as was required in 1970–75 to build the units needed to meet the demand arising if the quality of new units is upgraded as assumed in response to income growth. This growth is much larger than the growth in the labor supply of 2.66 times (Table 8.5) and larger than the growth in labor demand given in Chapter 3.

Only if future residential construction is limited to the level based on demographic factors alone does it appear there would be no upward pressure on real wage rates in this sector. However, the supply of labor to residential construction is likely to be relatively wage elastic both in the short and long run. The skills required for the construction trade are relatively easy to acquire. And there is "surplus" labor in the agricultural sector now and the prospect is that excess demand for labor in the twenty-first century will lead to more capital-intensive production and greater labor productivity in industry. The latter would not necessarily reduce residential construction expenditures below the levels forecast, but it could reduce the real resources required. These developments may not be sufficient to prevent the relative prices of new dwelling units from increasing if labor

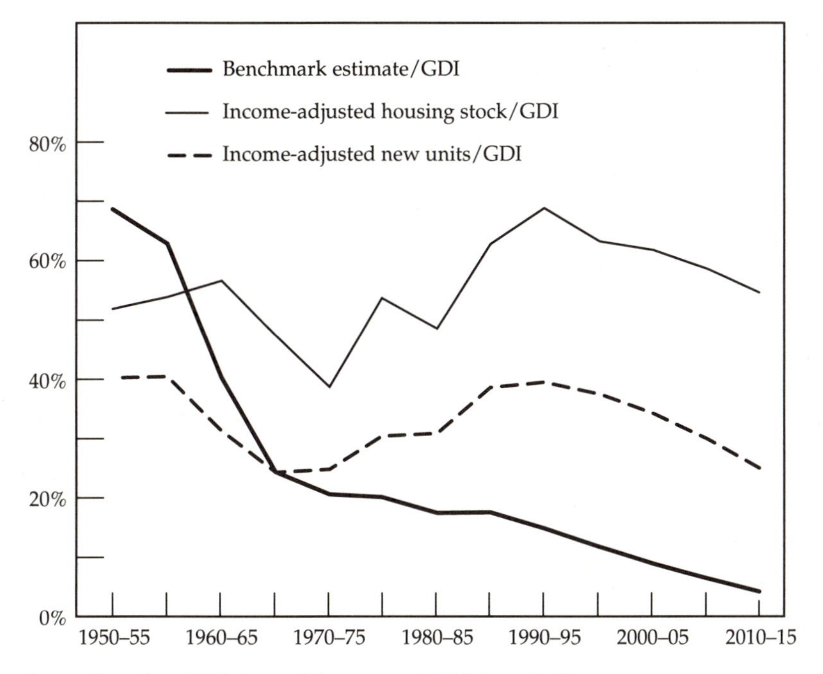

Source: Based on Table 8.4 and forecasts of GDI described in text.

Figure 8.13. Share of residential construction in GDI : 1950–55 to 2010–15

requirements increase as just noted and if there are no unprecedented increases in productivity in the construction sector.

Summary

Clearly, introducing an income elasticity of 1.0 has a very powerful effect, implying a large and continuing increase in the resources absorbed by the residential construction sector through 2010–15, rather than the increase and then significant decline suggested by the benchmark forecasts. And since there are so many economic activities complementary to residential construction, including furnishing the new dwelling units and the provision of utilities and transportation links for the units, the increases in real residential construction expenditures forecast would be much amplified in their impact on the Thai economy.

Further, if the estimated elasticity is close to correct, then the fact that income-adjusted estimates of real residential construction from 1960 to the present exceed actual real residential construction expenditures over the same period is significant. It suggests that in addition to the continuing

Table 8.5. Indices of labor force requirements in the residential construction sector: Various estimates

Period	Based on constant quality of new units	Based on upgraded quality of new units only	Based on upgraded quality of housing stock	Index of labor supply growth[a]
1950–55	54.95	27.10	22.17	55.48
1955–60	64.80	35.08	29.56	64.49
1960–65	64.26	42.17	47.13	75.17
1965–70	74.37	62.46	76.53	86.46
1970–75	100.00	100.00	100.00	100.00
1975–80	123.23	157.25	173.93	117.65
1980–85	138.66	209.69	208.66	138.97
1985–90	161.85	296.19	307.37	163.10
1990–95	180.49	409.04	451.81	181.33
1995–2000	193.35	525.21	563.58	209.02
2000–05	201.55	662.21	752.66	235.05
2005–10	198.38	796.75	984.38	249.94
2010–15	183.95	912.30	1,257.93	266.41

Note: The base quinquennia is 1970–75; all estimates assume the average product is fixed at the 1970–75 level.

a. Assumes participation rate is fixed at the 1970 level.

requirements of population and income growth there may be a large and growing backlog of demand in Thailand.[15]

If the backlog is ignored, forecasts of real residential construction based on quality changes only in newly constructed units show the share of residential construction in real GDP increasing to a peak in 1990–95 and then falling off. The share of real residential construction in GDP, however, remains above current levels until 2005–10.

Forecasts adjusted for income growth show that the share of real residential construction in real gross domestic capital formation increases through the mid-1990s. Thereafter the share of real residential construction falls off but remains above the 1980–85 level until early next century. Given the many other demands of growth on Thailand's savings and foreign resources, the

15. Whether this backlog reflects supply constraints or implies the income elasticity assumed is too high is moot. Adjusting either the income elasticity or growth rate assumptions downward by half does considerably decrease the forecast levels of residential construction, but it leaves the forecasts far above the zero elasticity level and the backcasts far above actual construction.

forecast of an increasing share of residential construction in gross capital formation has important implications for economic growth and suggests that some very difficult choices lie ahead—especially when the conservative nature of the forecast is considered.

One implication of these considerations is that the assumption of perfectly elastic supply on which our housing market forecasts are based is very likely to be breached. So is the implicit assumption that the relative price of housing will not change. Just how the housing market will react to these developments is uncertain. If the relatively elastic supply discussed does materialize, because the price elasticity of demand for housing units is generally thought to be low, our forecasts of residential construction expenditures and of real resource requirements may not be too far off target.

In sum, introducing the effect of income growth on the demand for housing quality in Thailand results in a residential construction boom in absolute terms that, at least for a time, is likely to be reflected in the relative share of the residential construction sector in the economy. Our estimates ignore the positive impact on construction of many factors, including the existing quality backlog and income-induced changes in headship rates and in doubling. The effects of internal migration and of related urbanization-induced changes in tastes are also ignored. Thus, the likelihood of a major residential building boom seems even greater than suggested by our estimates. In fact, a boom seems to be already underway. In any event, beyond the new construction involved, the growth forecast implies either major complementary expenditures for urban infrastructure or a rapid decline in the average quality of urban services. It also implies that some difficult land use and zoning decisions are ahead along with sharp shifts in land values.

International Effects

The final effects of a residential building boom involve the exchange rate and the balance of payments. Increased residential construction will increase demand for imports directly as some inputs are import-competing in both the construction industry and the industries complementary to residential building. Increased residential construction will also have an indirect effect through its impact on GDP and so on imports. Except for the minor possibility of better housing increasing productivity nationally, increased residential construction is not likely to increase exports and so the net effect of a residential building boom in Thailand should be to worsen the current account and depreciate the baht, other things being equal.

CONCLUDING COMMENTS

On balance, if the effects of income growth on the quality of housing are included, the forecasts presented point to a residential construction boom in Thailand, at least into the first decade of the twenty-first century. Further support for this conclusion derives from the fact that the estimates presented most likely err on the conservative side since, for example (1) no makeup of any actual quality backlog is accounted for, (2) a zero income elasticity of "undoubling" and of household formation is assumed, (3) internal migration does not leave any regional markets with an excess of housing while creating an excess demand for housing elsewhere, and (4) shifts in demand between types of housing (e.g., as the age composition changes) are not considered as a source of net excess demand.[16]

The present analysis was able to set out the possibilities for the housing market and the assumptions upon which these possibilities are based. It will aid in the advance planning that is so important for rational decision making in both the private and public sectors. Additional research to examine the premises on which the forecasts are based is needed to narrow the range of possible outcomes. Useful work can also be done relating household characteristics to the kind and quality of housing occupied as the requisite sample survey data become available.

16. In both circumstances new units are required even if there is no population change.

Appendix 8.1
ESTIMATION OF THE OCCUPIED HOUSING–HOUSEHOLDS RATIO (A_f) IN THAILAND

Estimates of the number of occupied housing units are available for 1970 (two estimates), 1975, and 1980 from the Registration Record (unpublished) of the Ministry of the Interior. Estimates of the number of occupied units are also available for 1970 based on sample surveys of heads by tenure type and heads by character of living quarters conducted for the 1970 Population and Housing Census. These various estimates are not the same, ranging from 5.608 to 5.923 million occupied housing units. Both these extreme values come from Ministry of the Interior records. The census estimates fall in between at 5.857 and 5.856 million.

The total number of households reported by the 1980 census was 6.211 million. Combined with the foregoing estimates of occupied housing, this number of households yields the following range of A_f ratios: .903, .943, .945, .954. Since there is little basis for choosing between the four available estimates of the occupied housing stock, we decided to take the average of four estimates—.936 as the 1970 value of A_f.

As shown in Appendix Table 8.1.1 this puts the A_f for Thailand just slightly above the level for Malaysia, where there is a similarly large proportion of the population in rural areas, and considerably above the A_f found in the almost entirely urban countries of Singapore and Hong Kong. Thus the estimate used seems quite reasonable.

However, because the evidence elsewhere as well as one Thai[1] estimate clearly shows that ratios of occupied housing units to the household population differ between urban and rural areas, some adjustment for the growth in the relative size of the urban population over time was necessary. This was accomplished by assuming that the 1970 estimate of A_f given is correct for the country as a whole and that Thailand's urban ratio of occupied housing units to the household population is the same as in urban Malaysia (.8333). The implicit rural ratio (A_{fr}) for Thailand was then found by solving the following equation using the 1970 shares of the urban (.1418) and rural (.8582) populations.

$$A_{fr} = [.936 - .8333\ (.1418)]/(.8582) = .953$$

The urban and rural ratios are assumed to remain unchanged over time and so the national A_f changes with the percentage of the urban and rural populations in the total population. The latter was estimated by one of the authors from a trend equation using the percentage share of the urban population reported in the 1960, 1970, and 1980 censuses as the base points. Finally, a zero level of "doubling" or an A_f of 1.00 was used as an upper limit and one of .90 was used as a lower limit for purposes of sensitivity analysis.

1. See NSO, *Report of the Labor Force Survey* (1977: table A, p. 26).

Appendix Table 8.1.1. A_f's in selected countries

Country	A_f
Hong Kong	0.7692
Malaysia	0.9259
Peninsula Malaysia (urban areas)	0.8333
Singapore	0.8333

Sources: Data on Hong Kong, Peninsula Malaysia (urban areas), and Singapore are from Yeh (1975). Data on Malaysia are from Yeh and Laquian (1979).

Appendix 8.2
ESTIMATED "NORMAL" VACANCY RATIOS (A_{v1}) FOR THAILAND

Since there are no data on vacancies available for Thailand,[1] a range of ratios from other ASEAN countries is used instead. Data on the vacancy ratio are available for Singapore and the Philippines (Appendix Table 8.2.1).[2]

Considering that Singapore is an urban area and that vacancy ratios in urban areas are generally higher than in rural areas, the Singapore A_v's can be assumed to be higher than those normally found in Thailand. The structure of the economy of Thailand is similar to that of the Philippines in many respects, and the reported A_v's for that country, ranging from 1.5 percent to 3.1 percent, seem more likely benchmarks for the Thai estimates. Consequently, the standard, noncyclical vacancy rate used in the estimates presented is 2 percent and the maximum value used, for comparative purposes, is 4 percent.

Appendix Table 8.2.1. Vacancy ratios: Singapore and the Philippines

Country	Year	Vacancy ratio (%)
Singapore	1970	5.92
	1980	9.86
Philippines	1960	3.07
	1970	1.48
	1980	3.05

Sources: Singapore: 1970 data are from Arumainathan (1973:211); 1980 data are from Kim (1981:9). Philippines: 1960 data are from Bureau of Census and Statistics, Philippines (1963:23); 1970 data are from the National Census and Statistics Office, Philippines (1974:635); 1980 data are from private communication.

1. Data on vacancies were collected in the 1980 Population and Housing Census, but the National Statistical Office has not released these data.

2. Data are also available for Malaysia but they are so far out of line with experience elsewhere that they must be seriously questioned. They suggest a vacancy ratio of 15 percent in 1947 and of 11 percent in 1970 in a predominantly rural country with a growing rural and urban population!

Appendix 8.3
ESTIMATED WITHDRAWAL RATES (A_w) IN THAILAND

Since there is no direct information on total withdrawals from the housing stock in Thailand, it is not possible to calculate the withdrawal rate directly. Instead, the rate must be inferred from the implications of different withdrawal rates or based on more complete data collected elsewhere or on the partial estimates available for Thailand. These approaches were all considered, with the first given precedence and the others used as a check on the relations assumed.

Using the forecasts of the housing stock presented in Table 8.1 as a starting point, the implications of a 3 percent, a 2 percent, and a 1 percent per annum withdrawal rate were analyzed.

If future withdrawals occur at a 3 percent per annum or 15 percent per quinquennium rate (ignoring as is done throughout, intra-quinquennium compounding) then the cumulated withdrawals from the housing stock, beginning in 2015 and summing backward, will exceed the 2015 housing stock sometime late in the 1985–90 quinquennium. The implication of this assumption is that all of the housing stock of 2015 will be 25 years old or newer.[1] Since it seems unlikely that actual withdrawals will ever reach and certainly are not likely to exceed 3 percent per annum, this rate is taken as an upper bound.

Making the same calculation for a 2 percent rate, we find that the 2015 stock will be 35 years old or less and that 93 percent will have been built after 1985. Finally, a 1 percent withdrawal rate implies that the 2015 housing stock includes only houses 50 years old or less and that 81 percent of the housing stock in 2015 will have been built after 1985.

These results can be given perspective by contrasting them with what would happen if the required withdrawal rate were zero. In this case 60 percent of the 2015 housing stock would have been built after 1985 (or, alternatively, 40 percent of the 2015 stock would be over 30 years old). From this starting point, it seems reasonable to take 1 percent per annum withdrawals as a lower bound and 2 percent per annum (10 percent per quinquennium) as the standard case.

All of these assumed withdrawal rates make no adjustment for the effects of industrialization and rising incomes. The same is assumed to apply throughout the period covered. Although a case could be made for moving the rate from the lower to the upper bound through time, this seemed simply to compound the guesswork already involved. For similar reasons, the more complicated approaches to inferring withdrawal rates originally worked through (e.g., estimating the age composition of the stock

1. It would be more correct to say "almost all" of the housing stock. Some of the withdrawals will be the result of random disasters (or economic events) affecting new as well as old units so the numbers given do not rule out the possibility that some other units will remain.

from experience and forecast housing stock data; using data on the materials composition of the stock to forecast dwelling unit aging) were discarded.

Looking at experience elsewhere, the only regional data available are for Singapore. These would, of course, be greatly influenced by Singapore's pervasive public housing program. In any event, the Singapore rate was 2.8 percent per annum in the 1970s (National Statistical Office, Singapore, 1977). The United Nations estimates the standard or "typical" withdrawal rate to be 2 percent (United Nations 1973b). All in all these additional guesstimates give no reason to change the withdrawal rate range assumed for this study.

Appendix 8.4
DETAILED AGE-OF-HEAD PROJECTIONS

Appendix Table 8.4.1. Change in households by age of head in Thailand: 1950–55 to 2010–2015

Age of head	1950–55	1955–60	1960–65	1965–70	1970–75	1975–80	1980–85	1985–90	1990–95	1995–2000	2000–05	2005–10	2010–15
15–19	9,853	11,015	21,189	25,834	23,418	27,952	30,213	13,746	6,918	5,507	–3,126	–9,866	–6,802
20–24	62,729	72,807	71,202	81,395	122,040	128,173	137,890	154,760	66,042	28,740	27,176	-16,529	-53,605
25–29	95,539	112,260	65,422	70,566	222,013	166,675	253,673	230,599	258,457	103,686	46,517	47,354	-29,246
30–34	82,872	94,648	59,758	64,198	157,003	169,054	288,627	297,402	270,500	300,076	118,353	145,500	-33,373
35–39	61,932	68,665	92,901	106,534	68,227	175,372	184,547	318,786	326,978	295,495	329,476	126,811	60,569
40–44	56,986	63,696	91,305	106,484	103,993	184,080	80,200	201,921	345,896	353,397	318,580	355,903	134,941
45–49	54,538	62,751	75,901	89,161	97,953	155,618	141,340	82,434	209,077	358,985	363,470	327,915	367,539
50–54	55,109	68,069	45,719	54,829	116,143	119,002	131,463	139,953	80,255	210,602	360,442	362,751	325,506
55–59	45,500	62,326	34,712	48,523	59,568	89,368	130,728	123,373	133,212	74,170	199,887	344,361	345,116
60–64	32,406	53,739	19,065	39,012	54,788	63,508	67,062	116,200	108,397	118,127	65,862	181,431	309,663
65–69	17,849	21,834	26,428	32,984	35,052	59,288	36,769	55,799	96,741	89,360	98,372	54,505	152,905
70–74	11,347	13,785	19,335	24,601	16,119	52,832	17,921	27,349	43,604	73,284	68,590	76,700	44,228
75–79	6,527	7,885	7,378	8,628	12,474	22,291	14,799	14,560	17,442	24,688	39,494	45,228	52,025
80–84	3,453	4,390	2,230	2,458	5,176	12,651	6,842	6,634	7,928	11,206	18,177	20,788	23,998
85+	1,846	2,299	1,564	1,580	3,363	3,360	3,496	3,439	4,116	5,772	9,211	10,565	12,024

Source: Based on NSO (1970, 1980), HOMES forecasts (Chapter 2), and Appendices 8.1, 8.2, and 8.3.

Appendix Table 8.4.2. Value of required additions by age of head in Thailand: 1950–55 to 2010–15 (1970 prices; millions of baht)

Age of head	1950–55	1955–60	1960–65	1965–70	1970–75	1975–80	1980–85	1985–90	1990–95	1995–2000	2000–05	2005–10	2010–15
15–19	180	201	384	467	421	502	541	240	115	89	−68	−189	−134
20–24	1,334	1,548	1,498	1,710	2,563	2,680	2,876	3,215	1,333	541	500	−423	−1,194
25–29	2,040	2,397	1,375	1,481	4,692	3,497	5,327	4,811	5,379	2,085	865	863	−746
30–34	1,672	1,910	1,186	1,272	3,129	3,356	5,738	5,884	5,316	5,875	2,231	2,739	−810
35–39	1,314	1,457	1,951	2,234	1,415	3,666	3,845	6,644	6,782	6,087	6,755	2,486	1,091
40–44	1,143	1,278	1,815	2,113	2,054	3,641	1,559	3,966	6,798	6,911	6,181	6,866	2,486
45–49	1,053	1,211	1,450	1,702	1,863	2,960	2,675	1,535	3,939	6,769	6,813	6,090	6,796
50–54	1,095	1,353	896	1,074	2,283	2,329	2,566	2,719	1,531	4,075	6,976	6,972	6,202
55–59	700	958	526	737	902	1,353	1,979	1,857	1,996	1,090	2,982	5,136	5,114
60–64	433	718	250	515	723	835	879	1,524	1,413	1,533	837	2,342	4,000
65–69	254	311	373	465	492	832	511	776	1,347	1,237	1,355	733	2,095
70–74	139	169	235	298	194	639	213	326	520	875	813	904	510
75–79	78	94	87	102	147	264	174	170	203	287	459	523	599
80–84	35	44	22	24	51	126	68	65	78	110	178	202	233
85+	21	26	18	18	38	38	39	38	46	64	103	117	133

Source: See Table 8.4.

Appendix 8.5
ESTIMATES OF THE PRICE OF HOUSING

The distribution of rents by age of head in 1970 was used to compute the average value of units occupied by heads in each age group. To do this the average monthly rent for each age group was computed and multiplied by 12 to find the average annual rent paid by heads in each age group. These rents are shown in Appendix Table 8.5.1. To adjust for the inclusion of land costs in the rents paid, the average annual rent paid was then divided by 15 percent to estimate the price of a dwelling unit that would generate the estimated average annual rent paid by each age group. This divisor derives from the assumption that rents paid average 10 percent of the value of the property rented, a common rule of thumb, and the assumption that, on average, land accounts for one-third of the value of the property rented. The resulting estimates of the average value of dwelling unit occupied in each age group are also given in Appendix Table 8.5.1.

The estimates shown implicitly assume that the average value of the rental units occupied by each age group of household heads is the same as the average value of the owner-occupied units in each age group. With rental units accounting for such a small portion of the total housing stock and with renters as a group being considerably different in location (more in urban areas) and age (younger) than the general population, this assumption obviously can be questioned. The procedure followed most likely underestimates the average value of housing occupied by older heads, which will lead to underestimating residential construction as the share of older heads in the housing population increases.

On the other hand, the procedure used probably tends to overestimate the average value of housing in all age classes since it is more heavily weighted by urban dwellings than is the actual housing stock, and urban housing, based on very partial data, appears to be more costly on average than rural.

Because of the uncertainty surrounding the procedure used to estimate house prices, we used other approaches, different but equally uncertain, to cross check our estimates. These included using (1) aggregative data on residential construction and the number of additional households (there are no data on housing starts) and (2) information on the rural and urban prices of dwellings classified by different building materials along with data on the number of households in housing classified by building materials in a slightly different manner.

The range of resulting estimates of the average value of a dwelling unit in 1970 was from 17,100 baht to 21,200 baht. The average value based on the procedure used in the text falls in the middle of these two estimates at 19,230 baht.

Thus, the approach is probably reasonable in terms of the average value implied and has the distinct advantage over any of the other possible approaches of giving a breakdown of the average value by age of head. This,

Appendix Table 8.5.1. Average rents and housing prices by age of head

Age group	Average monthly rent (1)	Average price of housing (2) = [(1) × 12] ÷ 0.15
15–19	237	18,986
20–24	276	22,119
25–29	278	22,208
30–34	262	20,990
35–39	276	22,071
40–44	261	20,871
45–49	251	20,077
50–54	258	20,674
55–59	200	15,994
60–64	174	13,895
65–69	185	14,795
70–74	159	12,714
75–79	156	12,443
80–84	131	10,465
85+	149	11,918
Weighted average A	252	20,150
Weighted average B		19,230

Note: Weighted averages A and B were weighted by the number in each age group.

A—252 is the weighted average of the rent paid household sample; 20,150 is the average price of housing based on a monthly rent of 252 baht.

B—19,230 is the weighted average value of the average price of housing by age of head.

of course, makes possible tracing the impact of the significant coming shifts in the age composition of households on residential construction.

In looking at the variation among age groups in the average rent paid (Appendix Table 8.5.1.), the fact that the younger age groups tend to spend more on average on housing than do older age groups stands out. This could reflect the variation in rental occupancy over the life cycle, with mostly households at the bottom end of the income ladder continuing to rent as they grow older, or it could reflect the concentration of the impact of industrialization and economic growth at the earlier life-cycle stages. If the latter is the main reason, then the procedure used will clearly underestimate the average expenditures on housing of people now at the early life-cycle stages as they age.

For all the foregoing reasons and because it is almost certain that the average value of additions to the housing stock will be greater than the average value of the entire housing stock, the forecasts of residential construction presented in the text are likely to be considerably on the low side.

APPENDIX A
Household Characteristics and Household Projections Using HOMES

by Andrew Mason

The purpose of this appendix is to provide a more detailed look at the data on the demographic characteristics of Thai households compiled from the 1970 and 1980 censuses of population (NSO 1970, 1980). We have several objectives in mind in providing this information. First, it will provide a clearer, more detailed understanding of the living arrangements in Thailand that are the basis of the HOMES projections. Second, it provides information that can be used to assess the stability assumption implicit in HOMES. The current version of HOMES assumes that the basic rules governing living arrangements are not changing. As examples, headship rates and the probabilities that children at each age continue to live in their parents' home are assumed to remain constant between 1980 and the end of the projection period (2015). Of course, there will be some change in these rules and they may turn out to be quite significant. But by examining the differences between 1970 and 1980, we obtain some notion of how rapidly Thailand is experiencing change. Third, the material presented here should provide the reader with a more detailed understanding of the Thai household and the ways in which changes in its demographic profile will affect social and economic trends.

This appendix is not intended to serve as a technical appendix and it does not provide comprehensive documentation for the HOMES model. The mainframe version of the model is documented in Mason (1987). Persons or institutions interested in learning more about the microcomputer version of the model can write directly to HOMES Project, Program on Population, East-West Center, Honolulu, HI 96848.

PROJECTING THE NUMBER OF HOUSEHOLDS

HOMES projects the numbers and types of households using an elaboration of the headship-rate method. The basic approach relies on headship rates calculated in the base year (1980) as the proportion of men and women in each five-year age group who are the head of a household. The numbers of households are projected by multiplying the projected number of men and women in each five-year age group by the base-year headship rates.

Headship rates for 1980 and 1970 are charted in Figure A.1. As can be seen in the figure, the overwhelming majority of all men head a household at some time during their lives. The peak in 1980 occurred among men in their 50s—95 percent were household heads. The rise in headship observed among men in their 20s and 30s accompanies the rise in the number married, but couples in Thailand frequently delay establishing their own households for a number of years after their marriage and live with the wife's or husband's parents. The decline in headship at older ages is significant in that the headship mantle is being passed on to the next generation. Headship rates are low among women in their 20s and 30s but rise steadily with age. By the time women reach their 60s and 70s, nearly a third are household heads.

A comparison of headship rates in 1970 and 1980 shows that the relationship between population and the number of households has been relatively stable. Headship rates showed evidence of very modest declines at young ages and somewhat more substantial increases at older ages among men. Among women, headship rates increased marginally at the young ages between 1970 and 1980 and somewhat more significantly among older women.

The overall headship rates shown in Figure A.1 conceal important changes that occur in living arrangements as adults progress through their lives, however. Among young adults, intact households, i.e., those with both head and spouse present, predominate, but as families age alternative forms become increasingly important. Table A.1 shows detailed rates for single, primary-individual, and one-person household headship for men and women in Thailand in 1980. Several features of the table are noteworthy. First, primary-individual headship is rare—for no age or sex group does the headship rate reach 1 percent. Second, one-person households are uncommon. A little over 1 percent of young men and a little under 1 percent of young women live alone. But among older men and women, living alone is somewhat more common. Of those over 65, around 2 to 3 percent of men and 5 to 6 percent of women live in one-person households. Third, being the single head of a household is quite common, particularly for women. Even among women in their late 40s, nearly 15 percent are single heads and around one-quarter of all women 55 and older head households

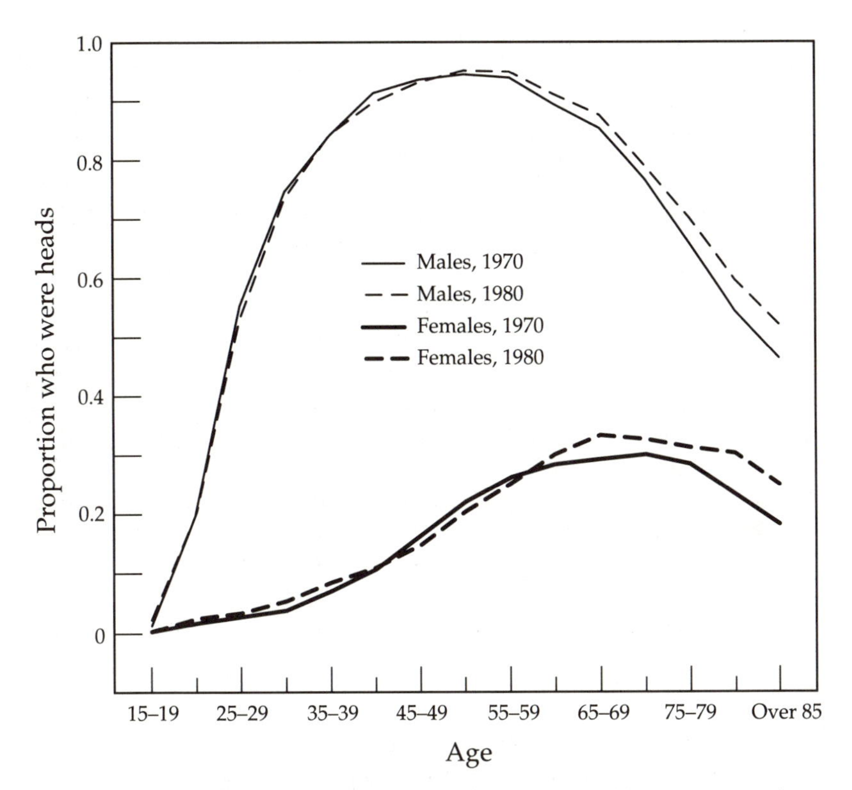

Source: The data in this figure and all subsequent figures and tables in this appendix are from the 1970 and 1980 population censuses (NSO 1970, 1980)

Figure A.1. Headship rates for men and women: 1970 and 1980

without a husband present. Men are considerably less likely to be single heads—single headship rates are close to 10 percent for those over 55.

Although the data reported above emphasize the household head, for many purposes and particularly for analyzing household composition, the wife of the household head plays a critical role.[1] Above all, the presence of children depends on childbearing, which is closely associated with the age of the wife. Table A.2 shows, for women in selected age groups in 1980, the proportion married to men in the same age group and adjacent age groups. As is true in most countries, Thai women are likely to be married

1. Household headship is self-reporting in the Thailand census and some intact households report female heads. To ease computation, reporting, and international comparisons, we have followed the convention of designating the male as the head and the female as the marker or spouse in all intact households.

Table A.1. Headship rates for non-intact households: 1980

Age of head	Single head		Primary individual		One-person	
	Male	Female	Male	Female	Male	Female
15–19	.0034	.0035	.0015	.0007	.0028	.0019
20–24	.0139	.0138	.0055	.0025	.0110	.0051
25–29	.0183	.0246	.0061	.0036	.0124	.0057
30–34	.0190	.0427	.0029	.0014	.0113	.0069
35–39	.0208	.0718	.0034	.0016	.0107	.0069
40–44	.0274	.0996	.0020	.0014	.0113	.0074
45–49	.0422	.1421	.0019	.0005	.0121	.0098
50–54	.0560	.1933	.0014	.0014	.0132	.0156
55–59	.0802	.2340	.0020	.0023	.0174	.0235
60–64	.1016	.2684	.0015	.0010	.0245	.0311
65–69	.1091	.2826	.0008	.0042	.0282	.0531
70–74	.1397	.2627	.0031	.0036	.0258	.0635
75–79	.1612	.2541	.0000	.0022	.0311	.0612
80–84	.1356	.2335	.0073	.0014	.0313	.0698
85+	.1163	.1991	.0000	.0000	.0445	.0552

Table A.2. Proportion of women at selected ages who are the spouse of a head in selected age groupings: 1980

Age of woman (X)	Proportion who are spouse of head age					Ages of head combined
	X–5	X	X+5	X+10	X+15	
20–24	.003	.093	.156	.053	.014	.330
30–34	.047	.242	.264	.094	.030	.699
40–44	.057	.282	.273	.103	.026	.779
50–54	.058	.255	.217	.085	.031	.687
60–64	.047	.170	.150	.060	.015	.477
70–74	.037	.096	.057	.017	.007	.240

to heads that are older, but the age difference between heads and spouses is not particularly high by Asian standards, and Thai women are somewhat more willing to marry younger men. As couples age, the average age gap declines. This occurs, of course, because younger husbands are more likely to survive and not because the age difference between newlyweds has been increasing over time.

ISSUES ABOUT HOUSEHOLD HEADSHIP

Headship rates are used to project the number of households, but the accuracy of the procedure depends on whether changes in headship rates from year to year are small or can be adequately predicted. A comparison of Thailand's 1970 and 1980 headship rates indicates that, for the most important age groups, i.e., those with the largest numbers of people, overall headship rates have been relatively stable. At the older age groups, headship rates have risen modestly, but for reasons that are not altogether clear. Increased headship rates accompany increased nuclearization of households, because older adults and their offspring establish separate households. That headship rates have not increased among adults under 55 suggests that this may not be occurring. For men, most of the increase in headship between 1970 and 1980 has been an increase in intact households. This might very well be a product of increased longevity among spouses, reducing the number of joint households, i.e., those containing siblings, aunts, and uncles, etc. Evidence presented below supports this view.

For Thai women, the proportions of single heads were relatively stable for women under 60 but increased by 2 to 8 percentage points between 1970 and 1980 for women 60 and older. The greatest increases occurred for women age 85 and older. The proportion living in one-person households and in primary-individual households was relatively constant during this period. Again, the rise in the proportion of single heads may be a consequence of increased longevity among women, i.e., because more women were outliving their husbands. This is speculative at the moment but warrants further investigation.

CHILDREN OF THE HEAD

The number of children refers to surviving offspring of the household head and his wife who have not established separate households. Also included are stepchildren, adopted children, and husbands or wives of the head's children. The number, age, and sex of children in the household are products of two factors: the candidates for household membership, consisting primarily of surviving offspring, and the rules that govern the likelihood that offspring will continue to live in their parents' household or that of their spouse's parents.

The number of surviving offspring for an individual couple depends on the couple's past childbearing and the mortality experience of their children. Likewise, for a cohort of women the number of surviving offspring of each age and sex depends on the cohort's fertility experience and the mortality history of the cohort's offspring.

Using techniques described in detail elsewhere (Mason and Martin 1982), the number of surviving offspring per woman is calculated and presented in Table A.3. Only offspring below the age of 30 are reported in Table A.3

Table A.3. Surviving offspring per woman: 1980

Age of women	Age of surviving offspring						
	0–4	5–9	10–14	15–19	20–24	25–29	0–29
Male offspring							
15–19	0.036	0	0	0	0	0	0.036
20–24	0.265	0.039	0	0	0	0	0.304
25–29	0.319	0.232	0.031	0	0	0	0.583
30–34	0.259	0.342	0.237	0.022	0	0	0.860
35–39	0.186	0.292	0.384	0.212	0.016	0	1.090
40–44	0.116	0.222	0.364	0.378	0.201	0.017	1.297
45–49	0.051	0.166	0.316	0.402	0.383	0.209	1.528
50–54	0.006	0.067	0.245	0.388	0.451	0.423	1.580
55–59	0	0.008	0.093	0.273	0.405	0.471	1.251
60–64	0	0	0.010	0.091	0.254	0.385	0.740
65–69	0	0	0	0.012	0.093	0.267	0.372
70–74	0	0	0	0	0.011	0.100	0.111
75–79	0	0	0	0	0	0.013	0.013
80–84	0	0	0	0	0	0	0
85+	0	0	0	0	0	0	0
Female offspring							
15–19	0.034	0	0	0	0	0	0.034
20–24	0.254	0.038	0	0	0	0	0.291
25–29	0.306	0.223	0.030	0	0	0	0.559
30–34	0.248	0.329	0.228	0.021	0	0	0.827
35–39	0.178	0.281	0.369	0.207	0.016	0	1.051
40–44	0.111	0.214	0.350	0.367	0.196	0.016	1.254
45–49	0.049	0.161	0.304	0.392	0.372	0.204	1.481
50–54	0.006	0.064	0.236	0.377	0.438	0.412	1.534
55–59	0	0.008	0.089	0.266	0.393	0.459	1.214
60–64	0	0	0.010	0.089	0.247	0.375	0.721
65–69	0	0	0	0.011	0.090	0.261	0.362
70–74	0	0	0	0	0.011	0.096	0.108
75–79	0	0	0	0	0	0.013	0.013
80–84	0	0	0	0	0	0	0
85+	0	0	0	0	0	0	0

because few offspring over age 30 are the child of a head; however, a complete table is used to project the number of children as reported below. The value of Table A.3 is twofold—it not only quantifies the number of children available for household membership but also identifies the households to which they would belong. Children under age 5, for example, will be concentrated in households with a wife of the head in her 20s or early 30s. Children 20–24 years of age, by contrast, would be concentrated in households in which the spouse of the head is in her 40s or 50s.

As the fertility transition proceeds in Thailand, the number of children in households will be influenced by both the decline in childbearing and changes in the timing of fertility. Fertility decline will mean fewer children per household and changes in the timing of fertility will influence the character of households in which children live. In general, fertility tends to be compressed into fewer years as older women, in particular, bear fewer children and in some cases fertility among very young women declines as well. The characteristics of households in which children are found will change correspondingly: the greatest decline in the number of children will be in older households. Such a pattern of change has characterized Thailand's fertility transition to this point. Figure A.2 shows that the number of offspring under age 15 per adult declined only for women in their late 30s or older between 1950 and 1980. But by 2010, dramatic declines are expected among all those 30 and older and more modest declines among women in their 20s.

The number of surviving offspring quantifies only the supply of potential children of the head. But the number who are the child of the head varies systematically with the age of the child and with the age of the mother. For the most part, young children are most likely to be the child of a head. Table A.4 reports the proportions of children who were the child of a head in 1970 and 1980.

Children 0–4 years of age in Thailand are actually less likely to be the child of the head than those who are somewhat older. This is a relatively common phenomenon in societies where extended households are prevalent: almost all who are not the child are the grandchild of the head. After 15 years of age, the proportion who are the child of a head declines steadily as offspring establish separate households. In general, the proportions decline more rapidly for women, reflecting their earlier age at marriage. But the proportions are roughly equal for those over 30. An unusually high percentage of older Thais are the child of the head. The proportions for those over 30 years of age are substantially higher than comparable values in Indonesia, South Korea, Malaysia, Taiwan, or the Philippines (Mason 1987). The likelihood of being a child of the head declined between 1970 and 1980 for young offspring, which is consistent with an increase in grandchildren or three-generation families. Among older offspring the propor-

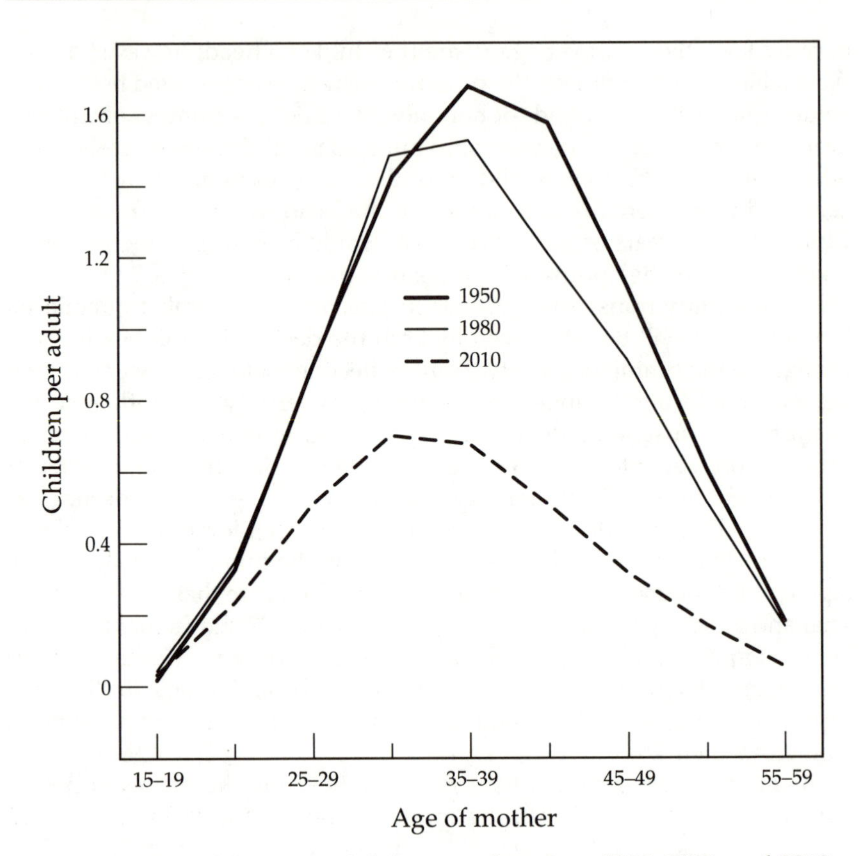

Figure A.2. Children per adult by age of mother: 1950, 1980, and 2010

Table A.4. Proportion of population who were the child of a head: 1970 and 1980

	1970		1980	
Age	Male	Female	Male	Female
0–4	.807	.819	.744	.747
5–9	.870	.872	.849	.852
10–14	.877	.876	.875	.872
15–19	.832	.788	.841	.786
20–24	.654	.532	.661	.540
25–29	.360	.300	.387	.329
30–34	.190	.167	.211	.210
35–39	.112	.102	.121	.123

tions who are the child of the head increased between 1970 and 1980, again consistent with a rise in three-generation families. It is not at all clear if this change reflects a behavioral change, i.e., an increased preference for the extended family. At least in part, the change may be a consequence of increased survival among the men and women who are the parents of these offspring. But whether the source of change is behavioral or demographic, the fact remains that the transition to headship and the likelihood of being in a lineal, three-generation family has increased in Thailand. This is a surprising result and contrary to the view that modernization has eroded traditional values and, in particular, the extended family.

The likelihood that offspring will be the child of the head also depends on the age of their mother. Figure A.3 plots the likelihood of being the child of the head (the ratio of children to surviving offspring) against age of spouse. For offspring under age 10, the likelihood of being the child of the head increases with the mother's age because older mothers are more likely to have established separate households. For offspring 15 and older, the likelihood of being the child of the head decreases with the mother's age. There are two obvious explanations for this phenomenon. First, offspring of older women are more likely to be orphaned. Second, within any age group the offspring of older mothers will be older, on average, than the offspring of younger mothers and more likely to have established a separate household.

The offspring and likelihood data in Figure A.3 address the questions of whether offspring are children of the head and, if so, how old are their mothers? But in what type of household will these children reside? As a first approximation, one might expect that each type of household would have on average the same number of children. But this is unlikely for three reasons. First, intact households do not have any apparent interruption to their childbearing due to the separation of head and spouse. Other factors aside, intact households should have higher childbearing, particularly in recent years, than households with single heads. Second, the choice of residence for children may not be independent of the sex of the parent. In the case of divorce, for example, children may be more likely to live with their mother than their father. Thus, the number of children per household would be disproportionately small for households headed by single men. Third, the existence of a separate household may depend on the number of children. Single women with a few or no surviving offspring may return to their parents' household, for example, whereas single women with many children may maintain separate households. Thus, households headed by single females might have larger than average households.

The net effect of these various factors can be assessed by comparing the observed number of children per household with the expected number if the average number is independent of household type. The ratios, calcu-

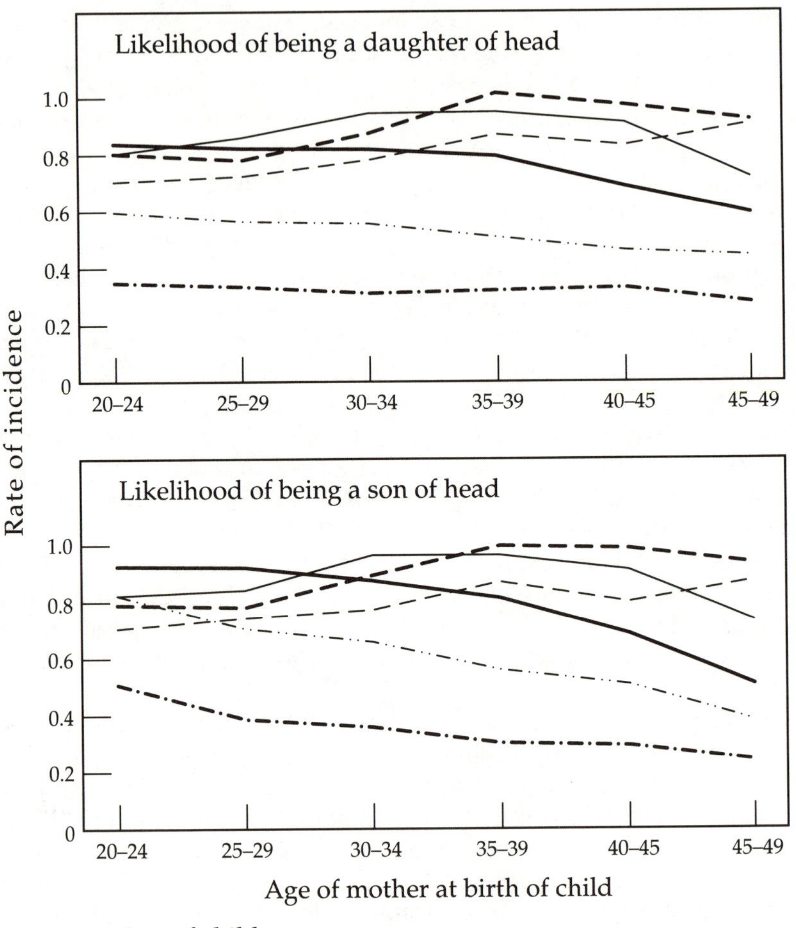

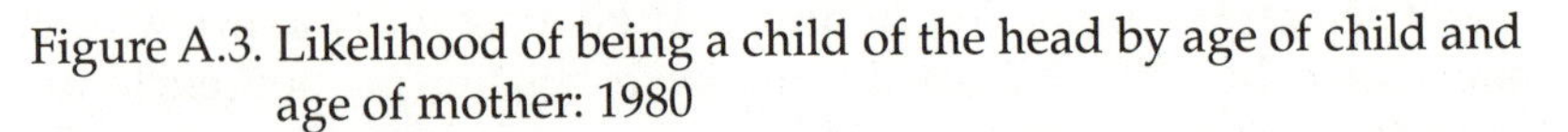

Figure A.3. Likelihood of being a child of the head by age of child and age of mother: 1980

lated from 1980 data, are presented for daughters at selected ages in Table A.5.

The number of children per household is apparently quite sensitive to household type. Disproportionately small numbers of young children are in single-headed households, particularly those headed by males. Obviously, the expected number of young offspring would be more closely associated with the current absence of a spouse than would the number of

Table A.5. Ratio of observed to expected daughters per household: 1980

Age of offspring	Age of mother at time of birth							
	15–19	20–24	25–29	30–34	35–39	40–44	45–49	50–54
Intact households								
0–4	1.12	1.07	1.05	1.05	1.07	1.10	1.16	1.16
10–14	1.02	1.03	1.04	1.04	1.08	1.10	1.10	1.04
20–24	0.89	0.99	0.99	1.01	1.04	1.04	1.06	0.80
30–34	0.73	0.94	0.98	0.93	0.85	1.03	0.84	1.15
Single head, male								
0–4	0.05	0.07	0.12	0.20	0.25	0.23	0.32	0.55
10–14	0.83	0.47	0.49	0.54	0.49	0.49	0.76	1.65
20–24	3.26	1.06	0.85	0.85	0.84	0.93	1.32	2.04
30–34	3.86	4.53	1.58	1.18	1.04	1.02	1.10	1.34
Single head, female								
0–4	0.31	0.46	0.54	0.52	0.56	0.53	0.41	0.56
10–14	0.69	0.81	0.81	0.86	0.77	0.79	0.82	0.76
20–24	1.33	1.03	1.07	1.01	0.94	0.94	0.85	0.96
30–34	1.24	1.04	0.99	1.12	1.18	0.95	1.04	0.83

older surviving offspring. Moreover, young children are most likely to live with their mothers. The picture is quite different for older children, however. Households with single heads have a disproportionately large number of older children. This is understandable because the great majority of people with spouses absent would have lived with their spouses 20 to 30 years earlier so that the expected number of surviving offspring 20 or 30 years old will not be highly correlated with current household type. That the ratios for single-headed households are frequently greater than 1.0 suggests that children in single-headed households are less likely to leave than are those in intact households. This appears to be an example of how the family institution operates to mitigate the impact of exogenous shocks, e.g., mortality among household members.

GRANDCHILDREN

That virtually all young offspring who are not sons or daughters of the head are grandchildren of the head is confirmed by Table A.6, which reports the proportion who were grandchildren according to the 1970 and 1980 censuses. In 1980, one child in five under age 5 was the grandchild of the household head, but the proportion declines rapidly with age as young parents establish their own households. Even so, nearly 4 percent of those in their

Table A.6. The proportion of grandchildren: 1970 and 1980

	1970		1980	
Age	Male	Female	Male	Female
0–4	.162	.152	.216	.215
5–9	.089	.088	.114	.109
10–14	.051	.052	.071	.066
15–19	.030	.025	.036	.034
20–24	.013	.010	.018	.014
25–29	.003	.003	.007	.005

late teens were the grandchild of the head in 1980. Although other Asian populations analyzed using HOMES show significant numbers of grandchildren, only in Malaysia are the rates as high as in Thailand among those over age 5. No other country approaches the prevalence of grandchildren of the head for the under-5 population in Thailand. The proportions increased notably between 1970 and 1980. As noted above, this phenomenon may reflect nothing more than increased survival among grandparents.

The proportions in Table A.6 are a by-product of several processes, in particular, the relationship between bearing children and establishing separate households. A pure nuclear system would dictate that women establish separate households prior to the birth of their first child, in which case all proportions in Table A.6 would be zero. Under one characterization of the extended family system, childbearing and the mother's relationship to head would be independent. In this case, the proportion of offspring who are children will be determined entirely by the *independent* decision of women of childbearing age about establishing a separate household. In actual cases, the decision to bear a child and relationship to head are anything but independent. On the one hand, the birth of a child provides the impetus to establish a separate household. On the other hand, childbearing in extended families may be encouraged by the presence of a grandparent who can assume some of the childrearing responsibilities. Or it may be that a traditional outlook or other factors jointly affect living arrangements and childbearing. Whatever the cause, the interdependence of childbearing and living arrangements is a critical determinant of the prevalence of grandchildren in any society.

Table A.7 provides a means by which the dependence of childbearing and living arrangements can be assessed. Census data described above report the number of daughters of childrearing age, i.e., 15 and older, who are the daughters of a head. If their childbearing is the same as that of the general population, the number of surviving offspring will equal that of

Table A.7. Ratio of observed grandchildren to "expected grandchildren"

Age of grandchildren	Age of head						
	40–44	45–49	50–54	55–59	60–64	65–69	70–74
Intact households							
Male							
0–4	0.78	0.83	0.93	1.00	1.00	1.07	1.30
5–9	0.58	0.50	0.68	0.70	0.67	0.82	1.09
10–14	0.63	0.50	0.67	0.80	0.62	0.81	1.14
15–19	1.14	0.35	0.54	0.69	0.60	0.62	0.87
Female							
0–4	0.76	0.85	0.94	1.04	0.92	1.06	1.16
5–9	0.42	0.46	0.68	0.67	0.66	0.74	1.09
10–14	0.67	0.59	0.66	0.71	0.65	0.69	0.81
15–19	1.14	1.18	0.78	0.51	0.67	0.62	0.97
Single male head							
Male							
0–4	0.86	0.95	1.02	1.05	1.04	1.02	1.00
5–9	0.75	0.76	0.82	0.83	0.86	0.89	0.85
10–14	0.56	0.72	0.75	0.73	0.73	0.74	0.77
15–19	0.38	0.43	0.51	0.53	0.60	0.64	0.61
Female							
0–4	1.03	1.03	1.06	1.17	1.26	1.19	1.06
5–9	0.68	0.69	0.75	0.81	0.85	0.87	0.92
10–14	0.54	0.56	0.61	0.61	0.64	0.68	0.72
15–19	0.45	0.45	0.55	0.60	0.64	0.63	0.63
Single female head							
Male							
0–4	1.17	1.08	1.12	1.02	1.11	1.14	1.15
5–9	0.44	0.67	0.79	0.79	0.79	0.78	1.01
10–14	1.22	0.63	0.54	0.88	0.84	0.76	0.80
15–19	1.75	1.06	1.14	0.76	0.71	0.68	0.61
Female							
0–4	1.15	1.21	1.20	0.97	0.99	1.09	1.00
5–9	0.79	0.66	0.80	0.81	0.73	0.76	0.87
10–14	1.07	0.74	0.97	0.86	0.72	0.70	0.81
15–19	1.91	0.86	0.67	1.04	0.54	0.66	0.66

the general population. The product of the two factors will give the number of grandchildren expected per household *if childbearing and living arrangements are independent*. Dividing the observed number of grandchildren by the "expected" number provides an index of the dependence between childbearing and residence. A value less than 1.0 indicates that daughters of the head have fewer children; an index greater than 1.0 indicates that daughters of the head have more children than the population at large.

These figures exhibit several interesting patterns. The values are near 1.0, and are often larger than 1.0, for children under age 5. This suggests that having a young child does not push the mother out of the household and that living in an extended family may encourage higher childbearing to a limited extent. The values in Table A.6 generally are below 1.0 for children older than five, indicating that having older children is associated with the establishment of a separate household, although there is no way to say that the older child itself is the motivating factor. The values are clearly and positively associated with the age of the head or his spouse (the grandparents). This would be expected if, for example, all but one offspring established separate households as childbearing began. Among older households, a high percentage of those who were the remaining child of the head would be a "permanent" household member, with childbearing independent or even positively associated with his or her status as the heir apparent.

PARENTS

One of the remarkable features of the parent-of-head proportions is that in both 1970 and 1980 fewer than 50 percent of any age and sex group, save one, were the parent of a household head. That sole exception was for women over 85 years of age in 1970. In general, women were more likely than men to be the parent of a household head, and older adults were more likely to be parents of the head than younger adults. Between 1970 and 1980, the proportion who were the parent of a household head rose very substantially in all age and sex categories (Table A.8). This trend is similar to those noted above in that an increasing number of household members have a direct lineal relationship to the household's head.

Whether or not parents of the head reside in a given household depends on a number of factors. First, it depends upon the availability of surviving offspring. The greater the number of surviving offspring 40–44 years of age, for example, the greater the chances that those 75–79 will live in households headed by someone 40–44. Second, it depends on competition among surviving offspring. If those 75–79 also have many surviving offspring 45–49 years of age, the likelihood that they will live in a household with a head 40–44 are thereby diminished. These two demographic components are both captured by a single measure—*parents per offspring*. The measure is an estimate of the expected number of parents living with offspring if all parents

Table A.8. Proportion of population who were parents of head: 1970 and 1980

Age	1970		1980	
	Male	Female	Male	Female
45–49	.001	.012	.003	.018
50–54	.006	.027	.011	.046
55–59	.015	.062	.022	.087
60–64	.040	.108	.060	.175
65–69	.053	.152	.101	.260
70–74	.102	.208	.166	.356
75–79	.162	.282	.253	.434
80–84	.225	.286	.338	.472
85+	.294	.287	.330	.557

lived with offspring (and the offspring lived separately.) For example, in a family with three surviving brothers, two surviving sisters, and two surviving parents, *parents per offspring* would be two parents divided by five offspring which equals 0.4 parents per offspring.

Table A.9 reports the number of surviving parents per 100 surviving offspring for selected age groups. The highlighted row indicates that in 100 households with a head or a spouse 50–54 years of age we would find 6.3 mothers of the head if all mothers lived with their offspring, their offspring all headed households, and if the choice of household for the mother was independent of the age of the offspring. If both the head and spouse were 50–54, then the "supply" of mothers would be 12.6. Of the 6.3 women, 2.00 would be 70–74 years of age, 2.28 would be 75–79, and 1.30 would be 80–84.

Figure A.4 compares calculated parents per offspring with observed mothers of the head per household living in households with a marker 50–54 years old. The total mothers of the head per 100 households varied from 3.65 for intact households to 4.43 for households headed by single men, or about one-half to two-thirds of the potential number. The observed parents per household has roughly the same shape as the parents per offspring index but there are disproportionately more parents in the youngest and oldest age categories. There are a variety of explanations for such a pattern. Parents may have a preference for living with older or younger offspring, for example. But there may also be errors in the data—either in the census data, e.g., age misreporting, or in the construction of the parent-per-offspring index. Furthermore, the observed values are based on very small numbers, in some cases no more than 3 or 4 observations.

Table A.9. Surviving parents per 100 surviving offspring: 1980

Age of offspring	Age of parents 55–59	60–64	65–69	70–74	75–79	80–84	85+	Combined*
Fathers								
15–19	1.58	0.45	0.04					20.98
20–24	2.77	1.48	0.36	0.03				18.28
25–29	3.76	2.61	1.21	0.31	0.02			16.34
30–34	4.11	3.47	2.11	1.03	0.20	0.01		14.37
35–39	2.62	3.80	2.80	1.78	0.66	0.10		12.09
40–44	0.26	2.43	3.04	2.36	1.15	0.33	0.03	9.61
45–49		0.22	1.86	2.54	1.53	0.60	0.13	6.88
50–54			0.17	1.55	1.64	0.79	0.29	4.44
55–59				0.14	0.99	0.84	0.51	2.50
60–64					0.09	0.51	0.75	1.36
65–69						0.05	0.90	0.94
Mothers								
15–19	1.63	0.46	0.04					21.77
20–24	2.86	1.52	0.41	0.04				19.11
25–29	3.88	2.69	1.40	0.40	0.03			17.20
30–34	4.24	3.58	2.44	1.33	0.28	0.02		15.45
35–39	2.71	3.91	3.24	2.31	0.92	0.17	0.01	13.59
40–44	0.27	2.51	3.52	3.05	1.59	0.55	0.05	11.54
45–49		0.22	2.15	3.29	2.13	0.98	0.23	9.00
50–54			**0.20**	**2.00**	**2.28**	**1.30**	**0.53**	**6.30**
55–59				0.19	1.38	1.38	0.93	3.89
60–64					0.13	0.84	1.37	2.34
65–69						0.08	1.63	1.70

*Includes parents under age 55.

OTHER HOUSEHOLD MEMBERS

The percentage of any age group categorized as "other household members" varied from about 1 percent up to about 12 percent depending upon the sex and age group in question. About one out of every 10 men and women in their late teens and early 20s were "other household members." Very few of those between 25 and 64 years of age fell into this category, but the likelihood increases for those over 65 years of age.

The age pattern observed in Thailand in 1970 was similar to the 1980 pattern with one important exception. The proportions among the middle aged and elderly who were "other household members" decreased substantially

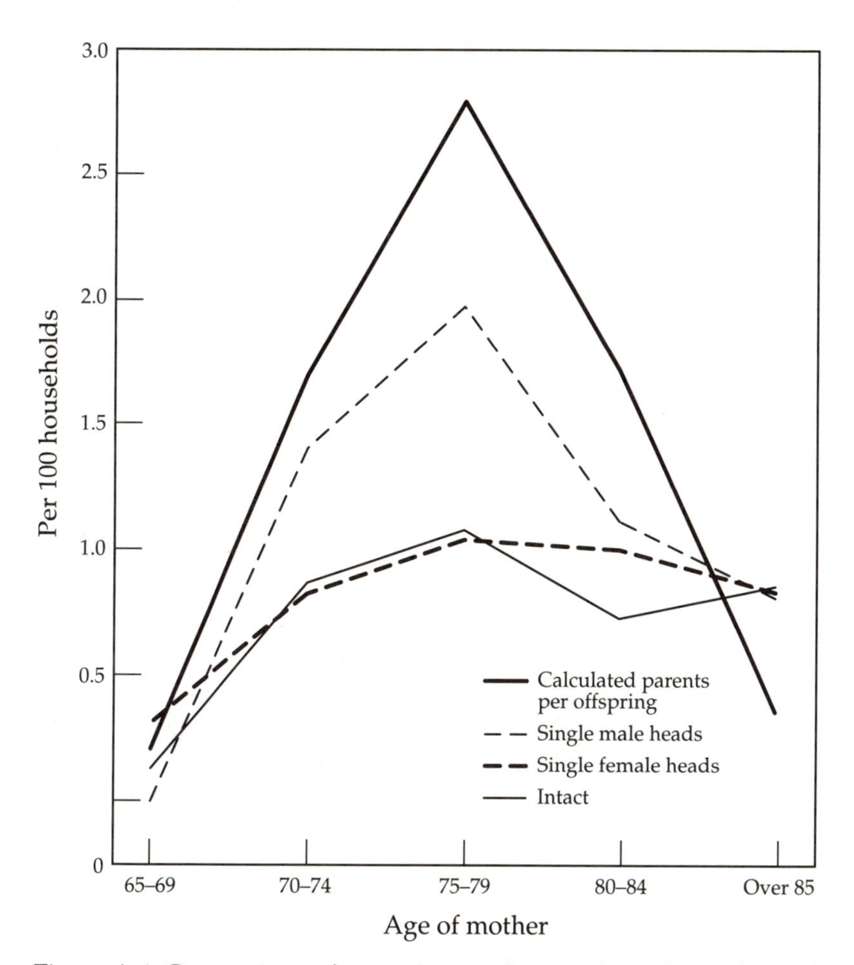

Figure A.4. Comparison of surviving mothers with mothers of head by age of mother for households with heads 50–54 years of age in 1980

between 1970 and 1980. In 1970, 24 percent of males and 47 percent of females 85 and older were categorized as "other household members." The enormity of the shift is readily apparent in Figure A.5.

To understand the source of such a dramatic change requires first some notion about the kinds of people included in this residual category. The 1970 and 1980 censuses break the data down into other relatives, nonrelatives, and servants. In addition, the 1980 census reports information about the number of grandparents of the head. The number of servants is negligible, reaching 1 percent only for women 15 to 19 years of age. Data

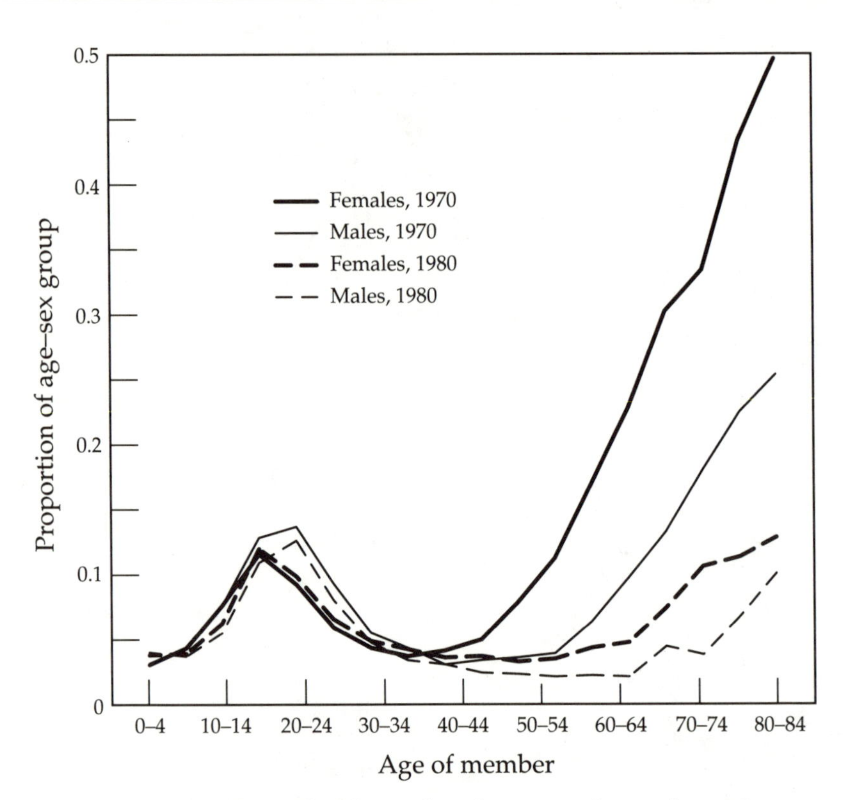

Figure A.5. Other household members by age and sex of members: 1970 and 1980

on grandparents and other related and unrelated household members are reported for selected age groups in Table A.10.

In all age categories, the great majority of members are related to the head and non-relatives make up a distinct minority. Furthermore, the declines in the proportions are concentrated among relatives rather than non-relatives. In 1980, among those 75–79, a third or less of relatives were grandparents of the household head, the rest being nonlineal relations, e.g., aunts, uncles, cousins, nieces, etc. There is no way of knowing for sure whether the decline between 1970 and 1980 was among grandparents or among nonlineal relatives. But indirect evidence suggests a decline in both. It is clear that the decline in the proportions among those 50–54 occurred among nonlineal relatives of the head, because this group is too young to be grandparents of a household head. Thus, this provides clear evidence of a decline in the importance of the joint extended family between 1970 and 1980.

Table A.10. Proportions of other household members: 1970 and 1980

	Unrelated		Related		Grandparents	
Age/year	Males	Females	Males	Females	Males	Females
0–4						
1970	.003	.003	.027	.026	u	u
1980	.005	.005	.033	.031	.000	.000
25–29						
1970	.023	.010	.062	.042	u	u
1980	.024	.015	.052	.043	.000	.000
50–54						
1970	.009	.007	.024	.066	u	u
1980	.008	.005	.014	.025	.000	.000
75–79						
1970	.022	.027	.148	.288	u	u
1980	.009	.020	.027	.079	.009	.021

Note: Grandparent values are not available for 1970; values for members related to the head include grandparents.

u—unavailable.

The available evidence suggests that the decline in other members 75-79 years of age is accounted for by a decline in both grandparents and nonlineal relatives of the head. The distribution of other members in 1980, shown in Figure A.6, exhibits two concentration points—one among households with middle-aged heads and the other among households with young heads. Because the category "other relatives" does not include parents, other relatives of heads 45–49 years of age or in adjacent age categories must be aunts or uncles or other nonlineal relatives. (The grandparents reported in the 50–54 age category is probably a coding or response error.) Other relatives of heads in their 20s are about evenly divided among grandparents and other relatives. A puzzling feature of the figure is the substantial difference in "generation lengths" as measured from the mid-point of the 75-79 age category to the two peaks. The 30-year interval from 75-79 to the 45-49 peak is probably reasonably close to the mean generation length of a high-fertility regime, which undoubtedly characterized fertility among women who are now elderly. But the peak-to-peak interval of 22.5 years is short of the mean generation length for women who were in their late 40s in 1980. The shorter interval undoubtedly reflects truncation of the distribution of members of the third generation—younger members would not be household heads.

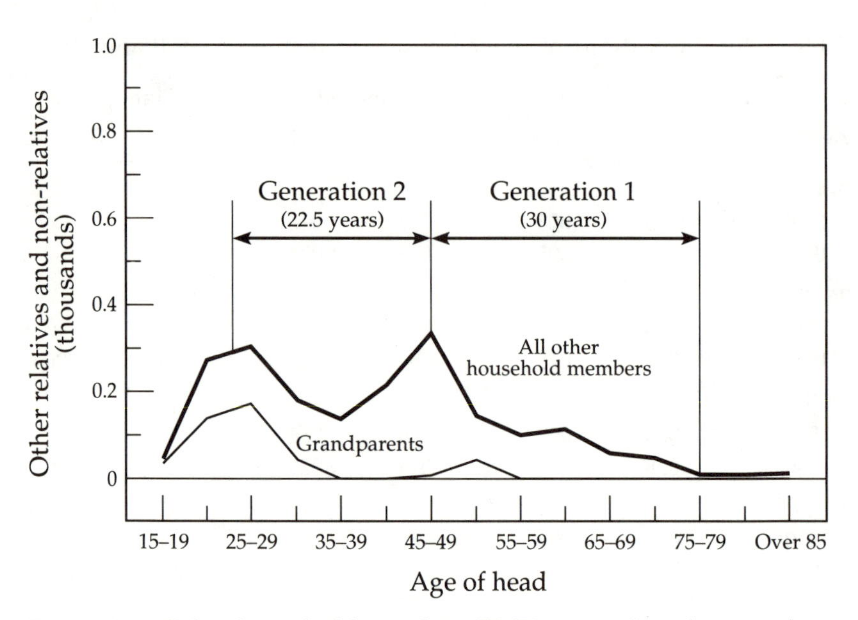

Figure A.6. Other household members 75–79 years of age by age of household head: 1980

The 1970 pattern is quite different and cannot be untangled with complete certainty because grandparents were not tabulated separately in the 1970 census (Figure A.7). Other household members 75–79 years of age are concentrated among households with heads 35–39 years of age and in adjacent age groups. Although the initial reaction might be that the distance to the peak represents two generations, 40 years is too short. More likely, the peak represents the sum of overlap of members in the second and third generations. Then the decline in other elderly members between 1970 and 1980 would represent, in part, a decline in households with a grandparent of the head, but a more significant decline in households with nonlineal ancestors one or two generations removed from the household head. Thus, the importance of the joint extended family apparently has declined over the last 10 years.

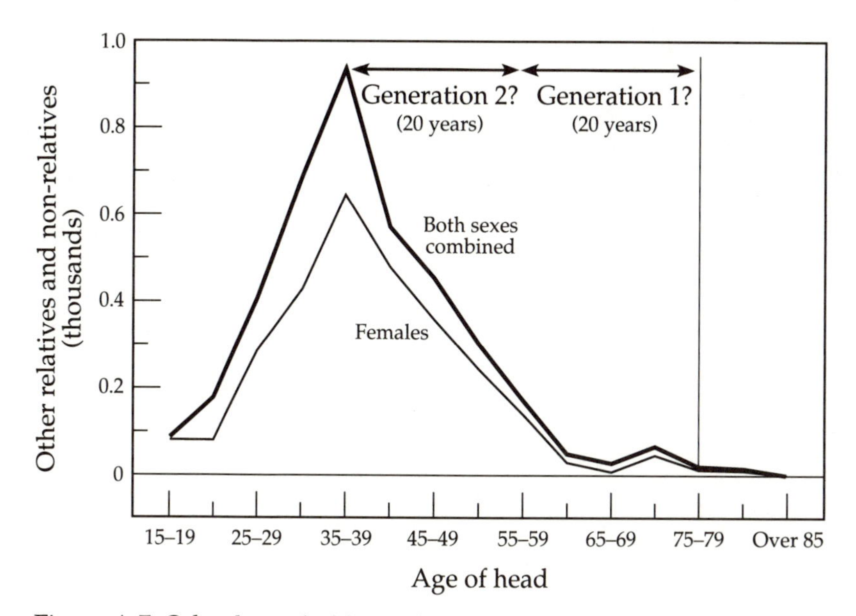

Figure A.7. Other household members 75–79 years of age by age of household head: 1970

References

Abbott, Graham J. 1984. **[4]** National saving and financial development in Asian developing countries. *Asian Development Review* 2(2):1–22.

Ahlburg, Dennis, Eileen M. Crimmins, and Richard A. Easterlin. 1981. **[6]** The outlook for higher education: A cohort size model of enrollment of the college age population, 1948–2000. *Review of Public Data Use* 19:211–227.

Ando, Albert. 1985. **[4]** The savings of Japanese households: A micro study based on data from the National Survey of Family Income and Expenditure, 1974 and 1979 (June).

Arumainathan, P. 1973. **[8]** *Report of the Census of Population 1970, Singapore,* Vol. I. Singapore: Dept. of Statistics.

Asian Development Bank (ADB). 1991. **[1]** *Key Indicators.* Manila: ADB.

Bangkok Metropolitan Administration, and Office of Local Education, Ministry of the Interior, Thailand. Various editions. **[6]** *Educational Report.* Bangkok.

Becker, Gary S. 1964. **[6]** *Human Capital.* New York: Columbia University Press.

Becker, Gary S., and H. Gregg Lewis. 1974. **[6]** Interactions between quantity and quality of children. In T. W. Schultz (ed.), *Economics of the Family.* Chicago: University of Chicago Press.

Bertrand, T., and L. Squire. 1980. **[3]** On the relevance of the dual economy model: A case study of Thailand. *Oxford Economic Papers* 32(3):480–511.

Blinder, Alan. 1976. **[3]** Dogmatism in human capital theory. *Journal of Human Resources* XI(1):8–22.

Bongaarts, John, Thomas K. Burch, and Kenneth W. Wachter, eds. 1987. **[2]** *Family Demography: Methods and Their Application.* Oxford: Clarendon Press.

Bowen, William G. 1981. **[6]** Market prospects for Ph.D.s in the United States. *Population and Development Review* 7 (September):475–488.

Budget Bureau, Ministry of Finance, Thailand. Various editions. **[6]** *Annual Government Expenditure Report.* Bangkok.

Bureau of the Census and Statistics, Philippines. 1963. **[8]** *Census of the Philippines: Population and Housing 1960,* Vol. II. *Summary Report.* Manila.

Burkner, Hans Paul. 1981. **[4]** *Savings Behavior and Savings Mobilization in Developing Countries: A Comparative Analysis of the Philippines and Thailand.* Bochum: Studienverlag Brockmeyer.

Chaipravat, Olarn. 1979. **[3]** *Bank of Thailand Model of the Thai Economy.* Bangkok: Department of Economic Research, Bank of Thailand.

Clark, B. Kim, and Richard B. Freeman. 1980. **[3]** How elastic is the demand for labor? *The Review of Economics and Statistics* 62(4):509–520.

Cochrane, Susan H., Valerie Kozel, and Harold Alderman. 1989. **[4]** Household consequences of high fertility: The case of Pakistan. Mimeo (March).

Deaton, Angus, and John Muellbauer. 1980. **[5]** *Economics and Consumer Behavior.* Cambridge: Cambridge University Press.

Deaton, Angus S., Javier Ruiz-Castillo, and Duncan Thomas. 1989. **[5]** The influence of household composition on household expenditure patterns: Theory and Spanish evidence. *Journal of Political Economy* 97 (February): 179–200.

Dresch, Stephen P. 1975. **[6]** Demography, technology, and higher education: Toward a formal model of educational adaptation. *Journal of Political Economy* 83:535–569.

Eilenstine, Donald, and James P. Cunningham. 1972. **[5]** Projected consumption patterns for a stationary population. *Population Studies* (July):223–231.

Evenson, R. E., and Suthad Setboonsrang. 1985. **[3]** Research, extension, literacy and productivity in the agricultural sector in Thailand. Unpublished paper.

Feldstein, Martin. 1983. **[4]** Domestic saving and international capital movements in the long run and the short run. *European Economic Review* (March/April): 129–151.

Feldstein, Martin, and C. Horioka. 1980. **[4]** Domestic saving and international capital movements. *Economic Journal* 90:314–329.

Fry, Maxwell J. 1984. **[4]** Terms of trade and national saving rates in Asia. Mimeo.

Fry, Maxwell J., and Andrew Mason. 1982. **[4]** The variable rate of growth effect in the life-cycle saving model. *Economic Inquiry* (July):426–442.

Gunderson, Morley. 1974. **[7]** Retention of trainees: A study with dichotomous dependent variables. *Journal of Econometrics* 2:79–93.

Hammermesh, S. Daniel. 1976. **[3]** Econometric studies of labor demand and their application to policy analysis. *Journal of Human Resources* 11(4):507–525.

Heckman, James. 1980. **[3]** Sample selection bias as a specification error. In James Smith (ed.), *Female Labor Supply: Theory and Estimation.* Princeton: Princeton University Press.

Institution of Higher Education, Office of University Affairs, Thailand. Various editions. **[6]** *Education Report.* Bangkok.

International Monetary Fund (IMF). 1992. **[1]** *International Financial Statistics.* August. Washington, D.C.: IMF.

Jones, Gavin. 1971. **[6]** Effects of population growth on the attainment of educational goals in developing countries. In National Academy of Sciences, *Rapid Population Growth.* Baltimore: The Johns Hopkins University Press.

Jones, Gavin. 1975. **[6]** *Population Growth and Educational Planning in Developing Nations.* New York: Irvington Publications.

Jones, Gavin, and Chet Boonpratuang. 1972. **[7]** *The Effect of Population Growth and Urbanization on the Attainment of Public Health Goals in Thailand.* Bangkok: Manpower Planning Division, National Economic and Social Development Board of Thailand.

Keilman, N., A. Kuijsten, and A. Vossen, eds. 1988. **[2]** *Modelling Household Formation and Dissolution.* Oxford: Oxford University Press.

Kim, Khoo Chian. 1981. **[8]** *Census of Population 1980, Singapore: Release No. 6, Households and Houses.* Singapore: Dept. of Statistics.

King, M. A., and L.-D. L. Dicks-Mireaux. 1982. **[4]** Asset holdings and the life-cycle. *The Economic Journal* 92:247–267.

Kleinbaum, Robert M., and Andrew Mason. 1987. **[4]** Household consumption and savings in South Korea. Paper presented at the Population Association of America Annual Meeting, Chicago.

Kmenta, Jan. 1971. **[5]** *Elements of Econometrics.* New York: The Macmillan Company.

Kotlikoff, Laurence J. 1988. **[4]** Intergenerational transfers and savings. *The Journal of Economic Perspectives* 2 (Spring):41–58.

Kotlikoff, Laurence J., and Lawrence H. Summers. 1981. **[4]** The role of intergenerational transfers in aggregate capital accumulation. *Journal of Political Economy* 89:706–732.

Leff, Nathanial H. 1969. **[4]** Dependency effects and savings rates. *American Economic Review* 59 (December):886–895.

Mason, Andrew. 1987. **[2,8,App. A]** *HOMES: A Household Model for Economic and Social Studies, Reference Guide for Household Projections, Version 1.0.* Papers of the East-West Population Institute, No. 106. Honolulu: East-West Center.

Mason, Andrew. 1988. **[4]** Saving, economic growth, and demographic change. *Population and Development Review* 14 (March):114–144.

Mason, Andrew, and Linda G. Martin. 1982. **[App. A]** The intergenerational distribution of income: An analysis of Japan. *Population and Development Review* 8, Supplement, *Income Distribution and the Family.*

Maurer, Kenneth, R. Ratajezak, and T. P. Schultz. 1973. **[3]** Marriage, fertility, and labor force participation of Thai women. A report prepared for AID and the Rockefeller Foundation. Santa Monica, CA.: Rand Corporation.

Meesook, Oey Astra. 1976. **[3]** Working women in Thailand. Paper presented at the Conference on Women and Development, Wellesey College, Massachusetts, 2–6 June.

Mincer, Jacob. 1985. **[3]** Intercountry comparisons of labor force trends and of related developments: An overview. *Journal of Labor Economics* 3(1), pt. 2.

Ministry of Health, Malaysia. 1982. **[7]** *Annual Report 1980.* Kuala Lumpur.

Ministry of Public Health (MOPH), Thailand. 1981. **[7]** *Statistical Report, 1981.* Bangkok.

Ministry of Public Health (MOPH), Thailand. 1985. **[7]** *Health Profile 1985.* Bangkok.

Ministry of the Interior, Thailand. 1970, 1975, 1980. **[8]** Registration record (unpublished).

Modigliani, Franco. 1988. **[4]** The role of intergenerational transfers and life cycle saving in the accumulation of wealth. *The Journal of Economic Perspectives* 2 (Spring):15–40.

Myers, Charles N., Dow Mongkolsmai, and Nancyanne Causino. 1985. **[7]** Financing health services and medical care in Thailand. Development Discussion Papers, No. 209, Harvard Institute for International Development.

National Census and Statistics Office, Philippines. 1974. **[8]** *1970 Census of Population and Housing,* Vol. II. *National Summary.* Manila.

National Economic and Social Development Board (NESDB), Thailand. 1985a. **[4]** *National Income of Thailand*. Bangkok: Office of the Prime Minister.

National Economic and Social Development Board (NESDB), Human Resource Planning Division, Thailand. 1985b. **[2]** *Population Projections for Thailand, 1980–2015.*

National Economic and Social Development Board (NESDB), Thailand. 1987. **[3]** *Projection of Labor Supply and Employment in the Sixth Plan (1986–1991)* (in Thai). Bangkok: Division of Human Resource Planning.

National Education Commission (NEC), Thailand. 1985. **[6]** *The Cost of Higher Education in Thailand* (in Thai). Bangkok: Office of the Prime Minister.

National Education Commission (NEC), Thailand. 1987. **[6]** *The Sixth National Education Plan (1987–1991)* (in Thai). Bangkok: Office of the Prime Minister.

National Epidemiology Board of Thailand (NEBT). 1987. **[7]** *Review of the Health Situation in Thailand: Priority Ranking of Diseases.* Bangkok.

National Statistical Office, Singapore. 1977. **[8]** *1976 Housing Survey.* Singapore.

National Statistical Office (NSO), Thailand. 1960. **[3]** *1960 Thailand Population Census.* Bangkok: NSO.

National Statistical Office (NSO), Thailand. 1970. **[3,8,App. A]** *1970 Population and Housing Census.* Bangkok: NSO.

National Statistical Office (NSO), Thailand. 1971–85. **[3]** *Report of the Labor Force Survey, Rounds 1–2.* Bangkok: NSO.

National Statistical Office (NSO), Thailand. 1977. **[8]** *Housing Survey 1976.* Bangkok: NSO.

National Statistical Office (NSO), Thailand. 1980. **[8,App. A]** *1980 Population and Housing Census.* Bangkok: NSO.

National Statistical Office (NSO), Office of the Prime Minister, Thailand. 1985. **[1,4,5,6,7]** *Summary Report of the 1981 Socio-Economic Survey, Whole Kingdom.* Publication Series E-Sur-Soc-No. 6-85. Bangkok: NSO.

National Statistical Office (NSO), Office of the Prime Minister, Thailand. 1991a. **[1]** *Report of the Labor Force Survey: May 1989 (Round 2).* Bangkok: NSO.

National Statistical Office (NSO), Office of the Prime Minister, Thailand. 1991b. **[1]** *Report of the 1988 Household Socio-Economic Survey, Whole Kingdom.* Bangkok: NSO.

National Statistical Office (NSO), Office of the Prime Minister, Thailand. 1992. **[1]** *Advanced Report: 1990 Population and Housing Census.* Bangkok: NSO.

National Statistical Office (NSO), Office of the Prime Minister, Thailand, and Office of the Undersecretary, Ministry of Education, Thailand. Various editions. **[6]** *Final Report on Education Statistics.* Bangkok: NSO.

Nitungkorn, Sukanya. 1981. **[3]** Labor force participation of married women in Thailand (in Thai). *Thammasat University Journal* 10(3):110–119.

Ogawa, Naohiro. 1985. **[7]** Population growth and the costs of health care: The case of Malaysia. EPU Discussion Paper No. 13, Prime Minister's Office, Government of Malaysia.

Ogawa, Naohiro, et al. 1986. **[7]** A long term perspective based on demographic, economic and medical model (Phase II). Tokyo: Nihon University Population Research Institute.

Paitoonpong, Srawooth. 1976. **[3]** The labor supply of Thailand: An empirical analysis of the determinants of participation rates. Ph.D. dissertation, University of Hawaii.

Pichaisanit, Pensri, et al. 1984. **[7]** Role of government hospitals in national health services. Faculty of Public Health, Mahidol University, Bangkok.

Poapongsakorn, Nipon. 1979. **[3]** Labor supply, demand for children and wage rates of paid employees in Thailand. Ph.D. dissertation, University of Hawaii.

Poapongsakorn, Nipon. 1984. **[3]** Unemployment issues in Thailand (in Thai). *Thammasat University Journal* 10(3):6–86.

Poapongsakorn, Nipon. 1986. **[3]** Employment in Thailand. A paper prepared for the World Bank's 1986 Country Economic Report for Thailand.

Pollak, Robert A., and Terence J. Wales. 1980. **[5]** Comparison of the quadratic expenditure system and translog demand systems with alternative specifications of the demographic effects. *Econometrica* 48 (April): 1,533–51.

Pollak, Robert A., and Terence J. Wales. 1981. **[5]** Demographic variables in demand analysis. *Econometrica* 49 (November).

Pongpaichit, Pasuk, and C. J. Baker. 1984. **[3]** Bertrand's choice and seasonal unemployment reconsidered. Unpublished paper, Faculty of Economics, Chulalongkorn University.

Robinson, Warren. 1975. **[6]** *Population and Development Planning.* New York: The Population Council.

Robinson, Warren C. 1986. **[7]** The economic and social impacts of declining fertility in Thailand and the policy options. Paper prepared for the National Economic and Social Development Board of Thailand.

Schultz, T. Paul. 1980. **[3]** Estimating labor supply functions for married women. In James P. Smith (ed.), *Female Labor Supply: Theory and Estimation.* Princeton: Princeton University Press.

Schultz, T. Paul. 1987. **[6]** School expenditures and enrollments, 1960–80: The effects of income, prices, and population growth. In D. Gale Johnson and Ronald D. Lee (eds.), *Population Growth and Economic Development: Issues and Evidence,* pp. 413–478. Madison: University of Wisconsin Press.

Sussangkarn, Chalongphob, Teera Ashakul, and Charles Myers. 1986. **[3,7]** Human resources management. Paper presented at Thailand Development Research Institute 1986 Year-end Conference on Human Resource Management, Pattaya, 13–14 December.

Tengumnuay, Malinee. 1981. **[4]** Household saving behavior in Thailand. Master of Economics thesis. Thammasat University, Bangkok.

Thai Population Information Center, Family Health Division, Department of Health, Ministry of Public Health, Thailand. 1992. **[1]** *Selected Population and Family Health Statistics, 1991.* Bangkok.

Thailand Development Research Institute (TDRI). 1985. **[3]** New dimensions for development. Paper presented at TDRI Year-end Conference, Pattaya, 14–15 December.

United Nations (U.N.), Department of Economic and Social Affairs. 1973a. **[2]** *Methods of Projecting Households and Families, Manual VII.* New York: U.N.

United Nations (U.N.). 1973b. **[8]** *World Housing Survey.* Report of the Secretary General. New York: U.N.

United Nations (U.N). 1985. **[6]** *Proceedings of the United Nations Ad Hoc Expert Group Meeting on the Manual on Integrating Population Variables into Development Planning, New York, 11–14 December 1984.* New York: U.N.

United Nations (U.N.). 1990. **[1]** *National Account Statistics: Main Aggregates and Detailed Tables, 1988.* New York: U.N.

Wachter, Michael L., and William L. Wascher. 1984. **[6]** Leveling the peaks and troughs in the demographic cycle: An application to school enrollment rates. *Review of Economics and Statistics* 66 (May):208–215.

Wattanavitukul, Somluckrat. 1980. **[4]** *Cash Expenditure, Own Consumption and Income in Thailand.* Council for Asian Manpower Studies Discussion Paper Series 79–07. Diliman, Quezon City, Philippines: Council for Asian Manpower Studies.

Wibulpolprasert, Suwit. 1991. **[7]** Health status, health policy objectives, health services, infrastructures, and utilization in Thailand. Prepared for the Regional Conference on Priority Health and Population Issues, 25–28 February, East-West Center, Honolulu, Hawaii.

Willis, Robert. 1974. **[6]** A new approach to the economic theory of fertility. In T. W. Schultz (ed.), *Economics of the Family.* Chicago: University of Chicago Press.

World Bank. 1983. **[3]** *Growth and Employment in Rural Thailand.* Report No. 3906–TH, April. Washington, D.C.: World Bank.

World Bank. 1984. **[4]** *World Development Report 1984.* New York: Oxford University Press.

World Bank. 1985. **[4,5]** Thailand poverty review. Mimeo (March).

Yeh, S. H. K. 1975. **[8]** *Public Housing in Singapore: A Multi-Disciplinary Study.* Singapore: Singapore University Press.

Yeh, S. H. K., and A. A. Laquian. 1979. **[8]** *Housing Asia's Millions.* Ottawa: IDRC.

Index

Age: dependency ratio and, 22–23; disease patterns and, 247–250; educational attainment and, 16–17; enrollment and, 193–195, 198; expenditure patterns and, 26–27, 163; health care and, 40–43, 231–233, 236, 238, 242–244, 255–257; household composition and, 65, 67; household expenditure and, 146–147, 155–156, 172; housing demand and, 47–49, 276–278, 288–289; labor force and, 19, 93–100, 107; saving and, 22–25, 139–141. *See also* Head of household age

Age distribution: of heads of households, 58, 73; health care expenditure and, 236, 238; households and, 7–8, 61–64, 72–74, 77; housing and, 276, 288–289; of labor force, 98; population and, 66, 68–69, 81

Age structure: disease patterns and, 247–250; savings and, 141; of Thai population, 2

Aging: employment and, 107; health care and, 39–43; household, 6–11; household composition and, 5–6, 55, 66; household expenditure patterns and, 30, 33; housing demand and, 285–286; labor force and, 18–20, 95, 107, 112; population and, 2, 68; of Thai market, 26–27; of Thai population, 2

Agricultural sector: domestic markets and, 168; household expenditure and, 168; household saving and, 141; labor and, 84, 87, 108; residential construction and, 287

AIDS: health care analysis and, 236; health care expenditure and, 238, 247, 260–261

Alcohol, household expenditure and, 30 n.16, 32–33, 144, 151, 154, 156–157, 166, 169

Amphoe, use of term, 121 n.3

Annual Government Expenditure Report, 186

Asia: domestic resource mobilization in, 116; saving patterns in, 117–118, 141

Asian Development Bank, 116

Baker, C. J., 87

Balance of payments, 299

Bangkok, 52; health care and, 244–245, 247, 252–253, 260; wages in, 101–104

Bangkok metropolis: education in, 188; health care in, 229; sampling procedure in, 121–123

Bangkok Metropolitan Administration, 186

Bertrand, T., 87

Birth rate, 1–2, 41, 81

Building industry: housing projections and, 286; residential housing and, 46

Business, domestic resource mobilization and, 117–118

Capital accumulation, household saving and, 21

Capital expenses: education and, 206–207; health care expenditure and, 236

Census data: children and, 10–11; HOMES and, 55–56; household aging and, 9; household composition and, 4; housing and, 272; population and, 10

Chaipravat, Olarn, 108

Changwat, use of term, 121 n.3

Child, use of term, 61

Child care: health care and, 39; labor supply and, 20–21; projected demand for, 113–114

Childrearing, household life cycle and, 6

Children: consumption ratios and, 130–131; "cost" of, 173; economic value of, 130; education of, 33–34, 186–187; employment projections and, 113–114; enrollment and, 193–199; health care and, 39–43, 254–258; household composition and, 6–7, 10–11, 55, 61–62, 72, 80, 113–114; household expenditure and, 27–28, 30, 160, 172–173, 258; household saving and, 119–120, 139–141; labor-force participation of, 195–196; mortality rates for, 10; number of, 33–34, 185; opportunities for, 192–193; saving ratio and, 23

Chulalongkorn University, 208

Civil Service Act, 188

Clark, B. Kim, 108 n.15

Class size, educational policy and, 35. *See also* Student–teacher ratio

Climate, labor-force participation and, 86–87

Clothing, household expenditure and, 30-32, 144, 157, 166, 169
College of Technology and Vocational Education, 207
Colleges, 189
Communication, household expenditure and, 31-32, 151, 154-155, 167, 169
Condominiums, 283-284
Consumption analysis, variables used in, 122
Consumption ratio, household, 126-127, 129-135, 172
Costs: educational, 206-214; health care, 41; *See also* Expenditure
Current Population Surveys, fertility and, 9-10

Data: education costs and, 207; enrollment projections and, 186; health care expenditure and, 230-233, 236; health care projections and, 247; household expenditure analysis and, 147-149; household saving and, 121; inadequacies of, 101-102; morbidity, 247; for Socio-Economic Survey of 1981, 124, 126-128; sources of, 186
Data collection, 124, 129
Defense, government expenditure and, 207
Demographic change: education and, 33-38, 185, 214-216; enrollment and, 192, 199; health care and, 38-44, 229, 259-260; household expenditure and, 143, 169-171; households and, 1-11; housing and, 44-52, 269-271, 279-282, 285-286; savings and, 118; social policy and, 52
Demographic processes, household composition and, 65-66
Department of General Education, 186, 207
Department of Physical Education, 186
Department of Teacher Training, 186
Department of Vocational Education, 186, 207
Dependency ratio: age and, 22-23, 72; household composition and, 6, 72; household life cycle and, 7-8, 61, 64; household saving and, 22-23; labor force and, 20-21, 113
Discretionary items: household spending patterns and, 28, 30; use of term, 28 n.14
Disease patterns, 247-251
Doctors, 244-247, 249, 260
Domestic market: agriculture and, 168; aging of, 26-27; economic growth and, 16, 21
Domestic resource mobilization: analysis of, 118-135; in Asia, 116
"Doubling rate," housing and, 272, 280

Economic behavior, households and, 53-54. *See also* Household expenditure; Saving
Economic change, demographic factors and, 81
Economic development: enrollment ratios and, 190; schooling and, 192-193
Economic growth: employment and, 12; expenditure patterns and, 31; government and, 16; household expenditure and, 30-33, 144, 169-171; household saving and, 21; labor market and, 12, 14-15
Economic policy: demographic change and, 52-53; housing and, 44
Economy, Thai: demographic change and, 11; economic growth and, 17; household expenditure and, 168; household saving and, 141; housing demand and, 270; labor supply and, 12, 14; residential construction and, 48-51, 291, 294-297. *See also* Gross domestic investment; Gross domestic product; Gross national product
Education: academic, 188; consumption ratios and, 130-131; cost of, 206-214; demographic change and, 33-38, 185; government expenditure on, 206-212; higher, 189; household expenditure and, 32-33, 144, 157-158, 166, 168-169, 212-214; human capital and, 191-193; labor force and, 16-17, 90, 92, 94-97, 111; preprimary, 186-187; private spending on, 215-216; public expenditure and, 35; quality of, 188-189; social benefits of, 111; university, 33; wages and, 102. *See also* Enrollment
Education, primary, 16-17, 34, 186-188; cost of, 209; enrollment and, 215
Education, secondary, 16, 34, 187, 203; enrollment and, 205-206, 215; government expenditure and, 207; teacher training and, 209
Education, tertiary, 16; enrollment and, 205-206; government expenditure and, 207
Education, vocational, 186-187, 189, 203, 205, 207-208; costs and, 209-210; enrollment and, 215

Educational attainment: education sector growth and, 185; enrollment and, 193–194, 197; inpatient rates and, 255; labor force and, 12, 16–18, 88–90, 93–97, 111–112; school attendance and, 35
Educational performance, 186–189
Educational policy, 185–189, 198, 200–202, 205; demographic change and, 35–38; labor force and, 18; population growth and, 214–215
Educational Report, 186
Elderly: health care and, 39, 40–43, 243–244, 255; household composition and, 6–7, 113; household saving and, 23–24, 119, 131–132; labor-force participation and, 113–114
Employment: agricultural, 84, 168; in formal sector, 87; growth of, 12, 14–15, 84; projections, 101, 105–107, 109–111; residential housing and, 49–50; seasonal, 87–88; teacher, 35–38; teenage, 130; urban, 87–88. *See also* Labor-force participation; Labor market
Employment growth rate, 84
Employment target, Sixth Plan, 105–106
Enrollment: definition of, 197; determinants of, 192–193; educational policy and, 36–38; labor-force projections and, 88–89; projected, 185–186, 189–206; trends for, 33–35; university, 34–35
Enrollment models, 191–199
Enrollment ratios, 189–191; age and, 198; calculation of, 203–204; education and, 33–35; projected, 196–199
Entrepreneurial class, household saving and, 141
Estimation procedure: household expenditure and, 147–161; residential construction expenditure and, 287–290; Socio-Economic Survey of 1981 and, 126–128
Evenson, R. E., 108
Exchange rate, residential construction and, 299
Expenditure: consumer, 148, 166–170; living standards and, 143; as measurement of income, 148; private, 39; recurring, 41; on residential construction, 287–299; use of term, 126. *See also* Government expenditure; Health care expenditure; Household expenditure
Expenditure elasticity, calculation of, 151
Expenditure equations, specifications of, 145–147
Experience, wages and, 102, 104
Export quotas, 84
Exports: agricultural, 168; labor shortage and, 16; residential construction and, 299; taxes and, 84

Family: health care and, 39, 42, 44; household composition and, 3–4. *See also* Households; Household types
Feldstein, Martin, 116
Fertility, declining, 1–2, 9–10, 22; education demographics and, 185; employment projections and, 105; enrollment and, 192; health care and, 243, 254, 256, 260; household composition and, 113; labor-force participation and, 111; saving and, 118, 139, 141
Final Report on Education Statistics, 186
Food: household expenditure and, 144, 151, 154, 156–157, 158, 166–167; spending patterns and, 28, 30–32
Formal sector, wages in, 87
Freeman, Richard B., 108 n.15

Gender: consumption ratios and, 133–134; disease patterns and, 248; educational attainment and, 16–17, 94–95, 111–112; enrollment and, 193–195, 197; heads of households and, 3, 58–60, 62–64, 70; health care and, 40–43, 231–233, 255–258; household composition and, 65, 67; household projections and, 56; labor-force participation and, 85–86, 93–99, 101–105, 111, 113; labor-force projections and, 90, 92; labor-market adjustment and, 101; labor supply and, 88 n.4; life expectancy and, 1–2, 10; saving and, 119–120, 131, 138–139; spending patterns and, 30 n.16, 155–158, 160–163, 166; wages and, 101–105, 107
Government, Thai: agricultural sector and, 84; domestic resource mobilization and, 117–119; economic growth and, 16; educational policy and, 187–188, 214–216; health care and, 41–42, 229, 236–249, 252–261; housing, 46, 270, 274, 276. *See also* names of government agencies
Government expenditure: on defense, 35, 207; education and, 39, 206–212, 215; health care and, 229–231, 233, 236–244
Grandchildren, household composition and, 60, 62, 72, 80
Greater Bangkok Metropolitan Area. *See* Bangkok metropolis

Gross domestic investment (GDI): health care and, 240–241; housing and, 49–51, 294–295, 297
Gross domestic product (GDP): agriculture and, 84; employment projections and, 105–106; growth of, 14; health care expenditure and, 240–241; household saving and, 21; housing and, 48–50, 294–296, 298; labor market and, 12, 14–15, 108–112; wages and, 109–111
Gross national product (GNP): health care and, 41, 229; housing and, 50

Head of household: cohorts of, 77, 80; demographic change and, 3; dependency ratio and, 22–23; educational attainment of, 35, 193–194, 197; gender and, 70; household members and, 58; household projections and, 72; use of term, 125
Head of household age, 5, 55, 73; consumption ratios and, 130–134; education expenses and, 212–214; enrollment and, 193–194, 197; household characteristics and, 58, 72–73, 81; household life cycle and, 6–11, 77, 80; housing and, 48–49, 276–278, 288, 292; labor force and, 20–21, 93, 98–100; living standards and, 113; outpatients and, 241–242; saving and, 22–24, 139–140; spending patterns and, 26–27, 146, 158–159
Headship rates, HOMES use of, 56
Health and Welfare Survey (1981), 38, 230, 254
Health care: demographic change and, 38–44, 259–260; Ministry of Public Health and, 236–249, 252–259; subsidized, 243
Health care expenditure, 41–42, 44, 229–247, 252; AIDS and, 260–261; government and, 39, 41, 229–231, 233, 236–244, 259–261; household expenditure and, 28, 30–32, 144, 156–158, 166, 168–169, 257–259; number of patients and, 236–241; private, 39
Health care facilities, 244–247, 249, 252, 254–257, 260–261
Health care policy: demographic change and, 260–261; disease patterns and, 249; expenditure and, 41–42, 243–244
Health insurance, 39, 42
Health personnel, 244–247, 249, 260
Health profiles, Bangkok, 252–253
Heckman, James, 101
HOMES. *See* Household Model for Economic and Social Studies
Horioka, C., 116
Hospital beds, 244, 260
Hospitals, utilization of, 256. *See also* Health care facilities
Household characteristics: consumption ratios and, 129–135; current, 57–64; demographic change and, 2–6, 81; educational expenditure and, 212–214; enrollment and, 185–186, 193–199; factors affecting, 64–65; HOMES and, 54; household expenditure and, 145–149, 162–166; household saving and, 119; labor-force projections and, 89; projected, 64–66; used in Socio-Economic Survey, 127
Household composition: children and, 10–11; consumption ratios and, 130–132; demographic change and, 3–6; elderly and, 113; factors affecting, 64–66; in family households, 58, 60–64; health care and, 40, 255–256; HOMES and, 54; household income and, 95; household life cycle and, 7–8; household projections and, 55, 72–77, 80; housing and, 47–49; labor force and, 20–21, 88–90, 98–101; relationship to head and, 58, 60–64, 67, 80; saving and, 23, 119–120; Socio-Economic Survey and, 127; spending patterns and, 27–30, 33, 145, 155–156, 160, 169–170; wages and, 102
Household expenditure, 26–33, 121; demographic change and, 143; education and, 212–214, 215–216; enrollment and, 197; factors affecting, 144–147; health care and, 28, 30–32, 40, 144, 156–158, 166, 168–169, 241–244, 257–259; household composition and, 27–30; household types and, 241–244; housing and, 45, 47, 288; projected, 31, 144, 161–172; statistical analysis of, 145–161; use of term, 125
Household income, 121; disposable, 125; education and, 35, 212; health care expenditure and, 258; household composition and, 89, 95, 119, 136; household expenditure and, 149, 151, 154; housing and, 288; living standards and, 53–54; measurement of, 126; use of term, 125
Household members: characteristics of, 58, 60–62, 65, 136–137; household projections and, 74–75; number of, 57, 73–75, 136–137, 196–197; relationship to head and, 56–57, 61, 63, 67; use of

term, 125. *See also* Household composition
Household Model for Economic and Social Studies (HOMES), 30; education and, 186, 212; enrollment projections and, 191–199; expenditure and, 161–162, 212, 230–231, 236, 241; health care and, 230–231, 236, 241, 241 n.7; household expenditure and, 161–162; housing, 44, 270, 272, 284–285; labor force and, 83, 88–89, 92–93, 95, 99; methodology and, 54, 88–89; overview of, 55–57; population projections and, 66, 68; savings ratio and, 135–136
Household projections, 64–66, 68, 70–77, 79; calculation of, 56–57; uses of, 53–54
Household size: consumption ratio and, 132–133; decline of, 5, 55, 57, 70, 72, 81, 136; household expenditure and, 151, 154, 162, 164; household saving and, 120; household type and, 58; inpatient rates and, 255; labor-force participation and, 21, 98; life cycle and, 7–9; projected, 283
Household types, 56–59, 70–72; consumption ratio and, 133–134; expenditure patterns and, 143, 156–158, 162–166, 241–244; health care and, 241–244, 260; household saving and, 120; labor force and, 83, 93, 99–100. *See also* Households: intact, nonfamily, one-person, primary-individual, single-headed
Households: age composition of, 61–62; demographic change and, 1–11; establishment of, 26, 77; extended, 4–7, 55; family, 5, 55–58, 60–64, 70, 195–196; farm, 135; health-seeking behavior of, 254; housing stock and, 277; intact, 56, 58, 61, 64, 70, 72, 98, 101, 143, 162; lineal, 6, 55; nonfamily, 5; nuclear, 4, 7; number of, 3–5, 54–55, 57–60, 64–65, 70–77, 79, 285–286; one-person, 3 n.3, 5, 55–56, 58, 133–134, 157–158, 162, 197; primary-individual, 55, 56, 58; projected, 4–6; purchasing power of, 26–27; single-headed, 56, 58, 61, 98; use of term, 3 n.2, 124–125
Housing: demographic change and, 44–52, 270–286; household expenditure and, 30–32, 151, 154, 158, 168–169; owner-occupied, 283–285; rental, 282–285, 287–288
Housing market, 275, 279
Housing stock, 44–47, 52, 273–274; demand for, 270–286; demographic change and, 269–271; projected, 286; required, 279–282; withdrawals and, 279–282
Housing Survey of 1976, 272
Human capital: education and, 191–193; investment in, 107, 130

Immigration, population projections and, 66
Immunization, 247, 249
Income, 101–102; expenditure patterns and, 145–146; farm, 124; housing and, 45, 47; measurement of, 148; national, 21; residential construction and, 288–293, 295, 297–300; savings ratio and, 21, 135–136; unearned, 102. *See also* Household income
Income, per capita: disposable, 125, 135, 148; enrollment and, 195; expenditure analysis and, 149, 151; health care expenditure and, 254; household expenditure and, 158, 169; housing and, 44–45, 288–289
Industrial growth, 12
Informal sector, wages in, 87
Infrastructure: disease patterns and, 247; housing and, 45, 51–52; urbanization and, 299
Inpatients, 40–43, 252, 254–257; disease patterns and, 248; health care expenditure and, 230–234, 238–239, 252; household types and, 242–244
Institution of Higher Education, 186
Institutions, population projections and, 68
Interest rates, savings and, 118
Investment: domestic, 116–117; human capital, 107, 130; saving rates and, 22, 116–117
Investment ratio, calculation of, 115

Japan: health care and, 39, 232–233, 235, 240, 244; saving and, 118, 141

Khon Khaen University, 208
Korea, saving in, 118, 120, 141

Labor demand: market adjustment and, 108; projected, 106–107, 112
Labor force: age distribution of, 98; aging and, 18–20, 95, 107, 112; agricultural, 168; children in, 195–196; demographic change and, 12–21; educational attain-

ment of, 111–112; fertility rate and, 105; growth of, 12–13, 84–85; health services and, 244–247; housing and, 49–50, 287, 294–296, 298; participation rates and, 84–87, 89, 93–94, 107; projections for, 88–101; quality of, 16–20, 112; women in, 20–21, 85–86, 93–94, 101–105, 113–114
Labor-force participation, 91; of children, 195–196; factors affecting, 111; HOMES and, 88–92; household composition and, 20–21; household life cycle and, 7–8; use of term, 90; wages and, 101–105
Labor-force participation model, 91
Labor-force participation rate, 83–87, 89, 93–94, 107
Labor Force Survey (1984), 83, 90, 92, 101–102
Labor market: adjustment and, 101–112; economic growth and, 12, 14–15; manufacturing sector and, 84, 87; overview of, 84–88; rural, 87; segmentation and, 87; unemployment and, 83
Labor shortages: economic growth and, 15–16; planning for, 112–113; wages and, 15–16
Labor supply: aging population and, 112; demand for, 12–15; demographic change and, 12–21; employment projections and, 105; gender and, 88 n.4; models for, 88–92; projected, 105–107, 108–109, 111–112; residential construction and, 295–296, 298; wages and, 104–105
Land, residential, 286
Legislation, minimum wage, 87
Life cycle, household: age composition and, 61–62; aging and, 6–11; household projections and, 77–80; spending patterns and, 26–27
Life expectancy: estimated, 10–11; gender and, 1–2; population projections and, 66
Living standards: expenditure patterns and, 143, 151, 163; health care and, 258; households and, 53–54, 151; investment and, 115; labor-force projections and, 113

Mahidol University, 208
Malaysia, health care expenditure in, 236
Manufacturing sector, labor market and, 84, 87
Markets. *See* types of markets
Marriage, 3
Mason, Andrew, 56
Medical care: household expenditure and, 144, 156–158, 166, 169; spending patterns and, 28, 30–32. *See also* Health care
Medical personnel. *See* Health personnel
Men: educational attainment and, 16–17, 94–95; as heads of households, 3, 58–60; health care and, 40; labor-force participation and, 85, 93–94, 101, 103–105; life expectancy and, 1–2, 10. *See also* Gender
Methodology: educational cost projections and, 209–210; employment projections and, 105; enrollment projections and, 185–186, 189–206; expenditure equations and, 145–147; fertility rate calculation and, 9–10, 66; forecasting of expenditure patterns and, 30; health care analysis and, 38–39; health care expenditure and, 230–233, 236; HOMES, 54, 55–57, 88–89; household demographics and, 52; household expenditure projections and, 147–150, 161–162; household saving analysis and, 119, 120–128; housing demand and, 270–286; inpatient rates and, 255–256; labor-force projections and, 88–92, 101–104, 111; labor-market projections and, 107–108; problems of, 88 n.4, 101–102; reliability of, 170, 172; residential construction and, 287–292; savings ratio estimation and, 135–136; wage rate projections and, 108–109, 111
Migration: housing stock and, 273; residential construction and, 299; rural–urban, 168; seasonal, 87–88
Ministry of Education, 186
Ministry of Public Health (MOPH), 38; health care and, 229–231, 233, 236–249, 252–259
Ministry of the Interior, 186
MOPH. *See* Ministry of Public Health
Morbidity: disease patterns and, 247–248, 250; health care projections and, 247
Mortality, 1–2; disease patterns and, 248; gender and, 10; improved, 81; population projections and, 66

National Economic and Social Development Board (NESDB), 55, 83; employment projections and, 101; labor demand and, 109; population projections and, 236
National Education Commission, 208
National Education Plan (1987), 205

National Epidemiology Board of Thailand, 247
National Statistical Office of Thailand, 38, 83, 121; education statistics and, 186; expenditure analysis and, 147-149; health care expenditure and, 231
National University Bureau, 207
Negative shares, household expenditure projections and, 172
NESDB. *See* National Economic and Social Development Board
Nonalcoholic beverages, household expenditure and, 144, 166
Nonthaburi, 122
Nurses, 244–247, 260

Occupation: consumption ratios and, 130; household expenditure and, 159; household saving and, 120; use of term, 126
Office of Local Education, 186
Office of National Primary Education, 186, 207
Office of Private Education, 186
Office of the Prime Minister, 186
Office of the Undersecretary, 186
Office of University Affairs, 186
Operating costs: for education, 206–208; health care expenditure and, 236
Outpatients, 40–43; disease patterns and, 248; health care expenditure and, 230–234, 236–238, 252; household types and, 241–244; projected number of, 252

Pakistan, household saving in, 120
Parents, 3-6, 55, 60–61, 63, 80
Participation probits: for Bangkok women, 103; labor-force projections and, 90, 92
Pathumthani, 122
Patients, 39–40, 42. *See also* Inpatients; Outpatients
Pensions: private, 113; as saving motivation, 119
Personal care, household expenditure and, 151, 157, 166, 169
Pongpaichit, Pasuk, 87
Population, 57-58; aging of, 2, 236, 238; children, 55; enumerated, 1, 10–11; household composition and, 66; housing demand and, 273; outpatient, 231; projected, 10–11; school age, 33–34
Population growth, 54–55, 57; changes in, 1-2; decline in, 83–84; education and, 33, 214–215; enrollment and, 203; housing and, 285–286; rural, 284; urban, 283–284
Population projections, 2, 66–69; assumptions underlying, 68; enrollment projections and, 204–205; relationship to head and, 79; uses of, 53
Population pyramids, 67, 69
Preschoolers, 114
Prices: consumer expenditure and, 173; farm-gate, 84; housing and, 46–48, 51, 288, 296-297; spending patterns and, 145
Private sector: education and, 187-188; health care and, 42, 229, 247, 252, 257, 260
Privatization of health care, 42
Probit models, labor-force projections and, 90, 92
Productivity: aging labor force and, 18, 20; educational attainment and, 112; employment projections and, 105-107; expenditure patterns and, 143
Public sector. *See* Government, Thai; names of government agencies
Purchasing power, 26–27

Quality control, survey data and, 124

Ramkhamkang University, 20 n.11, 189
Reading, household expenditure and, 144, 154–155, 166, 169
Real wage rate, 86; residential construction and, 296; stagnation of, 84
Real wages, 109
Recreation, household expenditure and, 144, 154-155, 157, 166–167, 169
Relationship to head: HOMES and, 56–57; household composition and, 58, 60–64, 67, 72, 76-77; population and, 76, 79
Reliability: of enrollment projections, 204–206; of health care expenditure projections, 231–232; of household expenditure projections, 170, 171
Rents, 287-288
Reporting error, statistical analysis and, 129
Reservation wage, 102
Residence, household expenditure and, 159. *See also* Housing
Residential construction: demographic change and, 270–271; expenditure on, 287-299; government and, 274, 276; income and, 297-300; projected, 44–47, 293; Thai economy and, 48–50, 294–297; withdrawal rates and, 280–282

Residual analysis, expenditure projections and, 170, 171
Retirement: household saving and, 21, 24–25; labor force and, 20
Rural areas: enrollment in, 195; health care in, 229–230; housing demand in, 45; labor-force participation rates in, 87; migration from, 168; teacher quality in, 188

Sabbatical system, educational policy and, 37–38
Sampling procedure, for Socio-Economic Survey of 1981, 121–124
Samutprakarn, 122
Saving: aggregate, 24; aging and, 20; business, 22; corporate, 22; domestic, 115–118; gender and, 131; household, 21–25, 117–128, 136–141; investment and, 116–117; national, 21–22, 116–118, 141, 269
Saving rates: investment and, 116–117; national, 118
Saving ratios, 21–22, 24; elderly and, 131–132; estimation of, 135–136; household types and, 133–134; projected, 135–141
Scale economies, household expenditure and, 151, 154
Scale effects, household expenditure and, 151
Scaling, demographic, 146
Scaling factors, labor-force projections and, 93
Schools: demonstration, 188, 207; health care and, 42; population growth and, 33; private, 188; public, 33; vocational, 207–208. *See also* Education; types of education
Seasons, labor-force participation and, 86–88
Selectivity bias, employment projections and, 101
Service ratios, health care and, 244–245, 247
Service sector, labor force and, 84
Setboonsrang, Suthad, 108
Sex ratio: health care expenditure and, 236; household characteristics and, 64. *See also* Gender
Sierra Leone, 115
Sixth National Economic and Social Development Five Year Plan, 105–106, 109
Sixth National Education Plan, 198, 200–202
Social behavior, households and, 53–54
Social change: demographic factors and, 81; household projections and, 70, 72
Social policy, demographic change and, 52–53
Socioeconomic characteristics, household saving and, 120
Socioeconomic status: consumption ratio and, 134–135; determinants of, 126; enrollment and, 193, 195–196; health care expenditure and, 257; hospital use and, 254; household expenditure and, 159; measurement of, 148–149
Socio-Economic Survey (1981): consumer expenditure and, 143; descriptive statistics from, 128; education and, 212–214; enrollment and, 191, 193–194, 215; health care and, 38, 230, 257; household expenditure and, 145–149, 212–214; household saving and, 121–128; statistical analysis and, 129–135; summary statistics from, 152–153
Socio-Economic Survey (1988), spending patterns and, 31–32
Squire, L., 87
Statistical analysis: enrollment projections and, 197; household expenditure and, 129–135, 147–161
Student–teacher ratio: educational costs and, 209; educational policy and, 35–37
Subsidies, for medical care, 243
Sukhothai Thammathirat, 189
Survey of Health Resources (1984), 244
Surveys of Population Change, 10
Sussangkarn, Chalongphob, 87–88

Taxes: disposable income and, 148; exemption from, 84; export, 84;
Teachers: benefits for, 188; employment of, 35–38; numbers of, 36; qualifications of, 188, 209
Teacher training, 35–38, 188, 203; cost of, 208, 210; educational policy and, 187
Teenagers, economic value of, 130
Tenure composition, housing demand and, 282–285
TFR. *See* Total fertility rate
Thai Demographic and Health Survey, 10
Thammasat University, 208
Tobacco: household expenditure and, 151, 154, 156–157, 166; spending patterns and, 30 n.16, 32–33
Total fertility rate (TFR), 9–10, 66. *See also* Fertility, declining
Trade, 12

Transition-rate method, 189-191, 200-204; educational costs and, 208-209; enrollment and, 200-204
Transportation, household expenditure and, 31-32, 151, 154-155, 167, 169

Unemployment, 12; education and, 112; gross domestic product and, 84; household composition and, 21; projected, 107; seasonal, 87
Unemployment rates, 83, 85-86
Union movement, 33
Unit costs, education and, 207-211
Universities: closed, 34-35, 189, 203, 208; government and, 187; open, 20, 33, 189, 203, 205, 208; public, 203
Urban areas: enrollment in, 196; labor market in, 87; migration to, 168. *See also* Bangkok
Urban growth, housing and, 45, 52, 283-284
Urbanization: household saving and, 141; inpatient rates and, 256; residential construction and, 299
Urban market, dualism and, 87

Vacancy rates, housing and, 272, 279-280

Wage differentials, 87
Wage elasticity, labor-market projections and, 107-108
Wage equations, 102-104
Wage rate, 108-111
Wages: aging of labor force and, 20; economic growth and, 12, 14-15; factors affecting, 87-88; gender and, 101-105; inflation and, 14 n.7; informal sector, 87; labor-force participation and, 101-105, 111; labor-force projections and, 89-90; labor market and, 83; labor supply and, 15-16; legislation and, 87; market, 89; projected, 112-113; reservation, 89-90; residential housing and, 49-50
Wealth: household expenditure and, 159; intergenerational distribution of, 20
Withdrawal rates: housing stock and, 279-282; residential construction and, 288, 292
Women: educational attainment and, 17, 94-95; as heads of households, 20, 58-60, 62-64; health care and, 39-43, 258; household saving and, 119-120; labor force and, 20-21, 85-86, 93-94, 101-105, 113-114; life expectancy and, 1-2, 10. *See also* Gender
Workers, discouraged, 90. *See also* Labor force
World Bank, 87, 115, 129, 149

Yemen, 115

East-West Center

The U.S. Congress established the East-West Center in 1960 to foster mutual understanding and cooperation among the governments and peoples of the Asia-Pacific region, including the United States. Officially known as the Center for Cultural and Technical Interchange Between East and West, it is a public, nonprofit institution with an international board of governors. Principal funding for the Center comes from the U.S. government, with additional support provided by private agencies, individuals, corporations, and more than 20 Asian and Pacific governments.

The Center promotes responsible development, long-term stability, and human dignity for all people in the region and helps prepare the United States for constructive involvement in Asia and the Pacific through research, education, and dialogue. It provides a neutral meeting ground at which people with a wide range of perspectives exchange views on topics of regional concern. Eighty researchers pursue individual and cooperative projects, provide policy advice to Asian and American public and private agencies, and work with 275 Center-funded students from Asia, the Pacific, and the United States, who are simultaneously enrolled at the University of Hawaii. Some 2,000 scholars, government and business leaders, educators, journalists, and other professionals from throughout the region annually work with the Center's staff to address topics of contemporary significance.

The Center focuses on four interconnected region-wide policy issues: post-Cold War regional security arrangements; social and cultural change; the domestic political evolution of Asian and Pacific nations, and rapid economic growth and its interrelated consequences (especially environmental concerns, energy needs, and demographic change).

Asian Development Bank

The Asian Development Bank, a development finance institution consisting of 52 member countries, is engaged in promoting the economic and social progress of its developing member countries in the Asian and Pacific region. The Bank started functioning in December 1966 with its headquarters in Manila, the Philippines. It is owned by the governments of 36 countries from the region and 16 countries from outside the region.

In 25 years of operations, the Bank has become a major catalyst in promoting the development of the most populous and fastest-growing region in the world today. The Bank's principal functions are: (1) to make loans and equity investments for the economic and social advancement of developing member countries; (2) to provide technical assistance for the preparation and execution of development projects and programs and advisory services; (3) to promote investment of public and private capital for development purposes; and (4) to respond to requests for assistance in coordinating development policies and plans of member countries. In its operations, the Bank also pays special attention to the needs of smaller or less-developed countries and gives priority to regional, subregional, and national projects and programs that will contribute to the harmonious economic growth of the region as a whole.

The Bank's operations cover the entire spectrum of economic development, with particular emphasis on agriculture, energy, capital market development, transport and communications, and social infrastructure. Although most Bank financing is designed to support specific projects, the Bank also provides program, sector, and multiproject loans.